BEYOND THE RANDOM WALK

**Financial Management Association
Survey and Synthesis Series**

BEYOND THE RANDOM WALK

A Guide to Stock Market Anomalies and Low-Risk Investing

VIJAY SINGAL
PH.D., CFA

OXFORD
UNIVERSITY PRESS

OXFORD
UNIVERSITY PRESS

Oxford University Press, Inc., publishes works that
further Oxford University's objective of excellence
in research, scholarship, and education.

Oxford   New York
Auckland   Cape Town   Dar es Salaam   Hong Kong   Karachi
Kuala Lumpur   Madrid   Melbourne   Mexico City   Nairobi
New Delhi   Shanghai   Taipei   Toronto

With offices in
Argentina   Austria   Brazil   Chile   Czech Republic   France   Greece
Guatemala   Hungary   Italy   Japan   Poland   Portugal   Singapore
South Korea   Switzerland   Thailand   Turkey   Ukraine   Vietnam

First published by Oxford University Press, Inc., 2004
198 Madison Avenue, New York, NY 10016
www.oup.com

First issued as an Oxford paperback, 2006

ISBN-13: 978-0-19-530422-0
ISBN-10: 0-19-530422-5

Library of Congress Cataloging-in-Publication Data
Singal, Vijay.
Beyond the random walk : a guide to stock market
anomalies and low-risk investing / by Vijay Singal.
p. cm.—(Financial Management Association survey
and synthesis series)
Includes bibliographical references and index.
ISBN 0-19-515867-9
1. Investments.
2. Stock exchanges.
I. Title.
II. Series.
HG4521.S576 2004
332.6—dc21
2003008016

9 8 7 6 5 4 3 2 1

Printed in the United States of America
on acid-free paper

This book is dedicated to my wife, Manisha,
and my teenage sons, Ashish and Akshay,
who, apparently believing that the book is perfect,
refused to read beyond the title page.

Contents

Preface to the Paperback Edition

First, I want to thank readers and buyers of the hardcover edition. The book went out of print in less than 18 months. Many reviewers helped promote the book by saying more good things than bad things about the book. Full-length reviews or references to the book have appeared in magazines and newspapers such as *SmartMoney*, *Money*, *New York Times*, *Fortune*, *UBS's Wealth Management*, and *CFA Magazine*; in journals like *Financial Analysts Journal*, *Journal of Financial Research*, *Journal of Investment Management*, and *Journal of Social, Political, and Economic Studies*; and in non-print media like Bloomberg Radio, CNN-fn, PBS, Briefing.com, and quizzes on Yahoo! Finance. All reviews can be found at http://www.BeyondTheRandomWalk.com/reviews. The book is also used in several investments courses as a supplement or as the main text. The ultimate accolade: my son, Ashish, not only read beyond the title page (see the Dedication), but successfully experimented with several strategies.

Second, I am happy to report that no significant changes in the strategies described in the book have taken place since publication of the hardcover edition. This is not unexpected, considering that the anomalies in the book are based on one or more decades of research. Nonetheless, it is heartening to note that the strategies have withstood the test of time.

I must mention, however, that one of the strategies is now more difficult to trade thanks to Eliot Spitzer. He has made it more difficult to time mutual funds (Chapter 6) by very effectively publicizing the strategy. Did he read my book? Now almost all mutual funds with stale prices have a short-term trading fee. However, you can still optimize your entry and exit from these funds.

Finally, changes have occurred in the reference list, especially for purveyors of investment advice. I have always been of the opinion that investment newsletters are notorious for disappearing after a short period of success. But I was not prepared for changes that I actually observed in the last two years. Out of eleven sector fund newsletters that I mentioned in the hardcover edition, only six still exist. The initial set of newsletters was not picked at random but was deliberately chosen based on independent certification of a track record of at least five years. Just goes to illustrate the severity of survivorship bias in financial markets.

I must end now. I have work to do for trading the January effect. But be sure to write to me. Your feedback in any form, suggestions, compliments, and even brickbats, is very welcome.

Dr. Vijay Singal
January 2, 2006

Preface

This book is about anomalies in financial markets. While most people believe that markets are generally efficient, there is a consensus that pockets of inefficiency exist within broad market efficiency. Both academics and practitioners share this view. As a finance professor remarks, "You find more and more academics willing to concede that the market doesn't look as efficient as they once thought." For instance, Gus Sauter, who runs Vanguard Group's massive stock indexing operations, valued at over $100 billion, says, "I don't believe markets are perfectly efficient."[1]

In an attempt to discover market inefficiencies, academics and practitioners have expended tens of thousands of man-years researching mispricings and anomalies. As the April 2001 issue of the *Journal of Finance* notes, "[T]housands of papers have . . . investigated the statistical behavior of stock returns and the extent to which stock prices reflect all available information." In the process of examining the behavior of returns, the finance profession has uncovered many mispricings or inefficiencies where the direction of price movements is predictable and may suggest the formation of certain profitable trading strategies.

Unfortunately, much of current academic research in finance is not accessible to most individual and institutional investors due to its complexity.

Moreover, academic research usually stops short of suggesting practical applications. The purpose of this book is to address those limitations.

The discussions of the anomalies have two main components. The first component attempts to make relevant academic research available in a form that is understandable to practitioners, investors, students, and academics not in that particular field. It describes the anomaly, empirical evidence, and possible explanations for the anomaly, and it explores reasons for the persistence of the anomaly. The second component of each chapter introduces and implements trading strategies designed to capture the mispricing, along with a discussion of the risk and return. In addition, the step-by-step trading strategy is illustrated with real data from a recent period so that an ordinary investor would find it easy to duplicate the strategy. Readers, if they so desire, will be able to further explore literature on the subject by perusing the extensive bibliography throughout the book and by possibly conducting additional empirical analysis independently.

This book is intended for any individual interested in mispricings in the stock market. It does not presume a deep understanding of financial markets, just an interest in the stock market and a thirst for knowledge. Investors and practitioners will gain from a summary of the current research on anomalies and evidence of the success of low-risk investment strategies based on those anomalies. Their trading activities may even make the markets more efficient! Academics can use the book as a starting point for an understanding of the large field of market efficiency. The references should help steer the academic community in the right direction to further explore this exciting and important area of research. The book can help students at all levels (advanced undergraduates, MBAs, and PhDs) enhance their understanding of financial markets.

Most but not all anomalies are expected to generate tradable profits. Even if generating trading profits is not possible, information about an anomaly will help the reader better understand the mispricing and, perhaps, modify trading behavior to avoid being hurt by it.

Description of Content

This book begins with a description of market efficiency and anomalies so that readers can fully comprehend the nature of the anomalies discussed. The discussion of market efficiency and its importance is followed by answers to questions such as: What is mispricing? How do you detect a mispricing? Is there really a mispricing after correcting for biases? Why does a mispricing persist? My intent is for you to be able to judge whether the anomaly is believable and continues to exist. This is the only chapter that I recommend you read before reading any other chapter in the book.

The introductory chapter (Chapter 1) is followed by the main part of the book (Chapters 2 to 11), where ten mispricings are discussed. Each chapter discusses one anomaly in detail along with the description, evidence, explanations, and risks and rewards of the investment strategy associated with that anomaly. I have kept each anomaly independent of the others so that if you are interested in the forward rate bias, for example, you can jump to Chapter 11 without having to trudge through the first nine anomalies. The summary at the beginning of each chapter and Table 0.1 allow you to preselect the anomalies that you are interested in reading about. While most anomalies have seemingly rational explanations related to institutional features, there are others for which rational explanations have yet to be discovered. Even if an explanation is known to exist, a nagging question remains: Why doesn't the mispricing disappear because of the actions of arbitrageurs or smart investors? That question is frequently difficult to answer. Limits of arbitrage activity are one possible explanation. Fortunately, trading by individual investors can relax that constraint, and the investors can gain while making the market more efficient. I hope this book will enable small investors to uncover and trade on the mispricings discussed.

A chapter devoted to a discussion of behavioral finance follows the individual anomalies. Whereas finance theory is based on rational investor behavior, behavioral finance theory is based on psychological precepts that generate irrational investor behavior, or at least behavior that is irrational from an economic standpoint. In the context of anomalies, the chapter on behavioral finance performs two functions. First, it provides an alternative way of thinking about the rationale behind some of the anomalies. Second, it provides useful information about mistakes that investors make, mistakes that investors should consciously try to avoid.

The last chapter of the book is a collection of other possible mispricings and is directed to readers whose appetite for anomalies is not satisfied. The most promising mispricings are described in that chapter, along with an extensive list of references that allow the reader to explore beyond the confines of the book.

The three appendices at the end of the book contain useful information for people who are new to certain aspects of trading strategies. Appendix A contains information about financial instruments, their availability, trading costs, and trading restrictions. The purpose is to provide practical information on selecting appropriate instruments for trading. Appendix B covers the intricacies of short selling.

Table 0.1: Summary of Anomalies discussed in the book

Chapter Number	2	2	3	4	5
Chapter Title	The January Effect	The New December Effect	The Weekend Effect	Short-Term Price Drift	Momentum in Industry Portfolios
Frequency of mispricing	Once a year	Once a year	Once a weekend	Daily	Daily
Level of difficulty in understanding the mispricing	Easy	Easy	Easy	Not difficult to marginally difficult	Not difficult to marginally difficult
Abnormal return based on past evidence*	Not possible. Theoretically, 10%.	About 2%	0.20% per weekend	1.5% to 3% per stock. 18–36% annualized	0%–5% per year
Abnormal return using real time data*	1% every January. Investors can also change trading patterns.	1.5% to 3.0% in December. Investors can also change trading patterns.	Not possible. But investors can change trading patterns.	30 to 38% annualized	10% per year
Financial Instruments for arbitrage	Mutual funds	Mutual funds, ETFs, and futures	Not applicable	Individual stocks; short-selling only for stocks with negative news	Mutual funds
Level of difficulty in strategy implementation	Easy	Easy	Easy	Easy to marginally difficult without short-selling	Easy
Time commitment per transaction	one hour	one hour	—	two hours	three hours
Transactions per year	One; change in trading patterns	One; change in trading patterns	Change in trading patterns	Many	10–12

6	7	8	9	10	11
Mispricing of Mutual Funds	Trading by Insiders	Changes to the S&P 500 Index	Merger Arbitrage	International Investing	Forward Rate Bias
Event based	Daily	Event based	Event based	Continuous	Continuous
Not very difficult	Easy	Easy	Not difficult to marginally difficult	Not difficult to marginally difficult	Difficult
1% to 50% annualized	7% to 10% annualized	36% to 48% annualized	4% to 10% annualized	2% to 8% per year	2% to 5% per year
5% to 7% annualized	30% to 57% annualized	> 100% annualized	16% annualized	Not available. But investors must include foreign stocks.	13% to 15% per year
Mutual funds	Individual stocks; short selling is optional	Individual stocks; short-selling is optional	Individual stocks; short selling only for stock mergers	Mutual funds; American Depository Receipts; ETFs	Currency futures
Easy with funds already identified; difficult to find new funds	Not difficult without short-selling	Easy without short-selling	Easy for cash mergers; marginally difficult for stock mergers	Easy	Easy
30 minutes	one hour	two hours	three hours	one hour	three hours
15–50	Many	About 50	20 to 100	A few	10–12

*Abnormal return is the return in excess of the normal return associated with this level of risk.

Buying stocks or selling stocks that you own is easy. However, short selling (selling stocks that you do not own) is a somewhat different and more complex strategy and is described in that appendix. Appendix C explains the basics of hedging. Hedging can be used to control risk associated with certain trading strategies. The appendices are not required reading for frequent traders.

Why Did I Write This Book?

> If stock market experts were so expert, they would
> be buying stock, not selling advice.
>   *Norman R. Augustine*

I share the skepticism of this statement and agree with the assertion that any person will use his informed position to make profits for himself first. However, the statement implicitly assumes that strategic trading will generate arbitrage profits that have no risk and require no investment. Unfortunately, arbitrage is rarely risk free or costless (see next chapter for an in-depth discussion on the *limits of arbitrage*). So, although I have the knowledge, the ability, and the willingness to craft an informed trading strategy that outperforms the market, I am constrained by the lack of adequate financial resources (I am only a professor of finance after all!) to take advantage of the many profitable opportunities that I discuss in this book.

Not to say that I have not profited from my expertise—as a small investor I have implemented, and continue to implement the strategies in this book—generally, managing to beat the market and make the desired level of profit. Yet, due to the resource constraint mentioned above, it is more profitable for me, both personally and professionally, to leverage my know-how in the form of this book, than to try and earn direct profits through the implementation of the strategies I have highlighted in the pages that follow.

In one sense then, this book itself can be treated as an anomaly (considering the above quotation), which, if fully exploited by its audience, would help to push the market back to its ideal of efficiency. This is another reason why I am writing this book instead of using my knowledge only for personal benefit.

Notes

1. Both quotes in this paragraph are from the August 2001 issue of the *Institutional Investor,* 30–33.

Acknowledgments

I would like to acknowledge with great appreciation the support and encouragement of Art Keown. As editor of the Financial Management Association Survey and Synthesis series, author of many books, and a colleague, Art facilitated the approval of this idea by the Financial Management Association's Survey and Synthesis Board and the publisher. He has also been an active participant in various stages of the project, a constant source of encouragement and help, and a sounding board, for which I am extremely grateful.

Paul Donnelly, executive editor of finance at Oxford University Press, has been a strong believer in this book from the start and has been instrumental in its quick acceptance at all levels. He has helped me write this book for the right audience and provided continuous feedback and encouragement in this endeavor. I owe him a debt of gratitude.

I would like to express my sincere appreciation to the editorial, production, and marketing groups at Oxford University Press for doing an outstanding job in producing a high quality product that reaches as many potential interested readers as possible. In particular, my thanks go to Helen Mules, Woody Gilmartin, and Sue Warga.

I thank the reviewers of this book, who worked hard to tell me what was missing and what needed more work. In particular, I would like to acknowledge the help of Rakesh Bali of Adelphi University, Dan Strachman of Answers and Company, Will Glasgow of U.S. Trust, Mahesh Pritamani of Frank Russell and Co., Venkat Ramaswamy HSBC, Bhoopat Jadeja of Tibco, and Harry Larsen of Fundbuster.com

    Finally, and most importantly, I appreciate the work put in by committed individuals who read the book in its entirety and provided detailed feedback. They include MBA students Stephen Deutsch, Virginia Benczik, Wes Gatewood, Huanmin Xu, Ajay Bhootra, and Robert Ratcliff and doctoral students Tunde Kovacs and Don Autore at Virginia Tech, Prasad Polamraju of Celanese Hoechst, Professors Dilip Shome and Randy Billingsley of Virginia Tech, Kathy Sevebeck of K&B Designs, and especially, Sonia Mudbhatkal of Virginia Tech.

Chapter Summaries

Chapter summaries below are reproduced from each chapter for ready reference. A table of the 10 anomalous price patterns is given on pages xiv and xv.

Chapter 1—Market Efficiency and Anomalies

This chapter addresses common questions related to market efficiency and anomalies. If prices properly reflect available information, then markets are said to be efficient. Although markets are known to be broadly efficient, there may be pockets of inefficiency that lead to mispricings or anomalies. In general, claims of anomalous pricing must be viewed with skepticism. The discussion describes reasons for skepticism as well as causes for persistence of some anomalies. You will also learn that even if profits can't be made by trading on anomalous prices, it may be possible to alter your trading behavior in view of the anomalies.

Chapter 2—The January Effect and the New December Effect

Small loser stocks are known to appreciate considerably in January, giving rise to the so-called January effect. The primary explanation for the January effect is tax-loss selling by investors in December to realize capital losses that are used to offset capital gains. When the selling pressure abates in January, the loser stocks appreciate. Unfortunately, it is not possible to arbitrage the January effect, though investors can gain by changing their trading patterns.

The December effect is similar in spirit to the January effect. Stocks that have done well in the January-November period are not sold by investors in December because selling those stocks will result in taxable capital gains. By waiting a few days, investors can postpone payment of capital gains taxes by almost one year. It is relatively easy to gain from the December effect, as popularly available indexes can be used for trading.

Chapter 3—The Weekend Effect

The weekend effect refers to relatively large returns on Fridays compared to those on Mondays. Whereas the Friday returns exceed 0.20%, the Monday returns are close to zero or negative resulting in a weekend effect for an equally weighted index of 0.34 percent.

Short sellers may be responsible for the weekend effect because they do not want to keep speculative positions open around the weekend. Accordingly, they close the short positions by buying back on Fridays and reopen them by short selling on Mondays causing higher returns on Fridays and lower returns on Mondays.

It is, however, not easy to capture the weekend effect with current financial instruments because the trading costs can be large. Nonetheless, investors should recognize the weekend effect and avoid buying on Fridays and selling on Mondays. Instead, they should buy stocks on Mondays and sell on Fridays.

Chapter 4—Short-Term Price Drift

Events associated with high-quality information signals tend to exhibit price continuations. The quality of information is characterized by the magnitude of price change, volume, and public dissemination of information. There is evidence to suggest that a large price change accompanied by high volume and a public announcement is followed by a drift in prices. A trading strategy designed to capture this short-term price continuation will earn annual abnormal returns of 15–36 percent after transactions costs.

Chapter 5—Momentum in Industry Portfolios

There is evidence to suggest that industry portfolios exhibit momentum. Industries that have done well in one period also do well in the next period. Moreover, industries with no related futures markets are likely to show greater momentum than industries where information regarding the real assets is aggregated in futures prices. Industry portfolios constructed in this manner generate returns that may be much larger than the S&P 500 return.

Chapter 6—Mispricing of Mutual Funds

The net asset values (NAVs) of mutual funds may be based on prices that are several hours old. That means the NAV may not reflect the most recent market movements. For small-cap funds with many illiquid stocks and international funds where markets close several hours before 4 P.M., the NAVs may be severely mispriced, especially on volatile days when large price movements occur.

Investors can use this information in at least one of two ways. They can construct a trading strategy to earn abnormal returns by buying funds when NAVs undervalue the stocks they hold and selling those funds a few days later. Second, they can protect themselves against other short-term traders by not investing in funds that use stale prices but do not take steps to restrict opportunistic trading.

Chapter 7—Trading by Insiders

Trading by insiders potentially conveys new information about the prospects of a company. Insiders have far superior knowledge about the company and the industry than the market. With this knowledge, their predictions of future trends are likely to be more accurate than the predictions based on publicly available information. Therefore, mimicking the trades of insiders generates above-normal annual returns of 10–15 percent.

To mimic insider trades, however, outsiders must first learn about those trades. A change in the SEC reporting requirement makes the information relating to insider trades more current and more readily available. Insiders are now required to report large trades to the SEC within two business days. Earlier, insiders could have waited as long as forty calendar days before reporting trades.

Chapter 8—Changes to the S&P 500 Index

Firms in the S&P 500 are occasionally replaced by new firms because the existing firm is no longer representative of the economy or the firm ceases to exist (goes bankrupt or is acquired by another firm). In general, the changes are announced about a week before they become effective.

Evidence indicates that a firm added to the index typically rises in value, while a firm dropped from the index falls in value. Not all of this change takes place on the announcement date; rather, it continues to occur until the effective date. However, after the effective date, the price change reverses itself. The added firms give up some value, and the deleted firms regain nearly all of their lost value.

Investors and arbitrageurs can earn abnormal returns by buying (short-selling) the added firm (deleted firm) upon announcement and reversing the positions on the effective date. The new positions are held for about a month and then liquidated.

Chapter 9—Merger Arbitrage

When a merger is announced, the target's price should rise close to the bidder's offer for the target. However, in most cases it does not. Two reasons account for the difference. First, successful completion of the merger is not a certainty. Second, shareholders of the target firm must earn a positive return until consummation of the merger, which implies that the target's price must be less than the offered price. Based on past completion rates and completion periods, the difference in the bidder's offer and the actual target price after merger announcement is larger than what it should be.

Investors and arbitrageurs can earn annual abnormal returns of 4 to 10 percent by buying the target upon a cash merger announcement, and by buying the target and short-selling the bidder upon announcement of a stock merger. The profitability of merger arbitrage can be improved by carefully selecting mergers in which large arbitrageurs are unlikely to participate but which generate higher abnormal returns.

Chapter 10—International Investing and the Home Bias

Financial economists have long maintained that all investors can improve the quality of their portfolios by investing a significant part of their portfolio in foreign securities. Including foreign assets reduces the risk of the portfolio due to low correlations between foreign stocks and domestic stocks without hurting return. However, individual investors routinely underweight foreign assets, perhaps due to their ignorance. While it is not possible to arbitrage home bias, investors should not suffer due to a home bias in their own portfolios.

Chapter 11—Bias in Currency Forward Rates

Currency forward rates are determined in accordance with interest rate parity, such that the total returns from investment in two risk-free assets are identical. Equivalence of returns implies that the forward rate foresees the currency with a higher interest rate falling in value. However, evidence reveals that currencies with higher interest rates do not actually fall as much as implied by the forward rate, creating the forward rate bias. A trading strategy that short-sells currencies with low interest rates and buys currencies with high interest rates can generate abnormal profits.

Chapter 12—Understanding and Learning From Behavioral Finance

While traditional finance is based on rational economic behavior of investors, behavioral finance claims that investors do not always behave rationally. This "irrational" behavior causes prices to move in anomalous patterns that cannot be explained by traditional finance theory but can be explained by behavioral finance. To be sure, traditional finance does allow some investors to behave irrationally, but those investors lose and are quickly driven out of the market by smart investors. Behavioral finance, on the other hand, believes that smart investors do not necessarily have the resources to dominate other investors. For example, limits on arbitrage (see Chapter 1) point to the limited nature of arbitrage activity, which may cause irrational investors to persist and may allow them to influence prices in a significant manner.

Whether or not the assumptions of behavioral finance are realistic, there are investors who suffer from behavioral biases. To earn optimal returns, investors are well advised to avoid those biases.

Chapter 13—A Description of Other Possible Mispricings

Ten pricing anomalies are discussed in Chapters 2 through 11. However, there are many more perceived anomalies in financial markets—probably hundreds. Some of the so-called anomalies have little basis or research associated with them. For example, street folklore would have you believe that an NFC win in the Super Bowl is good for the stock market. Whether true or not, there is no scientific or economic basis for such an assertion. This chapter briefly discusses many mispricings that have not been disproved by academic research. The list of references at the end of each mispricing allows the reader to learn more about that mispricing.

BEYOND THE RANDOM WALK

1

Market Efficiency and Anomalies

This chapter addresses common questions related to market efficiency and anomalies. If prices properly reflect available information, then markets are said to be efficient. Although markets are known to be broadly efficient, there may be pockets of inefficiency that lead to mispricings or anomalies.

In general, claims of anomalous pricing must be viewed with skepticism. The discussion describes reasons for skepticism as well as causes for persistence of some anomalies. Moreover, even when profits can't be made by trading on anomalous prices, it may be possible to alter trading behavior to avoid losses due to these anomalies.

What Is Market Efficiency?

Market efficiency in this book refers to the informational efficiency of markets as opposed to structural efficiency, administrative efficiency, or operational efficiency. That is, this chapter focuses on the efficiency with which information is reflected in prices. If new information becomes available about a stock (change in earnings), an industry (change in demand), or the economy (change in expected growth), an efficient market will reflect that information in a few minutes, even a few seconds. However, if only half of that information is reflected in the stock price immediately and the remaining half takes several days, then the market is less than fully efficient. Markets that are less than fully efficient open an opportunity for making profits because the inefficiency causes a mispricing in stocks. If a stock is slow to react and takes several days to fully reflect new information, then buying the stock immediately after good news and holding it for a few days would generate extra profit. However, if many people know about this inefficiency, they will all act the same way. As a result, the price will reflect the new information more quickly and the inefficiency will eventually disappear.

The idea behind efficient capital markets is quite simple but compelling. If you know that a stock is undervalued, then you will buy the stock until it is fairly valued. Or if the stock is overvalued, then you will sell the stock until it is fairly valued. Thus, market participants will ensure that prices are always accurate based on publicly available information.[1] The implicit assumption here is that trading based on nonpublic information, that is, insider trading, is illegal. Markets are said to be "semi-strong" form efficient if the prices are unbiased based on all publicly available information. If prices are unbiased based on all information (public and private), then markets are "strong" form efficient. Empirical evidence suggests that markets in the United States and other developed countries are essentially informationally efficient in the semi-strong form, though pockets of inefficiency may exist.

Who Cares about Market Efficiency?

Market efficiency is important for everyone because markets set prices. In particular, stock markets set prices for shares of stock. Currency markets set exchange rates. Commodity markets set prices of commodities such as wheat and corn. Setting correct prices is important because prices determine how available resources are allocated among different uses. If the price of a product is low relative to its cost, the investment in that product will fall. On the other hand, high prices encourage a greater allocation of resources. Thus, correct prices are important for resource allocation and, consequently, for economic growth. Unfortunately, correct prices are impossible to achieve because they require perfect foresight and information. The best a market can do is to form prices that reflect all available information.

Now, consider market efficiency for each constituent in turn: investors, companies, the government, and consumers. Investors are suppliers of capital that companies need for investment and operations. The investors earn a return on the capital they supply. If investors find that prices are predictable, then smart investors can earn extra return at the expense of naive or unsophisticated investors. This implies that unsophisticated investors earn a return that is less than the return that they should receive. In such an environment, unsophisticated investors will be reluctant to supply capital. The reduction in the availability of capital means that companies must pay a higher return for the capital due to restricted supply. However, the investors' capital does not disappear from the market altogether. The money not invested in corporate securities may be deposited with financial institutions, which may then lend that money to corporations. However, the cost of that money will be higher than if the companies could borrow directly from investors.

Besides the cost implication, companies care about market efficiency in another way. If markets are efficient aggregators of information, then companies can learn from the stock price reaction. For example, when AT&T bid for NCR in December 1990, AT&T's stock price promptly fell more than 6 percent, while NCR's price jumped 44 percent. Robert Allen, AT&T chairman, chided the markets for not appreciating the long-term benefits that would accrue to AT&T as a result of this combination. It took five years, but the market was proven right. AT&T bought NCR for $7.48 billion in 1991 but, after losses totaling $3.85 billion over the next five years, it was forced to spin off NCR in 1996 at less than half the purchase price, about $3.5 billion. Most companies, however, listen to the market's verdict on big decisions. Some mergers are aborted because of tepid reception by the market.

In addition to investors and companies, the government and the public are concerned about market efficiency because of the effect on economic growth. If the markets do not set prices based on all available information, then allocation of resources based on market prices will be flawed. Industries that deserve more capital will not get that capital, while industries that are not deserving of greater investment will. For example, if technology companies are overvalued by the market, then too many resources will be invested in technology companies, resulting in a misallocation. Also, market inefficiency in the form of speculative bubbles can affect the financial institutions and, through them, the entire economy. For example, Japan's stock market and real estate bubble in the 1980s has left the Japanese banking sector with nonperforming assets, affecting the country's economy.[2] Improper utilization of limited capital means suboptimal use of funds and underachievement in terms of growth and social welfare. Under such conditions, it is the government's responsibility and duty to intervene in financial markets to ensure optimal resource allocation. Whether the government can achieve the desired effect is an open question.

Thus, market efficiency is important so that optimal investment ensures optimal growth and maximizes social welfare.

Can Capital Markets Be Fully Efficient?

While market efficiency is desirable, there are three limitations in achieving that ideal: the cost of information, the cost of trading, and the limits of arbitrage. Strictly speaking, *arbitrage* refers to a profit earned with zero risk and zero investment. However, in this book the term is used in its more popular interpretation, that is, a superior risk-return trade-off that probably requires both risk and investment.

LIMITATION 1: COST OF INFORMATION

In an article aptly titled "On the Impossibility of Informationally Efficient Markets," Sandy Grossman and Joe Stiglitz go about proving just that. The concept behind the impossibility of informationally efficient markets is straightforward. Let us assume that markets are fully efficient, that is, they instantaneously reflect new information in prices. If that is the case, then no investor or market participant has any incentive to generate or report new information because the value of that information is zero. That is, when a company announces its earnings, no one wastes time trying to analyze that information because the price already reflects it. There is no value in even reading the corporate announcement. But if no one has any incentive to react to new information, then it is impossible to reflect new information in prices.

The implication of this is that markets can't be fully efficient because no one has the incentive to make them so. Market participants must be compensated in some way for making the market more efficient. Arbitrageurs and speculators must get something in return. Thus, instead of achieving instantaneous adjustment to new information, prices can adjust to new information only with a time lag. This time lag allows market participants to earn a reasonable return on their cost of obtaining and processing the information. If the return is abnormally high, it will attract more information processors, leading to a reduction in time lag. The net result is that prices take time to reflect new information because obtaining and processing that information is costly. However, if the delay is short enough (a few minutes), the markets are still considered efficient. But if they take several hours or several days, then the markets are not efficient.

LIMITATION 2: COST OF TRADING

Like the cost of information, traders incur costs while trading: their time, brokerage costs, and other related costs (see Appendix A for a discussion). When the cost of trading is high, financial assets are likely to remain mispriced for longer periods than when the cost of trading is low. In essence, like with the cost of information, the arbitrageurs or other traders must get an adequate return after accounting for costs to engage in an activity that makes the market more efficient. To the extent that trading activity is limited, prices will not reflect all available information. One factor that can have a large influence on prices is the difficulty in short selling. If short selling (that is, selling a stock that you do not own) is more difficult than buying long (that is, buying a stock that you do not own), then prices are likely to be biased upward. And if certain stocks are more difficult (and therefore more costly) to short-sell, the upward bias in prices is likely to be greater for those stocks. Thus, the greater the cost of trading, the greater the mispricing.

LIMITATION 3: LIMITS OF ARBITRAGE

The above discussion on why markets should be efficient suggests the presence of investors who would trade if they see a price that is inconsistent with their information, and would continue to trade until the price reflects the information they have available. On a simpler scale, consider two financial assets (say, stocks X and Y) that are equally risky but generate different returns. Obviously, one of the two assets is mispriced. If asset X generates the higher return and has a lower price, while asset Y generates the lower return and has a higher price, then to take advantage of the mispricing, arbitrageurs would buy asset X while at the same time short-selling Y. With the activities of like-minded arbitrageurs, the prices will converge and make them reflect the fundamental value associated with each asset.

There are four problems with this ideal scenario, however. First, it is not clear when, if ever, the prices will return to equilibrium levels or when the mispricing will disappear. If uninformed traders can continue to influence prices, then the prices of X and Y may actually diverge even more before eventually converging. If the divergence is significant, arbitrageurs may be forced to close their positions prematurely. Arbitrageurs who took short positions in Internet stocks in 1998 or 1999 on the belief that the stocks were overvalued would have been wiped out before the prices eventually fell. In fact, many short sellers went bankrupt in the late 1990s due to the ascent of the stock market. Even Warren Buffett, whom many regard as a smart investor, proclaimed that he had misread the new economy by not riding the technology wave. Today we know that he was correct to be skeptical of high Internet stock valuations, but at the time the prolonged period over which the mispricing seemed to persist caused him to accept defeat.

Second, it is rare to find two assets with exactly the same risk. Assume that X gives a higher return because it has a slightly higher risk than Y. However, smart investors believe that X's return is much higher than it should be based on differences in risk. Accordingly, they would like to implement a strategy of buying X while short-selling Y. But the risk inherent in such a strategy may deter them from arbitraging the mispricing. Thus, in cases where no close substitutes are available, the mispricing of a security may continue indefinitely.

Third and probably more important, we implicitly assumed that arbitrageurs have an unlimited amount of capital to take advantage of mispriced assets. That is not true. Just like everyone else, arbitrageurs have a limited amount of capital, which they devote to the most profitable strategies or to the most egregious mispricings while ignoring the remaining mispricings. The problem of limited capital becomes more severe in a bull market. Though there are potentially more mispricings in a bull market, the arbitrage capital is even more limited because most investors want to ride the market rather than find nebulous mispricings that generate relatively small returns.

Finally, most arbitrageurs act as agents because they manage other people's money. As agents, arbitrageurs must abide by the constraints imposed on them by the owners of capital (the principals). The principals are unwilling to give the agents a free hand in the pursuit of extra returns because the principals are concerned that the agents may not actually earn those extra returns and that the risk associated with those returns may be unacceptably high. Therefore, the typical mandate given to an agent will specify permitted strategies, the amount of capital at risk including the effects of leverage, and the maximum possible loss. For example, an arbitrageur may be allowed to invest only in merger arbitrage securities or only in distressed securities, with loss limited to 10 percent of the capital invested. While these constraints protect the owners of capital, they also limit the operation of arbitrage activities in the market. In addition, an arbitrageur's ability to attract more capital can be severely constrained when opportunities become more attractive if principals use an arbitrageur's past performance to judge his ability. Assume that an arbitrageur believes that a stock is undervalued by 10 percent and buys that stock. Assume further that the mispricing gets worse over the next few weeks and the stock becomes undervalued by 20 percent. The arbitrageur should probably increase his stake in the stock. However, in the meantime, due to the worsening mispricing, the arbitrageur has lost 10 percent of the capital. Principals observe the loss of 10 percent and may not believe that the arbitrageur has any superior skills. Instead of giving him or her more capital, they may ask the arbitrageur to immediately sell that stock, further depressing the stock price and making the mispricing even more acute. It is easy to see that there are serious limits of arbitrage activity that may cause mispricings to persist.

What about the small investor? Why can't the millions of small investors seek out and trade on these mispricings, especially the small mispricings that are ignored by professional arbitrageurs or where arbitrage activity is limited by constraints imposed on the arbitrageur? In general, the small investors do not have the expertise and knowledge to identify and profitably trade mispricings. If this book is able to educate investors so that they trade away the mispricings or trade in a more rational manner, the markets will become more efficient aggregators of information, with concurrent improvement in social welfare.

What Is a Pricing Anomaly?

A mispricing is any *predictable* deviation from a normal or expected return. For example, assume that IBM's stock is expected to earn a normal return of 15 percent a year. If the current stock price is $100, then the price should increase to $115 after one year, assuming that IBM does not distribute any dividends. If a market timer *predicts* that IBM will actually appreciate by 20 percent or more this year, and IBM does earn more than the normal return repeatedly and consistently in a predictable manner, then it is a mispricing. Similarly, a *predictable* deviation on the downside (less than 15 percent) is also a mispricing. On the other hand, an unpredictable movement in price is not a mispricing. For example, if the actual price after a year is $90 or $130, that is not a mispricing even though the actual return is different from the expected return. Deviations from the normal return are expected and, by definition, must occur for risky securities. On average, however, the deviation must be close to zero.

If a mispricing is well known and persistent, then it is referred to as an anomaly. In their article on anomalies in the *Review of Financial*

Studies, Michael Brennan of UCLA and Yihong Xia of the University of Pennsylvania define an anomaly as "a statistically significant difference between the realized average returns . . . and the returns that are predicted by a particular asset pricing model." Thus, persistent realization of abnormal returns (actual return minus the expected return) is referred to as an anomaly. The persistence in abnormal returns results in predictability of returns.

When Is a Mispricing Not a Mispricing?

Investment professionals, academics, and novice traders spend a great deal of time and effort to discover mispricings because these phenomena have the potential to make someone very rich. Therefore, mispricings are frequently touted by market timers, brokers, and other investment professionals. It is important to know how to judge the validity of a mispricing. In this section, the limitations and biases in the process of discovering mispricings are discussed along with simple tests to detect whether the mispricings can be attributed to such limitations. An understanding of these biases can be used to test other mispricings. Moreover, it will be natural to become more skeptical of mispricings or anomalies that are frequently cited as evidence against market efficiency. The intent here is not to actually check for limitations of the mispricing, but to judge whether flaws in the discovery process may have caused the observed mispricing.

MEASUREMENT OF ABNORMAL RETURN

If markets are efficient, then the expected *abnormal* return is zero. On the other hand, if the abnormal return is nonzero *and* it is possible to predict the direction of the deviation, then the pricing constitutes an anomaly. Since abnormal return is the actual return minus the normal return, a problem arises in defining the normal return (the term is used interchangeably with *expected return*). How do you define or measure normal return?

In the IBM example, it was assumed that the normal return is 15 percent. Is the 15 percent assumption correct? Who can say? Unfortunately, there is no accepted method for estimating a stock's normal return. Theoretical models include Nobel laureate William Sharpe's capital asset pricing model (CAPM) and Steve Ross's arbitrage pricing theory (APT). APT cannot be applied in a practical way because there are too many unknowns. CAPM is deterministic, but the CAPM does not have much empirical support. In the words of Eugene Fama, "[I]nferences about market efficiency can be sensitive to the assumed model for expected returns" (Fama 1998, 288).

Other models exist using alternate measures of risk derived from statistical methods and historical returns. Researchers have also discovered that stock return depends on such factors as size, the ratio of market value to book value, beta, momentum, and so on. However, these are empirical returns that do not necessarily have strong theoretical support. Further, there is no guarantee that these factors will continue to have explanatory power in the future. So, the question remains: what is IBM's normal return? There is no exact and generally accepted measure of expected return. However, it is possible to say that a particular return is too high or too low. For example, a normal return of 50 percent for IBM is too high and a return of 0 percent is probably too low. One way of getting a reasonable estimate is to estimate its relative return—relative to another firm with similar characteristics. The idea is to identify a similar (or control) firm—similar on several dimensions known to explain the cross section of returns, such as size, market-to-book ratio, and so on. Then measure the abnormal return for the sample firm as the difference between the sample firm's return and the control firm's return. Coke and Pepsi are good examples. If Coke and Pepsi are considered similar firms, then to find Coke's abnormal return, Pepsi's return would be used as the normal return. The difference between Coke's actual return and Pepsi's return is the abnormal return earned by Coke. Generally, it is better to use a group of firms as a control instead of using a single control firm so that one firm's chaotic price movements don't significantly influence the abnormal return calculation.

How critical is it to estimate IBM's normal return accurately for detecting a mispricing? Should it be 15 percent or 25 percent per year? The normal return becomes crucial only in long-term mispricings. Consider that IBM's return based on a particular mispricing is 25 percent over one year. The return is abnormal if the normal annual return is assumed to be 15 percent, but not if the normal annual return is 25 percent. On the other hand, if the mispricing occurs over short periods of time, then the normal return becomes essentially inconsequential. If IBM's stock earns 1 percent in a *day*, then the normal return does not really matter—whether it is 0.06 percent per day (15 percent per year based on 250 trading days per year) or 0.1 percent per day (25 percent per year). In either case, the mispricing is large: 0.94 percent or 0.90 percent for a day. This means that, holding the magnitude of mispricing constant, long-term mispricings should generally be subject to a much greater degree of skepticism than short-term mispricings.

As Fama states, "[A]n advantage of this approach [short-period event studies] is that because daily expected returns are close to zero, the model for expected returns does not have a big effect on inferences about abnormal returns" (Fama 1998, 283). He continues to stress the problem with long-term normal returns: "the bad-model problem is ubiquitous, but it is more serious in long-term returns. The reason is that bad-model errors in expected returns grow faster with the return horizon than the volatility of returns" (Fama 1998, 285).

DATA MINING

If you look hard enough at almost any bunch of numbers, you can find a pattern. Since anomalies are predictable patterns in returns, a person who studies hundreds of different relationships and millions of different observations is likely to find a pattern; this is called data mining. For example, try to find a relationship between the stock return and any number of different variables, such as the weather in New York, the number of sunspots, the height of ocean waves, growth in world population, or the number of birds in San Francisco. Given a large enough number of possible relationships and enough tries, it is possible to find a statistically significant relationship between a stock return and another variable. That relationship does not really exist: it is there just by chance. Further, as Fama states, "splashy results get more attention, and this creates an incentive to find them" (Fama 1998, 287). Fischer Black once said, "[M]ost of the so-called anomalies that have plagued the literature on investments seem likely the result of data-mining" (Fischer Black 1993, 9).

An example of data mining is illustrative. Take a researcher who believes that Nasdaq 100 returns are predictable on an intraday basis. He is determined to find this predictability to impress his boss. He can generate and test for thousands of different relationships to discover a pattern. He begins by calculating the six one-hour returns for each day: 10 A.M.–11 A.M. return, 11 A.M.–12 noon return, and so on. He analyzes the hourly returns to see whether the return during the first hour is related to the return during the second hour, whether the second-hour return is related to the return during the third hour, and so on. Then he tries to find significant correlations among 13 half-hour returns, and among 26 quarter-hour returns, and among 78 five-minute returns, and among 390 one-minute returns. Unsuccessful but persistent, he introduces filters, that is, selects only those observations where the Nasdaq 100 return is more than two standard deviations away from the mean. Again he fails to discover anything interesting. Next he introduces volume as a variable. Only those observations that have trading volume in the top 10 percent are selected. He continues this process until he discovers a pattern. Finally he finds that on high-volume days, a negative Nasdaq 100 return in the 3:00–3:30 P.M. period is followed by a negative return in the 3:30–4:00 P.M. period with a 90 percent probability. This is data mining at its best, but the boss is not impressed, and I hope you are not either.

Artificial anomalies need to be separated from real anomalies. Perhaps the most important thing is to assess the intuitiveness of the relationship discovered by researchers. Does it make sense? Can the number of birds in San Francisco really mean anything for stock returns? If it doesn't make intuitive and economic sense, then it is probably a case of data mining. Another way to check for data mining is to use an out-of-sample test, which is testing the same relationship using data from a different country or for an entirely different period. If data mining worked in this case, it may not work for a different sample. If it is not possible to get another data set, then test the relationship over subperiods of the data. The results must hold for subperiods as well as for the whole period unless there is a valid reason for a change in the observed relationship.

SURVIVORSHIP BIAS

Another source of unreliability of an anomaly is survivorship bias, which exists whenever results are based on existing entities. For example, a simple study of existing mutual funds will find that mutual funds, on average, outperform their benchmarks. The problem with such a sample is survivorship. Only well-performing funds continue to survive, while the underperformers die. Thus, a sample of existing mutual funds will not contain funds that underperformed and died. If all funds, dead and alive, are included in the sample, then the funds, on average, do not outperform their benchmarks. The sample of existing mutual funds has a survivorship bias and will result in an overestimation of fund performance.

Survivorship is important in market timing studies, as market timing newsletters or services use many strategies and frequently add new strategies and discontinue others. Which ones does the market timer add? The ones that have shown great promise based on past trends. Which ones are discontinued? The ones that no longer show continuing profitability. The record displayed by the market timer shows only the successful strategies and not the unsuccessful strategies, giving readers the false impression of market timing prowess where none exists.

Survivorship bias is widespread in many spheres of the investment world. People with a good investment record are retained, while others are dumped. It seems as if all the investment firms have analysts who can predict the market. What about the guests on CNBC? Are they really good stock pickers, or are they simply lucky?

SMALL SAMPLE BIAS

Mispricings may be caused by a small sample bias. Usually the small sample refers to the period of observation. For example, riskier stocks should earn higher returns than other stocks. Since stocks with small market capitalization (size) are considered riskier than large-size stocks, small-size stocks are expected to earn higher returns. However, during the 1995–99 period, the large-size stocks outperformed the small-size stocks. Looking at this limited time period, one may conclude that a mispricing exists. However, over long periods (1926–2002 or 1962–2002) small-size stocks did earn higher returns than large-size stocks. The small sample bias is especially relevant to anomalies that do not have a reasonable explanation, especially if it appears that the mispricing has occurred just by chance.

SELECTION BIAS

Another bias that may creep into the discovery of mispricings is selection bias, that is, the sample may be biased in favor of finding the desired result. Assume you want to measure the ownership of cell phones in the general American population. If you polled only people working in Manhattan, your estimate will be biased upward because the sample is biased and the result is falsely attributed to the entire American population, including rural and less urban areas.

In the case of stock market studies, a selection bias can creep in when the results arise from a certain part of the sample but seem to be representative of the entire market. For example, consider the January effect. According to the January effect, firms gain abnormally in the first few days of January. However, the effect is not broad-based; rather, it is due to firms that are small in size. Once the small firms are removed, the January effect disappears. The discovery of the small-firm effect is important, because it is necessary to attribute the effect to only the small firms and not to the entire stock market.

Nonsynchronous Trading

Stocks trade with different frequencies. Some stocks may trade continuously, that is, several times a minute, such as Pfizer, Intel, and Cisco. Other stocks may not trade for several hours or even several days. If a stock trades only once every day, at 10 A.M., the return based on that day's 10 A.M. trade will capture market movements that took place over the last twenty-four hours. The closing price at 4:00 P.M. will reflect the price of the last trade, which actually took place at 10 A.M., without accounting for any market movements that have taken place since 10 A.M. If the market jumped after 10 A.M., then the next day's return (but not today's return) of this stock will reflect the increase in price. If you construct a portfolio of such inactively traded stocks, then it will seem that these stocks have predictable returns—that is, the stock price will change in accordance with the market, but with a delay. Since you can predict returns, a natural strategy is to buy this portfolio whenever the market goes up after 10 A.M. and sell this portfolio if the market goes down after 10 A.M. The problem with returns caused by nonsynchronous trading is that those returns are not actually tradable. The 10 A.M. price is not a price at which a trade can be executed. As soon as any trader tries to trade, the price will move to reflect market movements, and the excess returns will disappear.

There is a way to take advantage of stocks that trade infrequently or at different times: trade mutual funds, where a buy does not necessarily trigger a trade in the underlying stock. Those cases are discussed in Chapter 6, "Mispricing of Mutual Funds."

Risk

Most investors demand a higher return for a riskier position than for a less risky position. That is why bank deposits give a lower return than stocks, because stocks are riskier than bank deposits. Small-size stocks have higher returns than large stocks because small stocks are riskier than large stocks. This means that a riskier strategy must also generate a higher return. Therefore, it is important to control for risk when comparing trading strategies designed to take advantage of mispricings. Further, historical risk estimates may not be appropriate if the mispricing is around certain corporate or market events, because volatility, and hence risk, generally increases around those events. Thus, anomalies that are event-driven must generate higher returns to compensate for the risk associated with those events. However, risk is probably not important if only a short holding period is required.

In any case, the abnormal returns computed for any mispricing must account for the level of risk inherent in exploiting that anomaly. Inaccurate estimates of risk are more likely to affect anomalies that require long holding periods or anomalies that have very small abnormal returns even with short holding periods. Therefore, care must be taken to ensure that adequate compensation is provided for risk.

Explanation for the Mispricing

It is necessary to reiterate the importance of a reasonable and intuitive explanation as a basis for the anomaly. Anomalies that are based on reasonable explanations are less likely to be the figment of someone's imagination or data mining and are more credible. Some anomalies exist because of government regulations or arise from institutional constraints. For example, the January effect is best explained by capital gains taxes. That is not to say that all anomalies must have rational explanations. However, an anomaly with a rational explanation is more believable than one without.

Can New Mispricings Be Discovered?

Until now, the discussion has focused on known anomalies. But investors, academics, and practitioners are constantly trying to discover new mispricings. Any new mispricing can potentially result in large profits to the explorer. While one must be skeptical of new mispricings—whether it is predicting when a stock split will be announced or which firm will be acquired—one must acknowledge the possibility of discovering new mispricings. Just because a pattern can't be discovered may not mean that it doesn't exist. At the same time, one must be wary of new mispricings and ensure that they meet the tests listed above.

Why Does a Mispricing Persist?

If a mispricing exists, then smart investors and arbitrageurs should take advantage of it to earn abnormal returns. As more and more arbitrageurs participate, the mispricing should disappear. In general, persistence of an anomaly is a cause for concern. However, there could be a number of reasons for an anomaly's continuation, as discussed below.

The Mispricing Is Not Well Understood

It is possible that a mispricing is well known but not well understood. For example, the weekend effect is well known. According to the weekend effect, first discovered in the 1970s, the return on the last trading day of the week is highly positive. On the other hand, the return on the first trading day of the week is usually negative. Until recently the weekend effect did not have a good explanation. Without a satisfactory and intuitive explanation, the mispricing does not meet one of the key conditions for acceptance. Though there is overwhelming evidence of its existence based on past data, investors are wary of trading on it because the mispricing may cease to exist at any time or may not occur during the current period. As Gabriel Hawawini and Donald Keim remark, "[that] effects have persisted for nearly 100 years in no way guarantees their persistence in the future" (Hawawini and Keim, 2000, 35).

Further, without knowledge of a reason, it is difficult to identify stocks that will exhibit the mispricing. Is it only among small stocks? Is it among large stocks? Is it among stocks that have listed options? Or maybe among stocks that just issued new equity? It becomes very risky for an arbitrageur to try to profit from a mispricing without knowing why it exists. As a consequence, the mispricing may not be arbitraged by risk-averse investors.

Arbitrage Is Too Costly

Sometimes the anomaly is known and understood but the arbitrage is too costly to transact. These costs have three components. The first component is the bid ask spread, which is the difference between the highest price that any buyer is willing to pay (the bid price) and the lowest price that a seller wants (the asking price). As all arbitrage strategies require a buy and a sell, the spread contributes to the total cost of transacting. Second, brokerage fees must be paid. Finally, each large trade can have a market impact. Even an actively traded stock such as General Electric may find it difficult to absorb a million-share order without moving the price. A large buy will cause the price to rise, meaning you pay more than the price indicated by the quotes. Similarly, a large sell will cause the price to decline. In both cases, the market impact of the order has the effect of increasing the trading costs.

Anomalies with high transactions costs may persist because large institutions or arbitrageurs may be reluctant to trade if large dollar positions cannot be taken without moving the price or if the bid-ask spreads are large. For example, the January effect has been known for decades and is caused by tax-loss selling of small-size stocks. Nonetheless, the January effect persists because it is necessary to trade hundreds of small-size stocks. Small stocks have high bid-ask spreads and low liquidity, making the potential benefit insufficient to offset the transaction costs.

PROFIT POTENTIAL IS INSUFFICIENT

Certain anomalies may generate small profits that cannot be multiplied easily. In those cases, institutions may not be interested because there is a limited profit potential. Imagine a $1 billion mutual fund trying to make a profit of $10,000 on a few trades. The return is only 0.001 percent. The fund manager could probably spend time more profitably on other pursuits. This is especially true of trading in small-cap stocks, where the institutions can't take large positions for fear of moving the price. Such mispricings are ideally suited to individual trading.

ARBITRAGE IS NOT POSSIBLE DUE TO TRADING RESTRICTIONS

A known mispricing may persist if institutional features limit trading. This is especially true for restrictions on short selling. For example, it is not possible to short-sell initial public offerings (IPOs) for a few days after the issue because shares are not available to borrow. The mispricing, if any, may persist for a few days, until short selling becomes possible. Again in the case of IPOs, the underwriters engage in price stabilization activities that can, in some cases, keep the price at an inflated level for almost a month.

A case in point is the spin-off of Palm by 3Com. 3Com sold a fraction of Palm as an IPO in March 2000 but retained 95 percent of its shares. At that time it announced that it would spin off the remaining shares to 3Com shareholders at the rate of 1.5 Palm shares for every 3Com share. Even assuming that 3Com was worthless without Palm, 3Com's share price should have been approximately 1.5 times Palm's share price because a single 3Com share gave the right to own 1.5 Palm shares. On the first trading day after the IPO, Palm's price was $95. Using the ratio of 1.5:1, 3Com's price should have been about $142.50. However, 3Com's price was only $82. A simple strategy to earn an arbitrage profit would have been to buy 1 share of 3Com and short-sell 1.5 shares of Palm. But arbitrageurs could not employ this strategy because shares of Palm were not available to short-sell. In this case, the mispricing existed, and persisted for several days, because of trading restrictions.

BEHAVIORAL BIASES MAY AFFECT INVESTMENT DECISIONS

If investors are reluctant to realize losses, are quick to take profits, do not diversify enough, and suffer from other instances of irrational behavior, then mispricings may occur. They may persist because investors do not change their behavior even in light of new information. The behavioral biases and the manner in which they affect investment decisions are discussed in Chapter 12.

Underreaction to earnings news can be explained by behavioral biases. If the earnings announcement is positive, the stock price rises. But the rise is stymied by the premature selling initiated by individual investors who sell to realize gains. As the selling pressure abates, the stock price slowly rises to the correct level. On the other hand, if the earnings announcement is negative, the stock price falls. But it does not fall sufficiently because individual investors continue to hold on to the stock hoping to recoup their losses. The stock eventually reaches the correct price but with a delay due to the behavioral biases of the investors.

However, irrational investor behavior can explain persistence only in conjunction with other explanations. Even if some investors are irrational, arbitrageurs should take advantage of that irrationality and in the process cause the mispricing to disappear.

Until investors learn to think and act rationally and minimize emotional trades, mispricings are also likely to be caused by irrational behavior.

LIMITS OF ARBITRAGE REVISITED

One reason for persistence of mispricings is the limits of arbitrage. As discussed in "Can Capital Markets Be Fully Efficient?" earlier in this chapter, arbitrageurs may not have the capital or the freedom to pursue the mispricings as aggressively as they would otherwise. However, the limits placed on arbitrageurs allow individual investors to gain from the knowledge provided in this book. If individual investors begin to target mispricings effectively, there will be one less reason for the persistence of mispricings in financial markets.

Can Valid Anomalies Be Unprofitable?

Besides analyzing anomalies, this book contains suggestions for implementing trading strategies designed to take advantage of mispricings. Many anomalies are especially suited to individual investors because the profit potential is small by institutional standards, the mispricing appears infrequently, or the trading costs are high. Where trading costs are high, individual investors, like institutional investors, cannot make arbitrage profits. However, individual investors can alter the timing of their trades so that they are not negatively affected by known mispricings. For example, based on the weekend effect, if an investor wants to sell a stock, he should sell it on a Friday instead of the following Monday.

At the same time, readers must recognize the limitations of this book and factors that may make these anomalies disappear or appear not to exist.

Documented Anomalies Are Based on Averages

Just because an anomaly exists does not mean that all trades will be profitable. For example, in the case of changes to the S&P 500, stocks deleted from the S&P 500 index lose value and will usually recoup their losses within a few weeks. This statement is based on an analysis of over three hundred deletions between 1962 and 2002. Does it imply that the next stock deleted from the index is *likely* to appreciate? Yes. But *will* it appreciate? Maybe not. Similarly, the results do not imply that the next twenty stocks deleted from the index will necessarily appreciate, though they are likely to. But the results do imply that if you follow this strategy for the next two to three years *and no significant changes take place in how the market reacts to these deletions*, then you will earn risk-adjusted returns that are larger than the normal return. However, an unsuccessful run of any mispricing can cost the investor a significant loss of capital.

Positive Abnormal Returns Do Not Mean Positive Returns

The anomalous evidence presented generally focuses on abnormal returns. Since an abnormal return is the actual return minus the normal return, the actual return could be negative even though the abnormal return is positive. Consider implementing a trading strategy with a 10 percent annual abnormal return. If the market drops 23 percent during a year, as it did in 2002, then the actual return is only −13 percent. Though −13 percent is much better than −23 percent, it is still a loss. Therefore, the anomalies discussed do not suggest absolute profitability, only profitability relative to the normal return.

Conditions Governing Anomalies May Change

An anomaly may disappear because of a change in conditions. In many cases the anomalies exist because of individual or institutional reasons. For example, the January and December effects are related to taxes. If the government reduces the capital gains tax (as in 2003), then the January and December effects are likely to slightly weaken. Similarly, it is possible to time mutual funds that hold foreign stocks because they use stale prices in computing net asset values (see Chapter 6). If the fund companies revise their rules for pricing, then the gains due to timing will disappear.

The foregoing discussion assumes that a valid explanation exists for each anomaly. That is not always the case. There are anomalies, such as the home bias, for which no reasonable explanation exists. Home bias is the tendency of investors to underweight foreign stocks compared to an optimally diversified portfolio. In other cases, the explanation, though supported by empirical evidence, may be incorrect. Whenever explanations are either false or unavailable, the anomaly is likely to disappear without any warning.

ANOMALIES MAY BE ARBITRAGED AWAY BY TRADING

If markets are efficient and investors are rational, then the more popular this book becomes, the greater the chance that people will trade on these anomalies until they are no longer profitable. To profit from this book, however, it is not necessary to trade on the anomalies listed. The primary objective is to ensure an understanding of these anomalies so that investors can sidestep unprofitable situations or marginally alter their trading patterns in beneficial ways.

Role of Individual Investors

The fact that the market cannot be fully efficient in spite of the personal profit motive and the presence of arbitrageurs and other smart investors provides the basis for this book. As noted above, constraints placed on arbitrageurs allow many mispricings to continue. On the other hand, individual investors are free to invest and trade in any way they want, with few constraints. Unlike professional arbitrageurs, individuals can continually change the strategy they use. Trades of individual investors will not have a significant effect on price. A profit of $5,000 on a few trades is sufficient to compensate individuals for their time and effort. Individuals can design and implement an exit strategy by using limit orders and stop limit orders (see Chapter 12). Arbitrageurs are loath to take on very risky positions. They prefer small margins but work with very high volume. As a result, currency markets and bond markets attract significantly more arbitrage activity than stock markets. Stock markets can be more effectively tapped by individual investors.

Why aren't individual investors more active in arbitraging mispricings? The primary reason is that their knowledge of anomalies is limited. The purpose of this book is to identify anomalies and make them accessible to investors, professionals, and academics.[3] I hope that trading based on these anomalies will improve market efficiency with the associated benefits of superior resource allocation and enhanced social welfare.

Key Points

- Markets are said to be efficient if publicly available information is reflected in prices in an unbiased manner.

- Efficient markets are desirable for the society because prices determine allocation of resources.

- Markets cannot be fully efficient because of the cost of collecting and analyzing information, cost of trading, and limits on the capital available to arbitrageurs.

- All anomalies must be viewed with caution and skepticism, as spurious mispricings can surface for a variety of reasons, such as errors in defining normal return, data mining, survivorship bias, small sample bias, selection bias, nonsynchronous trading, and misestimation of risk.

- Though anomalies should disappear in an efficient market, they may persist because they are not well understood, arbitrage is too costly, the profit potential is insufficient, trading restrictions exist, and behavioral biases exist.

- Documented and valid anomalies may still be unprofitable because the evidence is based on averages (and may include a large fraction of losers), conditions responsible for the anomaly may change, and trading by informed investors may cause the anomaly to disappear.

References for Further Reading

Alexander, Colin. 1999. *Streetsmart Guide to Timing the Stock Market: When to Buy, Sell, and Sell Short* (New York: McGraw-Hill). The author uses basic technical tools from futures markets to pick stocks.

Black, Fischer. 1993. Return and Beta. *Journal of Portfolio Management* 20(1), 8–18.

Brennan, Michael, and Yihong Xia. 2001. Assessing Asset Pricing Anomalies. *Review of Financial Studies* 14(4), 905–42.

Cooper, Michael, Robert Gutierrez, and William Marcum. 2003. On the Predictability of Stock Returns in Real Time. *Journal of Business,* forthcoming.

Fama, Eugene F. 1998. Market Efficiency, Long-Term Returns, and Behavioral Finance. *Journal of Financial Economics* 49(3), 283–306.

Fosback, Norman G. 1976. *Stock Market Logic: A Sophisticated Approach to Profits on Wall Street* (Fort Lauderdale: Institute for Econometric Research).

Grossman, Sanford J., and Joseph E. Stiglitz. 1980. On the Impossibility of Informationally Efficient Markets. *American Economic Review* 70(3), 393–408.

Haugen, Robert. 2002. *The Inefficient Stock Market: What Pays Off and Why* (Upper Saddle River, N.J.: Prentice Hall).

Hawawini, Gabriel, and Donald B. Keim. 2000. "The Cross-Section of Common Stock Returns: A Review of the Evidence and Some New Findings." In Donald B. Keim and William T. Ziemba, editors, *Security Market Imperfections in Worldwide Equity Markets* (New York: Cambridge University Press).

Keim, Donald B., and William T. Ziemba (editors). 2000. *Security Market Imperfections in Worldwide Equity Markets* (New York: Cambridge University Press). The book is a collection of academic articles.

Lo, Andrew W., and Craig MacKinlay. 1990. Data Snooping Biases in Tests of Financial Asset Pricing Models. *Review of Financial Studies* 3, 431–67.

———. 1999. *A Non-Random Walk Down Wall Street* (Princeton: Princeton University Press).

Malkiel, Burton. 1989. A *Random Walk Down Wall Street* (New York: Norton).

Michaud, Richard O. 1999. *Investment Styles, Market Anomalies, and Global Stock Selection* (Charlottesville, Va.: Research Foundation of the Institute of Chartered Financial Analysts). The book focuses on global factor-return relationships for institutional equity management and style analysis.

Noddings, Thomas C. 1985. *Low-Risk Strategies for the High-Performance Investor* (Chicago: Probus). This book focuses on convertible bonds.

O'Shaughnessy, James P. 2001. *What Works on Wall Street: A Guide to the Best-Performing Strategies of All Time* (New York: McGraw-Hill).

Shefrin, Hersh. 2000. *Beyond Greed and Fear: Understanding Behavioral Finance and the Psychology of Investing,* Financial Management Association Survey and Synthesis Series (Boston: Harvard Business School Press).

Shleifer, Andrei, and Robert W. Vishny. 1997. The Limits of Arbitrage. *Journal of Finance* 52(1), 25–55.

Shleifer, Andrei. 2000. *Inefficient Markets: An Introduction to Behavioral Finance* (Oxford: Oxford University Press).

Thaler, Richard H. (editor). 1993. *Advances in Behavioral Finance* (New York: Russell Sage Foundation).

Notes

1. Correct prices are difficult to obtain because it is impossible to predict the future. However, market efficiency requires only that prices be based on all *available* information.
2. The government must recognize and respond to the market's signals. Heizo Takenaka, Japan's financial services minister appointed in mid-2002, is the first "Japanese bank czar who seems sympathetic to the market's dim view of the [Japanese] financial system's health. Mr. Takenaka's predecessors all claimed there was nothing wrong with the quality of big banks' capital—a claim disputed by the rating agencies. But Mr. Takenaka admits there are problems. 'Technically, it's OK,' he said in an interview last week. 'But the market doesn't think so.'" Quoted in Phred Dvorak, "Japan's Financial Crisis Makes a Comeback," *Wall Street Journal*, November 22, 2002.
3. Many academics in finance routinely use their knowledge and research to manage hedge funds or other investment portfolios. For example, Dimensional Fund Advisors, which manages more than $30 billion in assets, is associated with Eugene Fama of the University of Chicago, Ken French of Dartmouth College, and two of their former students, David Booth and Rex Sinquefield. LSV Asset Management, which manages about $8 billion, is owned by Josef Lakonishok of the University of Illinois, Andrei Shleifer of Harvard, and Robert Vishny of the University of Chicago. Long Term Capital Management, whose failure shook world financial markets in 1998 and which had to be rescued by a group of large banks prodded on by the Federal Reserve, was advised by Nobel laureates Robert Merton and Myron Scholes.

2

The January Effect and the New December Effect

Small loser stocks are known to appreciate considerably in January, giving rise to the so-called January effect. The primary explanation for the January effect is tax-loss selling by investors in December to realize capital losses that are used to offset capital gains. When the selling pressure abates in January, the loser stocks appreciate. Unfortunately, it is not possible to arbitrage the January effect, though investors can gain by changing their trading patterns.

The December effect is similar in spirit to the January effect. Stocks that have done well in the January-November period are not sold by investors in December because selling those stocks will result in taxable capital gains. By waiting a few days, investors can postpone payment of capital gains taxes by almost one year. It is relatively easy to gain from the December effect, as popularly available indexes can be used for trading.

Description

Academics, practitioners, and investors have known about the January effect for decades.[1] It is generally accepted that the January effect is a consequence of tax-loss selling. Since investors must pay taxes on *net* capital gains, investors sell losers toward year-end to realize capital losses that can offset capital gains. Thus, past losers experience abnormal selling pressure in December. In January the selling pressure is relieved, resulting in large gains for loser stocks. Evidence of large January returns for loser stocks is dubbed the *January effect*.

Another relatively unknown activity driven by the tax code is tax-gain selling. If investors realize capital losses to offset capital gains, it is also natural for investors to postpone realization of capital gains so that they can postpone payment of taxes on capital gains. Thus, rational investors will sell winners in January instead of December. By waiting a few days, it is possible to defer payment of taxes by almost one year. The selling pressure on winners will be small in December, causing the price of winners to rise. The incidence of large December returns for winner stocks is called the *December effect*. The media sometimes refer to this as the Christmas effect.

Evidence

DAILY RETURNS BY MONTH

The average daily returns, in percent, by month over the entire 1963–2001 period are reported in Table 2.1 for all NYSE, AMEX, and Nasdaq stocks. At the top of the table, equally weighted and value-weighted returns are reported. Equally weighted return is the mean return to all stocks, with all stocks carrying equal weights. Value-weighted return is the mean return to all stocks where each stock's weight is equal to its market capitalization. Thus, General Electric's return will carry a weight larger than Dell Computer's because GE's market capitalization is larger than Dell's.

It can be seen from Table 2.1 that, contrary to media reports, the December return is similar to the return in other months.[2] There is no evidence of a broad-based December rally. The value-weighted daily return in December is 0.055 percent, compared with 0.070 percent in January and 0.072 percent in November. The returns in April, August, and October are also at least as large as those in December. The equally weighted daily return in December is 0.056 percent, the third lowest among all months, and larger than only the returns in March and May.

However, the results are different if firms are grouped based on market capitalization and return. Market capitalization is the market value of a firm, computed as the product of the price and number of shares outstanding. The groups are constructed as follows. Each month, all firms are categorized into size deciles (ten groups with the same number of firms in each group) based on the market capitalization at the end of the previous month from 1963 to 2001. Within each size decile, return quartiles (four groups with the same number of firms in each group) are formed based on the price drop from the maximum price attained over the previous eleven months to the price at the end of the preceding month. Average daily returns

Table 2.1. Daily Returns by Month

Size Decile	Return Quartile	Jan.	Feb.	Mar.	Apr.	May	Jun.	Jul.	Aug.	Sep.	Oct.	Nov.	Dec.	Annual
Equally-weighted returns		0.101	0.074	0.041	0.070	0.053	0.057	0.056	0.065	0.056	0.061	0.075	0.056	0.065
Value-weighted returns		0.070	0.048	0.034	0.057	0.047	0.041	0.049	0.055	0.040	0.063	0.072	0.055	0.053
Small Loser Firms														
1	1	1.029*	0.192+	0.052	0.025	0.007	-0.050	-0.029	-0.088	-0.050	-0.143+	-0.183+	-0.202+	0.045
2	1	0.616*	0.003	-0.050	-0.097	-0.071	-0.130*	-0.122+	-0.154+	-0.178+	-0.247*	-0.189+	-0.220*	-0.071*
Large Winner Firms														
9	4	0.016	0.052	0.013	0.050	0.013	0.011	-0.008	0.017	0.011	-0.037	0.075+	0.113*	0.027*
10	4	0.008	0.043	0.010	0.039	0.012	0.016	0.000	0.011	-0.011	0.002	0.077*	0.090*	0.025*

Returns are reported in percent. Statistical significance is at better than 1 percent for returns marked with * and at better than 5 percent for returns marked with +.

in percent are reported for each month in each of the categories. Firms in the smallest size decile (decile 1) and the lowest return quartile (quartile 1) within that decile are called small loser firms. Firms in the largest size decile (decile 10) and the highest return quartile (quartile 4) within that decile are called large winner firms. Returns for the next size decile are reported for comparison.

The returns for the select groups are more interesting. On average, the small loser firms earn significantly positive returns only in January and February and significantly negative returns in October, November, and December. In fact, the January return is 1 percent per day, a gain of more than 20 percent for January (assuming twenty to twenty-two trading days per month), compared with a loss of 4 percent in December. On the other hand, the large winner firms gain significantly only in November and December. For the remaining months of the year, the returns are not significantly different from zero. The return in December is about 2 percent for those firms. For both small loser firms and large winner firms, the differences between December and January returns are statistically significant. The median returns, though not reported, are similar in magnitude. Also, see the graphs in Figure 2.1 and 2.2.

Besides returns, volume can provide insights into the behavior of stock prices. The mean daily turnover for small loser stocks is 0.302

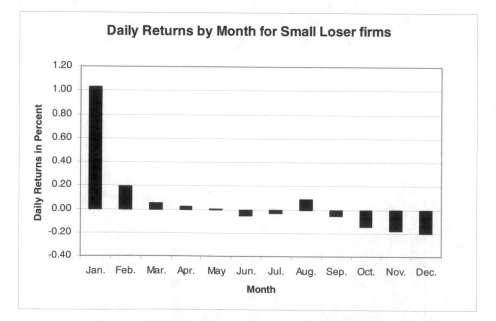

Figure 2.1   The figure shows the daily returns by month for firms in the smallest size decile and the lowest return quartile over the 1963–2001 period.

Figure 2.2   The figure shows the daily returns by month for firms in the largest size decile and the highest return quartile over the 1963–2001 period.

percent in December, which is greater than the turnover in all other months. In particular, the turnover in January (0.235 percent) is about 20 percent *less* than the turnover in December for small loser firms. On the other hand, the December turnover for large winner firms is among the lowest of all calendar months, while the January turnover is among the highest. In contrast to the small loser firms, the January turnover (0.242 percent) for the large winner firms is about 20 percent *more* than the December turnover (0.206 percent).

The return and turnover patterns suggest that the small loser firms and the large winner firms behave differently. The higher returns in December coupled with higher turnover in January for the large winner firms are consistent with the December effect. At the same time, the higher returns in January coupled with higher turnover in December for the small loser firms are consistent with the January effect.

Returns Around the Turn of the Year

Table 2.1 depicts the returns by month as an aggregate over the entire sample period. In Tables 2.2 and 2.3 you can view the results from a closer angle: around the turn of the year and by year from 1988 to 2000 (until January 2001). Only the period since the Tax Reform Act of 1986 is considered because of tax changes affecting mutual funds. Under the act, all mutual funds are required to use

October as the end of their tax year. Thus, any year-end tax effect caused by mutual fund trading has moved from December-January to October-November. However, the December-January period continues to be the relevant period for individual investors.

Stocks most likely to experience the January and December effects are identified by measuring each stock's drop from the high price attained during the year to the twelfth last trading day of the year (roughly the middle of December). Winners are defined as stocks in the smallest potential for tax-loss selling (PTS) decile, that is, stocks with the smallest price decline from the high price, while losers are stocks in the highest PTS decile, those with the largest price decline from the high price.

Characteristics of loser stocks are presented in Table 2.2. Loser stocks fall 74.5 percent from the highest price achieved during the year. These stocks have a low price and low market capitalization. For 2000, the median reference price is $1.14, the mean market capi-

Table 2.2.   January Effect for Loser Firms

Years	Drop in Price (%)	Median Price ($)	Median Size ($ million)	Mean Dec. 5-Day Return (%)	Mean Jan. 5-Day Return (%)	Jan. 5-Day Return Minus Dec. 5-Day Return (%)
1988	70.7	0.69	4.28	2.87	6.89	4.02
1989	72.0	0.66	4.74	1.86	6.53	4.67
1990	83.1	0.50	4.35	−1.48	7.15	8.63
1991	71.9	0.69	4.87	4.90	18.27	13.37
1992	72.1	1.25	8.96	2.99	9.74	6.75
1993	65.6	2.00	14.85	3.49	9.21	5.72
1994	74.6	1.50	12.59	−0.49	10.75	11.24
1995	66.3	1.75	13.73	0.52	10.10	9.58
1996	71.7	1.88	18.31	−4.18	13.69	17.87
1997	73.4	1.69	21.35	−3.43	10.66	14.09
1998	81.0	1.50	17.50	3.31	16.11	12.80
1999	72.2	2.94	36.72	5.14	7.95	2.81
2000	93.1	1.14	26.05	−1.04	28.01	29.04
1988–2000	74.5	1.50	13.73	1.11	11.93*	10.82*

The five-day December return is measured from the close of the seventh trading day before the end of the year to the close of the second trading day before the end of the year. The five-day January return is for the first five trading days in the following calendar year. If the five-day December return is for 2000, then the corresponding five-day January return is for 2001. Statistical significance is at better than 1 percent for returns marked with * and at better than 5 percent for returns marked with +.

talization is $108 million, and the median market capitalization is $26 million. Next, the returns are reported for five-day periods in December (excluding the last trading day) and in January.[3] The five-day January returns are large throughout 1988–2000 at 11.93 percent. Compared with the five-day December return of 1.11 percent, the five-day January return is 10.8 percent larger for the loser stocks. Though not reported here, the volume for loser stocks is about 35 percent smaller in January than in December. For 2000, the volume is about 45 percent less in January than in December.

Similar to Table 2.2 for loser stocks, Table 2.3 reveals that the winner stocks fall only 1.6 percent from the highest price achieved during the year over the 1988–2000 period. In 2000, the average price drop for winners is only 1.8 percent from the highest price. In general, winners are high-priced stocks but not necessarily the largest stocks by market capitalization. For 2000, the median reference price is $24.47, the mean market capitalization is $4,125 million, and the

Table 2.3.   December Effect for Winner Firms: Turn of Year

Years	Drop in Price (%)	Median Price ($)	Median Size ($ million)	Mean Dec. 5–Day Return (%)	Mean Jan. 5–Day Return (%)	Jan. 5–Day Return Minus Dec. 5–Day Return (%)
1988	1.2	17.25	71.45	0.46	0.80	0.34
1989	0.5	22.25	175.90	1.57	−0.25	−1.82
1990	3.6	22.75	221.14	−0.12	−3.64	−3.52
1991	0.8	22.44	118.12	4.78	1.44	−3.35
1992	0.6	24.00	167.49	1.43	−0.64	−2.07
1993	1.5	21.50	141.34	0.98	0.20	−0.78
1994	3.4	22.00	147.08	1.13	−0.56	−1.68
1995	0.2	27.50	331.37	1.79	−1.13	−2.91
1996	1.1	22.00	158.21	1.08	0.38	−0.70
1997	0.6	33.00	323.61	1.94	−2.64	−4.59
1998	3.7	31.88	721.05	2.62	0.60	−2.02
1999	2.1	23.91	243.65	3.96	−1.97	−5.93
2000	1.8	24.47	397.95	6.48	−3.66	−10.14
1988–2000	1.6	22.75	175.90	2.16*	−0.85	−3.01*

The five-day December return is measured from the close of the seventh trading day before the end of the year to the close of the second trading day before the end of the year. The five-day January return is for the first five trading days in the following calendar year. If the five-day December return is for 2000, then the corresponding five-day January return is for 2001. Statistical significance is at better than 1 percent for returns marked with * and at better than 5 percent for returns marked with +.

median market capitalization is $398 million. The mean return for the winner stocks in the five-day December period for 2000 is 6.48 percent. Compared to the gain in December, these stocks lose 3.66 percent in the first five days of the following January (2001). Consistent with the evidence discussed above, the volume for the winner stocks is significantly lower in December than in January, in accordance with postponement of tax-gain selling to January.

Overall, the absolute return for winner stocks is 3.01 percent greater for the five-day December period than for the five-day January period. The turnover is more than 40 percent greater for the five-day period in January than for the five-day period at the end of December.

A comparison of Tables 2.2 and 2.3 reveals striking differences. The winner stocks gain in December with significantly lower turnover in that month, a phenomenon that is consistent with tax-gain selling in January. On the other hand, the loser stocks gain in January with a significantly lower turnover, consistent with tax-loss selling. The results are depicted in Figures 2.3 and 2.4.

A close-up view of the monthly returns for the winner stocks is presented in Table 2.4. The difference of 0.12 percent per day is approximately 2.5 percent for the whole month. From Table 2.3, the five-day December return is 3.01 percent higher than the five-day

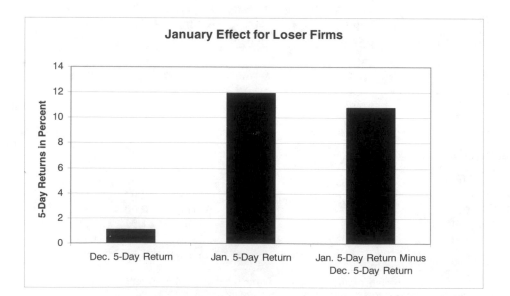

Figure 2.3   The five-day December return and the five-day January return are depicted in the figure along with a difference between the two five-day returns for loser firms over the 1988–2000 period.

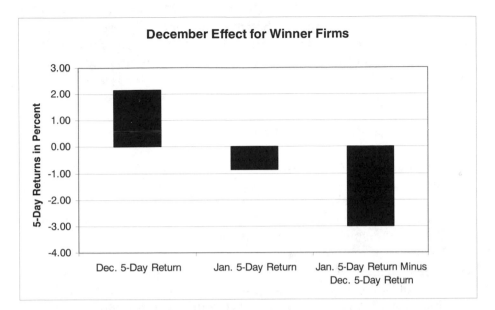

Figure 2.4   The five-day December return and the five-day January return are depicted in the figure along with a difference between the two five-day returns for
winner firms over the 1988–2000 period.

Table 2.4.   December Effect for Winner Firms: December and January

Years	Median Price ($)	Median Size ($ million)	Mean Dec. Return (%)	Mean Jan. Return (%)	Jan. Return Minus Dec. Return (%)
1988	17.50	73.77	0.059	0.192	0.141
1989	21.25	130.73	0.075	–0.325	–0.401
1990	20.25	171.43	0.108	0.156	0.048
1991	17.88	66.81	0.216	0.169	–0.047
1992	21.69	194.28	0.156	0.198	0.042
1993	19.50	102.95	0.090	0.153	0.062
1994	20.56	135.43	0.039	0.008	–0.030
1995	27.75	309.34	0.137	0.011	–0.125
1996	29.00	353.26	0.041	0.113	0.075
1997	30.25	330.95	0.233	–0.118	–0.354
1998	30.75	666.30	0.293	0.088	–0.208
1999	22.00	266.55	0.390	–0.054	–0.448
2000	24.88	672.21	0.286	–0.078	–0.368
1988–2000	21.69	194.28	0.163*	0.040	–0.124+

Daily returns in percent. The January return is for the first month in the calendar year following the month of December. That is, if the December return is for 2000, then the corresponding January return is for 2001. Statistical significance is at better than 1 percent for returns
marked with * and at better than 5 percent for returns marked with +.

return in January, implying that the difference in performance is concentrated in the ten days around the end of the year. Further, the volume turnover for winners is significantly higher in January than in December.

Explanation

The primary explanation for the January effect is that it is related to tax-loss selling in December: in order to reduce the tax bill, investors sell losing stocks in December to realize capital losses that are set off against any realized capital gains. The selling pressure abates in January, causing the prices of those stocks to rise.

The primary explanation for the December effect is also based on tax-related selling. If realized capital losses are not available to offset the capital gains, then those gains are subject to taxation either at the ordinary income tax rate or at a preferential capital gains tax rate. Prudent investors postpone realization of capital gains and, consequently, payment of taxes as much as possible. This becomes especially important and easy at the end of the year, when a delay in the realization of capital gains can postpone payment of taxes by almost one year. Thus, it is expected that winner stocks will not be offered for sale toward the end of the year. Prospective buyers of winner stocks must bid high to induce shareholders of those stocks to part with their holdings, thereby causing the observed December effect.

The evidence strongly supports the case for tax-related selling by investors. First, winners earn higher stock returns in December than in January, and losers earn less in December than in January (see Table 2.1). This is further corroborated by the five-day periods surrounding the end of the year in Tables 2.2 and 2.3. Second, if tax-gain selling causes the abnormal returns for winner stocks, then the trading volume for those stocks in December should be less than in January.[4] And if tax-loss selling causes the abnormal returns for loser stocks, then the trading volume for those stocks in January should be less than in December. The evidence is consistent with greater trading volume for winner stocks in January than in December, and for greater trading volume for loser stocks in December than in January.

There are other explanations for the January effect, but these have much weaker support, such as window dressing by institutional managers, bid-ask bounce, and release of new information. There are no alternative explanations that are consistent with the December effect. Overall, tax-related selling is the primary candidate for explaining both the January and December effects.

Persistence

Why does the January effect persist? Because it is *not* possible to arbitrage this anomaly. Note that these stocks are really small: the January effect occurs only in the bottom 20 percent of all stocks that trade on organized exchanges and Nasdaq. Thus, out of 6,500 stocks, the January effect occurs in the bottom 1,300 stocks, which have a median market capitalization of about $25 million. Investors cannot buy these stocks in December and sell them in January because the trading cost is too high, much greater than the potential profit. There are alternatives to buying and selling stocks that can reduce trading costs: index futures, options, and mutual funds. However, none of the alternative financial instruments works for these small-capitalization stocks, as they are not part of any index, nor do they have traded options. Mutual funds have low transaction costs compared to stocks or futures. Unfortunately, none of the mutual funds fits the requirements—either they hold too many stocks or they hold stocks that are too large. Total market funds, such as Vanguard Total Market, hold about 3,500 of the largest stocks and do not include any of the smaller stocks. Vanguard Total Market fund's weighted market cap is $32.5 billion, much larger than the objective of a $25 million median market cap. Perhaps the best fit is the Dimensional Fund Advisors U.S. Micro Cap Portfolio (formerly U.S. 9-10 Small Company portfolio), which claims to invest in the "smallest 4 percent of the market universe." However, it holds 2,900 stocks that span the entire bottom 50 percent of the market. As a result, the average five-day January return over the most recent eleven-year period is 1.0 percent, compared with 10.8 percent for the January effect stocks. Though the DFA U.S. Micro Cap portfolio can capture part of the January effect, the remaining 90 percent of the effect is untouched. Other small-stock mutual funds have similar compositions, precluding trading strategies to arbitrage the January effect. Thus, the January effect persists because it can't be arbitraged away.

Why does the December effect persist? Why hasn't that been arbitraged away? Unlike other pricing anomalies, the December effect is not well known. Investors must know about an anomaly and be convinced of its existence before they will take action to construct trading strategies. Maybe evidence related to tax-gain selling is sparse and not yet compelling enough for smart investors to act. Therefore, the December effect persists. As it becomes better known the December effect will be arbitraged away and will become less attractive.

The December Effect:
The Trading Process and Implementation

As the January effect cannot be arbitraged, the remainder of the discussion focuses on the December effect alone. There are two alternatives for trading on the December effect: either take a position at the beginning of December or take a position six trading days prior to the end of December. Table 2.3 shows that large winner stocks gain an average of 2.2 percent during the last five trading days in December, equivalent to about 0.44 percent per day. In this five-day period during December 2000, as shown in Table 2.3, the winner stocks gain 6.48 percent (about 1.25 percent per day). From Table 2.4, the average return for the entire month of December for large stocks is 0.16 percent per day. In 2000 it is 0.286 percent per day. Nonetheless, the daily return for the entire month of December is much less than the daily return for the shorter five-day period. Therefore, the focus for investors is on trying to capture the five-day December return, though results for both the full month and the five-day period are reported.

INDIVIDUAL STOCKS

Since winner stocks are usually of large size, their bid-ask spreads are low. From Table 2.3, the median stock price is about $24.47. The bid-ask spread (two transactions) for such stocks is about 0.50 percent. Further, large stocks are unlikely to be affected by large trades because they tend to be highly liquid. Therefore, it would be relatively easy to identify the winners, buy these stocks at the end of the seventh trading day prior to year end, and sell them five trading days later, giving an average return of approximately 1.66 percent (2.16 percent less 0.5 percent for trading costs) over the five-day trading period, which is in excess of an annualized return of 75 percent.

FUTURES AND EXCHANGE TRADED FUNDS

It is also possible to use other financial instruments that have lower trading costs to capture the December effect. Because the December effect stocks are large, the S&P 500 index can possibly provide an efficient way to trade. The S&P 500 index futures can be traded at a cost of less than 0.1 percent. Similarly, the exchange-traded S&P 500 index fund (SPDR, AMEX: SPY) has a round-trip transaction cost of about 0.1 percent. The returns from using S&P 500 futures and SPDRs are given in Tables 2.5 and 2.6, assuming that the total S&P 500 return is equal to the return on SPDRs. For the period 1988–2001, the

Table 2.5. Trading Strategy for the December Effect: S&P 500 Futures

Year	Futures Price at Nov. End	Futures Price at 7th Last Day in Dec.	Futures Price at 2nd Last Day in Dec.	Futures Dec. Return (%)	Futures Dec. 5–Day Return (%)
1988	275.90	281.35	280.40	1.87	-0.34
1989	351.80	347.90	354.95	1.34	2.03
1990	327.20	332.75	331.55	1.16	–0.36
1991	377.60	388.35	416.40	10.75	7.22
1992	432.20	441.95	439.50	1.17	–0.55
1993	463.20	468.90	469.70	0.84	0.17
1994	457.05	464.80	464.40	1.00	–0.09
1995	612.50	612.80	618.20	0.97	0.88
1996	764.90	757.00	758.70	–2.63	0.23
1997	965.80	962.90	979.40	1.28	1.71
1998	1,174.00	1,215.50	1,242.00	6.13	2.18
1999	1,410.80	1,457.00	1,480.00	5.19	1.58
2000	1,341.20	1,279.60	1,353.20	–0.46	5.75
2001	1,141.50	1,142.30	1,159.30	0.68	1.49
1988–2001				2.09[+]	1.56[+]

The table shows the total returns for the month of December and the last five days of December (excluding the last day) from holding the March S&P 500 index futures contract. All returns are in percent for the entire holding period. Statistical significance at better than 5 percent for returns marked with [+].

Table 2.6. Trading Strategy for the December Effect: Mutual Funds and Indexes

Year	S&P 500 Dec. Return (%)	S&P 500 Dec. 5–Day Return (%)	Vanguard VFINX (%)	Dreyfus DSPIX (%)	Scudder BTIEX (%)	Nasdaq 100 Index (%)
1988	1.85	0.83	0.83			1.16
1989	2.27	2.34	4.08			3.91
1990	2.79	–0.38	–0.12			–1.04
1991	11.43	7.36	7.46			10.45
1992	1.34	–0.26	–0.26			1.21
1993	1.22	0.38	–0.18	0.40	0.30	2.40
1994	1.48	0.41	0.41	0.38	0.47	2.14
1995	1.78	1.37	1.40	1.33	1.35	1.21
1996	–1.98	0.69	0.73	0.73	0.74	–0.91
1997	1.64	1.81	1.86	1.86	1.84	2.34
1998	5.88	2.42	2.40	2.37	2.37	2.44
1999	5.95	2.02	1.98	1.97	1.98	3.41
2000	0.48	5.51	5.52	5.52	5.51	11.51
2001	0.89	1.85	1.88	1.86	1.87	4.09
1993–2001	1.93	1.83	1.78	1.82	1.83	3.18
1988–2001	2.64	1.88	2.00			3.17

The table shows the total returns for last five days of December (excluding the last day) from holding the S&P 500 mutual funds and the Nasdaq 100 index. All returns are in percent for the entire holding period.

December return is 2.09 percent using futures and 2.64 percent using SPDRs.[5] For the five-day December period, the returns are 1.56 percent and 1.88 percent, respectively. Accounting for the trading cost of 0.1 percent, the net five-day December return using SPDRs is at least 1.5 percent during the 1988–2001 period. Clearly, this is a large return for a short period and does not seem difficult to earn.

MUTUAL FUNDS

Many funds will not charge you a redemption fee provided you don't trade multiple times in a year. Since the December effect requires only one buy and one sell in a year, it is unlikely that there will be any fees. Large, no-load S&P 500 index funds that are open to retail investors include Vanguard's 500 Index Fund (VFINX), Dreyfus's index fund (DSPIX), and Scudder Equity 500 Index Investment Fund (BTIEX). The fund returns are reported in Table 2.6. The returns earned are almost identical to those earned by the S&P 500. However, since the transaction cost is close to zero, the net return is about 1.8 percent over a five-day period. Therefore, index mutual funds are a superior vehicle for capturing the December effect.

NASDAQ 100

In addition to the S&P 500, the Nasdaq 100 represents a group of large stocks. Since the Nasdaq 100 is constructed solely on the basis of market capitalization and consists of only 100 stocks, instead of 500 as in the S&P 500, it is likely to reflect a greater concentration of large stocks. However, on the downside, the Nasdaq 100 is significantly riskier and more volatile than the S&P 500. The five-day returns for the Nasdaq 100 index are reported in Table 2.6. It can be seen that the Nasdaq 100 generates a whopping return of 3.18 percent (and 3.08 percent after transaction costs) over the five-day period in December compared with a 1.56 percent return for the S&P 500.

TRADING STRATEGY AND RESULTS

To capitalize on the December effect, this trading strategy would be used:

1. Buy SPDR, go long in S&P 500 index futures, buy an index mutual fund, or buy the Nasdaq 100 toward the close of trading on the seventh last trading day in December.

2. Close the position toward the close of trading on the second last trading day in December. Buying on the seventh last trad-

ing day and selling on the second last trading gives the five-day return for capturing the December effect.

As shown in Tables 2.5 and 2.6, the five-day return in December is between 1.56 percent and 3.08 percent after transaction costs, depending on the type of instrument employed to capture the December effect.

The December Effect: Qualifications

The evidence presented in this chapter and the trading strategy recommendations are based on past data. Since future market conditions and market patterns may be completely different, there is no certainty that the December effect will continue or be profitable in the future.

Only the raw returns from capturing the December effect have been reported in the analysis. In addition, the risk of trading the December effect has not been considered in evaluating the return. If the risk in the last few days of December is significantly higher than usual, the attractiveness of the December effect will decline.

The January Effect: What Can Investors Do?

Though arbitraging a significant part of the January effect is not possible, investors *can* utilize this knowledge to change their own trading patterns. Instead of selling losers in December, they should wait until January. The cost of paying taxes a year earlier is much less than the expected appreciation of the stock they hold. This can be illustrated easily: Assuming an average capital loss of 65 percent and the new tax rate of 15 percent, the realizable tax benefit is 10 percent. Postponement of realization of this tax benefit by one year will cost the investor one percent at a 10 percent interest rate. The January effect of about 10 percent easily exceeds this loss due to postponement. Similarly, investors should advance their purchases, if any, of small-cap stocks from January to December. A change in the trading patterns can help investors from not being hurt by the January effect even if they can't directly use it to earn arbitrage profits.

Key Points

- Investors may choose not to sell their winners in December in order to postpone payment of taxes. By waiting a few days, they can postpone payment of taxes by almost a year. Since the supply of winner stocks will be restricted in December or in the last few days of December, winner stocks are likely to appreciate abnormally.

- Evidence shows that winner stocks earn about 2.16 percent in the last five days of December.

- As the winner stocks are generally large stocks, the December effect can be easily captured using instruments that track the S&P 500 index, such as spiders, index futures, and index funds, or those that track the Nasdaq 100. The five-day return is 1.56 percent for S&P 500–related instruments and 3.08 percent for the Nasdaq 100 index.

- While the January effect cannot be arbitraged easily, investors can alter their trading patterns so that they are not hurt by the January effect. In particular, investors should buy loser stocks in December instead of January, and they should sell loser stocks in January instead of December.

Bottom Line

The December effect refers to appreciation of winner stocks in the last few days of the year. This effect has been persistent over the last decade, even in 2000 and 2001, when not many stocks appreciated. The December effect of 1.5 percent could have been profitably exploited during that period using a simple technique: hold the S&P 500 index for about a week at the end of the year.

Internet References

http://www.cme.com: The Chicago Mercantile Exchange is the primary exchange for trading stock index futures.

http://www.indexfunds.com, http://www.etfconnect.com: Provide a list of indexed mutual funds and exchange-traded funds.

http://www.rydexfunds.com, http://www.profunds.com: Almost all mutual fund companies offer index funds. These two companies do not impose any penalty for frequent trading.

References for Further Reading

Agrawal, Anup, and Kishore Tandon. 1994. Anomalies or Illusions? Evidence from Stock Markets in Eighteen Countries. *Journal of International Money and Finance* 13(1), 83–106.

Barry, Christopher B., and Stephen J. Brown. 1984. Differential Information and the Small Firm Effect. *Journal of Financial Economics* 13(2), 283–94.

Bhabra, Harjeet S., Upinder S. Dhillon, and Gabriel G. Ramírez. 1999. A November Effect? Revisiting the Tax-Loss-Selling Hypothesis. *Financial Management* 28(4), 5–15.

Bhardwaj, Ravinder, and Leroy Brooks. 1992. The January Anomaly: Effects of Low Share Price, Transactions Costs, and Bid-Ask Bias. *Journal of Finance* 47, 552–75.

Chen, Honghui, and Vijay Singal. 2003a. The January Effect: A Re-Examination. Working paper, Department of Finance, Virginia Tech.

———. 2003b. A December Effect with Tax-Gain Selling? *Financial Analyst Journal*, forthcoming.

Constantinides, George M. 1984. Optimal Stock Trading with Personal Taxes: Implications for Prices and the Abnormal January Returns. *Journal of Financial Economics* 13(1), 65–89.

Haugen, Robert A., and Philippe Jorion. 1996. The January Effect: Still There After All These Years. *Financial Analyst Journal* 52(1), 27–31.

Haugen, Robert A., and Josef Lakonishok. 1988. *The Incredible January Effect: The Stock Market's Unsolved Mystery* (Homewood, Ill.: Dow Jones–Irwin).

Keim, Donald B. 1983. Size-Related Anomalies and Stock Return Seasonality: Further Empirical Evidence. *Journal of Financial Economics* 12, 13–32.

Lakonishok, Josef, Andrei Shleifer, Richard Thaler, and Robert Vishny. 1991. Window Dressing by Pension Fund Managers. *American Economic Review* 81, 227–31.

Poterba, James M., and Scott J. Weisbenner. 2001. Capital Gains Tax Rules, Tax-Loss Trading, and the Turn-of-the-Year Returns. *Journal of Finance* 56(1), 353–68.

Reinganum, Mark. 1983. The Anomalous Stock Market Behavior of Small Firms in January: Empirical Tests for Tax-Loss Selling Effects. *Journal of Financial Economics* 12, 89–104.

Wachtel, Sidney. 1942. Certain Observations on Seasonal Movement in Stock Prices. *Journal of Business* (April), 184–93.

Notes

1. This chapter is based on research in Chen and Singal (2003a, 2003b). Other works used in this chapter include Bhabra, Dhillon, and Ramírez (1999), Constantinides (1984), Keim (1983), Poterba and. Weisbenner (2001), and Haugen and Jorion (1996).

2. For example, see the *Wall Street Journal,* December 6, 2001.

3. Excluding the last day of the year is common in many studies because of low trading volume on that day.

4. The abnormal return is calculated as the actual return minus the expected return. Expected return is the risk-free rate plus market risk premium times the beta of the stock.

5. The difference in the return to SPDRs and futures may be attributable to differences in closing times.

3

The Weekend Effect

The weekend effect refers to relatively large returns on Fridays compared to those on Mondays. Whereas the Friday returns exceed 0.20%, the Monday returns are close to zero or negative resulting in a weekend effect for an equally weighted index of 0.34 percent. On the other hand, the weekend effect for a value-weighted index has fallen to zero during the 1990s.

Short sellers may be responsible for the weekend effect because they do not want to keep speculative positions open around the weekend. Accordingly, they close the short positions by buying back on Fridays and reopen them by short selling on Mondays causing higher returns on Fridays and lower returns on Mondays.

It is, however, not easy to capture the weekend effect with current financial instruments because the trading costs can be large. Nonetheless, investors should recognize the weekend effect and avoid buying on Fridays and selling on Mondays. Instead, they should buy stocks on Mondays and sell on Fridays.

Description

The *weekend effect* is best defined as a Friday's return minus the following Monday's return for a single security or a portfolio of securities.[1] This definition captures the preweekend positive returns (higher returns on Fridays) and the postweekend negative returns (lower returns on Mondays). In the absence of seasonality in returns, firms should, on average, earn the same return on all days of the week, especially on adjacent trading days. Thus, the weekend effect should be zero for all securities and should be unaffected by the risk or volatility of a security or by trends in returns.[2] In the discussion that follows, the last trading day of the week is called Friday, whether it is actually a Thursday or a Friday. Similarly, the first trading day of the week is called Monday, whether it is a Monday or a Tuesday.

Beginning with the discovery of the weekend effect by Frank Cross in 1973 and Arthur Merrill in 1975, there is much evidence in support of higher returns on Fridays and lower returns on Mondays. Numerous academic and practitioner papers have examined the existence and causes of the weekend effect and discovered many stylized facts, such as the weekend effect has been in existence for more than a hundred years, Friday returns are lower when there is Saturday trading, the weekend effect is larger around long weekends, a larger number of stocks rise before a holiday than after the holiday, and the weekend effect has been weakening over the past decade. Even a book based on the weekend effect was published in 1986: Yale Hirsch's *Don't Sell Stocks on Monday*. A detailed discussion of the weekend effect follows.

Evidence

An examination of daily returns for all common stocks traded on the NYSE, AMEX, and Nasdaq is instructive. The returns are presented in Table 3.1 for the period July 1962–December 2001. Two types of returns are reported: an equally weighted return (the mean return to all stocks with all stocks carrying equal weights) and a value-weighted index (the mean return to all stocks where each stock's weight is equal to its market capitalization). The first two rows have the returns for the entire period, while the remaining rows have returns by decades. The table shows that Monday returns are significantly negative, whereas Wednesday and Friday returns are significantly positive for both the equally weighted and the value-weighted indexes. For the equally weighted index, the Friday return is much larger than the return on any other day of the week, and the Monday return is the smallest. For the value-weighted index, the Friday and Wednesday returns are comparable, but the Monday return is again the smallest (most negative). It is no wonder that the weekend effect, which is the difference between the Friday return and the Monday return, is positive and significant.

Overall, the weekend effect for an equally weighted index is 0.339 percent. This translates into an annual return of about 17 percent. For a value-weighted index, the return is 0.15 percent, or about 8

Table 3.1   The Weekend Effect

		July 1962 to 2001: Daily Returns (in percent)				
	Mon.	Tue.	Wed.	Thu.	Fri.	Weekend (Fri.–Mon.)
Overall for July 1962 to 2001						
1962–2001						
EW	−0.093*	0.000	0.133*	0.125*	0.246*	0.339*
VW	−0.055+	0.044+	0.099*	0.047+	0.098*	0.153*
By Decades						
1962–1970						
EW	−0.105*	−0.008	0.176*	0.074+	0.218*	0.326*
VW	−0.124*	0.022	0.145*	0.028	0.131*	0.255*
1971–1980						
EW	−0.082+	−0.019	0.112*	0.115*	0.245*	0.327*
VW	−0.100+	0.035	0.098*	0.049	0.111*	0.211*
1981–1990						
EW	−0.173*	−0.038	0.108*	0.123*	0.231*	0.403*
VW	−0.078	0.062	0.112*	0.049	0.109*	0.187*
1991–2001						
EW	−0.021	0.056	0.144*	0.174*	0.283*	0.304*
VW	0.063	0.053	0.057	0.057	0.050	−0.013

The sample consists of all ordinary common shares traded on NYSE, AMEX, or Nasdaq. Monday refers to the first trading day of the week, while Friday refers to the last trading day of the week. The weekend effect refers to the difference between a Friday's return and the following Monday's return. The equally weighted index returns of all stocks are given in the rows titled "EW," while value-weighted index returns are in the rows titled "VW." Statistical significance is at better than 1 percent for returns marked with * and at better than 5 percent for returns marked with +.

percent per year. The value-weighted index is tilted heavily toward stocks with high market capitalization, such as General Electric and Microsoft.

Table 3.1 also depicts the time trend in the weekend effect. It can be observed that the weekend effect based on the equally weighted index is almost invariant with time. The weekend effect was 0.326 percent per weekend during the 1960s, 0.327 percent during the 1970s, 0.403 percent during the 1980s, and 0.304 percent during the 1990s. It is statistically significant in all four subperiods. In the last period, the Monday return is close to zero, but the Friday return is essentially unaltered. The story with the value-weighted index is

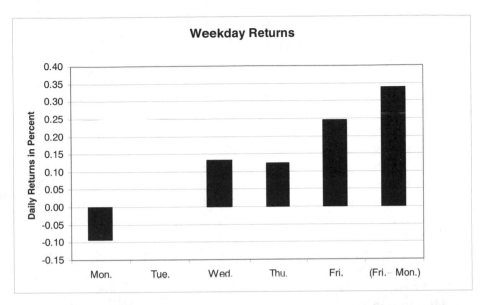

Figure 3.1 The first five columns show the weekday returns for an equally weighted index over the 1962–2001 period. The last column shows the weekend effect, which is the difference between the Friday return and the Monday return.

different. The difference among day-by-day returns becomes less and less important with time until it completely disappears in the 1991–2001 period. For the last decade, the value-weighted daily return is between 0.05 percent and 0.063 percent irrespective of the day of the week, which means that there is no weekend effect. Indeed, the last column shows that the weekend effect based on the value-weighted index falls gradually from 0.255 percent in the 1960s to 0.211 percent in the 1970s to 0.187 percent in the 1980s and to an insignificant –0.013 percent in the 1990s. It is important to note that the persistence of the weekend effect for the equally weighted index is broad-based and not due to one or two abnormal years. (As explained in subsequent sections, the weekend effect is due to short sellers, who migrate to the options market once options become available. Since options are more easily available and less expensive for large stocks, the weekend effect for the value-weighted index begins to disappear in later years. For an average stock, however, options are either unavailable or too expensive to trade, causing the weekend effect for the equally weighted index to be relatively unchanged.)

Short Selling as
the Primary Explanation

Given evidence of the weekend effect, what is the cause? The primary explanation for the weekend effect relies on the behavior of short sellers with regard to unhedged short sales, as distinct from hedged short sales.[3] Hedged short sales include merger arbitrage where an investor short-sells the bidder and buys the target (see Chapter 9), index arbitrage between futures and cash markets, short selling by put option writers to hedge their positions, shorting against the box (short-selling a stock that is held long in another account) to postpone realization of capital gains, and other similar activities where the short position is hedged by an offsetting similar position. On the other hand, unhedged or purely speculative short sales are naked positions based on the expectation (or hope) that the price of the shorted security will fall.

Hedged short sales are not very risky because an equivalent trade hedges the movement in the short-sold security. But speculative short positions are not hedged and require close monitoring. Unlike a long position, where the loss is limited to the value of the holding, the downside risk of a speculative short position is theoretically unlimited. A large price move can wipe out the owner's equity in an account. For that reason, "[p]ros warn that speculative short-selling, in which an investor simply sells a stock short hoping the price will fall, is one of the riskiest strategies going. . . . [I]t is not something a part-time investor should engage in" (Smith 1999).

While close monitoring during trading hours can limit the potential loss of a short seller, nontrading hours introduce special risk as the short sellers are unable to trade. The inability to trade implies that short sellers are unable to control losses that may occur due to news or stock price moves after market hours. Thus, short sellers are averse to holding positions over nonmarket hours and like to close positions at the end of the day and reopen them the next morning. However, the transaction costs of closing and opening a position, the uptick rule, and limited availability of shares to short-sell make it expensive for the short sellers to trade too often.[4] The weekend becomes a natural break point, as it is a long period (65.5 hours for a regular weekend and 89.5 hours for a long weekend) of nontrading compared to the normal interday period (17.5 hours) of nontrading.[5] Thus, the inability to trade over the weekend makes many short sellers close their speculative positions at the end of the week and reopen them at the beginning of the following week, leading to the weekend effect. The stock prices rise on Fridays as short sellers cover their positions, and fall on Mondays as short sellers reestablish new short positions.

EVIDENCE IN SUPPORT OF SHORT SELLING

If short selling is responsible for the weekend effect, then stocks with a higher level of short sales should have a stronger weekend effect. That is indeed the case. To relate the weekend effect to short sales, all stocks are divided into ten size deciles (ten equal groups based on market capitalization). Each size decile is then subdivided into four quartiles (four groups of equal size) based on relative short interest (RSI), where RSI is measured as the short interest divided by the number of shares outstanding. Stocks in the highest RSI quartile within a size decile have a weekend effect that is more than 40 percent greater than stocks in the lowest RSI quartile for the same size decile: the weekend effect increases from 0.27 percent for the lowest quartile to 0.39 percent for the highest quartile.

The weekend effect should depend on speculative short interest, not total short interest. However, the test discussed in the previous paragraph does not distinguish between speculative short interest and hedged short interest. Initial public offerings (IPOs) are ideal for testing the effect of speculative short sales on the weekend returns, because they are likely to have only speculative short positions. IPOs are not good candidates for hedged short sale activity because (1) they are usually not part of an index (no index arbitrage), (2) they are not likely to be takeover candidates (no merger arbitrage); and (3) the high volatility of IPOs inhibits other types of nonspeculative short sellers from trading them. Results with IPOs show that the weekend effect increases from 0.12 percent for the low RSI quartile to 0.59 percent for the high RSI quartile. The weekend effect is nearly four times greater for IPOs in the top 25 percent by RSI than for IPOs in the bottom 25 percent by RSI.

If speculative short sales are so risky that short sellers must resort to trading around the weekend, isn't there another way of trading on negative information? Unfortunately, there was no alternative until put options were introduced in 1977. Put options are considered a substitute for short selling, as they allow the buyer to gain from a fall in price. Put options are more expensive because of the option premium but entail lower risk. Speculative short sellers tend to prefer put options because of the high risk associated with speculative short positions, and would migrate to the options market if options are available. The consequent reduction in speculative short interest would then coincide with a reduction in the weekend effect. However, as traders are very concerned with the cost of trading, the migration to the options market will occur only for stocks with actively traded options. Otherwise, the high cost of trading in illiquid options markets makes it uneconomical to migrate.

Further evidence of the importance of short selling as an explanation for the weekend effect becomes apparent when a test is conducted to compare the weekend effect for the one hundred most actively traded stocks (by stock volume) with those of the one hundred least actively traded stocks. The test shows that the weekend effect weakens significantly after 1977 and disappears in the 1990s for the most actively traded stocks. On the other hand, the weekend effect continues unabated for the least actively traded stocks through the 1980s and 1990s. These results are reinforced by regression results that suggest that stocks with higher put option activity have a lower weekend effect, a finding that is consistent with the substitution agreement suggested in the preceding paragraph.

The evidence presented above supports the role of speculative short sellers in contributing to the weekend effect. Some other observed facts related to the weekend effect are also consistent with the short-selling explanation:

- The weekend effect has been in existence for more than a hundred years: Short selling has been permitted on U.S. exchanges since 1858. After the stock market crash in 1929, there was an attempt to curb the practice. However, short selling was actually disallowed on only two days in 1931. New rules governing short selling were introduced by the SEC under the Securities and Exchange Act of 1934.

- Friday returns are lower when there is Saturday trading: Consistent with the short selling explanation, short sellers may wait until Saturday to close their positions, reducing the Friday return.

- The weekend effect is larger around long weekends: When the market is closed for a holiday weekend, more short sellers are likely to close short positions by buying back on the last trading day of the week and reopen their positions after the market reopens. This will result in a larger weekend effect.

- A larger number of stocks rise before a holiday than after a holiday: Short sellers trade around holidays in the same manner as they do around weekends, giving rise to the returns documented around holidays.

- The weekend effect is more pronounced for stocks held by institutions: Since individuals tend not to engage in short selling, the weekend effect will be greater where institutional investors are more active.

- The weekend effect has become weaker for the most actively traded stocks during the 1990s: As explained above, the migration of short sellers to the options market will result in the disappearance of the weekend effect for the more actively traded stocks, which are usually firms with a large market capitalization.

Alternative Explanations

Many potential explanations have been proposed and investigated: measurement errors, specialist-related biases in prices, timing of corporate releases after Friday's close, reduced institutional trading and greater individual trading on Mondays, and Daylight Saving Time changes for two weekends a year. These explanations account for some portion of the weekend effect. For example, the announcement of earnings and dividends on Friday after the close, especially if the news is negative, can explain a small proportion (3.4 percent) of the weekend effect. Further, the tendency to postpone release of this news is not restricted to firms in any particular size decile. This delay in settlement of trades can explain about 17 percent of the weekend effect.

Another possible explanation relates to the bid-ask bounce. If stocks trade at the ask price on Fridays at market close and at the bid price on Mondays, it will seem that the Monday return is negative even when no change in price has taken place. For example, consider a stock that has a bid of $5.00 and an ask of $5.05. Assume that the price is unchanged on Friday and the following Monday. However, if the closing trade occurs at the ask price of $5.05 on Friday but the closing trade occurs at the bid price of $5.00 on Monday, the computed return for Monday will be −1 percent. This explanation implies that there is really no weekend effect—that the bid-ask bounce is misinterpreted as a weekend effect. However, estimates indicate that the bid-ask bounce can account for 32 percent of the observed weekend effect, but only for small stocks. For large stocks, the bid-ask bounce can explain less than 10 percent of the observed returns.

From the above, it can be seen that all of the alternative explanations account for only a small portion of the weekend effect. Though short selling may not be the only explanation, it can explain at least 30 percent and up to 80 percent of the weekend effect. Therefore, trading strategies constructed here are based on the assumption that speculative short selling is the primary explanation.

Persistence

Since existence of the weekend effect has been known for more than twenty years, why hasn't it been arbitraged away? There are two possible reasons. First, the cause of the weekend effect was unknown until the discovery of the short-selling explanation in a paper published in 2003. An anomaly without a reasonable explanation is very risky for an arbitrageur because the mispricing can unpredictably cease to exist; in fact, the weekend effect has disappeared for actively traded stocks. Further, if the arbitrageur does not know the reason, it is not possible to refine the trading strategy for capturing the highest return. This leads to the second reason for persistence: the weekend effect is not large. For an equally weighted index, the weekend effect was about 0.3 percent during 1990–2001. For a value-weighted index, the weekend effect does not exist. As the equally weighted index consists of small stocks, the trading costs may be larger than the weekend effect unless the investor can narrow the list of stocks to a few that can be selectively traded.

The Trading Process

This section attempts to construct a trading strategy in which the costs of trading are smaller than the weekend effect.

The evidence relating to the weekend effect reveals many determinants. These factors will help in identifying stocks that exhibit the greatest weekend effect. Since it is not possible to distinguish between speculative and nonspeculative short interest, only those firms that are not good candidates for hedged short sales will be selected.

- The stock should have a high level of relative short interest. A minimum RSI of 5 percent is appropriate.

- The stock should not have actively traded options. The maximum average daily option volume should be one thousand contracts (one hundred thousand shares). Fewer than five hundred stocks have actively traded options.

- The stock should not be engaged in any significant corporate events such as mergers, equity issues, and so on, because these events may result in hedged short selling.

- The stock should not be part of the S&P 500 index or the Nasdaq 100 index. These stocks are subject to significant hedged short-selling activity.

- To minimize the transaction costs, the stock price must be at least $10 and the daily stock volume should exceed one hundred thousand shares.

- Stocks trading on Nasdaq are better suited to the weekend effect than NYSE stocks because Nasdaq stocks are smaller in size and are of greater interest to short sellers due to their volatility.

It is anticipated that a carefully selected set of stocks may generate a weekend effect of about 0.50 percent. In addition to capturing the weekend effect by trading individual stocks, investors could alter their trading behavior at little or no extra cost. In particular, stocks not in the top five hundred stocks by volume should be bought on Mondays and sold on Fridays rather than on other days of the week.

Strategy Implementation

As mentioned in the summary at the start of this chapter, it is not possible to generate large tradable profits from the weekend effect based on financial instruments available at the present time. Nonetheless, this section shows the construction of a trading strategy and the results using a variety of different instruments.

The criteria for selection of stocks outlined in the previous section imply that selected stocks should not be large because they will have actively traded options for which the weekend effect has disappeared. At the same time, the stocks should be somewhat liquid so that the trading costs are low. Short sellers will not trade illiquid stocks. For example, firms in the bottom 10 percent by size have close to zero short interest. Only the top 50 percent, by size, have a significant level of short interest (more than 1 percent of shares outstanding). The Russell 2000 index, while not perfect, comes closest to capturing the stocks with the highest weekend effect. The index excludes stocks that fall in the bottom half of the market and also excludes large stocks (the top one thousand) that are likely have actively traded options. However, the Russell 2000 contains many stocks with insufficient volume or with a very low stock price.

Table 3.2   Weekend Effect During 1992–2001 (in percent)

Year	Russell 2000 Weekend Effect	Equally Weighted Index Weekend Effect	Russell 1000 Weekend Effect	Value- Weighted Index Weekend Effect
1992–1993 mean	0.126	0.253*	−0.189+	−0.152+
1992–1993 median	0.027	0.232*	−0.134+	−0.099
1994–1995 mean	0.137+	0.291*	−0.017	0.013
1994–1995 median	0.106	0.296*	0.054	0.048
1996–1997 mean	0.017	0.176+	−0.106	−0.079
1996–1997 median	0.027	0.137*	−0.027	−0.025
1998–1999 mean	0.179	0.365*	0.128	0.117
1998–1999 median	0.107	0.295*	0.303	0.213
2000–2001 mean	0.352	0.292+	−0.104	−0.083
2000–2001 median	0.142	0.208+	0.056	0.146
Overall mean	0.167*	0.304*	−0.057	−0.013
Overall median	0.070+	0.232*	0.000	−0.000

The weekend effect refers to the difference between a Friday's return and the following Monday's return. Statistical significance is at better than 1 percent for returns marked with * and at better than 5 percent for returns marked with +.

Returns for the Russell 2000 are presented in Table 3.2 for the 1992–2001 period in two-year intervals. In addition, returns for the Russell 1000 (the large-cap stocks) and the equally weighted index and the value-weighted index are given for comparison. It can be seen that the weekend effect for the equally weighted index is positive and significant throughout the entire period, with an average of 0.3 percent. On the other hand, the weekend effect for the value-weighted index is never positive and significant. The overall mean weekend effect for the value-weighted index is an insignificant −0.01 percent. The Russell 2000 has a positive weekend effect that is significant for the overall ten-year period, with a mean of 0.17 percent. However, it is not significant for any of the biennial periods except 1994–95. Thus, the Russell 2000 index fares much worse than the equally weighted index in Table 3.1. However, the Russell 2000 is our best bet for capturing the weekend effect, as the equally weighted index is not available in a tradable form.

Four financial instruments related to the Russell 2000 and individual stocks as vehicles for capturing the weekend effect are described below.

EXCHANGE TRADED FUNDS

The first financial instrument for the Russell 2000 is an exchange-traded fund, iShares Russell 2000 (AMEX: IWM). The fund has a daily volume in excess of 1.5 million shares. However, the bid-ask spread is approximately 0.10 percent, which implies that two round trips to capture the weekend effect will cost 0.20 percent. As the weekend effect associated with the Russell 2000 is estimated at 0.17 percent, the transactions costs are actually greater than the weekend effect. Thus, ETFs are not appropriate.

MUTUAL FUNDS

Mutual funds are another possible vehicle for capturing the weekend effect. There are many mutual funds that track the Russell 2000, including Vanguard's Small Cap Index, E*trade Russell 2000 Index, Federated Mini-Cap Index, and Merrill Lynch Small Cap, to name a few. However, the typical mutual fund company does not allow one trade per weekend or fifty trades a year. Fortunately, two mutual fund companies, Rydex and ProFunds, offer funds without restrictions on the frequency of trading. Rydex has one fund that tracks the Russell 2000, while ProFunds has three funds related to the Russell 2000, including one that is the inverse of Russell 2000. Unfortunately, the funds do not have a long enough history for any reliable conclusions. The Rydex Mekros Fund was first offered in November 2000, the ProFund Small Cap in September 2001, the ProFund UltraSmall-Cap in February 2000, and the ProFund Short Small-Cap in May 2002. At least five years of historical data should be available to evaluate the performance of a fund with reference to its benchmark.

FUTURES

Russell 2000 futures contracts provide one more avenue for trading. Unfortunately, the trading in Russell 2000 futures is quite limited, averaging between two thousand and five thousand contracts per day. Thus, the round-trip trading cost of 0.1 to 0.2 percent decimates the expected returns from the weekend effect. If trading in Russell futures becomes more active, then it might become possible to use futures contracts to capitalize on the weekend effect.

OPTIONS

In addition to options on individual stocks, options are available on popular indexes, including the Russell 2000. Unfortunately, as with futures, the Russell 2000 index options are very thinly traded, with a daily volume of fewer than one hundred contracts. Consequently, the bid-ask spread and the premium costs are too high for Russell 2000 index options relative to the weekend effect.

STOCKS

Stocks that meet the previously outlined conditions can be selected for trading. Begin with the short interest position of stocks made public by various stock exchanges in the third week of each month. The information containing the short interest positions also reports the average daily volume for the previous month. Since both short interest and volume are given, it is easier to calculate the short interest ratio (short interest divided by volume) than the relative short interest (short interest divided by number of shares outstanding). Therefore, the short interest ratio is used for the remaining analysis.

The month of analysis is December 1999. All stocks with a short interest ratio of at least five days and a daily average volume of at least one hundred thousand shares are selected. Instead of checking the option activity and index membership, both of which are time-consuming to verify, a market capitalization limit can be imposed. Since the largest company in the Russell 2000 has a market capitalization of a little in excess of $1 billion, the market capitalization of the selected companies must be at most $1 billion and the stock price must be at least $10. Sixty-five Nasdaq firms meet these criteria.

For the year 2000, the weekend effect for the sixty-five Nasdaq firms has a mean of 0.50 percent and a median of 0.62 percent. Though both of these are larger than the weekend effect for the equally weighted index, the bid-ask spread for these stocks is even larger, at 0.80 percent. Because the trading costs exceed the weekend effect, stocks cannot be used for capturing the weekend effect.

Qualifications

The evidence presented in this chapter is based on past data. Since future market conditions and market patterns may be completely different, there is no certainty that the past weekend price patterns will continue in the future.

Key Points

- The weekend effect, defined as the Friday return minus the subsequent Monday's return, should be zero.

- Evidence reveals that the weekend effect is about 0.34 percent for an equally weighted index and 0.15 percent for a value-weighted index. In general, the Monday return is negative and the Friday return is positive. Evidence also reveals that the weekend effect has weakened for actively traded stocks during the 1990s.

- It seems that speculative short sellers are largely responsible for the weekend effect. Since short positions are very risky, short sellers do not want to hold them over the weekend. Therefore, some of them close their positions on Fridays and reopen them on Mondays, causing the weekend effect. When options are available and actively traded, the short sellers migrate to the options market. This move makes the weekend effect disappear among large stocks with actively traded options. Alternative explanations of the weekend effect cannot explain a significant part of the weekend effect.

- Due to the small absolute magnitude of the weekend effect, it is not possible to arbitrage the weekend effect. New instruments with lower trading costs may present an opportunity to arbitrage in the future.

- In any case, investors must recognize the existence of the weekend effect. Accordingly, whenever it is possible to alter the timing of trades, investors should sell on Fridays and buy on Mondays.

Bottom Line

There is strong evidence regarding the weekend effect for stocks with a high level of short interest but without actively traded options. Typically, these are stocks that are not among the top five hundred stocks by market capitalization. The weekend effect for an equally weighted index is about 0.34 percent. No efficient trading strategies exist to arbitrage the weekend effect due to relatively high trading costs.

However, investors can still profit from the weekend effect by slightly altering their trading behavior. That is, investors should sell stocks on Fridays and buy them on Mondays.

Internet References

Short Interest Data

http://www.nysedata.com: Go to Data Products and then to Short Interest to buy data for all stocks. If you are interested in just a few stocks, finance.yahoo.com is good enough.

http:www.nasdaqtrader.com: Short interest data is available for purchase.

http://www.amex.com/amextrader/: Has historical short interest data for AMEX issues back to 1995.

Activity in Options Markets

http://www.cboe.com/data/AvgDailyVolArchive.aspx: Has options volume data for the Chicago Board Options Exchange, which accounts for roughly one-half the total options volume.

http://www.optionsclearing.com: Site of Options Clearing Corporation, which is responsible for all U.S. options exchanges.

Constituents of Equity Indexes

http://www.standardandpoors.com: Has a list of constituents of the S&P 500. You can choose either an Excel or .csv format.

http://www.nasdaq.com has a list of constituents of the Nasdaq 100.

http://www.russell.com/US/Indexes/US/membership.asp: For Russell 1000, Russell 2000, and Russell 3000.

References for Further Reading

Ariel, Robert. 1990. High Stock Returns Before Holidays: Existence and Evidence on Possible Causes. *Journal of Finance* 45, 1611–26.

Chan, Su Han, Wai-Kin Leung, and Ko Wang. 2003. The Impact of Institutional Investors on the Monday Seasonal. *Journal of Business*, forthcoming.

Chen, Honghui, and Vijay Singal. 2003. Role of Speculative Short Sales in Price Formation: Case of the Weekend Effect. *Journal of Finance* 58, 685–705.

Damodaran, Aswath. 1989. The Weekend Effect in Information Releases: A Study of Earnings and Dividend Announcements. *Review of Financial Studies* 2, 607–23.

Dyl, Edward A., and Stanley A. Martin Jr. 1985. Weekend Effects on Stock Returns: A Comment. *Journal of Finance* 40, 347–50.

Fosback, Norman G. 1986. Stock Market Logic. Institute for Economic Research, FL.

French, Kenneth R. 1980. Stock Returns and the Weekend Effect. *Journal of Financial Economics* 8, 55–69.

Gibbons, Michael R., and Patrick Hess. 1981. Day of the Week Effects and Asset Returns. *Journal of Business* 54, 579–96.

Hirsch, Yale. 1986. *Don't Sell Stocks on Monday* (New York: Facts on File).

Jaffe, Jeffrey, and Randolph Westerfield. 1985. The Week-End Effect in Common Stock Returns: The International Evidence. *Journal of Finance* 40(2), 433–54.

Kamstra, Mark J., Lisa A. Kramer, and Maurice D. Levi. 2000. Losing Sleep at the Market: The Daylight Saving Anomaly. *American Economic Review* 90, 1005–11.

Keim, Donald B., and Robert F. Stambaugh. 1984. A Further Investigation of the Weekend Effect in Stock Returns. *Journal of Finance* 39, 819–35.

Lakonishok, Josef, and Maurice Levi. 1982. Weekend Effects on Stock Returns: A Note. *Journal of Finance* 37, 883–89.

Lakonishok, Josef, and Seymour Smidt. 1988. Are Seasonal Anomalies Real? A Ninety-Year Perspective. *Review of Financial Studies* 1, 403–25.

Rogalski, Richard J. 1984. New Findings Regarding Day-of-the-Week Returns over Trading and Non-Trading Periods: A Note. *Journal of Finance* 39, 1603–14.

Sias, Richard, and Laura Starks. 1995. Day-of-the-Week Anomaly: The Role of Institutional Investors. *Financial Analyst Journal* 51(3), 57–66.

Smith, Geoffrey. 1999. "You, Too, Can Short Stocks." *Business Week,* March 22.

Wang, Ko, Yuming Li, and John Erickson. 1997. A New Look at the Monday Effect. *Journal of Finance* 52, 2171–86.

Notes

1. This chapter draws extensively from the author's prior work, in particular from Chen and Singal (2003). Other work used in this chapter includes French (1980), Gibbons and Hess (1981), Lakonishok and Smidt (1988), Keim and Stambaugh (1984), Jaffe and Westerfield (1985), Sias and Starks (1995), Ariel (1990), and Wang, Li, and Erickson (1997), which have documented discoveries relating to the weekend effect. These and Fosback (1986), Damodaran (1989), Kamstra, Kramer, and Levi (2000), Dyl and Martin (1985), Lakonishok and Levi (1982), Chang, Leung, and Wang (2003), and Chen and Singal (2003) examine potential explanations of the weekend effect.

2. Since Mondays follow days that are closed for trading, the Monday return should actually reflect the return for more than one day and, therefore, should be greater than the return on other days. Thus, the weekend effect should be negative for all securities.

3. See Appendix B for a discussion on short selling.

4. Under the uptick rule, an investor cannot short sell shares of a stock that is falling in price.

5. Since price volatility over nontrading hours is much smaller than during trading hours, it can be argued that nontrading hours are less important than trading hours in terms of volatility. However, note that as short sellers can monitor prices during trading hours and take action, the volatility during trading hours is inconsequential, even desirable. On the other hand, even a little volatility during nontrading hours can be devastating to the short sellers.

4

Short-Term Price Drift

Events associated with high-quality information signals tend to exhibit price continuations. The quality of information is characterized by the magnitude of price change, volume, and public dissemination of information. There is evidence to suggest that a large price change accompanied by high volume and a public announcement is followed by a drift in prices. A trading strategy designed to capture this short-term price continuation will earn annual abnormal returns of 15–36 percent after transactions costs.

Description

Predictably, there is much research on price continuations (also called price drift or price momentum) and price reversals.[1] It seems that there is momentum in stock returns over periods of six to twelve months—that is, if prices are rising, they will continue to rise, or if they are falling, they will continue to fall (see Chapter 5). Over longer periods extending up to five years, there is a tendency for mean reversion, that is, prices revert to normal levels. The medium- and long-term evidence suggests that there are cycles in price patterns. However, mispricings that rely on long periods are not interesting. First, it is not clear that those mispricings actually occur, given the noise in estimates. Second, trading strategies are not easily amenable to long holding periods.

Short-term price patterns considered here are of two kinds: the pattern could be a form of price drift, where the price continues to move in the same direction, or it could be a price reversal where the price moves in the opposite direction. These price patterns may be due to market frictions, a result of market inefficiency, or related to information arrival.

The earliest documentation of short-term price drift is related to earnings announcements, in which it was found that firms with surprisingly good earnings earn abnormal returns of about 2 percent in the following three months, whereas firms with surprisingly bad earnings lose abnormally. Evidence of price drift suggests that information in the earnings announcement is not immediately and fully reflected in prices. Other research has found that trading volume is important in evaluating the permanence of price changes. Stock prices, especially of inactively traded stocks, can be affected by medium-sized trades that do not contain any new information. A sell order driven only by a need for cash can push down the price artificially that reverses over the next few days. The type and quality of information determine whether the price impact is permanent or temporary.

What is information quality and how can it be measured? The quality of information signals can be measured on different dimensions: magnitude, precision, and dissemination. The first dimension, the size of a price change, captures the magnitude of the signal or the significance of the news. The second dimension is precision of information quality, which is measured by volume. If the information is precise, then more people are likely to trade as they rebalance their portfolios or take new positions in response to the new information. Finally, the third dimension of information quality is dissemination of new information and is determined by whether or not a public announcement is made. Since public announcements are more credible due to legal and reputation costs, they are likely to contain higher-quality information. However, any one of the proxies used captures only one of the three dimensions. Using all three quality-identifying proxies simultaneously should improve the detection of price patterns.

The idea is that if a stock experiences a large price change unaccompanied by high volume or a public announcement, then that price change may get reversed. On the other hand, a price change accompanied by high volume and a public announcement is likely to be permanent. Indeed, if large price changes are accompanied by an increase in volume and a public announcement by the management or analysts, then a price continuation is likely to result in a one-month abnormal return of about 3.5 percent for positive events and –2.25 percent for negative events. A trading strategy set up to exploit these price patterns can earn an abnormal return of 1.25 percent to 3 percent after transaction costs, that is, 15–36 percent annually.

Evidence

The evidence on the short-term price drift begins with a large price change as an indicator of a strong signal of new information. A large price change (stock return) can be defined in two different ways: as an absolute return or as a relative return. A 10 percent absolute return or a change in price from $50 to $45 (or to $55) obviously seems like a large price change. However, a 10 percent return in one day may be relatively common for riskier stocks, such as technology stocks. For example, Amazon.com's price changed by more than 10 percent fourteen times over the July 2001–June 2002 period. By comparison, General Electric's return crossed the 10 percent threshold only two times during that period. Further, the 10 percent limit becomes easier to cross for a stock with a price of less than $1 because a change of 10 cents in the price translates into a 10 percent return. ICGE, a stock with a price of less than $1, earned or lost more than 10 percent in a day forty-five times in a one-year period.

Due to the limitations of an absolute return, a relative return seems more appropriate. For one thing, the relative return criterion does not impose an ad hoc cutoff that is invariant across different kinds of stocks; rather, the threshold of relative return is based on the normal return and its volatility. In other words, if relative return is used to select large returns, then the top 1 percent of all returns, ignoring the sign, will be considered large for a particular stock.[2] Considering the top 1 percent of 250 daily returns of a stock (there are 250 trading days in a year) means that the top two or three returns every year are large. Continuing with the stocks considered in the previous paragraph, the two 10 percent returns for GE will be considered large, constituting the greatest 1 percent of all returns. For Amazon.com, only three of the fourteen returns fall in the top 1 percent category. For ICGE, three of the forty-five returns fall in the top 1 percent category. The advantage of using the relative return screen is that the selected sample will represent all firms equally, unlike the absolute return criterion, which is geared toward selecting more stocks that are riskier or low-priced. The disadvantage is that the relative return is different for each stock and requires computation for each individual stock to judge whether or not a particular return falls in the top 1 percent of all returns.

Results with Large Price Changes

Results presented in Table 4.1 are for all large price changes. The relative return criterion for the first two returns requires that the

Table 4.1 Price Continuations and Reversals Following Large Price Changes

	Period	Sample Size	Selection Criterion for Return on Day 0	Market Adjusted	Price Level	Volume Requirement	Average Return on Day of Large Change (Day 0)	Abnormal Return: Day 1 to Day 20
1.	1990–1992	2,919	Relative return (increase)	Yes	>$10	Yes	7.13%	0.08%
2.	1990–1992	1,954	Relative return (decline)	Yes	>$10	Yes	−7.13%	−0.48%
3.	1984–1987	1,276	>10%	Yes	>$10	—	12.31%	−2.13%
4.	1984–1987	840	<−10%	Yes	>$10	—	−13.83%	−1.12%

Abnormal return is defined as the raw return minus the S&P 500 return for a particular day. Event day is the day of the large price change. Sources: Pritamani and Singal (2001), Park (1995), and Cox and Peterson (1994).

selected return be an extreme price change for the firm that lies more than three standard deviations away from the mean. This means that approximately 0.25 percent of all returns for a particular stock are selected. The day on which the large price change occurs is referred to as day 0 or the event day.

The other conditions imposed for initial selection are also important. First, all returns are adjusted for the market. Imagine a day when the market falls by 5 percent. A large number of companies will fall in value, though the reason for the fall does not relate to the individual firm. Accordingly, an adjustment for market return is made before selecting firms.

One big concern with short-term drift is that patterns discovered may not represent a mispricing; rather, they may represent the bid-ask bounce (also see "Alternative Explanations" in Chapter 3). For example, consider a stock (say, ICGE) that trades at less than $1.00 a share. On a large price change day, assume the price falls from $0.60 with a closing bid price of $0.50 and a closing ask price of $0.51. Assume that the last trade on day 0 occurs at $0.50; that translates into a fall of 16.7 percent from a previous price of $0.60. Next day (day 1), nothing changes and the bid and ask prices remain at $0.50 and $0.51. If the last trade is a buy that takes place at the ask price of $0.51, the recorded closing price would be $0.51, which is an increase of 1 cent and a calculated return of 2 percent. Looking at the closing prices alone, it seems reasonable to conclude that there is a reversal following large price changes (–16.7 percent on day 0 followed by +2 percent on day 1), though nothing actually changed between day 0 and day 1. On the other hand, assume that the price falls from $0.60 to $0.51 on the event day, a drop of 15 percent. Again, assume that nothing changes on day 1, but the last trade is executed at the bid price of $0.50, a drop of 1 cent and a return of –2 percent. Now it seems reasonable to conclude that there is a continuation— a fall of 15 percent is followed by another fall of 2 percent on the next day. Though the assumptions about ICGE's stock price suggest that there is no change, the return calculations reveal a pattern because of closing trades bouncing between the bid and ask prices.

To guard against spurious results due to the bid-ask bounce, a $10 price limit is imposed. However, many stocks with a price of more than $10 can also have large bid-ask spreads. For example, Masonite International (NYSE: MHM) has a price of more than $10, but the bid-ask spread is about 1 percent. Also, imposing an additional condition of nonzero volume on any day can reduce the inclusion of infrequently traded stocks. Moreover, trading strategies will not work effectively with stocks that have large bid-ask spreads.

Instead of using objective criteria to screen stocks, it is significantly more effective just to make sure that stocks with a high cost of trading are not included in trading strategies.

Accordingly, stocks considered in Table 4.1 have a lower price limit and, in some cases, a minimum volume requirement. From the table, you can see that there are no consistent patterns. The abnormal return (raw return adjusted for the market) over 20 trading days is only 0.08 percent in the first row, –0.48 percent in the second row, a reversal of –2.13 percent in the third row and a continuation of –1.12 percent in the fourth row.[3] Thus, overall, for large price increases and declines, there is no evidence of a price drift.

RESULTS WITH LARGE PRICE CHANGES AND HIGH VOLUME

The second distinguishing feature of information quality is its precision. As the signal becomes more precise, it will lead investors to have more confidence in their valuation of the stock, and so they will be more willing to make large trades. For example, if a company announces surprisingly good earnings and high revenues and forecasts stronger results in the future, the investors are likely to believe that the stock's valuation should be higher, leading to active trading in that stock and significantly higher volume. On the other hand, postings on Internet message boards promoting a particular stock may not instill much confidence. Though the price might rise due to the trades of few people on low volume, especially in illiquid stocks, it is just as likely to fall quickly on subsequent days.

Volume is, therefore, generally viewed as an effective measure of information precision. In the same vein, chartists usually look at volume to confirm price trends. Price changes unaccompanied by high volume are considered suspect and require further review. Financial news services routinely report up-volume and down-volume to give an indication of the strength of market moves.

Just like with return, defining high volume becomes a challenge. The results presented in panel A of Table 4.2 assume that the trading volume on day 0 is in the top 10 percent of daily volumes over a sixty-day period, that is, among the top six volume days. Since an individual stock's volume, like its return, depends on market volume, it is appropriate to adjust the stock's trading volume by market volume.

The results in panel A of Table 4.2 reveal two return patterns. First, price changes that are accompanied by high volume have price continuations. Price increases with high volume are followed by subsequent increases of 0.20 percent and 0.95 percent over five-day

Table 4.2   Returns Following Large Price Changes, High Volume, and News

	Price Change	High Volume	Public News	Sample Size	Abnormal Return: Days 1–5 (%)	Abnormal Return: Days 1–20 (%)
Panel A: Large price changes with and without high volume						
1.	Increase	Yes	—	1,477	0.20	0.95
2.	Increase	No	—	1,442	−0.71	−0.67
3.	Decrease	Yes	—	1,142	−0.66	−0.65
4.	Decrease	No	—	812	0.49	−0.13
Panel B: Large price changes, high volume, and public news						
5.	Increase	Yes	Yes	603	0.54	1.98
6.	Increase	Yes	No	874	−0.09	0.03
7.	Decrease	Yes	Yes	653	−1.26	−1.68
8.	Decrease	Yes	No	489	0.63	0.52

Large price change is based on relative return. The return must lie more than three standard deviations away from the mean return calculated over the last one year. A stock is deemed to have a high volume if its volume on the event day lies in the top 10 percent of daily volumes over the previous sixty days. Abnormal return is defined as the raw return minus the S&P 500 return for that day. The event day is the day of the large price change. Source: Pritamani and Singal (2001).

and twenty-day periods. Similarly, price decreases with high volume are followed by further price decreases of 0.66 percent and 0.65 percent in the five-day and twenty-day periods. Price changes not accompanied by high volume have a slight reversal in returns.

RESULTS WITH LARGE PRICE CHANGES, HIGH VOLUME, AND NEWS

The third characteristic of signal quality is dissemination of information, proxied by announcement of the information. The primary source of information about a company is the company itself. Officers of a company cannot legally trade on material nonpublic information (see Chapter 7, on insider trading). Instead, the company is encouraged to make public any material information as soon as possible. That is why companies routinely preannounce their earnings estimates if they are significantly different from publicly available information. Security analysts can also generate new information based on their own reading of the industry or that particular firm. But their analysis is derived from information disclosed in corporate news releases. Analysts can, of course, choose not to publicly release their recommendations, as they are not subject to insider trading laws, provided that their analysis is based on publicly available information. On the other hand, analysts do have an incentive to publicize their recommendations because correct calls will enhance their reputation in the market. Thus, analysts will usually choose to publicize rating changes in which they have confidence, notwithstanding calls by Merrill Lynch's Henry Blodget on Internet stocks and Salomon Smith Barney's Jack Grubman on the telecom sector.

Large price changes can also occur in the absence of new information. For example, an institution may decide to trade a particular stock for portfolio rebalancing, selling it if it has become overweighted due to price appreciation or buying it if it has become underweighted due to a fall in the stock price. Or a large shareholder may sell a significant fraction of his shareholding because he needs the cash to diversify into real estate or buy an executive jet.

As these events contain no new information about the stock, they are unlikely to provide reliable predictions about price movements and should be excluded from further consideration. Results are presented with and without public news for comparison in panel B of Table 4.2. It can be seen that the distinction between the news sample and no-news sample is quite sharp. There is a definitive continuation in returns when price changes are accompanied by high volume and public news: price increases are followed by an increase of 1.98 percent in the subsequent twenty trading days, while price decreases are followed by a return of –1.68 percent. On the other hand, there is no pattern when price changes are not accompanied by a public announcement.

Type of News

The type of news is important to judge the probability of a price drift or momentum. Extremely precise information may not necessarily provide an opportunity to predict future movements in price. Cash mergers are one such case. For example, Regions Financial Corp. announced a cash bid for Morgan Keegan (NYSE: MOR) on December 18, 2000, at $27 per share (see Chapter 11, on merger arbitrage). The price of MOR jumped 35 percent to close at $26.13 on a volume of 576,400 shares, compared to a normal daily volume of less than 50,000 shares. The next highest volume in the prior three months was 113,600 shares. This particular instance meets the requirements for inclusion in the sample. However, there is no uncertainty about the target's price, assuming the merger is successful. Not surprisingly, the price moved within a narrow range of about 1 percent over the next several days.

On the other hand, Intel warned about impending underperformance after the close on June 6, 2002. The next day Intel fell from $27 to $22, a decline of 18.5 percent, on a volume of 152 million shares. The price change and the volume were among the highest ever. In spite of the announcement, there was great uncertainty about Intel's correct valuation. It seems obvious that if the preannouncement price of $27 was correct, the correct postannouncement value must be below $27. But the question is whether it should be $25, $20, $10, or $5. The price uncertainty surrounding big news is ideal for price continuations. Indeed, Intel's price fell by 12.1 percent over the next twenty days, while during the same period the Nasdaq 100 fell by 6.9 percent and the S&P 500 fell by 3.8 percent. Thus, Intel underperformed the market by at least 5.2 percent.

The implication for price drift is obvious from the two examples—that the type of news matters. The results for different kinds of news are given in Table 4.3. Actual earnings announcements or preannouncements by the management and analysts' reports are the most effective predictors of price drift. The abnormal returns after these public announcements can be large: about 1 percent within five trading days and 3.50 percent over twenty trading days after large price increases, and about –2.4 percent over twenty days after price decreases. Other news items have no predictive power in the case of positive events, though there is a price drift for negative events. A possible reason for this difference is discussed in the next paragraph. The abnormal returns have already been adjusted not

Table 4.3   Price Continuations Conditional on News Type

	Price Change	High Volume	News Type	Sample Size	Abnormal Return: Days 1–5 (%)	Abnormal Return: Days 1–20 (%)
1.	Increase	Yes	Earnings	226	1.03	3.50
2.	Increase	Yes	Analysts' reports	102	0.80	3.59
3.	Increase	Yes	Others	243	0.04	0.08
4.	Decrease	Yes	Earnings	337	–1.58	–2.37
5.	Decrease	Yes	Analysts' reports	217	–1.11	–2.39
6.	Decrease	Yes	Others	318	–1.08	–0.44

Large price changes are based on relative return. The return must lie more than three standard deviations away from the mean return calculated over the last one year. A stock is deemed to have a high volume if its volume on the event day lies in the top 10 percent of daily volumes over the previous sixty days. Abnormal return is defined as the raw return minus the S&P 500 return for that day. Event day is the day of the large price change. Source: Pritamani and Singal (2001)

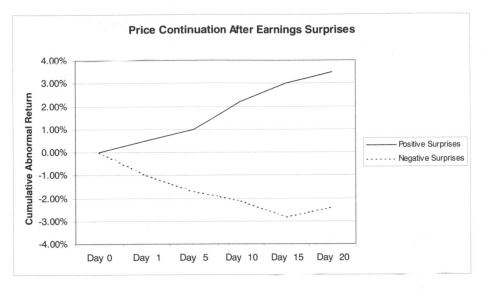

Figure 4.1   The day of the surprise announcement is day 0. The price drift over the twenty-day period after the announcement is shown in the figure for firms with large price increases, high volume, and a public earnings announcement.

only for the market in general but also for the particular firm's risk. So the risk adjustment is superior to a normal adjustment. However, it is known that firm risk normally increases around extreme events. The returns in Tables 4.1, 4.2, and 4.3 do not account for any additional event-related risk.

One interesting observation appears from a comparison between large price decreases and large price increases: the limitations imposed by short sales. In the case of large price increases, other types of news have no residual effect after the event day (see row 3 in Table 4.3), that is, all of the information is incorporated right away on the event day. However, in the case of large price declines, other types of news continue to impact the stock, as much as 1 percent in the first five trading days after the event (see row 6 in Table 4.3). Why does this difference exist? A natural reason for the difference is the cost of short selling. Consider IBM's surprisingly good earnings reported after the close of the market on October 16, 2002. Anyone who wanted to buy IBM as a result of this report could buy the stock. The current holders of IBM could buy more, and investors who did not own IBM could also buy IBM stock. On the other hand, consider AOL Time Warner's revelation of a fact-finding inquiry by the SEC into its accounting practices on July 24, 2002 (a negative event). Investors who owned AOL could sell the stock if they so desired. However, the only way investors who did not own AOL stock could trade on this information was by short-selling AOL stock. As explained in Appendix B, it is difficult and expensive to short-sell. Therefore, the price drift in stocks following large price declines may extend over a longer period than the price drift in stocks following large price increases.

TRADING COSTS

The results in Tables 4.1 to 4.3 do not consider the costs of trading. It is necessary to obtain an estimate of trading costs to accurately estimate realizable profits. The primary component of trading costs is the bid-ask spread. Brokerage commissions are usually negligible and there is not likely to be any significant price impact, as a typical investor's trade is small. On average, the bid-ask spread is about 0.5 percent. Therefore, the net abnormal return after trading costs will be about 3.0 percent over a twenty-day period following large price increases, or about 36 percent annually. In the case of price declines, the total cost of trading may be about 1.0 percent, as the trading strategy will entail short sales. Thus, the net abnormal return after trading costs is estimated to be about 1.4 percent following large price declines, or 16.8 percent on an annual basis.

Persistence

Evidence related to short-term price drift seems quite compelling. Moreover, price drift following earnings announcements (but not conditioned on volume or price changes) has been known to exist since the mid-1980s. Why did the short-term price drift continue to persist even in the late 1990s and continue today? Four possible explanations are discussed below.

First, information seems to come in cascades, that is, good information is followed by more good information, and bad information by more bad information. The assumption of cascades in information is not necessarily unreasonable. Positive earnings surprises are usually followed by analyst upgrades, while negative earnings surprises are followed by analyst downgrades. For example, Intel's warning on June 6, 2002, was quickly followed by downgrades by J. P. Morgan and CIBC World Markets. Morgan Stanley removed Intel from its Fresh Money list on June 11. On the same day, June 11, Intel followed up by reporting that its earnings visibility was impaired and the current environment was not good. On June 12, an analyst firm reported that there was an excess inventory of PC motherboards. Thus, in Intel's case, an initial warning is followed by recurring bad news over the next several days; in some situations there is new information, while in others old information is repackaged and presented in a different forum or through a different medium. If the assumption of cascading information is correct, prices might exhibit the momentum reported in the previous section.[4]

The second explanation for the price drift is related to strategic trading by large institutional investors. As institutions must trade large parcels of stock to significantly change their portfolios, they are concerned about how their trades will affect the price. Though the daily trading volume of many stocks runs into millions of shares, the stock price will still be negatively affected if an institution wants to sell several million shares of the stock and will be positively affected if the institution wants to buy the stock. Therefore, in order to minimize the price impact of their trades, institutions strategically divide their entire order into several smaller trades spread over one or many days. As repeated buy orders (or sell orders) appear in the market, they are likely to pressure the price to move up (or down). Large price changes considered in this chapter can become important events for investment portfolios triggering rebalancing of the portfolio because the price target has been reached, the stock is no longer worthy of inclusion in the portfolio, or the institution decides to buy the stock because its upside potential has improved. Thus, strategic trading by institutions may cause the observed price drift.

The third explanation suggests that short-term price drift actually does not exist once the risk of the event is considered. If the stock becomes riskier around an event because of greater uncertainty, it must earn a higher return as compensation for that risk. The returns in Tables 4.1 to 4.3 do not explicitly account for higher risk around public announcements. This explanation, however, has two shortcomings. First, the return that can be earned (3 percent in one month) is too high as compensation for typical estimates of event-related risk. Most risk-averse investors will find the excess return very attractive. Second, the explanation requires a positive return after both positive and negative events in order to compensate for the extra risk. The continuation of the negative price drift after price declines is inconsistent with this explanation.

Finally, prices may not react fully to new information because of investor behavior (see Chapter 12 for a discussion). As investors are slow to change their deeply held beliefs about a stock's value, they tend to underreact. According to this explanation, as investors realize their mistakes, they trade, but with a time lag, resulting in the price drift. In addition, investors are averse to selling at a loss and will continue to delay selling in the hope that the stock price will recover. As a result of this characteristic of investor behavior, the negative drift in price would be less than the positive drift in price. This prediction is supported by the data in Table 4.3.

Whether the price drift occurs due to strategic trading, information cascades, or irrational investor behavior, it is reasonable to claim that the drift will continue to persist.

The Trading Process

The process of identifying potential candidates for the trading strategy requires an analysis of all stocks at the end of the day based on closing prices by applying different criteria that have generated abnormal returns in the past. The trading strategy described below covers both large price increases and large price declines, though most investors would want to concentrate on the large price increase sample since it does not require short selling and is potentially more profitable.

Step 1: The first step is to pick stocks that experienced a large price change. As mentioned in "Evidence," earlier in the chapter, a large price change can be defined as an absolute return or a relative return. A 10 percent cutoff is deemed adequate to select stocks on an absolute basis. Implementation of the relative return criterion becomes difficult because each stock has its own cutoff. However, to make it simple, the relative return criterion can be combined with an absolute return screen. For example, first, all stocks that experienced a change of at least 5 percent are selected. Second, for each such stock with a return of at least 5 percent, the relative return criterion is applied by checking whether that day's return (ignoring the sign) falls in the top three returns for the year for that stock.[5] This process is performed at the end of each trading day.

Step 2: For the selected sample of stocks, stocks whose stock price is less than $10 before the large price change are excluded. In addition, it should be ensured that the same stock is not selected in the previous month, as this large price change should not be a continuation of an earlier price change.

Step 3: The second screen is related to volume. Exclude the firm if the stock's event day volume does not fall in the top 10 percent of daily volumes over the past sixty trading days. If it does, make sure that it still constitutes one of the six highest daily trading volumes when adjusted for market volume on the event day. Some data sources do not adjust the trading volume for stock splits. Check for any stock splits in the last three months and, if necessary, adjust the volume for the splits.

Step 4: The third screen is related to public announcement of news. The easiest way to look for news is to use the ticker symbol and type it into news services' search box. The news about the stock should be related to earnings announcements, earnings preannouncements, distributions, or analyst ratings of stock or debt. While earnings announcements by the management will be carried by all news services, some analyst ratings are first announced to their customers before being disseminated in the media. In any case, if no news item related to the stock can be found then drop that stock from the sample.

Step 5: Before placing trades for selected stocks, it is important to ensure that there are no company announcements scheduled for the twenty-day holding period after the event day. Scheduled announcements will unnecessarily increase the risk of the position, as the announcement can have a large positive or negative effect on the company's stock price.

Step 6: For stocks that experience large price increases, put in an order to buy at the opening price. For stocks that experience large price declines, put in an order to short-sell with the limit price set to the previous day's close.

Step 7: Four weeks (or twenty trading days) later, close all open positions.

Strategy Implementation

The process described above is actually employed in this section for the month of April 2002. For each day in April, an initial set of stocks is chosen from the Quotes-Plus database (see "Historical Price Data" in this chapter for details) that satisfy the following conditions: it is a common stock, it traded a minimum of one thousand shares on the previous trading day, and it earned a return of at least 5 percent plus the S&P 500 return for that day. The number of stocks selected, by day, is shown in column 1 of Table 4.4. On each day there are more than five hundred stocks that earned an abnormal return of more than 5 percent. Introducing the $10 price limit cuts the number of stocks to about one-quarter the original number. High volume and high return are the next two screens. In addition, the large price change must not be a continuation from another recent event. In other words, the current event must be the first eligible event over the prior twenty days. On average, only five or six stocks

Table 4.4 Stock Selection for April 2002

Date	Column 1[a]	Column 2[b]	Column 3[c]	Column 4[d]	Column 5[e]	Number of increases	Average increase (%)	Number of decreases	Average decrease (%)
April 1, 2002	631	128	32	7	2	1	17.4	1	−52.1
April 2, 2002	600	166	50	16	4	0	—	4	−19.0
April 3, 2002	509	122	33	5	2	0	—	2	−13.5
April 4, 2002	501	122	48	18	8	4	9.2	4	−20.9
April 5, 2002	513	105	38	12	5	3	11.0	2	−13.9
April 8–29, 2002	data not shown								
April 30, 2002	785	176	51	10	2	2	10.3	0	—
Total for April 2002	13,089	3,436	1,250	301	114	55	12.9	59	−16.9

[a]Column 1 = Stocks with volume 1,000 and absolute abnormal return of at least 5 percent.
[b]Column 2 = Column 1 + the price on the day before the event is greater than $10.
[c]Column 3 = Column 2 + volume in the top 6 out of previous 60 days.
[d]Column 4 = Column 3 + return in the top three among the last year.
[e]Column 5 = Column 4 but excluding continuations of earlier events.
The original data set is from Quotes-Plus.

satisfy these criteria each day. The total number of events selected for April 2002 is 114, including 55 price increases and 59 price declines. The average price increase is 12.9 percent on the event day, while the price decrease is –16.9 percent.

News Type

The selected stocks are further refined by searching for the type of news. Since April follows the quarter end in March, a large fraction of the large price changes can be attributed to earnings announcements. Thirty-two earnings announcements and preannouncements account for price increases, while thirty-nine are responsible for price declines. Announcements of distributions by the company fall into the same category as earnings announcements, though they are categorized differently in Table 4.5. There are eight rating changes by security analysts. These rating changes are not concurrent with or close to a corporate announcement. Finally, no news is found for twenty-four large price changes. Absence of news could be related to aggressive trading by an institution based entirely on its own assessment of the stock. Or it could be because analyst recommendations are disclosed only to the company's clients and not to other investors. Finally, the media may not have carried the news if the company is too small or if the news services did not consider the news important enough.

Results by News Type

The returns by news type for April 2002 are in Table 4.6. Announcements by the company that pertain to the company's financial performance (types 1 and 3) are reported in the first column. For the thirty-five stocks, the mean abnormal return is 3.36 percent over a twenty-day period after the large price increase. Two-thirds of the positions are winners. The costs of transacting have not been explicitly considered. As these stocks have an average price of $32 and are traded actively on days around the event, the bid-ask spread is unlikely to be more than 0.50 percent. Thus, the net return is 2.86 percent per month, or 34 percent annually.

The price drift after large price declines is similar. The sample firms lose 4.27 percent over the following twenty trading days. Adjusted for the market, the mean abnormal return is computed as –1.67 percent. As mentioned earlier, the trading strategy in the case of large price declines entails a short position. Therefore, the –1.67 percent actually reflects a gain of 1.67 percent. Considering 1 percent as the cost of a short sales transaction, the net profit is only 0.67

Table 4.5 Type of News Announced for Selected Firms in April 2002

Type of News	Description	Number of Firms	Number Included in Final Sample	Price Increases	Price Decreases
1	Actual earnings and earning forecasts	71	71	32	39
2	Analyst ratings not related to type 1	8	8	3	5
3	Distributions	3	3	3	0
4	Legal actions	1	0	0	1
5	Accounting-related	3	0	0	3
6	Pharmaceutical trials	1	0	0	1
7	News followed by scheduled earnings	2	0	0	2
8	No news	24	0	17	7
9	Miscellaneous	1	0	0	1
	Total	114	82	55	59

News items are searched on Bloomsberg.com's news archive, Briefing.com, and Bigcharts.com.
The news types are defined as follows:

News type 1: Earnings announcement or preannouncement by the company.
News type 2: Rating upgrade or downgrade by security analysts. The rating changes must not be in response to earnings announcements.
News type 3: Distribution announced by the company, such as a cash dividend or stock split, but not concurrent with news type 1.
News type 4: Legal actions initiated or concluded against the company.
News type 5: Any accounting irregularities disclosed by the company or alleged by a government agency.
News type 6: News related to the progress of pharmaceutical trials or application to the FDA.
News type 7: News that is immediately (one to two days) followed by a scheduled earnings announcement.
News type 8: No news found in the news services listed or on the company's website. However, this does not mean that there was no news—only that none could be found.
News type 9: Miscellaneous, not elsewhere classified. In this case, it is a complaint to the FCC.

Table 4.6   Returns for Stocks Selected in April 2002, by News Type

	Earnings and Distributions	Analysts' Ratings	No News	
Panel A: Price Increases				
Sample size	35	3	17	
Event day return	13.2%	19.5%	11.1%	
Average stock price	$32	$27	$26	
20-day raw return	1.03%	4.75%	1.27%	
20-day S&P 500 return	−2.33%	−2.78%	−3.52%	
Mean abnormal return	3.36%	7.53%	4.78%	
Median abnormal return	2.99%	15.27%	2.76%	
Percent positive	66%	67%	76%	
	Earnings and Distributions	**Analysts' Ratings**	**Other News**	**No News**
Panel B: Price Decreases				
Sample size	39	5	7	7
Event day return	−17.8%	−11.0%	−18.1%	−15.5%
Average stock price	$26	$22	$22	$24
20-day raw return	−4.27%	−12.98%	1.92%	−4.50%
20-day S&P 500 return	−2.60%	−2.35%	−1.07%	−1.77%
Mean abnormal return	−1.67%	−10.63%	2.99%	−2.73%
Median abnormal return	0.49%	−12.34%	6.84%	−6.20%
Percent negative	49%	100%	29%	71%

News items are searched on Bloomsberg.com's news archive, Briefing.com, and Bigcharts.com.

percent. As shown in Table 4.3, the lower profitability after large price declines is not unexpected. Moreover, the median abnormal return is positive, and only 49 percent of the positions are winners. Given the evidence in Table 4.3, the evidence in Table 4.6 for April 2002, and the difficulty in short selling, it is probably best to exclude stocks with large price declines while constructing a trading strategy.

News type 2 refers to rating changes by analysts. If a rating change occurs concurrently with an earnings announcement, the news is classified as type 1. Thus, these rating changes are isolated events usually far removed from any other significant news related to the company. News about changes in analyst ratings has the most significant price drift, at least for the stocks selected in April 2002. The mean return is 7.53 percent following large price increases and −10.63 percent following large price declines. Though the sample size calls for caution, the returns are large and attractive.

Other news items—accounting irregularities, legal problems, and progress of pharmaceutical trials—are announced only for price declines. These news releases result in an overreaction for the month of April 2002.

Surprisingly, the no-news sample (type 8) also exhibits significant price drift: an average of 4.78 percent following price increases and –2.73 percent following price decreases. There are two possible explanations. First, the media did not carry information about the companies, though that information was important. Second, the month of April 2002 just happens to be different from other months.

Nonetheless, the primary evidence of price drift following large price changes in section 4.2 is reconfirmed by the results for April 2002. Relying on large price increases due to announcements by the management and analyst rating changes would have generated an average abnormal return of 3.19 percent (average of returns to types 1, 2, and 3) over a twenty-day period following large price increases, or an annualized return of 38 percent.

Annualized returns are used for a better understanding of the magnitude of gains. To annualize the abnormal return calculated above, it is assumed that the same return can be earned for multiple events in a sequential manner. For example, if an abnormal return of 5 percent is earned over a period of twenty trading days, it is assumed that we will earn the same 5 percent abnormal return in subsequent twenty-day periods. Thus, the annualized return is calculated simply as the 5 percent abnormal return times 12, since there are 250 trading days in a year or approximately twelve twenty-day periods.

Qualifications

The evidence and the trading strategy recommendations presented in this chapter are based on past data. Since future market conditions and market patterns may be completely different, there is no certainty that the short-term price drift will continue in the future or be profitable.

In addition, all of the evidence suggests positive abnormal returns. However, even with positive abnormal returns, one might lose money if the market return is sufficiently negative. It is known that there is an increase in risk around important events. While the abnormal returns have been adjusted for normal levels of risk, they do not account for heightened event-related risk. Finally, hedging against market movements with S&P futures is appropriate to reduce one's risk and increase the chances of earning the abnormal returns documented here.

Key Points

- Do prices exhibit any patterns after large price changes? Is there an overreaction or an underreaction? It seems that the discovery of patterns depends on the quality of information. Quality of information is proxied by price changes, volume, and news.

- The evidence reveals that there is no predictability in returns following large price changes. However, the returns become predictable if the price changes go together with extraordinarily high volume. Announcement of public news further improves the reliability of forecasts. For different types of news, price changes following earnings announcements and analysts' reports can continue to drift over the next twenty days. The annualized abnormal return is approximately 36 percent following large price increases and 18 percent following large price declines.

- The explanations for this phenomenon are varied. There has not been much research aimed at explaining short-term price drift. One of the possibilities is information cascades, that is, good information is followed by more good information because information comes in bits and pieces. Another explanation is based on strategic trading by institutions. As institutions must trade large quantities, they break their orders into small parcels to reduce the price impact. Irrational investor behavior could be another reason if investors are slow to sell their losers and quick to sell their winners causing prices to drift for several days.

- A trading strategy can be devised and applied to real data. The strategy reveals an abnormal return of 38 percent per year by capturing the drift following large price increases in the month of April 2002. The success ratio is 66 percent.

Bottom Line

In general, there is no evidence of tradable price regularities following large price events. If large price changes are accompanied by other traits of information, such as high volume and public dissemination of news, the patterns become stronger. Evidence of price continuation becomes very important for news relating to earnings, distributions, and analyst recommendations, where the postevent twenty-day price drift is +3.50 percent for positive events and –2.25 percent for negative events. The annualized return after transactions costs can be estimated at 36 percent annually for positive price changes and 15 percent for negative price changes. This strategy works even in bear markets!

Internet References

Historical Price Data
http://www.qp2.com: Quotes-Plus contains all stocks traded on NYSE, AMEX, and Nasdaq. It provides daily updates.

http://www.fasttrack.net, http://www.msodata.com: These are some other sources that provide data needed for this chapter.

News Services
http://www.bigcharts.com: Very comprehensive site—one is more likely to find a press release on this site than anywhere else. However, the site does not contain information about announcements that are not publicly released, such as some rating changes. For those types of news, Briefing.com is better. In addition, the site does not provide information carried exclusively by Reuters.

http://www.briefing.com: Abridged news articles are available for most companies and for several years in a nice accessible format. Requires a subscription.

http://online.wsj.com: Articles up to thirty days old are available without extra payment. Requires a subscription.

http://finance.yahoo.com, http://moneycentral.msn.com: These sites contain news from all major news services but do not archive news stories.

References for Further Reading

Chan, Wesley S. 2003. Stock Price Reaction to News and No-news: Drift and Reversal After Headlines. *Journal of Financial Economics,* forthcoming.

Cox, Don R., and David R. Peterson. 1994. Stock Returns Following Large One-Day Declines: Evidence on Short-Term Reversals and Longer-Term Performance. *Journal of Finance* 49, 255–67.

Fehle, Frank, and Vladimir Zdorovtsov. 2002. Large Price Declines, News, Liquidity, and Trading Strategies: An Intraday Analysis. Working paper, Department of Finance, University of South Carolina.

Larsen, Stephen J., and Jeff Madura. 2003. What Drives Stock Price Behavior Following Extreme One-Day Returns. *Journal of Financial Research* 26(1), 129–46.

Nofsinger, John R. 2001. The Impact of Public Information on Investors. *Journal of Banking and Finance* 25, 1139–366.

Park, Jinwoo. 1995. A Market Microstructure Explanation for Predictable Variations in Stock Returns Following Large Price Changes. *Journal of Financial and Quantitative Analysis* 30, 241–56.

Pritamani, Mahesh, and Vijay Singal. 2001. Return Predictability Following Large Price Changes and Information Releases. *Journal of Banking and Finance* 25(4), 631–56.

Ryan, Paul, and Richard J. Taffler. 2002. What Firm Specific News Releases Drive Economically Significant Stock Returns and Trading Volumes? Working paper, School of Management, Cranfield University.

Notes

1. The chice of the top 1 percent or the top 5 percent of all returns for construction of the sample is arbitrary.
2. This chapter is based primarily on the author's work with Mahesh Pritamani (2001). This research was among the first to recognize the importance of quality of information as revealed by large price changes, high trading volumes, and news. In addition, the chapter relies on work by Park (1995), Cox and Peterson (1994), Chan (2003), Nofsinger (2001), Fehle and Zdorovtsov (2002), and Larsen and Madura (2003).
3. Note that a typical week has five trading days. Twenty trading days are approximately equal to one month.
4. If more analysts are likely to provide updated analysis after good news (so that their customers can buy those stocks) than after bad news, the effect of information cascades will be reflected as a larger price drift after positive surprises than after negative surprises.
5. If the 5 percent cutoff generates too many stocks, the absolute level can be raised to 7.5 percent. If there are too few stocks, then the level can be lowered to, say, 2.5 percent.

5

Momentum in
Industry Portfolios

There is evidence to suggest that industry portfolios exhibit momentum. Industries that have done well in one period also do well in the next period. Moreover, industries with no related futures markets are likely to show greater momentum than industries where information regarding real assets is aggregated in futures prices. Industry portfolios constructed in this manner generate returns that may be much larger than the S&P 500 return.

Description

Investment practitioners believe that asset allocation among bonds, domestic stocks, and foreign stocks should be altered over time depending on individual circumstances and economic conditions.[1] This chapter proposes taking asset allocation a step further, to allocation among different industries. One industry may be hot today and another may be hot next month depending on changing fads, individual preferences, national requirements, or political expediency. For example, after the terrorist attacks on September 11, 2001, the defense and security industry did exceptionally well, as demand for such equipment and personnel increased. Similarly, bad weather or continued drought can affect production of commodities and hurt industries that use those inputs.

If changes in an industry are not fleeting but sustained, then a change in stock prices should mirror changes in the industry. However, if changes in an industry occur gradually, then stock prices may also change gradually. Evidence tends to support gradual movement in industries and in returns of industry portfolios. This means that compared to an industry that underperforms, an industry that does well in one period is more likely to do well in the next period. Such predictability of returns enables the creation and implementation of profitable trading strategies.

Evidence

Before presenting evidence related to industry momentum, it is instructive to discuss momentum in individual stocks. There is extensive empirical evidence to suggest profitability of trading strategies based on buying and holding winner stocks. In a typical strategy, an investor buys a group of stocks that have done well over a specified period (winner stocks) and short-sells another group of stocks that have done poorly over the same period (loser stocks). Evidence suggests that this zero investment strategy generates a positive annual return of up to 12 percent. The strategy doesn't work for short periods of less than one month or long periods of more than twenty-four months, but it has proven to be successful in the six-to-twelve-month range. Some researchers believe that the momentum is due to herding by institutional investors, when many institutional investors buy the same or similar securities. Others believe that irrational individual investor behavior is responsible for the profitability of momentum strategies.

There is other evidence to suggest that momentum among individual stocks actually arises from industry momentum. Once individual stock returns are adjusted for industry effects, momentum-based trading strategies are much less profitable and largely insignificant. This means that the primary reason for momentum is trends in industry. Therefore, industry-momentum-based trading strategies are likely to be better than strategies based on individual stocks without considering their industry group.

Evidence based on 1963–1995 data supports this conjecture. An industry-momentum-based trading strategy, where the three best-performing industries based on one month's return are bought and the three worst-performing industries are short-sold, generates an annualized profit of 12 percent over the following one month. If the industry effect in the momentum strategy is neutralized, then the return becomes much smaller.

Although these returns are large and significant, implementing such a strategy is entirely another matter. There are at least two limitations. First, strategies involving momentum-based trading of individual stocks require extensive short selling. Hedged short sales, as in the case of merger arbitrage, may be acceptable to most investors, but open, unhedged short positions are generally avoided by individuals and institutions alike. Therefore, ideally a trading strategy should not contain any speculative short sales. Second, trading in individual stocks can become expensive. Moreover, trading multiple stocks within each industry to control risk raises transaction costs with the consequent decimation of returns.

FIDELITY SECTOR MUTUAL FUNDS

A study of Fidelity sector mutual funds provides more evidence. Fidelity Select funds are undiversified single-industry mutual funds designed to capture industry movements with a few stocks. The advantage of Fidelity Select funds over homemade industry portfolios is that the cost of trading and maintaining a portfolio of Fidelity Select funds is relatively small. Trading among Fidelity sector funds can be costless if the portfolio is held for at least thirty days and traded via the Fidelity website without the assistance of a Fidelity representative. The short-term trading fee is 0.75 percent if the fund is held for less than thirty days, and exchanges through a Fidelity representative cost $7.50.

There are two potential limitations of Fidelity sector funds. First, these portfolios reflect gains or losses due to active management by the fund manager. The fund manager will alter the portfolio depending on his perception of the prospects of a particular company. If the manager is uncertain about the whole industry, he may reduce exposure by holding cash, making exposure to the industry incomplete. Second, the fees and expenses associated with the portfolios can be large. The expense ratio, which includes administrative costs and management fees, is about 2 percent per year. Additionally, nearly all sector funds have annual turnovers in excess of 100 percent. This means that, on average, all stocks are traded at least once a year. Such frequent trading will affect returns negatively. The transaction costs, such as the bid-ask spread and brokerage fees, are not part of the expense ratio. In spite of these shortcomings, Fidelity sector funds are a superior vehicle for industry-momentum-based strategies.

The trading strategy is implemented in the following manner: the best-performing fund over a six-month period is chosen and held for the subsequent six-month period. For instance, using data for the November 1988 to April 1999 period, the first estimation

Table 5.1 **Returns for Trading Strategies with Fidelity Sector Funds, May 1989 to April 1999**

	Holding Period: 6 Months	Holding Period: 12 Months	Holding Period: 6 Months	Holding Period 12 Months
Number of industries	3	6	6	6
6-month estimation period (%)	18.7 (25.7)	20.2 (25.5)	20.0 (21.2)	22.7 (22.1)
12-month estimation period (%)	22.2 (23.9)	26.5 (24.6)	20.5 (21.3)	22.1 (22.1)
S&P 500 return (%)	18.7 (15.7)	18.7 (15.7)	18.7 (15.7)	18.7 (15.7)
Wilshire 5000 (%)	17.7 (15.8)	17.7 (15.8)	17.7 (15.8)	17.7 (15.8)
Russell 2000 (%)	12.0 (19.1)	12.0 (19.1)	12.0 (19.1)	12.0 (19.1)

All returns are annualized, and the standard deviations of returns are in parentheses. This table is derived from O'Neal (2000).

period for selection of the best-performing fund is from November 1988 to April 1989, and the first holding period for the identified fund is from May 1989 to October 1989. The second estimation period is from May 1989 to October 1989, and the second holding period is from November 1989 to April 1990. There are twenty nonoverlapping six-month periods over the May 1989–April 1999 period. The aforementioned trading strategy would have generated an annualized return of 22.4 percent over the ten-year period. Instead of using just the single best-performing industry, the risk can be slightly reduced by holding the top three industries. With three industries, the annualized return falls to 18.7 percent. Results for various strategies are summarized in Table 5.1, which shows that returns improve with longer estimation and longer holding periods. This result is slightly different from the earlier result, where industry-momentum strategies are most profitable for one-month evaluation and one-month holding periods.

Risk becomes important in momentum-based trading strategies because the portfolio is inadequately diversified—only a few industries are selected for investment. From Table 5.1, it is apparent that these strategies are clearly riskier than holding a broader market portfolio. A simple and commonly used measure of the risk-return trade-off is the Sharpe ratio.[2] The ratio is calculated as:

$$\frac{\text{Portfolio return} - \text{Return on Treasury bills}}{\text{Standard deviation of portfolio return}}$$

The Sharpe ratios are reported below based on the average short-term interest rate and annual returns for two trading strategies and three indexes over the May 1989–April 1999 period.

6-month estimation period, 12-month holding, 3 industries	0.58
12-month estimation period, 12-month holding, 3 industries	0.86
S&P 500 holding return	0.86
Wilshire 5000 holding return	0.78
Russell 2000 holding return	0.35

Sector fund trading strategies do not outperform the S&P 500 after accounting for risk. However, the trading strategies are generally superior when compared with other mutual funds, and other indexes. If only the beta risk (or systematic risk) is considered (assuming the sector funds are held in an otherwise well-diversified portfolio), the sector fund trading strategies are superior, in general, to almost all other mutual funds, including the S&P 500 index funds. All of the data presented in this section for Fidelity sector funds are based on long holding periods. Later in this chapter we will see that Fidelity sector funds perform quite well over shorter holding periods. Those results are similar to the results reported earlier in this section.

Explanations

The momentum in individual stock returns and industry returns suggests underreaction to new information that may be inconsistent with market efficiency. What can explain the observed momentum in industry portfolios? There are two broad categories of explanations: one is based on irrational investor behavior, and the other is based on efficient markets.

Behavioral finance theories (see Chapter 12) attribute underreaction and overreaction to investor irrationality. According to this explanation, investors are reluctant to change their beliefs quickly even in the face of convincing new information. As a result, they underreact, giving rise to momentum. Smart investors may be unable to take advantage of these biases because their actions are often limited by capital availability and uncertainty. For example, the exploding Internet valuations in 1999 and 2000 could not be controlled despite strong beliefs among smart investors that these were overvaluations.

Another explanation is related to lags in revisions by analysts. Firms that are industry leaders are followed by many stock analysts, while smaller firms in the same industry are followed by fewer analysts. The extent of coverage affects the frequency with which those stocks are reviewed. Leader stocks tend to get reviewed early, with dissemination of new information and the consequent price impact. Other industry stocks are reviewed later but experience a similar price impact. The lead-lag relationship in information dissemination can result in the observed momentum.

Besides the behavior of irrational individual investors, institutional managers can be responsible for momentum. It is always less risky for a manager to go with the crowd than to stick his neck out. Therefore, when a few institutional managers begin to buy a particular stock, other managers may feel safe in buying the same stock, resulting in momentum. This is popularly known as herding.

Finally, a rational explanation that is consistent with momentum arises from the relationship between financial markets and real assets. While financial asset prices *can* reflect all available information, prices of real goods are known to be sticky. Prices of real goods, such as food and housing, move slowly because the demand for these products changes slowly. Since financial markets reflect expectations related to markets for real goods, financial asset prices also move slowly. One can rightly claim that financial markets should be able to forecast industry profitability depending on forecasts of supply and demand. The problem is that financial markets that can aggregate information related to forecasts of futures prices do not exist for all industries. Consider the semiconductor industry. An analyst can forecast semiconductor prices for the next few months. However, that forecast represents a single data point and may not reflect the market wisdom. Many well-informed market participants may choose not to participate or may be ignored by market analysts. If futures prices did exist for the semiconductor industry, as they do for crude oil on the New York Mercantile Exchange, the semiconductor futures prices would more accurately reflect an aggregation of market information. For industries with futures prices, the forecasts are much easier and more accurate, and there may be a smaller momentum effect.

To illustrate momentum in an industry where futures prices are not available, consider the demand for security and defense equipment after September 11, 2001. The stock prices of security equipment providers rose immediately on anticipation of increased demand. However, no one knew exactly how much the demand would rise. The companies themselves were in the dark. Corporate estimates were based on actual sales rather than anticipated sales. As the orders for security and defense equipment kept pouring in, first from U.S. agencies and then from foreign government agencies, the demand estimates were continually revised upward. Consequently, the stock prices continued to rise. The returns to Fidelity's sector fund for the defense industry (ticker: FSDAX) are given below along with the S&P 500 return for comparison:

Month	FSDAX Return (%)	S&P 500 Return (%)
October 2001	3.6	1.9
November 2001	3.8	7.7
December 2001	4.1	0.9
January 2002	5.8	−1.6
February 2002	2.3	−1.9
March 2002	4.6	3.8
April 2002	2.0	−6.1
May 2002	0.7	−0.7
June 2002	−3.0	−7.1

The FSDAX return is positive for eight out of nine months following the attacks, and becomes negative only in the last month. Compared to the S&P 500 return, the return for the defense industry is also larger in eight out of nine months. Overall, the defense sector earned a return of 23.9 percent versus a return of −3.0 percent for the S&P 500 over the nine-month period.

Why couldn't the increase in demand be anticipated more accurately? On average, the demand forecasts should equal the actual demand. The main reason may be the *absence* of financial markets that aggregate available information. Futures markets for commodities such as crude oil, orange juice, lumber, hogs, chicken, coffee, cotton, and so on aggregate all publicly available information. No such mechanism or financial market exists for futures prices of security and defense equipment. The primary sources of information are corporate officers and financial analysts, who tend to be conservative in revising estimates, possibly contributing to the momentum in stock prices.

Persistence

Given the evidence related to industry momentum, a natural question that follows is: Why does it still persist? There may be several reasons. First, there is a fair amount of skepticism relating to momentum in spite of the evidence. More work is needed to convince investors that individual stock momentum or industry momentum exists. Once that happens, investors may feel more confident about taking positions to arbitrage and eventually eliminate momentum. Second, no clear explanations have emerged to explain momentum. Besides failing to convince the ordinary investor, behavioral explanations introduce greater risk and uncertainty because investor behavior can change without warning. Lack of an adequate explanation increases the skepticism with the results. Third, the evidence related to individual stock momentum not attributable to industries is strongest at periods of intermediate length (six to twelve months). Whenever mispricings occur at intervals in excess of about one month, estimation of risk and computation of abnormal returns can become important. The evidence indicates that industry based momentum is also strong at short intervals of about one month. Therefore, misestimation of abnormal return becomes less of an issue with industry-based momentum. However, the skepticism of industry momentum mentioned above becomes more critical because the evidence of industry-based momentum is new.

Trading Process and Strategy Implementation

IMPLEMENTATION WITH MANY MUTUAL FUNDS

Evidence supporting the existence of industry momentum presented in the "Explanations" section is limited to reliance on individual stocks and Fidelity's sector funds. While the use of mutual funds is preferred to individual stocks, there is no need to restrict the choice to Fidelity funds alone. Many other fund families, such as Rydex, ProFunds, Icon, and Invesco, offer sector funds. A combination of mutual funds for a particular industry from different fund families is likely to reduce manager-specific risk and probably more fully span the industry than a single sector fund. It is worth exploring the profitability of trading strategies based on a larger sample of mutual funds.

The construction of the mutual fund sample and results are described below. The period analyzed here is January 1997 to December 2001. In the next section, the same strategy is employed for the first half of 2002.

Step 1: The first step is to identify and choose broad industries. Fidelity's forty-one sector funds are a good starting point. However, each fund need not represent a distinct industry. Some of the Fidelity funds belong to the same industry and even have considerable overlap. For example, Select Computers and Select Software and Computers can be merged into a single industry. In order to have sufficient historical data, only funds that were established before 1997 are considered. The assignment of the forty-one Fidelity funds into distinct industries is shown in Table 5.2. The final sample consists of twenty-four industries.

Step 2: In addition to the Fidelity funds, pick other sector mutual funds that fit into the twenty-four industries, irrespective of the fund family. These other funds come from Morningstar's Principia Pro, which has a fairly broad coverage of mutual funds. Sector funds are usually, but not always, categorized by Morningstar under "Specialty." Therefore, besides identifying funds from the "Specialty" category, it is desirable to peruse all funds offered by Fidelity, Rydex, Invesco, ProFunds, and Icon individually.

Step 3: To make the sample of mutual funds accessible to most investors, several screens are imposed for selection. First, the minimum purchase amount must not exceed $25,000. Actually, the minimum amount is typically $1,000 to $5,000. Only Rydex has a minimum amount of $25,000. Second, only one fund is chosen when funds with multiple classes are offered. The selection process is biased toward using funds with zero or low loads and funds with a high asset base. After these screens, up to the top five funds in each industry by assets are selected. The funds are listed by ticker symbols in Table 5.3.

Step 4: The next step is to obtain historical prices, including distributions, for the funds selected in the previous step. The weekly return is computed as the return from Wednesday close to the next Wednesday close. If Wednesday is a nontrading day, then the next business day's close is considered. You can compound five weekly returns to get a five-week return that is a close approximation to the monthly return.

Step 5: To select funds for the trading strategy, calculate the periodic return (either weekly or for periods of five weeks) for each sector. Then calculate the mean overall return for twenty-four industries.

Table 5.2 Fidelity Sector Funds and Industry Categories

	Name	Ticker	Inception Date	Industry Assignment	Reason for Nonassignment
1.	Fidelity Select Air Transportation	FSAIX	Dec. 1985	Airlines	
2.	Fidelity Select Automotive	FSAVX	Jun. 1986	Transportation	
3.	Fidelity Select Banking	FSRBX	Jun. 1986	Banking	
4.	Fidelity Select Biotechnology	FBIOX	Dec. 1985	Biotechnology	
5.	Fidelity Select Brokerage and Investment Management	FSLBX	Jul. 1985	Banking	
6.	Fidelity Select Business Services and Outsourcings	FBSOX	Feb. 1998	No assignment	Sector is too new
7.	Fidelity Select Chemicals	FSCHX	Jul. 1985	Basic materials	
8.	Fidelity Select Computers	FDCPX	Jul. 1985	Computers	
9.	Fidelity Select Construction and Housing	FSHOX	Sep. 1986	Real estate	
10.	Fidelity Select Consumer Industries	FSCPX	Jun. 1990	Consumer	
11.	Fidelity Select Cyclical Industries	FCYIX	Mar. 1997	No assignment	Sector is too new
12.	Fidelity Select Defense and Aerospace	FSDAX	May 1984	Defense	
13.	Fidelity Select Developing Communications	FSDCX	Jun. 1990	Communications	
14.	Fidelity Select Electronics	FSELX	Jul. 1985	Electronics	
15.	Fidelity Select Energy	FSENX	Jul. 1981	Energy	
16.	Fidelity Select Energy Services	FSESX	Dec. 1985	Energy services	
17.	Fidelity Select Environmental	FSLEX	Jun. 1989	No assignment	Sector is too narrow
18.	Fidelity Select Financial Services	FIDSX	Dec. 1981	Financial services	
19.	Fidelity Select Food and Agriculture	FDFAX	Jul. 1985	Food	
20.	Fidelity Select Gold	FSAGX	Dec. 1985	Gold	
21.	Fidelity Select Health Care	FSPHX	Jul. 1981	Health care	
22.	Fidelity Select Home Finance	FSVLX	Dec. 1985	Banking	

(continues on next page)

Table 5.2 Fidelity Sector Funds and Industry Categories (*continued*)

	Name	Ticker	Inception Date	Industry Assignment	Reason for Nonassignment
23.	Fidelity Select Industrial Equipment	FSCGX	Sep. 1986	Industrials	
24.	Fidelity Select Industrial Materials	FSDPX	Sep. 1986	Basic materials	
25.	Fidelity Select Insurance	FSPCX	Dec. 1985	Financial services	
26.	Fidelity Select Leisure	FDLSX	May 1984	Leisure	
27.	Fidelity Select Medical Delivery	FSHCX	Jun. 1986	Health care	
28.	Fidelity Select Medical Equipment and Systems	FSMEX	Apr. 1998	Health care	
29.	Fidelity Select Multimedia	FBMPX	Jun. 1986	Communications	
30.	Fidelity Select Natural Gas	FSNGX	Apr. 1993	Energy	
31.	Fidelity Select Natural Resources	FNARX	Mar. 1997	Natural resources	
32.	Fidelity Select Networking and Infrastructure	FNINX	Sep. 2000	No assignment	Sector is too new
33.	Fidelity Select Paper and Forest Products	FSPFX	Jun. 1986	Natural resources	
34.	Fidelity Select Pharmaceuticals	FPHAX	Jun. 2001	Health care	
35.	Fidelity Select Retailing	FSRPX	Dec. 1985	Retailing	
36.	Fidelity Select Software and Computer Services	FSCSX	Jul. 1985	Computers	
37.	Fidelity Select Technology	FSPTX	Jul. 1981	Technology	
38.	Fidelity Select Telecommunications	FSTCX	Jul. 1985	Telecommunications	
39.	Fidelity Select Transportation	FSRFX	Sep. 1996	Transportation	
40.	Fidelity Select Utilities Growth	FSUTX	Dec. 1981	Utilities	
41.	Fidelity Select Wireless	FWRLX	Sep. 2000	No assignment	Sector is too new

Table 5.3 Sectors and Sector Funds Used in Analysis

	Sector Name	Ticker Symbols
1.	Airlines	FSAIX
2.	Banking	FSRBX, FSLBX, FSVLX, FRBCX, RYKIX
3	Basic Materials	FSCHX, ICBMX, FSDPX, RYBIX, BMPIX
4.	Biotechnology	FBIOX, FBDIX, DRBNX, RYOIX, ORHBX
5	Communications	FSDCX, TCFQX, FBMPX, FTICX, FCTYX
6.	Computers	FDCPX, FSCSX
7.	Consumer	ICCCX, RYCAX, FSCPX
8.	Defense	FSDAX
9.	Electronics	FSELX, RYSIX, FELCX, SMPIX
10.	Energy	VGENX, FSTEX, FSENX, FSNGX, UMESX
11.	Energy Services	FSESX, RYVIX
12.	Financial Services	FSPCX, FSFSX, FIDSX, PRISX, PBTAX
13.	Food	FDFAX
14.	Gold	VGPMX, FSAGX, INIVX, SCGDX, USAGX
15.	Health Care	VGHCX, FSPHX, FHLSX, SCHLX, FSMEX
16.	Industrials	ICTRX, FSCGX
17.	Leisure	FLISX, FDLSX, ICLEX, RYLIX
18.	Natural Resources	PNRBX, FRNRX, BGRIX, MBGRX, PRGNX
19.	Real Estate	CSRSX, VGSIX, RRESX, CREEX
20.	Retailing	FSRPX, RYRIX
21.	Technology	TVFQX, PRSCX, FSPTX, JAGTX, FTCHX
22.	Telecommunication	ISWCX, PRMTX, FSTCX, FWRLX, ATINX
23.	Transport	FSRFX, FSAVX, RYPIX
24.	Utilities	VGSUX, IUTBX, EVTMX, MMUCX, FSUTX

Step 6: A very simple trading strategy is implemented. Usually, the simplest strategies are the most effective and longest-lasting. The strategy is to choose sectors whose return exceeds the mean return for all industries. Invest in these sectors over the next period. The results are reported in Table 5.4.

Two different holding periods, one-week and five-week, are considered for the rest of the chapter. The choice of these holding periods is primarily for convenience. Longer holding periods are not considered for two reasons. First, the study discussed in "Fidelity Sector Mutual Funds," earlier in this chapter, is already based on longer holding periods, and there is no reason to duplicate those results. Second, results with longer holding periods do not generate enough observations, making statistical testing ineffective. Eventually, the recommendation is to use a five-week holding period only. However, for the time being, both one-week and five-week holding periods are considered.

For each of the two holding periods, three different estimation periods are used, ranging from one week to twenty-five weeks. An

Table 5.4 Returns to Industry-Momentum-Based Trading Strategies (1997–2001)

Estimation Period	Holding Period	Mean Return to Sectors Held (%)	Annualized Return to Sectors Held (%)	Success Ratio (%)	Mean Return to Sectors Not Held (%)	Number of Observations
Panel A: Sectors with above-average return held for 5 weeks						
5 weeks	5 weeks	1.9*	21.6 (23.2)	61	0.7	51
15 weeks	5 weeks	2.2**	25.4 (24.8)	67	0.6	49
25 weeks	5 weeks	2.4**	28.0 (26.4)	66	0.1	47
Panel B: Sectors with above-average return held for 1 week						
1 week	1 week	0.37**	21.2 (19.5)	60	0.14	259
3 weeks	1 week	0.39**	22.4 (19.5)	59	0.07	257
5 weeks	1 week	0.41**	23.7 (18.7)	58	0.06	255
Panel C: Sectors with above- average and positive return held for 5 weeks						
5 weeks	5 weeks	1.9*	21.6 (23.5)	57	0.7	49
15 weeks	5 weeks	2.2**	25.4 (24.8)	63	0.6	49
25 weeks	5 weeks	2.2*	25.4 (25.5)	66	0.1	47
Panel D: Sectors with above-average and positive return held for 1 week						
1 week	1 week	0.35*	19.9 (21.6)	59	0.14	250
3 weeks	1 week	0.39**	22.4 (19.5)	57	0.07	249
5 weeks	1 week	0.42**	24.4 (18.7)	56	0.06	248
S&P 500 annualized return			13.0 (18.2)			

The number of observations corresponds to the periods for which funds are held. When estimation period returns must be positive, as in panels C and D, no positions are taken in a few cases. In those instances, the number of observations is smaller. Standard deviation is in parentheses for the annualized return. ** implies significance at the 5 percent level, and * implies significance at the 10 percent level.

estimation period is the prior period over which actual returns are measured to categorize the sectors as underperforming or overperforming sector. The holding period is the subsequent period during which the trading strategy is implemented by investing in only the overperforming sectors.

Results for a holding period of five weeks are reported in panels A and C of Table 5.4. The estimation periods for portfolio formation are five weeks, fifteen weeks, and twenty-five weeks. Funds in industries that exceed the mean return during the estimation period are held for a subsequent five-week period. The return for the five-week holding period with a five-week estimation period is 1.9 percent, or 21.6 percent annualized, significantly greater than zero in a statistical and economic sense. The return is positive 61 percent of the time. At the same time, funds in industries that earned below the mean return in the preceding period earned only 0.7 percent, in the holding period, which is statistically not different from zero. During the same 1997–2001 period, the S&P 500's return was a statistically insignificant 1.2 percent.

Table 5.4 shows that returns and success ratios are generally higher for very long estimation periods. This means that the past twenty-five weeks' return is a better predictor of the next period's return than the past five weeks' return. In addition, the return to sectors *not* held decreases as the estimation period increases, implying the superiority of the longer estimation period. On the other hand, the results are not very different across different holding and estimation periods.

In panel B, returns are reported for a one-week holding period based on one-week, three-week, and five-week estimation periods. The one-week holding period returns are almost as good as the five-week holding period annualized returns. There is no improvement in the success ratio as the estimation period is increased, though there is an improvement in return. In panels C and D, a slightly different selection process is used for choosing the sectors to be held. Instead of holding all sectors with a return above the mean in the estimation period, an additional condition is imposed: the return of the sector must be positive. However, the results reveal that neither the return nor the success ratios are higher with this additional condition than the results in panels A and B without the added screen. Accordingly, all future analysis is presented based on the simple strategy of holding sectors above the mean return.

Until now, the risk level of the positions was ignored. However, it is important to take risk into account because industry-momentum-based trading strategies are clearly riskier than holding a broader market portfolio. The Sharpe ratio is used to compare the risk-adjusted returns.[3] Sharpe ratios are reported below based on annual returns for the best-case scenarios, an average return of 4 percent for short-term Treasury bills during 1997–2001, and standard deviations (reported in parentheses) in Table 5.4.

25-week estimation period and 5-week holding period	0.91
5-week estimation period and 5-week holding period	0.76
5-week estimation period and 1-week holding period	1.05
S&P 500 holding return	0.49

Since higher Sharpe ratios indicate superior investment, the best results are for the one-week holding period, with a ratio of 1.05. The five-week holding period with a twenty-five-week estimation period is only slightly lower at 0.91. Moreover, once short-term redemption fees are considered, it may be desirable to hold the sectors for five weeks rather than just one week. In any case, all three industry-momentum-based trading strategies have a significantly better Sharpe ratio than a buy-and-hold S&P 500 strategy, which has a Sharpe ratio of only 0.49.

The difference in returns between sectors held and sectors not held is reassuring because it suggests that superior performance of sectors held is unlikely to be accidental.

IMPLEMENTATION FOR INDUSTRIES WITH AND WITHOUT FUTURES MARKETS

It is possible to improve returns from an industry-momentum-based trading strategy by relying on the rational explanation that industry momentum probably exists for industries that do not have futures markets (see "Explanations" above). Futures markets, like other financial markets, are aggregators of information. Since commodity futures prices capture information about trends in commodity prices, participants in financial markets can make better-informed decisions in industries dependent on commodities with traded futures markets than in industries without futures markets.

If the futures markets' explanation is indeed true, then industries with futures markets will exhibit much less momentum than industries without futures markets. And selecting only industries without futures markets will sharpen and strengthen the gains due to industry momentum.

Of the industries listed in Table 5.3, commodity futures represent a significant part of the following industries:

- *Gold.* Futures exist for gold, silver, copper, platinum, and palladium.

- *Energy.* Futures exist for crude oil, heating oil, propane gas, and natural gas.

- *Energy services.* This demand is derived from energy prices.

- *Airlines.* Fuel constitutes a large portion of airline costs.

- *Natural resources.* Futures exist for oil, gas, and lumber.

- *Food.* Futures exist for corn, wheat, soybeans, coffee, orange juice, and sugar.

Sectors are divided into two groups: one where futures markets exist (the six industries) and the other where futures markets do not exist (the remaining seventeen industries). Industry-momentum-based strategies are constructed separately for the two groups but in a manner similar to that for Table 5.4.

The results are in Table 5.5. Three points need emphasis. First, in sectors with futures markets, there is no evidence of any industry momentum. Whether well-performing sectors are held or poorly performing sectors are held, the returns for the five-week holding period are in the 0.70–0.85 percent range. There is no perceptible difference between the well-performing and poorly performing subsamples. On the other hand, there is clear and strong evidence of industry momentum in sectors *without* futures markets. Well-performing sectors in the estimation period outperform the other sectors during the holding period. The results for the one-week holding period are similar to those for the five-week holding period. The obvious implication is that industry momentum occurs only for sectors where futures markets do not exist. Finally, the results based on sectors without futures markets are somewhat stronger than the results in Table 5.4. Therefore, it is preferable to concentrate only on sectors without futures markets when constructing trading strategies based on industry momentum. Accordingly, trading strategies in the remainder of this chapter are constructed on the basis of industries that do not have futures markets.

Implementation with Fidelity and Rydex Funds

The results in the previous sections are based on a large number of funds. While the large number is useful in spanning the entire industry and minimizing the risk of any one industry, many funds are inconvenient and costly to trade. For example, if about one-half

Table 5.5. Returns to Industries with and without Futures Markets (1997–2001)

Estimation Period	Holding Period	Sectors without Futures Markets		Sectors with Futures Markets		Number of Observations
		Sectors with above-average return in prior period (%)	Sectors with below-average return in prior period (%)	Sectors with above-average return in prior period (%)	Sectors with below-average return in prior period (%)	
5 weeks	5 weeks	2.32**	0.44	0.80	0.72	51
15 weeks	5 weeks	2.60**	0.42	0.78	0.84	49
25 weeks	5 weeks	2.82**	0.10	0.76	0.71	47
S&P 500 return	5 weeks	1.18	1.18	1.18	1.18	52
1 week	1 week	0.41**	0.18	0.31	0.06	259
3 weeks	1 week	0.49**	0.08	0.21	0.12	257
5 weeks	1 week	0.47**	0.08	0.21	0.14	255
S&P 500 return	1 week	0.23	0.23	0.23	0.23	260

Futures markets exist for the following industries: gold, natural resources, energy, energy services (derived demand from energy), food, and airlines (profitability depends on oil prices). ** implies significance at the 5 percent level. None of the returns in columns 4, 5, and 6 is significantly different from zero.

of the sectors are above the mean return, it implies that one would have to trade forty to fifty funds of five or six different mutual fund companies. While that is practical for large investors, it is not desirable for small investors. Therefore, it is worthwhile to explore whether intrafamily fund transfers are possible while earning reasonable returns.

The two firms with the largest number of sector funds, Fidelity and Rydex, are selected for this experiment. Although Fidelity has forty-one sector funds in twenty-four industries, only thirty-five funds in twenty-four industries that were in existence in January 1997 are considered. Rydex has seventeen funds spanning sixteen industries. Of these, only fifteen Rydex funds covering fifteen industries are chosen, all of which were created in April 1998.

As mentioned above, Fidelity allows costless exchanges through their website provided the sector fund is held for at least thirty days. Fidelity does have an initial sales load of 3 percent, but that load has to be paid just once. Fidelity usually waives the sales load for 401(k) and retirement accounts. Rydex allows exchanges among its various funds with no fees or constraints. Rydex funds are no-load funds, but entry into the Rydex family of funds requires a minimum initial investment of $25,000.[4]

The results of trading Rydex funds and Fidelity funds within each family are reported in Table 5.6. Fidelity sector funds perform at least as well as the universe of funds considered in Table 5.5. The twenty-five-week estimation period and five-week holding period returns are 2.82 percent for the sample of all funds in Table 5.5 but slightly higher at 2.94 percent for Fidelity funds. The one-week holding period returns for Fidelity funds and All funds are almost identical.

The performance of Rydex funds is not as good except for the twenty-five-week estimation period and five-week holding period strategy. However, the difference in returns could be attributed to different observation periods. The five-week S&P 500 return for the April 1998–December 2001 period is 0.54 percent, compared with 1.11 percent for the 1997–2001 period. If the abnormal return for Rydex funds is considered, it can be seen that performance of Rydex funds is comparable to that obtained for Fidelity funds. However, Fidelity funds are preferred because they cover more industries.

IMPLEMENTATION IN REAL TIME

The above strategy is implemented in real time for the January 2002–June 2002 period. The industry-momentum-based trading strategy that is adopted here consists of the following steps:

Table 5.6 Industry Momentum Returns for Rydex and Fidelity Funds

		Fidelity Funds: 1997–2001			Rydex Funds: April 1998–2001		
Estimation Period	Holding Period	Sectors with Above-Average Return in Prior Period (%)	Success Ratio (%)	Number of Observations	Sectors with Above-Average Return in Prior Period (%)	Success Ratio (%)	Number of Observations
5 weeks	5 weeks	2.31**	61	51	1.89	57	33
15 weeks	5 weeks	2.62**	59	49	1.88	58	31
25 weeks	5 weeks	2.94**	68	47	3.09*	66	29
S&P 500 return	5 weeks	1.11	N.A.		0.54	N.A.	
1 week	1 week	0.42**	60	259	0.30	57	171
3 weeks	1 week	0.49**	60	257	0.29	55	169
5 weeks	1 week	0.47**	59	255	0.40	56	167
S&P 500 return	1 week	0.21	N.A.	260	0.15	N.A.	172

Only sectors without futures markets. Rydex funds in existence as of April 1998 and Fidelity funds in existence as of January 1997. ** implies significance at the 5% level, and * implies significance at the 10% level.

- Select funds in each of the seventeen industries that do not have futures markets. If only Rydex or Fidelity sector funds are used, then those funds may not span all of the seventeen industries.

- Estimate the return over the estimation period. Funds that earn an above-average return are held during the holding period. The holding period must be at least thirty days for Fidelity funds.

- Repeat the previous step upon completion of the holding period.

The results are in Table 5.7. The stock market performed poorly during the January-June 2002 period. The trading strategies based on industry momentum convincingly outperformed the S&P 500; though in most cases the raw returns are negative, they are usually much less negative than the S&P 500. Using the sample of All funds generates a return of −1.5 percent for a five-week holding period with a twenty-five-week estimation period, and a return of −3.9 percent for a one-week holding period with a five-week estimation period. These returns are significantly superior to the S&P 500 returns of −8.8 percent and −15.9 percent, respectively. The Fidelity returns are similar to the returns for All funds, and occasionally better. However, the Rydex funds do not perform as well. They have

Table 5.7 Industry Momentum Returns for the January–June 2002 Period

| Estimation Period | Holding Period | Sectors with Above-Average Return in Prior Period | | |
		All Funds (%)	Fidelity Funds (%)	Rydex Funds (%)
There are five 5-week holding periods beginning on December 5, 2001, and ending on May 29, 2002. Total return for those periods is reported below.				
5 weeks	5 weeks	2.2	3.5	−0.1
15 weeks	5 weeks	−3.8	−0.5	−6.1
25 weeks	5 weeks	−1.5	−2.5	−8.1
S&P 500 return	5 weeks	−8.8	−8.8	−8.8
There are twenty-six 1-week holding periods beginning on December 26, 2001, and ending on June 26, 2002. Total return for those periods is reported below.				
1 week	1 week	−16.6	−15.3	−24.6
3 weeks	1 week	−13.5	−10.0	−16.8
5 weeks	1 week	−3.9	−3.9	−7.8
S&P 500 return	1 week	−15.9	−15.9	−15.9

Only sectors without futures markets are evaluated. Rydex funds in existence as of April 1998 and Fidelity funds in existence as of January 1997 are considered.

lower returns than Fidelity and the sample of All funds for all estimation and holding periods. The use of Fidelity funds continues to be the preferred mode of capturing industry momentum.

Overall, one can see that investing in sector funds that have done well in the prior period is a superior strategy compared to holding the broader market. As shown in this section, it is also a simple strategy to implement.

IMPLEMENTATION THROUGH SECTOR FUND NEWSLETTERS

As an alternative to designing the strategy, you can rely on sector fund newsletters. Sector fund switching is particularly popular in the newsletters. The newsletters will suggest when to switch into which industry, or how to "play the sector game." A word of caution is in order, however, as newsletters suffer from severe survivorship biases (see Chapter 1). To show a string of good results, the newsletters routinely abandon old, unprofitable strategies, create new ones based on past data that seem to work for some time, and then discard them once they cease to perform. *Hulbert's Financial Digest* (HFD) provides some guidance by tracking the performance of newsletters and their strategies. It rates the timing newsletters based on the actual return that could have been earned based on the recommendations. However, HFD also suffers from a survivorship bias, though less severe—only newsletters' portfolios that have continued to do well will be retained by the newsletters and, therefore, only the winning portfolios, by luck or design, will get covered by HFD.

The sector newsletters covered by HFD as of June 2002 are listed in "Sector Fund Newsletters" later in this chapter. Each newsletter offers many different portfolios and many different combinations that can often be confusing. Whether you should use a newsletter is a difficult question to answer. On one hand, newsletters use sophisticated technical analysis for making recommendations that may be superior to the simple strategy described herein. Also, it is a lot easier to pay a newsletter to make recommendations than to compute the returns every month. On the other hand, sophisticated technical analysis, which is usually devoid of economic content, may not be much better than data mining. If you decide to choose a newsletter, make sure it has at least a five-year record. Also, try to understand the system to determine whether it is following the strategies outlined and tested here. It is even more important to feel comfortable and trust the newsletter. You want to find one that is honest, discloses limitations of the strategy other than as a disclaimer, and does not constantly keep changing the rules. It is best to try out the newsletter for about six months before actually implementing its sector rotation strategy.

IMPLEMENTATION WITH RYDEX'S SECTOR ROTATION FUND

In addition to the newsletters, there is one sector rotation fund that explicitly tries to buy hot sectors and sell cold sectors. The Rydex Sector Rotation Fund (RYISX) debuted in March 2002. It ranks fifty-nine industries and picks the best-performing ones for investment. The fund is not based on the principles discussed in this chapter. It also invests in individual stocks and short-sells as necessary. Since the fund is new, it is difficult to evaluate its performance. However, so far its performance has not been particularly encouraging.

Qualifications

The evidence and trading strategy recommendations presented in this chapter rely on past data. Since future market conditions and market patterns may be completely different, there is no certainty

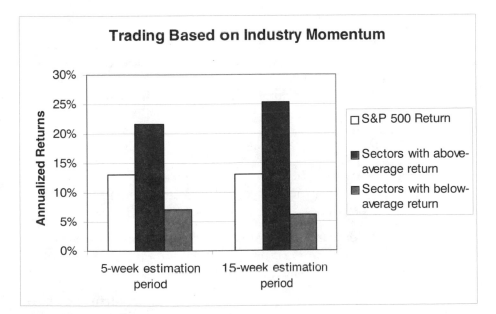

Figure 5.1   The figure shows the S&P 500 buy-and-hold return compared with the returns for above average and below average sectors based on five-week and fifteen-week estimation periods. The data are from 1997–2001 and represent a five-week holding period.

industry momentum will continue in the future or be profitable. Trading strategies based on momentum are particularly risky because only a few industries are held, resulting in inadequate diversification.

Key Points

- Research has discovered that stocks exhibit momentum. Stocks that have done well in one period are more likely to do well in the following period. Momentum among stocks is particularly high for intermediate holding periods ranging from about six to twelve months.

- Momentum among stocks seems to arise from industry momentum. If an industry is doing well, then it tends to continue to do well. Industry momentum occurs at short intervals (periods of one month) and at intermediate intervals of six to twelve months.

- Sector mutual funds can be used to study or benefit from industry momentum. Analysis of Fidelity sector funds reveals that higher returns, albeit with higher risk, can be earned by following an industry-momentum-based trading strategy.

- Irrational investor behavior can explain momentum, as investors often either chase winning stocks or underreact to new information. However, industry momentum may also occur because there is no mechanism to aggregate information about future prices of real goods. In the absence of this information, financial markets rely on companies and analysts who are slow in updating earnings forecasts.

- The evidence presented shows that industry momentum is profitable. The Sharpe ratio of returns for momentum strategies is almost twice as large as that for the S&P 500.

- A test of the explanation related to futures markets reveals that industry momentum is more profitable when only industries without futures markets are traded.

- Among fund families that offer sector funds, Fidelity is superior and as good as holding multiple funds in the same industry. Rydex funds, on the other hand, do not perform as well. Another possibility not considered explicitly in the book is the use of S&P sector exchange-traded funds.

- A trading strategy is employed for the January-June 2002 period. The strategy generates a negative return of –1.5 percent. However, this return is much better than the –8.8 percent earned by the S&P 500 over the same period.

- Numerous advisory services are available for timing industrial sectors, especially with Fidelity funds. According to *Hulbert's Financial Digest*, some of these services have a good record of outperforming the market.

Bottom Line

Momentum within an industry suggests that investors can actually chase winning sectors and profit from them. Fidelity sector funds offer an easy way to switch among different "hot" sectors. Industry funds that outperform the average industry fund over a six-month period are likely to generate annual abnormal returns of more than 10 percent. The Sharpe ratio, which accounts for risk, is much higher for an industry-momentum-based trading strategy than for the S&P 500.

Internet References

Historical Mutual Fund Price Data
http://www.qp2.com: Quotes-Plus has about fifteen thousand mutual funds in its database and provides about ten years of historical price data.
http://www.morningstar.com: For data about specialty funds and other mutual funds.

Fund Families with Sector Funds
http://www.fidelity.com: Go to "Investment Products," then to "Mutual Funds," followed by "Browse Fidelity's no-load mutual funds," and finally to "Sector-Fidelity Select Portfolios."
http://www.rydexfunds.com: The Rydex website.
http://www.invesco.com, http://www.profunds.com, and http://www.iconfunds.com: Other fund families.

Sector Fund Newsletters
http://www.allstarinvestor.com: Offers switching advice on Fidelity single-sector portfolio, Fidelity's multisector portfolio, Rydex funds, and ProFunds. Followed by *Hulbert's Financial Digest* since December 31, 1992. HFD ranks its single-sector portfolio as one of the top-performing portfolios.
http://www.dollarlink.com: Select Timing Service has been in existence for about 10 years. I know because I subscribed to this service a long time ago. Not very expensive but reliable.

http://www.topsectors.com: Mike Lottridge, the editor of this site, has tested his strategy in many different ways. Very impressive record but not followed by HFD and, therefore it cannot be verified. Very inexpensive.

http://www.fidelitytimer.com: Very inexpensive subscription service. This newsletter is not followed by HFD and, therefore its performance is not independently verifiable.

http://www.fidelitymonitor.com: Relatively inexpensive and has performed well. Concentrates on the Fidelity sector portfolio. HFD has followed the Fidelity Select system of this newsletter since December 31, 1986.

http://www.fidelityinvestor.com: Quite expensive but has performed well. Concentrates on the Fidelity sector portfolio. HFD has followed the Fidelity sector investor portfolio of this newsletter since December 31, 1999.

http://www.fund-track.com: This site has several trading strategies. Select the Fidelity Sector fund strategy. Inexpensive but performance has not been verified.

http://www.stockmarketcycles.com: Offers advice on Fidelity select switchers and on Rydex switchers. Reasonable performance with Fidelity. Followed by HFD since December 31, 1984.

http://www.timerdigest.com: Concentrates on the Fidelity select program. Good performer. Followed by HFD since December 31, 1987.

References for Further Reading

Dellva, Wilfred L., Andrea L. DeMaskey, and Colleen A. Smith. 2001. Selectivity and Market Timing Performance of Fidelity Sector Mutual Funds. *Financial Review* 36(1), 39–54.

Grundy, Bruce D., and J. Spencer Martin. 2001. Understanding the Nature of the Risks and the Source of the Rewards to Momentum Investing. *Review of Financial Studies* 14(1): 29–78.

Jegadeesh, Narasimhan, and Sheridan Titman. 1993. Returns to Buying Winners and Selling Losers: Implications for Stock Market Efficiency. *Journal of Finance* 48(1), 65–92.

Moskowitz, Tobias, and Mark Grinblatt. 1999. Do Industries Explain Momentum? *Journal of Finance* 54(4), 1249–90.

O'Neal, Edward S. 2000. Industry Momentum and Sector Mutual Funds. *Financial Analyst Journal* 56(4), 37–49.

Notes

1. Besides the author's own analysis, this chapter is based on O'Neal (2000), Dellva, DeMaskey, and Smith (2001), Moskowitz and Grinblatt (1999), Grundy and Martin (2001), and Jegadeesh and Titman (1993).

2. The Sharpe ratio is based on the assumption that the portfolio under consideration is held alone; hence the total risk of the portfolio, as measured by the standard deviation, becomes relevant. The Treynor ratio, not discussed here, relaxes that assumption. However, the Treynor ratio is more complicated to use, as it needs estimates of systematic risk (beta) and is not commonly used in the industry.

3. See the sub-section "Fidelity Sector Mutual Funds" under "Evidence" in this chapter for a definition of the Sharpe ratio.
4. In addition to Fidelity and Rydex, ProFunds also offers sector funds. However, ProFunds funds are not considered, as they are relatively new.

6

Mispricing of Mutual Funds

The net asset values (NAVs) of mutual funds may be based on prices that are several hours old. That means the NAV may not reflect the most recent market movements. For small-cap funds with many illiquid stocks and international funds where markets close several hours before 4 P.M., the NAVs may be severely mispriced, especially on volatile days when large price movements occur.

Investors can use this information in at least one of two ways. They can construct a trading strategy to earn abnormal returns by buying funds when NAVs undervalue the stocks they hold and selling those funds a few days later. Second, they can protect themselves against other short-term traders by not investing in funds that use stale prices while not taking steps to restrict opportunistic trading.

Description

The net asset value (NAV) of a mutual fund is the 4 P.M. price at which investors can purchase or redeem shares of the fund, usually at no additional cost.[1] The NAV is calculated based on the last traded price of stocks that the fund holds. If the last trade does not take place close to 4 P.M., the NAV may be based on stale prices and could be incorrect. Consider a mutual fund that holds stocks of companies with small market capitalization. Since small stocks do not trade very frequently, assume that the last trade for an average stock in the fund takes place at 2 P.M. Now the mutual fund's NAV calculated for 4 P.M. actually represents 2 P.M. prices. Add to that high volatility and you have a recipe for disaster—or a market timing opportunity. For example, on July 15, 2002, the Dow jumped more than 5 percent and the Russell 2000 more than 3 percent in the last hour of trading, between 3 P.M. and 4 P.M. A small-cap fund's NAV based on stale 2 P.M. prices would undervalue the fund by as much as 3 percent. All that a smart investor had to do was to buy the fund at the 4 P.M. closing price on July 15 and sell it the next day, pocketing an abnormal return of 3 percent.

This example is an extreme one. Most NAVs do not reflect such mispricing. Large-cap domestic funds are rarely mispriced because large-cap stocks trade almost continuously. Even small-cap funds are dominated by the largest of small stocks, which tend to trade often. Moreover, there are not many days when the market jumps 3–5 percent in the last hour. And, finally, if the market is highly volatile, then even the small stocks will trade more often, making the last traded price more current.

On the other hand, the situation can get much worse under two scenarios. The first is for funds that invest in foreign markets, and the second is for funds with illiquid assets. Foreign markets close several hours before the U.S. market closes. East Asian markets, including Japan, close by 1 A.M. Eastern time. The European markets close between 10 A.M. Eastern time and noon Eastern time. Thus, the East Asian prices are about fifteen hours stale, while the European prices are four to six hours stale. Compounding the stale stock prices for international funds is the staleness in exchange rates. Funds use a variety of exchange rates: the rate at the time the foreign market closes, the 12 noon rate, the 4 P.M. rate, or the rate at some other time. Thus, the mispricing of international funds can occur more often and be of a larger magnitude.

The second condition under which the NAV can get mispriced occurs for funds with a significant holding of illiquid assets—in particular, private equity or restricted securities. Private equity consists of shares in a non-publicly-traded firm and is usually held by small-cap funds or venture capital funds that invest in companies that are likely to go public. If the company does go public, the investment will generate a handsome return. However, if the brilliant idea doesn't materialize or the initial public offering gets delayed, then the private equity can quickly become worthless. The problem is that, unlike publicly traded securities, private equity is difficult to value. Moreover, the fund manager has an incentive to delay the write-down of private equity to avoid disclosing the magnitude of losses. Thus, the value of private equity may be not just a few hours stale but several months stale. If the broad market is doing well, private equity will be undervalued, but if the market is doing poorly, private equity will be overvalued. For example, the Van Wagoner

Table 6.1 Returns to Trading Strategy Designed to Arbitrage U.S.-Based Mispriced Mutual Funds

Fund Type (assets held by fund)	Observation Period	Number of Funds	Correlation with S&P	Correlation with Nikkei (1 A.M.–4 P.M.)
1. European	06/1990 to12/1996	1 (VEURX)	0.22	—
2. European	01/1990 to 07/1998	58	0.36	—
3. European	01/1998 to 10/2001	—	0.43 (11:30–4:00)	—
4. European	01/1997 to 11/2000	12	0.38	—
5. European	01/1997 to 11/2000	12	0.38	—
6. Japan	01/1990 to 07/1998	17	0.25	—
7. Japan	01/2000 to 10/2001	—	—	0.54
8. Japan	01/1997 to 11/2000	5	0.30	0.60
9. Japan	01/1997 to 11/2000	5	0.30	0.60
10. Pacific	06/1990 to 12/1996	1 (VPACX)	0.36	—
11. Pacific Asia	01/1990 to 07/1998	34	0.40	—
12. Pacific except Japan	01/1998 to 10/2001	—	0.24 (11:30–4:00)	0.40
13. Pacific except Japan	01/1990 to 07/1998	65	0.37	—
14. Emerging markets	05/1994 to 12/1996	1 (VEIEX)	0.11	—
15. Emerging markets	01/1990 to 07/1998	10	0.33	—
16. Foreign	02/1998 to 03/2000	139	—	—
17. Domestic funds	02/1998 to 03/2000	451	—	—
18. Domestic small-cap, high beta	02/1998 to 03/2000	21	—	—
19. Small growth	01/1998 to 10/2001	—	—	—

Information in this table is based on published work listed under "References for Further Reading."

[a] *Trading rule 1*: Buy the international fund at the close of trading when the S&P 500's return exceeds its mean by more than 1.5 times the standard deviation, measured over the last forty trading days. The fund is sold at the close on the next day, and the proceeds are kept as cash.

Trading rule 2: Buy the international fund whenever the S&P 500's daily return is positive. Sell the fund when the S&P 500 return is negative, and put the money in cash.

Trading rule 3: Buy the mutual fund whenever the S&P 500's return during the last two-hour period (1:55 P.M. to 3:55 P.M.) exceeds 0.94%. Sell the fund when the S&P 500 return is negative during the two-hour window, and put the money in cash. The number of buys is restricted to six in this strategy, to correspond with the trading restrictions imposed. The abnormal return is based on short-selling S&P 500 futures contracts simultaneously with mutual fund purchases.

Trading Rule[a]	Trades Per Year	Annual Return (%)	Abnormal Annual Return (%)	Percent Positive (%)	Time Invested (%)
Mean + 1.5σ [rule 1]	18	8.9	5.3	76	7.2
S&P 500 > 0 [rule 2]		28.0	16.3	—	—
Predicted return > 0 [rule 4]	66	—	37.0	—	—
Predicted return > 0.5% [rule 6]	18	21.7	10.8	77	13.9
Predicted return > 1.0% [rule 6]	3	8.8	–1.9	83	2.0
S&P 500 > 0 [rule 2]		20.5	23.8		
Predicted return > 0 [rule 4]			48.6		
Predicted return > 0.5% [rule 5]	28	41.5	34.2	76	26.8
Predicted return > 1.0% [rule 5]	10	18.7	11.4	87	8.8
Mean + 1.5σ [rule 1]	18	10.1	6.5	69	7.2
S&P 500 > 0 [rule 2]		26.5	27.0		
Predicted return > 0 [rule 4]	59		50.6		
S&P 500 > 0 [rule 2]		27.3	26.3		
Mean + 1.5σ [rule 1]	18	12.4	9.4	88	7.2
S&P 500 > 0 [rule 2]		22.8	19.8		
S&P 500 > 0.94% [rule 3]	6		10.4		
S&P 500 > 0.94% [rule 3]	6	8.4	1.20		
S&P 500 > 0.94% [rule 3]	6	21.3	5.3		
Predicted return > 0 [rule 4]	63		26.4		

Trading rule 4: Buy the fund when the expected return is positive. Expected return = Corr × Change in the relevant market return. Sell the fund when the expected relevant market return is negative, and put the money in cash. For European funds, the relevant market is the S&P 500 from 11:30 A.M. to 4:00 P.M.; for domestic funds, it is that day's S&P 500 return; and for Japanese and other Pacific Asia funds, it is the Nikkei index return from 1 A.M. to 4 P.M.

Trading rule 5: Buy the Japanese fund whenever the expected return exceeds 0.5 or 1 percent. Expected return = Corr × [Change in Nikkei between 1 A.M. and 4 P.M]. Sell the fund when the expected return is negative, and put the money in cash. The correlation is estimated over the past year.

Trading rule 6: Buy the European fund whenever the expected return exceeds 0.5 or 1 percent. Expected return = [Corr$_1$ × Change in S&P 500 from open to noon] + [Corr$_2$ × Change in S&P 500 from noon to close]. Sell the fund when the expected return is negative, and put the money in cash. The correlations are estimated over the past year.

Emerging Growth Fund (VWEGX) was the target of lawsuits and an SEC investigation for not revaluing private equity when the stock market dropped in 2000 and 2001. While there are no reliable statistics or studies that document mispricing in such funds, investors are cautioned against holding funds that invest more than 5 percent in private equity or other restricted securities.

Evidence

Not surprisingly, past empirical evidence has uncovered numerous instances of mispriced NAVs due to reliance on stale prices. In general, the discovery of mispriced net asset values consists of two steps. First, identify mutual funds whose next day's fund return is highly correlated with the previous day's broad market return. A high correlation means that if the market return is positive today, then the fund's return is likely to be positive tomorrow. Second, buy the mutual fund when the market return is large and positive, and sell the fund when the market return becomes negative. If this trading strategy generates a significant abnormal return, then a mispricing exists.

Results of past empirical evidence are summarized in Table 6.1 for U.S.-based mutual funds. The classification of fund types is as defined by Morningstar. The correlation of the fund return with the market return is measured by regressing the fund return on the prior day's market return.[2] Market return for the correlations depends on the fund type. In the case of European funds, the S&P 500 return is used as the market return. However, some researchers consider only the additional U.S. return after the close of European markets. For Japanese and Pacific funds, the Nikkei return from 1 A.M. to 4 P.M. is most appropriate. The Nikkei return can be estimated using Nikkei futures, traded on the Chicago Mercantile Exchange. The next column specifies the trading rule for execution of the trading strategy. Abbreviated trading rules are given in the table.

The annual return and the abnormal return in the table are not annualized returns; rather, these returns are earned during the time that the mispriced fund is held. If the fund is held for less than a full year, then the corresponding risk is also less. For example, in row 5, a return of 8.8 percent is earned by investing for only five days in a whole year or by investing for only 2 percent of the time. The abnormal return for this trading strategy is –1.9 percent because the one-year buy-and-hold return for someone who is fully invested is 10.7 percent. Obviously, an investor invested for only 5 days has much lower risk than one who invests for 250 days in a year. Thus, in many cases the abnormal return is misleading because it does not account for risk or the holding period. It is important to note that *all* of these trading strategies have less risk than being fully invested, because an investor employing these strategies will be holding cash for a significant period of time.

Table 6.1 reveals a high level of correlation between the S&P 500 or the Nikkei index and the *next day's* net asset values of funds. Correlations of 0.3 or 0.4 between same-day returns are not considered large. But a correlation between the current return and the previous day's return of 0.3 to 0.6 is extremely high and seemingly profitable. The following table, based on data from January 1990 to July 1998, illustrates the importance of the high lagged correlations:

	Average daily return if previous day's S&P 500 return is *positive* (%)	Average daily return if previous day's S&P 500 is *negative* (%)
Emerging market funds	0.17	−0.17
Pacific Asia funds	0.20	−0.23
Europe funds	0.21	−0.14
Japan funds	0.15	−0.21

The table shows that positive S&P 500 days are followed by positive return days for the international funds. Isn't it amazing that today's S&P 500 return can tell us so much about tomorrow's measured return for international funds? Even Japanese funds that declined during this period would have earned high positive returns by selective investing. As you will see, this pattern is borne out by the profitability of trading strategies.

Returning to Table 6.1, we can see that the annual return varies from 8.4 percent to 41.5 percent, while the abnormal return ranges from −1.9 percent to 50.6 percent.[3] The reason for the negative abnormal return, as discussed above, is the extremely short holding period of 5 days, or 2 percent of the entire year. In the case of the Japanese funds in row 8, an annual return of 41.5 percent could have been earned by holding the funds for only 67 days in a whole year. The trading strategies are profitable between 69 percent and 88 percent of the time. This success ratio compares favorably with a normal buy-and-hold strategy that has a maximum of 55 percent days with positive returns. It can also be seen from the table that the results vary considerably across fund types, observation periods, and trading rules.

The trading rules used in Table 6.1 are summarized below:

Trading rule 1: Buy the international fund at the close of trading when the S&P 500's return exceeds its mean by more than 1.5 times the standard deviation, measured over the last forty trading days. The fund is sold at the close on the next day and the proceeds are kept as cash.

Trading rule 2: Buy the international fund whenever the S&P 500's daily return is positive. Sell the fund when the S&P 500 return is negative, and put the money in cash.

Trading rule 3: Buy the mutual fund whenever the S&P 500's return during the last two-hour period (1:55 P.M. to 3:55 P.M.) exceeds 0.94 percent. Sell the fund when the S&P 500 return is negative during the two-hour window, and put the money in cash. The number of buys is restricted to six in this strategy, to correspond with the trading restrictions imposed. The abnormal return is based on short-selling S&P 500 futures contracts simultaneously with mutual fund purchases to reduce risk (also see Appendix C).

Trading rule 4: Buy the fund when the expected return is positive.

Expected return = Corr × Change in the relevant market return.

Sell the fund when the expected relevant market return is negative, and put the money in cash. For European funds, the relevant market is the S&P 500 from 11:30 A.M. to 4:00 P.M.; for domestic funds, it is that day's S&P 500 return; and for Japanese and other Pacific funds, it is the Nikkei index return from 1 A.M. to 4 P.M. Corr is the correlation between the fund return and the relevant market return. The correlations are estimated over the past one year.

Trading rule 5: Buy the Japanese fund whenever the expected return exceeds 0.5 percent or 1 percent.

Expected return = Corr × Change in Nikkei between 1 A.M. and 4 P.M.

Sell the fund when the expected return is negative, and put the money in cash. The correlation is estimated over the past one year.

Trading rule 6: Buy the European fund whenever the expected return exceeds 0.5 percent or 1 percent.

Expected return = [$Corr_1$ × Change in S&P 500 from open to noon] + [$Corr_2$ × Change in S&P 500 from noon to close]

Sell the fund when the expected return is negative, and put the money in cash. $Corr_1$ is the correlation between the fund return and the S&P 500 return from open to noon, while $Corr_2$ is the correlation between the fund return and the S&P 500 return from noon to close. The correlations are estimated over the past one year.

Trading rules that trigger execution of a strategy come in various styles. The simplest trading rule—to buy the fund if the S&P 500 return is positive and sell the fund if the sign is negative (rule 2)—applies to rows 2, 6, 11, 13, and 15. For this trading rule, only the sign of the raw S&P 500 return is considered. This strategy has the highest or second highest return within each fund type. This strategy will also have the highest number of trades and be invested for the longest period of time, which is not desirable. A related trading rule is rule 3, where the threshold return is not zero but 0.94 percent, as for rows 16–18.[4] Besides static trading rules, a dynamic trading rule, in which the mean and standard deviation are calculated every day based on the previous forty trading days (rule 1), applies to rows 1, 10, and 14. A trade is signaled when the S&P 500 return exceeds the mean by 1.5 standard deviations.

Rules 1, 2, and 3 discussed above do not consider the actual correlation between the fund return and the prior period's market return. Instead, they are based on the absolute value of the market return. Since the correlation between the fund and the market contains information regarding the expected movement in the NAV, rules 4, 5, and 6 use the information contained in the correlation by computing a predicted return. For example, the predicted return for the next day used in rule 6 for rows 4 and 5 is calculated as the correlation between the S&P 500 return and the fund return multiplied by the S&P 500 return for day t.

If the predicted return is positive, as for rule 4, or greater than 0.5 percent or 1.0 percent, as for rules 5 and 6, the buy signal is triggered. The period over which the correlation between the market return and the fund return is estimated should ideally be about a year.

Trading rules 5 and 6 allow a comparison of how the threshold return affects the results. Compared to a lower threshold of 0.5 percent, a higher threshold of 1 percent generates fewer trades, a smaller annual return, a higher success ratio, and fewer days for which the fund is held. For example, row 9, with a 1 percent threshold return, generates only ten trades, a return of 18.7 percent, and a success ratio of 87 percent by investing for only 8.8 percent of the time. On the other hand, row 8, with a 0.5 percent threshold, generates twenty-eight trades, a return of 41.5 percent, and a success ratio of 76 percent for a 26.8 percent investment period. Thus, depending on the restrictions placed by the fund, the threshold can be altered to obtain an optimal number of trades that maximizes the return earned without alerting the mutual fund management.

The profitability of trading strategies varies considerably by fund type and depends on the market chosen as relevant. When the S&P

500 return is used to signal buys and sells, Japanese funds outperform European funds in the case of rule 1, but European funds outperform Japanese funds with rule 2. However, if the Nikkei index is relied upon for signaling trades, Japanese and other Pacific Asia funds outperform European funds.

Domestic funds can also be profitable, but the profitability is much less than for foreign funds. Among domestic funds, small-cap and high-risk (beta) funds are the most attractive.

Generally, arbitrageurs can earn an annual return of 10–50 percent by arbitraging mispriced mutual funds. This return comes at significantly lower risk than for a fully invested portfolio, but the return estimates assume negligible trading costs and no restrictions on trading. In particular, the following fund types are likely to be mispriced and are ordered from high to low level of mispricing.

1. Funds heavily invested in Japanese and Pacific markets

2. Funds heavily invested in European markets

3. Funds invested in other foreign markets

4. Funds with a high fraction of private equity

5. Funds with a small median market capitalization

6. Funds that hold high-risk stocks (that is, stocks that move more than the market)

7. Funds with high market-to-book ratio

LIMITATIONS

There are two limitations of this evidence. First, most of the work is based on the data from the 1990s. The last decade was unique because the correlations among different markets were higher than usual. Since the profitability of trading strategies depends on the level of correlation, the returns earned would fall if the actual correlations during the current period are lower.

The second and possibly more important limitation relates to trading costs and restrictions. A few years ago it was possible to execute numerous trades without any restrictions. However, an increasing number of funds are imposing short-term redemption fees and limiting the number of round-trip trades that an investor can make in a year. Nonetheless, hundreds of funds still exist where no redemption fees are charged. Other kinds of trading restrictions, such as monitoring an individual account for the number of trades, are easy to overcome by routing trades through a supermarket, such as Charles Schwab or TD Waterhouse. Loads and redemption fees imposed by funds are more difficult to avoid. However, it is profitable to time the mutual funds even after payment of short-term trading fees, as shown in the section on "Strategy Implementation" later in this chapter.

Persistence

The main reason for mispricing of mutual fund NAVs is that the fund managers do not care or do not have acceptable solutions to eliminate mispriced NAVs. The background and the current solutions are discussed to highlight the reasons for persistence.

The mispricing of mutual funds took center stage during the East Asian currency crisis, when stock prices were flip-flopping. On October 27, 1997, the S&P 500 fell nearly 7 percent. The next morning, due to worsening conditions in East Asia and the drop in the S&P 500, the Hong Kong stock market fell 14 percent. However, the U.S. market, instead of falling further, rallied 5 percent on October 28, 1997. Since the U.S. market leads foreign markets, the Hong Kong market was expected to rally, and the futures prices for the Hong Kong stock market showed that the market would indeed rally. Many investors, believing that the Hong Kong market was undervalued or because they wanted to time the mutual funds, bought mutual funds exposed to Hong Kong on October 28, 1997, at their NAVs. The funds included Fidelity China Region Fund (FHKCX, with Hong Kong as the primary investment area), Investec China and Hong Kong Fund (ICHKX), U.S. Global China Region Opportunity (USCOX), and T. Rowe Price New Asia Fund (PRASX). Many investors who bought mutual funds exposed to Hong Kong on that day profited from their positions. ICHKX fell 11 percent on October 28, 1997, and rose 15 percent the next day; USCOX fell 10 percent on October 28, 1997, and rose 9 percent the next day; and PRASX fell 9 percent on October 28, 1997, and rose 9 percent the following day. Since these investors captured the return on October 29, 1997, they earned 9 percent to 15 percent in one day.

However, changes in Fidelity's Hong Kong fund were much smaller, with a fall of 5 percent on October 28, 1997, and a rise of only 2 percent the following day. Why did Fidelity's Hong Kong fund show much lower volatility? Because Fidelity relied on fair value pricing, whereas the other fund families did not. With fair value pricing, Fidelity used stock futures prices to value the Hong

Kong fund, reducing the staleness in its NAV. On the negative side, Fidelity could not report the NAV to Nasdaq until two days later because of intricate calculations required in the computation of fairly valued NAV. Moreover, and for all practical purposes, Fidelity did not allow trades on either October 28 or October 29, 1997.

The above incident illustrates that fund companies have been aware of mispriced net asset values for a long time. At the same time, it highlights the pros and cons of fair value pricing. There are many solutions to mispricing, as described below, in addition to fair value pricing. Though these solutions reduce the benefits from arbitraging any mispricing, they are either difficult to implement or do not completely eliminate opportunities for arbitrage.

POSSIBLE SOLUTIONS TO MISPRICING

Short-Term Redemption Fees

About 60 percent of international funds have adopted short-term redemption fees. With redemption fees, an investor is required to pay a fee ranging from 0.50 percent to 2.0 percent to the fund if the investment is liquidated in less than thirty or ninety days. While redemption fees can reduce the profitability and frequency of arbitrage trades, they have other shortcomings. First, investors don't like them because it takes away their ability to use mutual funds for parking money. Instead of bank accounts, many customers use brokerage accounts and write checks against the funds they hold. If investors are unable to redeem funds at will, it reduces the attractiveness of mutual funds as an investment vehicle. Second, many arbitrage trades are profitable even after allowing for redemption fees. Alternatively, arbitrageurs can wait out the redemption fee and still earn the abnormal returns, albeit at a higher risk. For example, the arbitrageur can hold the fund for thirty days if the short-term fee applies for holding periods less than thirty days. As Table 6.1 shows, many strategies require as few as six trades per year to earn an abnormal return of more than 10 percent per year.

Restrictions on Trading Frequency

A majority of funds either explicitly limit the number of trades per year or warn investors against frequent trading. As in the case of redemption fees, such restrictions reduce the attractiveness of funds to ordinary investors. However, it is easy to hide behind mutual fund supermarkets, such as Charles Schwab, TD Waterhouse,

Scottrade, and Brown and Co. Mutual fund supermarkets are usually permitted to indicate to the fund family a single consolidated trade for all of their accounts at the end of each trading day. As a result, the responsibility for monitoring the frequency of trades is delegated to the fund supermarket. However, supermarkets fail to perform this function effectively as long as the net trade amounts are not unusually large. In addition, it is very easy to shift money from one fund family to another without running afoul of trading restrictions imposed by the fund families.

Front-End Loads and Back-End Loads

Some people believe that load funds do not allow timing of mutual funds. This is true for arbitrageurs trying to time funds of different fund families. However, it is easy to time funds within a fund family because many of them allow unrestricted trading among their own family's funds once the investor puts his or her money in the fund family. Since almost all mutual fund families have an S&P 500 index fund as well as several foreign funds, it is easy for an investor to use the trading strategies outlined earlier. In addition, fund families do not usually impose loads on monies held in retirement accounts. Individual investors can use retirement accounts to time funds with stale NAVs.

Besides the inability to discourage timing, imposition of loads discourages investors from investing in the fund family because load funds do not generate superior performance when compared with no-load funds. Although opportunities for timing are reduced, loads are not normally favored by fund families as a way of limiting trading frequency.

Restricting the Trading Time

Another solution is not to allow trading in foreign funds while the U.S. market is open. For example, the last order for a foreign fund can be restricted to 9:30 A.M. Such time restrictions can reduce the opportunity for arbitrage, but they suffer from at least three limitations. Investors may not want to be constrained by the trading time. Second, the futures prices provide a reasonable approximation of the likely movement in stock prices. For example, the Nikkei futures contract before 9:30 A.M. can still capture anticipated movements in Japanese and other Pacific funds. Finally, stale prices also occur within a market, as shown in the last three rows of Table 6.1. Therefore, time restrictions may not be very effective in preventing arbitrage of mispriced mutual funds.

Fair Value Pricing

All of the solutions listed above try to prevent arbitrageurs from timing purchases and sales but do not really tackle the underlying problem of mispricing. Fair value pricing attempts to fairly value mutual funds. Instead of using stale prices, fund companies would update the stale prices with market movements to obtain a fair net asset value. The fair value pricing could be done for each individual security or for the fund as a whole. The idea is to make the correlation between the fund's return and the previous day's market return as close to zero as possible. If the correlation is zero, arbitrageurs cannot predict movements in fund net asset values, thereby eliminating any profit opportunities.

While the intuition behind fair value pricing is simple, implementation is another matter. The relevant market for a stock or a fund is not obvious. Some stock prices or fund NAVs may depend on multiple markets rather than just the S&P 500. And the correlation between a fund and a particular market may not be constant but may change continuously. Even when the relevant market is known and stable, there may be no way of accurately measuring the market's return. For example, small-cap stocks are correlated more closely with the Russell 2000 than with the S&P 500. But Russell 2000 exchange-traded funds and futures contracts themselves have stale prices because of low trading volume. In addition, imagine the computational complexity required at the end of each day. A delay of two days for pricing, as in the case of Fidelity in 1997, is generally unacceptable.

If fair value pricing is so complex, perhaps funds could use it only on days when there is extreme market movement. Some fund companies do selectively apply fair value pricing; selective application is good for publicity but does little else. Big price moves that warrant fair value pricing occur once or twice a year at best and account for less than 10 percent of the total arbitrage profit that can be earned. The remaining 90 percent can still be captured by the arbitrageurs by making numerous though relatively low-profit trades.

The Trading Process

How do you profitably trade mispriced mutual funds? The first step consists of identifying mispriced funds. This is followed by execution of an appropriate trading strategy. The process of discovering and trading mispriced funds described here is based only on a single index, the S&P 500. To extend the process to use other indexes or even multiple indexes, change the regressions in steps 5 and 7.

Step 1: Pick mutual funds that you are interested in. The size of the initial set of mutual funds will depend on computational and data resources. If resources permit, start with as large a data set as possible. The largest data set consists of more than fifteen thousand mutual funds.

Step 2: Exclude funds with less than $10 million in assets because their returns are likely to be very volatile. Also, exclude funds that are less than two years old because you will need at least two years of data to estimate the regressions. Keep only equity funds as the results documented above relate to equity funds alone. If it is not possible to screen out funds based on these criteria, keep the entire initial set and eliminate them from the short list that you would create in step 8.

Step 3: Obtain daily historical S&P 500 returns, including distributions such as cash and stock dividends. The S&P 500 index levels only give the returns excluding distributions. The daily returns including distributions can be obtained from Standard and Poor's. Unfortunately, the data are not available on their website, and they charge exorbitant fees for even small bits of data. A close approximation to the total S&P 500 return can be obtained by using the prices of the Vanguard 500 Index Fund (VFINX), adjusted for distributions that are available on Vanguard's website.

Step 4: Obtain historical daily fund prices adjusted for distributions for the funds you keep after step 2. It is especially important here to make sure that adjustments for distributions have been made. Most websites, including Yahoo!, do not accurately account for distributions such as cash dividends and capital gains distributions (see "Internet Resources" for data sources). Compute returns from daily fund prices.

Step 5: Run a regression of each fund's daily return on the previous day's S&P 500 return using the previous year's data. The previous year need not be a calendar year—only twelve consecutive months are needed. If you have only a few funds (ten to fifteen), the regression can be run in Microsoft Excel under Data Analysis.[5] If you have hundreds of funds that you are researching, a more powerful software package is required.[6] In the regression, only the previous day's S&P 500 return has been specified. However, that is not ideal. International funds are likely to be influenced by other indexes such as the Nikkei and will be more affected by the afternoon S&P returns than the whole day return. Small-cap domestic funds are affected by movements in the Russell 2000. These refinements are desirable but have not been included here in order to keep the implementation relatively simple and more accessible.

Step 6: Select funds with a coefficient (also called correlation in earlier sections of this chapter) of at least 0.30 on the previous day's S&P 500 return. Coefficients with higher values are preferred. In addition, make sure that the explained sum of squares (R-squared) is at least 10 percent.

Step 7: For the selected funds, redo the analysis in step 5 based on data for the year two years prior to the current year. This allows you to verify that the high correlation is persistent and not for just one year. Drop the funds that do not exhibit a coefficient of at least 0.30 and an R-squared of at least 10 percent.

Step 8: Take the short list of funds from the previous step and research their loads, redemption fees, and trading restrictions, if any. Keep only those funds that can be traded easily, preferably without any fees. If you end up with many funds, choose the ones with more assets (at least $10 million) and with higher coefficients. The number of funds will depend on trading fees, your investment amount, and the amount of risk you are willing to accept. If you choose only one fund, the strategy will be riskier than for a portfolio of five to ten funds.

Step 9: Set up a trading strategy that uses each fund's parameter estimate or coefficient. Say that the coefficient is 0.40. Then the predicted return for the next day for that fund = 0.40 × current S&P 500 return.

Step 10: Initially, begin with a trading strategy that buys if the predicted return is at least 1 percent. Sell when the predicted return is less than –0.10 percent. Based on the past year, calculate the number of trades that would be triggered by the strategy. If the fund will allow more trades, then lower the minimum predicted return from 1 percent to 0.75 percent. If there are too many trades, increase the minimum predicted return. Don't become very exact in choosing the threshold because return characteristics for the holding period are bound to be different.

Step 11: Do a dry run for about a month with the selected funds to become comfortable with the fund and to gain confidence in your strategy. If you like the results, go live!

Strategy Implementation

The above investment strategy is implemented in this section. The initial sample consists of 14,445 mutual funds, including equity, bond, and hybrid funds. Any nonequity funds will be automatically eliminated because their correlation with the S&P 500 is likely to be less than 0.30. If they still remain, they will be removed when the characteristics of each short listed fund are verified.

DISCOVERY OF MISPRICED FUNDS

Each fund's return for 2001 is regressed on the previous day's S&P 500 return. Funds that have a parameter estimate or coefficient on the lagged S&P 500 return of greater than 0.30 are selected. Out of an initial set of 14,445 funds, 607 have a parameter estimate greater than 0.30. The regressions and the screening are repeated with data from 2000. In this way, it can be ensured that the relationship that is observed in 2001 also existed in 2000. Again, the parameter estimate must be greater than 0.30. The number of funds that survive falls to 379. Besides elimination due to an unstable coefficient, some funds are lost because they did not exist in 2000.

Data relating to fund characteristics such as assets under management, category, and so on for the 379 funds is obtained from Morningstar's Principia Pro for December 2001 or from Standard and Poor's. Once these data are collected, two other conditions are imposed. First, the assets under management must exceed $10 million. With this screen, the number of funds falls to 245. Second, at least 10 percent of the return must be explained by the previous day's S&P 500 return. In other words, the R-squared from a regression must be at least 10 percent for both 2000 and 2001. A total of 214 funds satisfy this condition.

The top ten funds in each category, ranked by the average correlation for 2000 and 2001, are tabulated in Table 6.2, without regard to trading restrictions. Table 6.1 shows that trading restrictions reduce but do not eliminate the profitability. The restrictions are explicitly considered later in Tables 6.4 and 6.5. Some fund families have multiple classes for the same fund. Since fund classes vary only in loads and expenses, but really pertain to the same underlying portfolio, only the fund that is least restrictive in terms of trading is selected. Three categories are considered based on Morningstar's definitions: foreign, Europe, and Pacific Asia. The foreign category includes funds that are international in nature and not confined to a particular region.[7]

The thirty funds listed in Table 6.2 show significant mispricing. The regression coefficient varies from 0.34 to 0.69 for European stocks, from 0.32 to 0.57 for foreign stocks, and from 0.37 to 0.57 for Pacific Asia stocks. These coefficients are based on using the lagged S&P 500 return, though it may not necessarily be the relevant market for international funds. As mentioned earlier, using other market indexes or futures such as the Nikkei or Eurotop in the regression might improve the predictability.

Table 6.2 List of Top Ten Short-listed Funds by Category

These funds are ones whose prices are most mispriced. The estimate of mispricing is based on a regression of fund return on the lagged S&P 500 return for the years 2000 and 2001. Ten funds in each category with the largest coefficients and an R-squared of greater than 10% are included.

Ticker	Fund Name	Fund Size	Coeff. 2001	R^2 2001	Coeff. 2000	R^2 2000
European Stock						
PEAGX	Payden European Aggressive Growth	13.6	0.69	0.18	0.62	0.13
FEURX	INVESCO European Investor Class	352.9	0.41	0.12	0.55	0.15
AEDCX	AIM European Development C	32.9	0.34	0.15	0.59	0.18
GTGEX	AIM Euroland Growth A	212.4	0.40	0.11	0.52	0.13
PRBEX	Prudential Europe Growth B	57.0	0.42	0.13	0.43	0.15
UMPNX	Excelsior Pan European	63.4	0.36	0.13	0.46	0.20
LMEUX	Legg Mason Europe C	24.0	0.38	0.11	0.43	0.12
FNORX	Fidelity Nordic	103.8	0.38	0.13	0.43	0.11
LMEFX	Legg Mason Europe A	32.7	0.38	0.11	0.42	0.12
ANECX	Alliance New Europe C	35.0	0.34	0.10	0.42	0.15
Foreign Stock						
HAIGX	Harbor International Growth	405.9	0.57	0.18	0.51	0.14

PJRCX	Prudential Jenn International Growth C	24.1	0.54	0.17	0.53	0.13
CSQBX	Smith Barney International Aggressive Growth B	65.0	0.39	0.13	0.62	0.20
STISX	Strong International Stock	77.5	0.30	0.15	0.65	0.23
FPSSX	Dreyfus Founders Passport F	79.0	0.32	0.15	0.61	0.22
LINCX	Lord Abbett International C	11.4	0.43	0.20	0.50	0.22
SBIEX	Smith Barney International All Cap Growth A	199.1	0.40	0.14	0.52	0.14
UISLX	UM International Small Cap Equity	10.5	0.37	0.16	0.54	0.25
PRITX	T. Rowe Price International Stock	6,370.5	0.32	0.12	0.37	0.21
TWEGX	American Century International Discount	1,016.0	0.36	0.22	0.56	0.20
Pacific						
WPJGX	Credit Suisse Japan Growth Fund	52.5	0.57	0.11	0.81	0.15
ICHKX	Investec China and Hong Kong	77.1	0.51	0.15	0.80	0.30
PCASX	Pacific Cap New Asia Growth Y	19.6	0.51	0.16	0.68	0.29
EMCGX	Eaton Vance Greater China Growth B	42.3	0.45	0.15	0.67	0.27
MSCAX	Van Kampen Asian Equity C	15.5	0.47	0.16	0.64	0.26
MSAEX	Morgan Stanley Asian Equity A	49.0	0.45	0.15	0.63	0.25
SCOPX	Scudder Pacific Opportunity S	76.9	0.40	0.13	0.66	0.26
MDDRX	Merrill Lynch Dragon D	48.0	0.39	0.13	0.59	0.22
PRASX	T. Rowe Price New Asia	527.2	0.38	0.10	0.60	0.26
ASIBX	AIM Asian Growth B	28.1	0.37	0.16	0.60	0.23

Table 6.3 Returns from Trading Mispriced Mutual Funds During January–June 2002

Ticker	Predicted Return >0.5% and 1-Day Holding Period			Predicted Return >0.5% and 2-Day Holding Period		
	6-Month Return (%)	Number of Trades	Success Ratio (%)	6-Month Return (%)	Number of Trades	Success Ratio (%)
Vanguard Fund	1.2	9	33.3	0.1	7	42.9
Panel A: European Funds						
PEAGX	22.7	27	81.5	6.7	21	66.7
PRBEX	12.7	15	73.3	8.2	11	72.7
FEURX	11.8	14	64.3	7.1	11	54.5
GTGEX	14.2	14	92.9	9.8	11	63.6
LMEFX	11.0	14	78.6	7.3	11	54.5
LMEUX	10.8	14	78.6	7.4	11	54.5
FNORX	11.7	14	92.9	8.4	11	63.6
UMPNX	12.8	14	85.7	9.2	11	63.6
AEDCX	9.0	11	90.9	7.1	9	88.9
ANECX	10.0	12	75.0	5.7	10	60.0
Total Europe	12.7	15	81.3	7.7	12	64.3
Panel B: Foreign Funds						
HAIGX	9.1	24	66.7	2.2	19	63.2
PJRCX	13.3	23	69.6	7.4	19	57.9
LINCX	10.0	15	86.7	8.0	11	81.8
SBIEX	11.9	14	85.7	8.7	11	45.5
CSQBX	12.4	14	92.9	7.1	11	54.5
UISLX	10.2	14	78.6	9.7	11	81.8
FPSSX	6.8	9	88.9	7.3	7	71.4
PRITX	8.5	9	66.7	6.1	7	57.1
PINMX	7.8	9	66.7	6.2	7	57.1
STISX	7.4	9	55.6	5.1	7	57.1
TWEGX	11.2	13	84.6	8.5	10	60.0
Total Foreign	10.1	14	77.6	7.1	12	63.0
Panel C: Pacific Asia						
WPJGX	26.3	24	66.7	17.3	19	57.9
ICHKX	14.2	21	52.4	14.0	17	58.8
PCASX	18.2	21	71.4	18.5	17	64.7
MSCAX	12.7	18	72.2	11.0	14	57.1
EMCGX	11.1	17	58.8	8.9	13	46.2
MSAEX	13.2	17	70.6	9.8	13	53.8
MDDRX	12.6	14	71.4	7.8	11	45.5
SCOPX	13.6	14	71.4	10.0	11	45.5
PRASX	5.7	14	50.0	3.0	11	45.5
ASIBX	11.5	13	84.6	7.8	10	60.0
Total Pacific Asia	13.9	17	67.0	10.8	14	53.5
Total All 30 Funds	12.2	15	75.3	8.5	13	60.3

The first row reports the return for the S&P 500 as provided by the Vanguard fund. The remaining information is from trading funds identified in Table 6.2.

| Predicted Return >1.0% and 1-Day Holding Period | | | Predicted Return >1.0% and 2-Day Holding Period | | | | Correlation with S&P 500 |
6-Month Return (%)	Number of Trades	Success Ratio (%)	6-Month Return (%)	Number of Trades	Success Ratio (%)	Fund Return (%)	Lagged Return (%)
−1.4	1	0.0	−3.1	1	0.0	−13.2	0.30
12.5	13	84.6	5.4	10	80.0	−17.1	0.70
−0.3	2	0.0	−1.8	2	0.0	−6.3	0.42
−0.3	2	0.0	−2.6	2	0.0	−16.5	0.41
0.5	2	100.0	−1.5	2	0.0	−10.0	0.41
0.1	2	50.0	−1.5	2	0.0	−10.8	0.39
−0.0	2	50.0	−1.5	2	0.0	−11.1	0.39
0.7	2	100.0	−1.2	2	0.0	0.1	0.38
0.4	2	100.0	−0.6	2	0.0	−2.5	0.37
0.0	0	—	0.0	0	—	5.6	0.35
−0.4	1	0.0	−1.2	1	0.0	−8.1	0.35
1.3	3	53.8	−0.7	3	8.9	−7.7	0.42
6.7	9	77.8	4.7	7	71.4	−7.6	0.57
5.5	7	71.4	3.5	5	60.0	−6.9	0.54
2.5	3	100.0	1.6	3	100.0	−4.7	0.43
0.8	2	100.0	−1.5	2	0.0	−9.6	0.41
0.9	2	100.0	−1.9	2	0.0	−19.7	0.39
0.6	2	50.0	0.4	2	100.0	−0.3	0.38
0.2	1	100.0	0.4	1	100.0	4.1	0.33
0.0	1	0.0	−1.0	1	0.0	−3.7	0.33
−0.2	1	0.0	−0.3	1	0.0	−1.6	0.32
0.0	1	0.0	−0.7	1	0.0	−5.1	0.31
1.0	2	100.0	−0.6	2	0.0	3.9	0.36
1.9	3	69.9	0.5	3	42.1	−5.1	0.41
14.7	9	88.9	12.2	7	71.4	−6.1	0.58
8.2	6	66.7	7.3	5	60.0	−0.6	0.52
7.7	5	60.0	7.2	5	60.0	2.6	0.51
6.9	5	60.0	5.1	5	60.0	4.5	0.48
5.4	4	75.0	4.8	4	50.0	−1.0	0.46
4.9	4	50.0	3.0	4	50.0	7.5	0.46
−0.2	2	50.0	−3.4	2	0.0	1.7	0.40
0.2	2	50.0	−3.0	2	0.0	4.0	0.40
−2.1	2	0.0	−5.5	2	0.0	6.1	0.38
0.4	1	100.0	−1.3	1	0.0	3.3	0.37
4.6	4	60.1	2.6	4	35.1	2.2	0.46
2.6	3	61.3	0.8	3	28.7	−3.5	0.43

RETURNS FROM TRADING MISPRICED FUNDS

Once the grossly mispriced funds are identified using data from 2000 and 2001, actual returns from trading these funds during the *subsequent* six months are estimated and reported in Table 6.3. The following four strategies are employed. In all cases, the predicted return for the next day is calculated as the coefficient for 2001 times the current S&P 500 return. Since orders for mutual funds must be placed by 4 P.M., in reality, the S&P 500 return until 3:55 P.M. only will be considered. It is highly unlikely that the signal will change based on the S&P 500's movement during the last five minutes.

The four strategies are:

- Buy the fund when the predicted return for the next day is at least 0.5 percent, with a holding period of one day—that is, the fund will be sold the next day.

- Buy the fund when the predicted return for the next day is at least 0.5 percent with a holding period of two days. Some fund supermarkets do not allow investors to sell the fund until the day after it is settled. Settlement takes one business day for most mutual funds.

- Buy the fund when the predicted return for the next day is at least 1 percent, with a one-day holding period.

- Buy the fund when the predicted return for the next day is at least 1 percent, with a two-day holding period.

The first trading strategy (0.5 percent and one day) is the most profitable, as it imposes the fewest constraints on trading. The top ten European funds yield a return of 12.7 percent in 6 months compared with a buy-and-hold return of –7.7 percent. This is equivalent to an abnormal return of 20.4 percent for 6 months, or more than 40 percent per year. The success ratio is 81.3 percent. By comparison, a similar strategy employed for the Vanguard 500 Index Fund, as a proxy for the S&P 500, would have generated a return of 1.2 percent. Foreign funds and Pacific Asia funds are similar, with abnormal returns of 15.2 percent and 11.7 percent over six-month periods.

The returns are smaller for the other three strategies, although the success ratio improves for funds with more than three or four trades when the threshold is 1 percent. The two-day holding period returns for the selected categories are 7.7 percent for European funds, 7.1 percent for foreign funds, and 10.8 percent for Pacific Asia funds. In most cases the returns for 2002 correspond closely with the co-

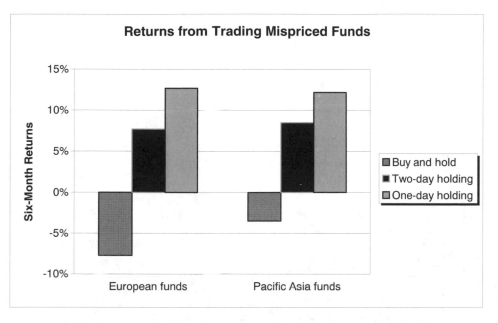

Figure 6.1   The returns from trading mispriced funds are compared with the fund's buy-and-hold return over the January-June 2002 period.

efficients reported in the last column. The close association between the January-June 2002 returns and the 2001 coefficients suggests that the pattern of returns is quite stable between 2001 and 2002 and is indicative of the future profitability of similar trading strategies.

The results in Table 6.3, shown in Figure 6.1, strongly suggest that mispricing of mutual funds can be exploited in real time.

RETURNS FROM MISPRICED FUNDS WITH NO TRADING RESTRICTIONS

Until now, trading restrictions have not been explicitly considered. They can reduce the profitability of strategies that require frequent trading. To account for any trading restrictions, all funds that have any kind of restriction on trading are excluded. Among the remaining funds, five funds are selected that have the highest estimated regression coefficients. The selected funds are in the first row of Table 6.4.

With the least restrictive trading strategy, these funds would have earned an average return of 6.9 percent over the January–June 2002 six-month period with a success ratio of 67.8 percent, compared to an average return of –0.6 percent for a buy-and-hold investor. The two-day return is 4.5 percent with a 0.5 percent threshold and –0.1 percent with a 1.0 percent threshold. The 1.0 percent threshold is probably too high, as it results in an average of only two trades over

Table 6.4 Returns from Trading the Top Five Mutual Funds by Mispricing*

Ticker	HAIGX	PRASX	STISX	FPSSX	NAGUX	Total
Loads	0.0%	0.0%	0.0%	0.0%	0.0%	0.0%
Redemption fees	0.0%	0.0%	0.0%	0.0%	0.0%	0.0%
Fund return	−7.6%	6.1%	−5.1%	4.1%	0.3%	−0.6%
S&P 500 return	−13.2%	−13.2%	−13.2%	−13.2%	−13.2%	−13.2%
1-Day Holding with Predicted Return > 0.5%						
Return	9.1%	5.7%	7.4%	6.8%	5.5%	6.9%
No. of trades	24	14	9	9	9	13
Success ratio	66.7%	50.0%	55.5%	88.9%	77.8%	67.8%
2-Day Holding with Predicted Return > 0.5%						
Return	2.2%	3.0%	5.1%	7.3%	4.8%	4.5%
No. of trades	19	11	7	7	7	10
Success ratio	63.2%	45.5%	57.1%	71.4%	71.4%	61.7%
2-Day Holding with Predicted Return > 0.5%—Hedged						
Return	6.5%	3.3%	3.8%	6.0%	3.7%	4.7%
No. of trades	19	11	7	7	7	10
Success ratio	52.6%	45.5%	57.1%	57.1%	42.9%	51.0%
2-Day Holding with Predicted Return > 1.0%						
Return	4.7%	−5.5%	−0.7%	0.4%	0.4%	−0.1%
No. of trades	7	2	1	1	1	2
Success ratio	71.4%	0.0%	0.0%	100.0%	100.0%	54.2%
2-Day Holding with Predicted Return > 1.0%—Hedged						
Return	3.3%	−4.2%	0.8%	1.8%	2.1%	0.8%
No. of trades	7	2	1	1	1	2
Success ratio	42.9%	0.0%	0.0%	100.0%	100.0%	68.6%

*All numbers are reported for the six-month period, January to June 2002.

a six-month period. However, the results for 0.5 percent and 1.0 percent thresholds are reported throughout this chapter.

The trading strategy is designed to predict the next day's return. However, sometimes investors are forced to hold the fund for two days and thus are exposed to unnecessary market movements on the second day. This risk can be reduced if the investor short-sells S&P 500 futures (or SPDRs) when he buys the fund at 4 P.M. on day 0. He would close the short position in S&P 500 at the close of day 1 and sell the fund at the close on day 2. In this way, any movement in the mispriced fund on day 2 due to S&P 500's return on day 1 is partially neutralized by the short position. The result is a hedged fund return.

The hedged two-day return with 0.5 percent and 1.0 percent thresholds are in Table 6.4 and show that the success ratio of a hedged strategy is not necessarily better. The return to a hedged strategy improves slightly primarily because the S&P 500 was falling during this period. In any case, and despite the mixed results, the hedged return has much less exposure to the market and therefore less risk than the unhedged return. More details about hedging market risk are in Appendix C.

Returns from a Fund with a Redemption Fee

It is possible to gain from mispricing even if you are not allowed to trade the fund for a prespecified period without paying a redemption fee. There are two approaches.

Wait Out the Redemption Fee

The basic idea behind the first approach is to wait out the minimum holding period. You would earn an abnormal return with each trade that you use to enter the fund, and then earn a normal return for the remaining holding period. With a thirty-day holding period, you may be able to execute between eight and eleven trades in a year. With an abnormal return of about 1.5 percent per trade, the annual abnormal return is likely to be approximately 12 to 15 percent.

As an illustration, consider the Payden European Aggressive Growth Fund (PEAGX), which has a coefficient of 0.69. The trading strategy is as follows:

- If the predicted return is greater than 1 percent, buy PEAGX.
- Sell the fund at the end of the holding period if the predicted return for that day is less than –0.1 percent.
- Repeat this process.

Table 6.5   Returns for a Mispriced Fund with Redemption Fee

Fund Name and Details

Payden European Aggressive Growth (PEAGX)

Period: January to June 2002.
Buy-and-hold return = –17.1% for 6 months
Correlation based on 2001 = 0.69
S&P 500 return = –13.2% for 6 months

Assumptions

A redemption fee of 1% applies if the fund is held for less than 30 days

Buy signal when the predicted return > 1.0% for both strategies below.

Strategy 1

Wait out the redemption fee. That is, once the fund is bought, it is not sold for 30 days.

Number of trades = 4
Return based on signals and holding for at least 30 days = –5.8%
Abnormal return = 11.3% for 6 months

Strategy 2

Pay the redemption fee if the predicted return is less than the redemption fee, that is, < –1.0%

Number of trades = 8
Gross return based on signals = –4.3%
Net return after payment of 7% in redemption fees = –11.3%
Abnormal return = 5.8% for six months

The results are reported in Table 6.5 for a thirty-day holding period. There are four signals during January–June 2002 with a 1.0 percent threshold. The total return is –5.8 percent. Compared with a buy-and-hold return of –17.1 percent, an investor would have earned an abnormal return of 11.3 percent over the six-month period, equivalent to an annual abnormal return of 22.6 percent even for a fund that has a thirty-day redemption fee. It is clear that a timing strategy is superior to a buy-and-hold strategy.

Pay the Redemption Fee

The second approach is to actually sell the fund even if you have to pay the redemption fee. However, the redemption fee is paid only when the predicted return is more negative than the redemption fee. Assuming a 1 percent redemption fee, there are eight buy signals for PEAGX over the January–June 2002 period. Seven of the eight buy signals are followed by sell signals that do not meet the thirty-day time limit. Thus, the redemption fee is payable in seven cases. The gross return is –4.3 percent without accounting for the redemption fees. Deducting a redemption fee of 7 percent for the seven premature sales generates a net return of –11.3 percent. Again, compared with the buy-and-hold return of –17.1 percent, an investor will earn an abnormal return of about 5.8 percent in a six-month period, or an 11.6 percent annual abnormal return, by paying the redemption fee each time it is less than the predicted return.

To conclude, it can be observed that mispriced mutual funds are attractive for the smart investor. The redemption fees make the trading less attractive, but the returns from timing are still reasonable and better than a buy-and-hold strategy. The returns can be improved with a refinement in the regression model that includes multiple index returns instead of just the S&P 500, as mentioned in "The Trading Process."

REFINEMENTS

Using futures contracts can reduce the risk of trading. Since the trading strategies are designed to capture mispricing of mutual funds and not market movements, it may be desirable to reduce market risk. If the signal is based on the S&P 500, then at the time the investor buys the fund, he can also short-sell an equivalent number of S&P 500 futures contracts. In this way, the investor is insulated against any market movements related to the S&P 500. However, the risk doesn't fall to zero, as the fund will continue to have idiosyncratic risk and the risk of any international markets that it is exposed to. S&P 500 futures contracts are appropriate for domestic and European funds, but Nikkei futures contracts are better suited to Japanese and Pacific funds. The hedging can also be performed by buying an inverse S&P fund such as Rydex Ursa instead of short-selling S&P 500 futures contracts.

By taking an exactly opposite position in futures, the return of the trading strategies can be improved by remaining fully invested. In this case, the investor would be holding futures contracts when he is not invested in the fund. Thus, when a sell signal occurs, the investor would sell the fund and buy S&P 500 futures contracts. When a buy signal occurs, he would sell the futures contracts and buy the fund. Since futures contracts do not need to be short-sold in this strategy, the investor can flip between the mispriced fund and an S&P 500 index fund, instead of trading futures contracts.

Action Plan for Investors

The evidence and the trading strategies illustrate the widespread mispricing of mutual funds. There are two alternatives open to mutual fund investors: arbitrage and protection. Pursuing both alternatives will reduce the mispricing of mutual funds.

ARBITRAGE THE MISPRICED MUTUAL FUNDS

The selection of mispriced mutual funds and execution of trading strategies leads to abnormal profits. If more and more investors begin to trade mispriced mutual funds, the mutual fund industry will be forced to take these mispricings more seriously and adopt one or more of the solutions highlighted in this chapter. Perhaps someone might even design a more effective model to price mutual funds.

INVESTOR PROTECTION

Whether you take advantage of the mispricings or not, you must not allow others to take advantage of you. International funds, small-cap funds, and many other funds are prone to timing by arbitrageurs. Small investors should certainly not be holding any of the funds listed in the tables here because these funds suffer from mispricing. Investors should also examine the safeguards that their funds have against frequent trading. Although investors may feel constrained by redemption fees and similar features, these are good in the long run because they limit the impact of mispriced NAVs. In addition, investors should urge their fund managers to implement fair value pricing in preference to imposition of redemption fees.

Qualifications

The evidence presented in this chapter and the trading strategy recommendations rely on past data. Since future market conditions and market patterns may be completely different, there is no certainty that mispricing of mutual funds will continue in the future or be profitable.

The trading strategies can easily become nonremunerative if the fund families begin to properly price NAVs or if they impose onerous restrictions on frequent trading. In particular, the funds listed in the tables are likely to attract significantly more attention, and it is very likely that investors will have to discover other funds that misprice NAVs.

Key Points

- Net asset values for mutual funds are set at the end of each day based on the last traded price. If the last trade occurs several minutes or hours before the close of the market, the mutual funds are likely to be mispriced.

- The mispricing problem is most severe for funds holding foreign stocks that stop trading several hours earlier. In addition, many small-cap funds hold stocks that do not trade frequently, and the NAV of these funds will also be based on stale prices. Funds that have significant holdings of private equity, such as venture capital funds, may have NAVs that are based on prices several days or weeks old.

- Evidence points to the profitability of trading strategies. For instance, foreign funds tend to have positive returns on days following a rise in the S&P 500 index.

- The annual return from these trading strategies varies between 8.4 percent and 41.5 percent in spite of holding the foreign fund only a quarter of the time. Moreover, the risk of these trading strategies is less than the risk faced by a buy-and-hold investor. The risk of the trading strategies can be reduced further by short-selling futures contracts.

- Transaction costs and restrictions on trading are a big concern. However, there are many mutual funds that do not have redemption fees or loads. Fund supermarkets such as Schwab can be used to avoid monitoring by mutual fund families.

- There are a few solutions to resolve the timing and mispricing problem, but they are either inefficient or difficult to implement. Mutual funds impose redemption fees or use fair value pricing to limit losses due to mispricing. Clearly, however, more needs to be done.

- It is easy to set up a trading strategy to time the mispriced mutual funds. First, find the mispriced mutual funds by regressing the fund's return on the previous day's market return. Buy the mispriced fund whenever the market rises abnormally, and sell otherwise.

- Investors should time mispriced mutual funds and ensure that their own fund cannot be timed by other people. One hopes the fund managers and the uninformed investors will wake up and adopt solutions to eliminate or reduce mispricing.

Bottom Line

The net asset values of mutual funds are mispriced when stale prices are used for computation. Investors can make abnormal profits by buying mispriced funds on days when the market rises abnormally and selling them on subsequent days.

Internet References

Historical Mutual Fund Price Data

http://www.qp2.com: Quotes-Plus has about fifteen thousand mutual funds in its database. Nearly all of the equity funds reflect distributions in a timely manner for the last four years. You also can see the distributions that have actually been considered in its price series giving you added confidence. Prices more than four years old are less likely to have been adjusted for distributions.

http://www.fasttrack.net: Fasttrack has about three thousand funds in its database, selected on the basis of the funds' popularity. Though the adjustment for distributions is not perfect, it is probably the best in the industry. In addition to prices, it provides extensive technical tools for detecting trends.

http://finance.yahoo.com: Inexpensive and easily accessible. However, this and similar sites have two limitations. First, these sites do not accurately and reliably adjust for all distributions, especially midyear distributions. Second, these sites do not allow users to download data for multiple funds at the same time.

http://www.vanguard.com: Reports distributions for Vanguard funds. Historical price data can be obtained from Yahoo! Distribution information for other fund families can usually be obtained from their websites or by phone.

Current Mutual Fund Data

http://www.morningstar.com: Morningstar is the leader in information about mutual funds. However, you must either have premium access to their site or subscribe to Principia Pro for mutual funds on a CD. Principia Pro is preferred over access to the website.

http://finance.yahoo.com, http://www.smartmoney.com, http://moneycentral.msn.com
http://money.cnn.com: Excellent sites to obtain profiles of mutual funds—category, assets held, and so on.

http://www.funds-sp.com: A competitor of Morningstar, Standard and Poor's also provides fund information.

Data About Index Returns

http://www.spglobal.com: Information about S&P 500. Unfortunately, no historical return information is provided.

http://www.barra.com: Contains monthly returns for S&P 500, including distributions.

http://www.cme.com: Website of the Chicago Mercantile Exchange. The site provides trading data for Nikkei futures and S&P 500 futures.

References for Further Reading

Bhargava, Rahul, and David Dubofsky. 2001. A Note on Fair Value Pricing of Mutual Funds. *Journal of Banking and Finance* 25, 339–54.

Bhargava, Rahul, Ann Bose, and David Dubofsky. 1998. Exploiting International Stock Market Correlations with Open-End International Mutual Funds. *Journal of Business Finance and Accounting* 25(5), 765–73.

Boudoukh, Jacob, Matthew Richardson, Marti Subrahmanyam, and Robert Whitelaw. 2002. Stale Prices and Strategies for Trading Mutual Funds. *Financial Analyst Journal* 58(5): 87–97.

Chalmers, John, Roger Edelen, and Greg Kadlec. 2001. On the Perils of Financial Intermediaries Setting Prices: The Mutual Fund Wild Card Option. *Journal of Finance* 56(6), 2209–36.

Goetzmann, William, Zoran Ivkovic, and K. Geert Rouwenhorst. 2001. Day Trading International Mutual Funds: Evidence and Policy Solutions. *Journal of Financial and Quantitative Analysis* 36(3), 287–309.

Zitzewitz, Eric. 2003. Who Cares About Shareholders? Arbitrage-Proofing Mutual Funds. *Journal of Law, Economics, and Organization*, forthcoming.

Notes

1. This chapter is based on the author's analysis, and research by Bhargava and Dubofsky (2001), Bhargava, Bose, and Dubofsky (1998), Goetzmann, Ivkovic, and Rouwenhorst (2001), Zitzewitz (2003), Chalmers, Edelen, and Kadlec (2001), Boudoukh et al. (2002), and Robert Whitelaw (personal communication). Many no-load funds with no transaction fees are available.

2. Regression is a simple statistical technique available in common software packages such as Microsoft Excel.

3. In row 11, the abnormal return is larger than the annual return in the previous column because the normal return for the thirty-four Pacific Asia funds during that period was negative.

4. The figure 0.94 percent is not arbitrary but corresponds to the top 5 percent of S&P 500 returns during the last two hours of trading.

5. Data Analysis is not part of the default installation of Excel. You must install it separately after the default installation, or perform a custom installation when installing Excel for the first time.

6. Most finance professionals use SAS, available from SAS Inc. However, SAS is expensive unless your organization has a site license. SAS also has a steep learning curve.

7. In addition, there are several domestic funds that have extremely high correlations, almost 1.0. Upon closer inspection, it is discovered that the high correlations occur for "fund of funds," that is, funds that invest in other funds that are otherwise inaccessible to individual investors. Since such funds must wait for the net asset values of the funds that they hold, their own NAVs are reported with a one-day delay. Once the data are corrected for delayed reporting, the high correlations for the domestic funds disappear, and no domestic fund remains with a coefficient greater than 0.30 and R-squared > 10 percent.

7

Trading by Insiders

Trading by insiders potentially conveys new information about the prospects of a company. Insiders have far superior knowledge about the company and the industry than the market. With this knowledge, their predictions of future trends are likely to be more accurate than the predictions based on publicly available information. Therefore, mimicking the trades of insiders generates above-normal annual returns of 10–15 percent.

To mimic insider trades, however, outsiders must first learn about those trades. A change in the SEC reporting requirement makes the information relating to insider trades more current and more readily available. Since September 2002, insiders are required to report large trades to the SEC within two business days. Earlier, insiders could have waited as long as forty calendar days before reporting trades.

Description

LEGAL AND ILLEGAL TRADES

Alleged insider trading by Martha Stewart made big news in 2002.[1] It is believed that she sold her holding of Imclone stock based on a tip from the then CEO of Imclone. The tip came a day prior to public disclosure of the FDA's decision to delay approval of a drug application submitted by Imclone. More than a decade ago, Ivan Boesky (see Chapter 9, on merger arbitrage) was jailed for insider trading and fined $100 million. Since the media focuses on illegal insider trading, many investors mistakenly believe that all insider trading is illegal. In reality, however, insider trading can be either legal or illegal.

Although the term "insider trading" connotes illegal trading to some people, the focus of this chapter is on legal insider trading. For ease of reference, in this chapter "insider trading" will always refer to legal insider trading. Whenever the reference is to illegal trading, "illegal insider trading" will be used. In addition, legal insider trading will also often be referred to as just "trading by insiders."

Illegal insider trading refers to trading by insiders on the basis of material and nonpublic information. Material nonpublic information is any information that is likely to have an impact on the stock price, such as information related to earnings, discovery of an oil field, start of a Securities and Exchange Commission (SEC) investigation, FDA approval or denial (as for Imclone), or a merger announcement. According to SEC regulations, such information must be publicly disseminated, and insiders may not trade on that information before it is made public. Besides officers and directors, for the purpose of insider trading laws other individuals who have a business relationship with the firm are also considered insiders. Trading by outsiders (such as Martha Stewart's trades in Imclone) is also referred to as illegal insider trading when outsiders obtain information from insiders who are aware of the potential impact of that information. Thus, investment bankers (such as Ivan Boesky), publishers of prospectuses, lawyers, and others, are subject to insider trading regulations.

However, insiders (officers or directors of the firm) must be allowed to trade. Insiders get company shares through the exercise of stock options, through corporate awards, and through voluntary purchase of those shares in the market. Consequently, a large fraction of the insiders' wealth can be tied up in the company's stock. Insiders will want to sell their holdings for two reasons. First, whenever large expenses arise, such as the down payment for a home, they may want to sell their company's stock to raise funds. Second, insiders' portfolios are usually poorly diversified because of large holdings in a single stock. Therefore, they may want to sell their company's stock to invest in other assets to diversify their portfolios.

SEC policies and regulations govern when and how insiders may trade. Unlike the broad definition of an insider for illegal insider trading, an insider is narrowly defined for legal trading. An insider is the chairman, CEO, or president (top executive), a senior executive (or an officer), a member of the board of directors (director), an owner of 10 percent or more of the firm's shares (a large shareholder), or a close relative of such persons. The key objective of the SEC regulations is to ensure that insiders do not trade based on material nonpublic information and do not speculate in their own stock. Besides the threat of prosecution for illegal insider trading, insiders are required to disgorge profits from offsetting trades (a buy and a sell) that occur within a six-month period when requested by either the SEC, other stockholders, or the company. Insiders are also prohibited from short-selling their own company's stock.

In addition to federal laws, many companies have internal rules that govern trading by insiders. First, insiders are not allowed to trade within certain blocks of time: usually beginning as many as thirty days before a scheduled or anticipated announcement and until one to two weeks after that announcement. Announcements include earnings, mergers, discoveries, and so on. Second, in many cases, insiders must seek approval of the company's compliance officer prior to trading in the company's stock and sometimes even for any trading in the insider's entire securities portfolio.

Informativeness of Trades

Under SEC regulations, insiders must report all trades to the SEC soon after they occur. Every year there are more than two hundred thousand trades by insiders reported to the SEC. What do these trades mean, and do they contain information that can be gainfully used by investors? The short answer is "yes."

Insiders, especially the top management, have a much better sense of how the company is doing and expected to do in the future than the market. As a matter of fact, the market gets a lot of its information about a company from the company itself. And the company routinely shares that information with the market. For example, the management discusses the company's future prospects at the time of an earnings announcement. Many corporate events also convey information about the management's beliefs about the true value of the company. Dividend increases, stock repurchases, and debt issues are usually interpreted as positive events. Dividend decreases and new stock issues are interpreted as negative events. At other times the management may voluntarily share information with the market. However, any voluntary sharing of positive information is usually discounted by the market unless the company is very selective about making such pronouncements.

It is important to note that insiders' knowledge of the company is usually superior to that of the market. Though insiders cannot trade on the basis of material information, they can trade in the normal course of firm operations. Insiders may have the same detail of information as external participants but interpret that information differently. Their interpretation, due to their expertise and knowledge, is considered to be superior to that of an external analyst. For example, it is common knowledge that the steel industry is fighting for survival. However, does it mean that the industry will die in five years, ten years, twenty years, or never? The opinion of the CEO of a steel company is probably more valuable than the opinion of anyone else. How do the insiders share that information? Their trading conveys that information in a credible way because insiders stand to lose or gain from their trades. Thus, trading by insiders has the potential to convey new information to the market.

EVALUATING INSIDER TRADES

Since there are hundreds of thousands of trades by insiders every year, how does one evaluate so many of them? And do they all contain useful information? In fact, there are many insider purchases and insider sales that contain no information. Sometimes insider buying is involuntary. For example, a new member of management may be required to purchase a hundred thousand shares of the company to align his or her personal incentives with those of the stockholders. Stock options are a popular form of compensation. When an insider exercises a call option (an option to buy stock at a predetermined price), he or she automatically acquires shares of a company. Many insiders will immediately sell the acquired shares so that their assets do not become even more concentrated in one stock. Typically, insiders exercise their options when they need to raise funds. A CEO may exercise his or her stock options, automatically receive one million shares, and sell them immediately in the open market. In addition to using options, insiders may liquidate part of their stock holdings to meet major expenses.

Besides the need to eliminate trades with no information, it is also necessary to distinguish among trades based on the amount of information. Do larger trades have greater predictability? Does company size make a difference? Is there a difference between insider selling and insider buying?

Evaluation of insider trades is not easy. The past performance of newsletters specializing in reading and interpreting trades of insiders has not been spectacular.[2] In fact, two newsletters followed by *Hulbert Financial Digest* underperformed the broader market though they pursued riskier strategies. *Insiders' Portfolio* gained 118.9 percent from January 1985 to June 1992, compared with a gain of 197.6 percent by the broader market, and *Market Logic* earned 339.2 percent from July 1980 to June 1992, compared with a gain of 432.7 percent for the Wilshire 5000. Neither of these letters exist any longer. In addition, *Inside Track, Insider Chronicle,* and *Insider Scores* have discontinued publication. The performance of one current newsletter is slightly better, with a return of 11.2 percent annually compared with 10.5 percent for the broader market. For details, see "Newsletters Based on Trading by Insiders" later in this chapter.

The past existence of many newsletters on insider trading suggests that market watchers consider those trades to be important. However, the performance of market pundits in analyzing trades suggests the need for a more careful analysis of what works and what doesn't, and how to more carefully interpret the data that are revealed by insiders. That is the purpose of the next section, which summarizes evidence related to how insider trading can predict future market returns.

Evidence

SOME BASICS

The evidence presented is based on data obtained from the Securities and Exchange Commission's Ownership Reporting System. However, the data can also be easily obtained from secondary sources (see "Internet References"). Since only open market trades of insiders contain information, private trades and trades with the company are excluded from consideration.

In a moment you will observe that insider selling is almost four times as large as insider buying. The main reason for the difference is that insiders have a large number of shares that are not acquired through open market buying, whereas all of their sales are in the open market. Although sales convey valuable information, it is the purchases by insiders that are more interesting and informative.

It is also important to define a metric for measuring the size of insider buying or selling. There are several ways of aggregating the numerous trades by insiders in a given month for a single company. Trading by insiders could be counted based on the net number of shares traded (buys minus sells), net number of transactions, net number of insiders (buyers minus sellers), and so on. Although the net number of insiders is important, the most effective way is to use the net number of shares traded. Accordingly, the results presented in the next two subsections are based on the net number of shares traded as the measure of insider trading.

BROAD EVIDENCE

The following evidence is based on an analysis of insider trades by major studies over a twenty-year period (1975–94) and a twenty-one-year period (1975–95). First, the results show that if insiders buy in one month, there is a 38 percent chance that they will buy in the following month and only an 11 percent chance that they will sell. A similar pattern exists for insider sales. This implies that insiders do not make all of their trades right away but do it slowly over a period of several months. One reason for splitting trades may be to minimize the price impact of trades by not alerting the media or other investors to their beliefs about the company. This is a common practice among large traders whenever trades are based on information: large orders are split into small orders spread over many trading days. The implication of this type of serial buying or serial selling is that the opportunities to trade do not disappear immediately, and so outsiders may be able to pattern their own trades using information from insider trades.

Second, a firm is likely to perform better following an insider buying month than an insider selling month. The difference in returns over the subsequent twelve-month period varies from 4.8 percent to 18.7 percent, as shown in Table 7.1.

Overall, it can be seen that stocks of firms where insiders have been actively buying outperform stocks where insiders have been actively selling. If one month's insider trades are used to signal a buy or a sell, stocks with net buys earn 24.0 percent, whereas stocks with net sells earn 15.1 percent in the subsequent twelve-month period. The performance improves if a three-month period for estimation is

Table 7.1.   Returns Following Insider Activity (in percent)

	Estimation period[a]		Estimation period[b]		Estimation period[c]
	12-month return	12-month return adjusted for market	12-month return	12-month return adjusted for market	12-month return
Transactions					
Buys	24.0	4.5	29.6	7.5	30.5
Sells	15.1	−2.7	10.9	−6.1	9.5

[a]Estimation period = 1 month.
[b]Estimation period = 3 consecutive months with the same signal.
[c]Estimation period = 12 consecutive months with the same signal.

chosen with the additional condition that each of the three months must be of the same sign (all three net buys or all three net sells). Adjusted for the market, measured as the equally weighted return on all stocks, a strategy of buying stocks with a history of three-month net buys by insiders earns a return of 7.5 percent more than the market, whereas a strategy of buying stocks with a history of sells would earn 6.1 percent less than the market. Extending the estimation period to twelve months of nonconflicting net buys or net sells results in a difference of 21 percent over the subsequent year. Clearly, the trading pattern of insiders is a useful indicator of future returns for the company.

Third, insiders seem to time their purchases and sales. If an insider wants to buy but thinks (or knows) that the stock is likely to fall in value, he will wait for the stock to fall before buying. Similarly, if an insider wants to sell but expects the stock to rise, he will wait before selling. The evidence indicates that the probability of selling by top executives increases to 69 percent if the stock has risen more than 10 percent in the last six months. On the other hand, the probability of selling is only 52 percent if the stock has fallen more than 10 percent in the last six months. Does this really indicate that insiders know what is going to happen to the stock, or is it simply that their price targets for trading have been met? Combined with the continuity in trading patterns and continuity in return patterns enumerated above, it seems that insiders do have the ability to time their trades.

Finally, if all insider trades are aggregated, they may provide some information about future economic growth. If insiders can provide information about their respective companies, then it seems reasonable that if all of those signals are consolidated, insiders may be able to predict the direction of the economy and the overall stock market. Indeed, that is true.

Table 7.2 is constructed by counting the number of firms with net insider buys and net insider sells during each of the estimation periods. A buy signal is issued if more than 50 percent of the firms have net insider buys, and a sell signal is issued if more than 50 percent of the firms have net insider sells. If trade signals are based on a three-month estimation period, then the return in the subsequent three-month period is 5.7 percent following buys and 3.9 percent following sells. The difference of 1.8 percent is equivalent to an annualized return of 7.2 percent. The prediction of future growth improves if longer estimation and holding periods are used. With a twelve-month estimation period and a six-month holding period,

Table 7.2   Determining Buy Signals Based on Insider Activity (in percent)

	Estimation period 3 months Holding period: 3 months		Estimation period: 12 months Holding period: 6 months	
	Adjusted return	Probability of an up market	Adjusted return	Probability of an up market
Buys	5.7	74.2	14.1	80.0
Sells	3.9	62.5	6.2	65.2

the difference in returns following buys and sells is 7.9 percent, which translates into an annualized return of 15.8 percent. That is a big difference. The probability of an up market is 80 percent for buys compared with 65.2 percent for sells.

The newsletter, *Vickers Weekly Insider,* uses aggregate trading by insiders to predict the direction of the market. It computes a sell-buy ratio based on insiders' trades, and claims that if the ratio is less than 2.00, the market is likely to rise, and if the ratio is greater than 2.50, the market is likely to fall. Note that 2.00 and 2.50 are used as cutoffs because there is significantly more insider selling than insider buying.

Some anecdotal evidence related to trading by insiders is illustrative. Until May 2000, insiders at Lucent Technologies were actively selling their stock at prices in the range of $40–70. Thereafter, there were relatively few trades by insiders. In August 2002 insiders became active once again. This time, the CEO and several directors were actively buying Lucent stock at a price of less than $2.00.

REFINING THE RESULTS

In addition to the broad evidence presented, there are a variety of characteristics of insider trades that can help refine and improve the predictability of stock returns for the insider's firm. In particular, the identity of traders, number of shares, firm size, type of trade (buy or sell), and consensus among insiders are factors that can significantly improve the results.

Identity of Insiders

It is reasonable to expect that top executives (chief executive officer, chief financial officer, and chief operating officer) will know the firm more intimately than anyone else in the organization. Other members of the senior management team may be well informed about their particular area but not necessarily about the whole organization. The board of directors provides overall direction to the company but is essentially given information by the top executives. Moreover, the board usually meets only a few times a year, so its access to information is somewhat limited. Large shareholders are outsiders and are not privy to any information unless they have representation on the board of directors.

The predictive power of insider trades is related to the amount of information the insiders have. The following table shows the percentage of average abnormal returns earned during the twelve months following insider purchases (or insider sales). Evidence indicates that it is best to ignore trades of large shareholders and pay close attention to trades of other insiders, especially the top executives.

Top executives	5.0
Officers	3.9
Directors	3.6
Large shareholders	0.7

Number of Shares Traded

It is natural to expect that larger trades will be more informative because insiders will trade more if they are more confident about their assessment. Small trades, on the other hand, will convey little information. The results are reported below by size (%) of the trade:

1–100 shares	0.8
101–1,000 shares	2.9
1,001–10,000 shares	4.0
10,001–20,000 shares	4.1
20,001–100,000 shares	4.8
100,001–1,000,000 shares	3.8
More than 1,000,000 shares	0.5

The evidence supports the expectation that larger trades are informative. However, once the number of shares traded becomes very large, the trades don't remain as informative. There are probably two reasons for this decline. First, large trades are likely to be scrutinized by the media and the SEC. Therefore, an insider will avoid large trades based on private information and will make large trades only when they are triggered for other reasons, such as a tax payment that can neither be avoided nor delayed. As mentioned above, large informative trades are usually split into slightly smaller trades.

Second, large trades are more likely to be sales than purchases. As you will see momentarily, sales have lower predictability than purchases. Therefore, large trades tend to contain less information.

Firm Size

Firm size can be an important factor in the predictive ability of insiders for several reasons. First, larger firms have many stock analysts who continually study and report on the firm. As a result, insiders' evaluation of the firm may not be as important as in the case of a smaller firm where no outsiders are actively producing and disseminating information about the firm. Second, any particular event is likely to have a much larger impact on a smaller company than on a larger firm. A new marketing relationship with AOL Time Warner will be more valuable to Flowers.com than to Amazon.com because Amazon.com is a much larger company with many established channels for selling. Consequently, the same piece of information may elicit a significantly larger price response from Flowers.com stock than from Amazon.com stock. Or, as in the case of Imclone, denial of approval of one drug by the FDA caused the stock price to plummet by 75 percent. The data below confirm the predictive ability of insider trading based on firm size.

Size	All insiders (%)	Officers only (%)	Top executives only (%)
<$25 million	6.2	7.0	7.8
$25–100 million	3.1	3.4	4.0
$100–1,000 million	2.3	2.5	2.9
>$1,000 million	1.7	2.0	3.9

The twelve-month market-adjusted return is much higher for smaller firms than for larger firms. The table also shows that trades by top executives can predict the future more accurately than trades by other insiders. If the size of trades is combined with firm size and the identity of insiders, the results are more promising. The twelve-month market-adjusted return following large trades (more than ten thousand shares) by top executives in firms with a market capitalization of less than $25 million is 9.8 percent, much higher than the 3.7 percent return for firms with a market capitalization of more than $1,000 million.

Purchases Versus Sales

On average, selling by insiders is nearly four times as large as buying by insiders. Moreover, selling is more likely to be involuntary, due to liquidity or diversification needs, whereas buying is more likely to be voluntary, for speculative reasons. Consequently, buying by insiders should be more significant than selling by insiders. The twelve-month return following trades by top executives is 8.9 percent for buys and –5.4 percent for sells (avoidance of a loss). For small firms and top executives, the twelve-month profits (or losses avoided for sales) are as follows:

	All insiders	*Officers*	*Top executives*
Buys	10.4%	11.9%	12.3%
Sells	–0.8%	–0.9%	–2.8%

The difference between purchases and sales is smaller but significant even for larger firms. Since selling is more common, it is natural to expect that a high level of sales is less abnormal than a comparable high level of purchases. Moreover, insiders may choose not to buy more stock even if they have positive information about the company, for two reasons. First, almost all purchases, except those made by new insiders, are likely to be based on special information and, therefore, subject to closer scrutiny. Second, purchasing additional shares of a company where the insider is already heavily invested increases his risk significantly. Therefore, insiders with positive information may choose not to sell instead of buying more shares. Thus, the absence of sales and purchases is also a strong signal of positive information, especially if the top executives are inactive.

Number of Insiders

Finally, the number of insiders who buy or sell can sharpen the informativeness of trades. If only one insider is selling, then that may simply be due to his personal situation. However, if several insiders are selling, it is easier to claim that the selling contains new information. The evidence supports this notion. If only one insider is selling, then the twelve-month abnormal return is 1.2 percent, which improves to 4.6 percent if three or more insiders are selling. On the other hand, insider buying is rare enough that even following the purchases of one insider will generate an abnormal return of 4.2 percent, which improves slightly to 4.7 percent with three or more buying insiders.

Overall, the evidence suggests that:

- Top executives know more.

- Large trades (up to 500,000 shares) reveal more.

- Purchases have better predictive ability.

- Consensus among insiders is important.

- It is easier to forecast returns for smaller firms than for larger firms.

Note, however, that the evidence presented does not account for transaction costs. Since those costs are high for small firms, and sometimes prohibitively high, it may be necessary to alter the above recommendations for implementation of a trading strategy.

Though it is important to keep the practicability of a trading strategy in mind, evidence reveals that copying the large trades (more than 10,000 shares) of top executives is profitable. Outsiders can mimic these trades and earn a return of 7 percent for purchases and 4.9 percent for sales over a twelve-month period after adjusting for the market and accounting for transaction costs.

If all trades (large and small) based on a six-month period are considered, the insider purchases outperform insider sales by 7.8 percent over the next twelve-month period. Adjustment for risk reduces the overperformance to 4.8 percent.

RESULTS BASED ON THE *WALL STREET JOURNAL'S* INSIDER TRADING SPOTLIGHT

Realizing the importance of insider trading to investors, the *Wall Street Journal* began publishing an "Insider Trading Spotlight" column in 1988. The column reports the top ten insider sales and the top insider purchases by dollar value reported to the SEC. Until early 2003, the column appeared weekly, but now it appears daily. The column is also available online. In addition to reporting the insiders with the largest buys and sells, the online version also reports companies with the most insider buying or selling activity. Similar information is also published by Barron's and several Internet sites such as Quicken and MSN Money. The availability of insider trading data is listed in "Internet References."

A few studies have examined whether trading based on top ten insider buys and sells is profitable or not. The research finds that on the day of publication there is an abnormal increase in the prices of stocks that had large insider buys and an abnormal decrease in the prices of stocks with large insider sells. The price change is about 1 percent, statistically significant, and accompanied by significantly higher volume. If only insider buys are considered, then the market-adjusted return on publication day is about 2 percent, but the cumulative market-adjusted return for a one-year period is small.

Because the data can be compiled independently without waiting for the print edition of the *Wall Street Journal*, this insider trading activity suggests a possible trading strategy. However, the above returns do not account for transaction costs, which can cut into the profitability of a trading strategy.

OVERALL EVIDENCE

The evidence indicates that trading by insiders reveals information about future stock price movements. Outsiders can benefit by observing and mimicking the insider trades. Among the two hundred thousand trades by insiders every year, large (but not too large) purchases by top executives, especially of small companies, are most informative. However, even trades publicized in the news media can be profitable and informative for investors.

Besides constructing a trading strategy based on trades by insiders, investors can use that information to reconfirm planned buys and sells. For example, if an investor is thinking of buying Pepsi stock but insiders are selling, then it may not be the best time to invest in that stock. Similarly, if an investor needs to liquidate some stocks to meet certain expenses, he should look at the trades by insiders and not sell the stocks that insiders have been buying.

Change in Reporting Requirements

The evidence presented above is based on SEC reporting requirements and data in secondary sources such as newspapers, magazines, and the Internet. However, recent SEC reporting changes accelerate release of insider trading information to the public and will probably improve outsiders' gains. The changes are discussed below.

Until August 2002, insiders had until the tenth day of the following month to report open-market trades, which meant that trades could be reported as many as forty calendar days after they occurred. For shares sold back to the company, insiders could wait to report until forty-five days after the start of the *next* fiscal year. However, in accordance with new SEC regulations, insiders are now required to report their large trades, typically the ones of interest to investors, within two business days. All other trades must be reported by the second business day of the following week. This is a significant change from the earlier regulation, under which the average delay in reporting was about twenty-seven calendar days and could be even longer.

Moreover, insiders must now file their reports electronically and post them on the company's website. Under the old regulations, insiders were required to file trades by the deadlines mentioned earlier. However, electronic filing was not required. As most of insider trading filings were on paper, there was an even greater delay before the filings were transcribed and entered into SEC's EDGAR database.

Finally, as mentioned above, the *Wall Street Journal*'s "Insider Trading Spotlight" column can be accessed online before it appears in print.

Persistence

While not entirely clear, the reasons for persistence of insider trading strategies are probably related to a lack of understanding and a lack of interest. There are few hedge funds, if any, that specialize in insider trading. It is possible that professional arbitrageurs are more attracted to strategies that are less uncertain and those that require a shorter holding period. Many other people seem to lack a complete understanding of insider trading. Newsletters devoted to strategies based on insider trading have not been particularly successful and have a low survival rate. The reason for their failure is most likely a lack of understanding. Many individual investors avoid any strategies related to insider trading because they mistakenly believe that all insider trading is illegal. Nejat Seyhun's book on insider trading, while a brilliant piece of work by an expert in the field, was largely inaccessible to the small, individual investor.

The changes in reporting mentioned in the previous section will definitely make trades by insiders more transparent and timely. Consequently, the evidence presented above and the results presented below will improve and become more rewarding to the investors. It is also anticipated that more investors will begin to construct strategies related to insider trading.

The Trading Process

There are two ways investors can use information related to trading by insiders: on an individual stock level or on an aggregate industry or market level. At an individual stock level, investors can use the data either to set up trading strategies or to alter trading behavior (for example, not buying an individual stock when insiders are selling it). The use of data on insider trading for predicting broad market movements and for altering individual trades is discussed in "Other Uses and Refinements of Insider Trading Information."

Institutions have access to large databases to screen stocks and identify those that may be of interest. However, the situation for individual investors is different. Unlike stock and mutual fund databases, which are freely available and easily accessible, databases that contain insider trading data are too expensive and generally inaccessible to individual investors.

There are a few sources [such as the *Wall Street Journal*, Vickers Stock Research (vickers-stock.com), and Thomson Financial Network (thomsonfn.com)] that provide information about stocks and insiders with very high levels of insider trading activity. This information is freely accessible to individual investors. However, the information in these sources is already prescreened and by their own criteria, not necessarily the criteria established based on the evidence presented in "Evidence" and "Change in Reporting Requirements," above. Therefore, the list of stocks obtained from these sources must be screened once again based on the criteria discussed above and enumerated in the following steps.

Step 1: Obtain a list of stocks for review from one or more of the sources in "Information on Trades by Insiders for Individual Stocks."

Step 2: Get insider trading data for each of the stocks from Quicken.com. In case any information is suspect, it can be verified with Vickers. Select transactions during the previous six months. The process can also be repeated by considering transactions only during the last three months.

Step 3: Exclude transactions that fall into the following categories:

- Trades by large outside shareholders, those who own more than 10 percent of the stock

- Individual transactions that are larger than 500,000 shares

- Individual transactions that are smaller than 101 shares

- Private trades, where no market transaction takes place

- Sales less than or equal to the exercise of options on the same date

- Planned sales reported on Form 144

- Initial trades reported on Form 3 and annual ownership on Form 5

Trading by insiders is reported to the SEC on four different forms. For the purpose of this chapter, Form 4 is the only relevant form. It is used to report trades of existing insiders to the SEC. Form 144 alerts the SEC to planned sales of restricted securities or securities held by an affiliate of the issuer; it is irrelevant because restricted securities are not of much interest to individual investors. Form 3 is the initial transaction by an insider after becoming an insider; initial purchases by an insider are usually required by the company and therefore are involuntary. And Form 5, the annual statement of ownership by insiders, contains no new information.

Step 4: Sum up the total number of shares sold and the total number of shares purchased. Compute the sales-to-purchase ratio (SP), provided the number of shares purchased is not zero.

Step 5: Repeat step 4 but use the number of unique insiders instead of the number of shares. Again compute the ratio of the number of unique insiders selling to the number of unique insiders buying (SIPI), provided the number of unique insiders buying is not zero.

Step 6: If SIPI and SP (calculated in steps 4 and 5) are dissimilar— say, different by more than 50 percent—then explore the reasons for the dissimilarity. If a single insider is making up the bulk of the purchases or sales, then the SIPI and SP are likely to be quite different. In such a case, one should rely more on SIPI than on SP, or should exclude that insider from all computations. For example, Bill Gates sold $1.1 billion worth of Microsoft stock in the first six months of 2002. Since no insider is likely to buy such a large quantity of Microsoft stock, are Bill Gates' sales a bearish signal? If you consider the past sales by Bill Gates, he sold $1.25 billion in the first six months of 2001 and another $1.25 billion in the second six months of 2001, it is obvious that the sale of $1.1 billion in the first six months of 2002 is unlikely to convey much information. So it may be best to exclude Bill Gates from computation of sales and purchases of Microsoft stock.

In any case, if no reasons can be discovered for an unusually large trade by an insider, go to step 7, which contains recommendations for trading.

Step 7: A buy is recommended under any one or more of the following conditions:

- There is *no* selling by insiders over the observation period (at least six months).

- If there is selling by insiders, then SIPI and SP are both less than 1, and the net number of insiders buying is at least 3.

A sell is recommended if the net number of insiders selling is at least three and SIPI and SP are at least 2.00. The remaining stocks are ignored.

Strategy Implementation

The trading process outlined above is applied to all stocks featured in the weekly "Insider Trading Spotlight" column of the *Wall Street Journal* (WSJ) during December 2001. The WSJ is selected because it is easily accessible to all investors. However, WSJ reports the largest trades by insider, not by company. Thus the same report may contain several insiders from the same company.

In December 2001 "Insider Trading Spotlight" appeared in the WSJ four times, each time listing the ten largest insider sales and the ten largest insider purchases. The total of forty insider purchases and forty insider sales represented sixty different companies. Using the steps in the trading process for each of these companies, the results are reported in Table 7.3. Firm size and the number of shares are as of the end of December 2001. The shares sold or bought and the insiders selling or buying are based on the July–December 2001 period. The SP and SIPI ratios are reported in the second and third last columns. Whenever the number of shares purchased is zero or the number of insiders buying is zero, the ratios cannot be calculated. In those cases, the ratios are indicated to be "high" (greater than 2.0).

In some instances there is no insider trade that qualifies for inclusion based on the criteria set out earlier. How can that be reconciled with the fact that the company was featured in the WSJ based on the size of trades? Typically, it means that the trade reported in the WSJ was related to the exercise of options. While sales related to an option exercise may have some information, the evidence indicates that the predictability of sales concurrent with an option exercise is close to zero. Hence all such trades are excluded. As a result, some companies have zero sales and zero purchases. When both sales and purchases are zero, the ratios are again undefined but indicated to be "low." Since the norm for a company's insiders is to be selling company stock, zero sales suggest a buying opportunity.

The last column in Table 7.3 has the recommendations based on step 7: fifteen sells and twenty-six buys. The stock returns for these recommendations are presented in Table 7.4. Of the fifteen stocks recommended as a sell, only two stocks earn a positive return in the following six-month period, January–June 2002. Overall, the fifteen

Table 7.3 Trading by Insiders of Firms Highlighted in the *Wall Street Journal*

Firms are taken from the "Insider Trading Spotlight" column of the *Wall Street Journal* during December 2001. Firm size and number of shares are as of the end of December 2001. Insider transactions are based on the July–December 2001 period. The last row has trading recommendations, where S is a sell and B is a buy. A — indicates that no trading recommendation can be made based on insider trading.

Ticker Symbol	Firm Size (millions)	Number of Shares (millions)	Shares Sold (thousands)	Shares Bought (thousands)	Insiders Selling	Insiders Buying	Ratio of Sales to Purchases (SP)	Ratio of Insiders Selling to Insiders Buying (SIPI)	Trading Recommendation
ADP	36,000	617	346	0	11	0	high	high	S
AHC	5,500	89	0	12	0	1	0	0	B
AMHC	460	14	151	0	6	0	high	high	S
APD	10,650	227	0	0	0	0	low	low	B
ATVI	1,350	52	135	0	2	0	high	high	—
AXR	40	7	0	555	0	1	0	0	B
BEN	9,200	261	234	0	12	0	high	high	S
BLS	71,600	1,877	0	0	0	0	low	low	B
BRCM	7,600	186	1,881	0	9	0	high	high	S
CAH	29,200	451	275	0	3	0	high	high	S
CB	11,700	170	2	10	1	1	0.2	1	—
CEC	1,210	28	0	30	0	1	0	0	B
CEFT	16,500	504	309	0	6	0	high	high	S
CLSR	315	13	87	3	4	1	29	4	S
COT	1,100	68	555	0	12	0	high	high	S
CSGS	2,150	53	810	50	4	1	16	4	S
DBRN	460	18	0	0	0	0	low	low	B
DCGN	525	54	94	0	1	0	high	high	—
DELL	70,900	2,607	1,970	0	7	0	high	high	S
DIAN	450	7	100	0	1	0	high	high	—
ESV	3,350	135	4	65	1	1	0.1	1	—

(continues on next page)

Table 7.3 Trading by Insiders of Firms Highlighted in the *Wall Street Journal* (continued)

Ticker Symbol	Firm Size (millions)	Number of Shares (millions)	Shares Sold (thousands)	Shares Bought (thousands)	Insiders Selling	Insiders Buying	Ratio of Sales to Purchases (SP)	Ratio of Insiders Selling to Insiders Buying (SIPI)	Trading Recommendation
FCBP	100	5	0	79	0	1	0	0	B
GNSS	2,050	31	450	9	12	1	50	12	S
GR	2,700	102	0	227	0	9	0	0	B
HCP	2,000	56	50	0	1	0	high	high	—
HIG	15,000	238	300	19	1	3	15	0.3	—
HMA	4,500	242	0	2	0	1	0	0	B
HU	1,325	46	17	40	2	6	0.4	0.3	B
IBM	20,800	1,723	71	5	3	1	14	3	—
ITT	4,625	92	0	0	3	0	low	low	B
JAKK	350	18	260	0	3	0	high	high	S
KG	10,300	246	267	2	2	2	high	1	—
KIND	900	17	400	0	1	0	high	high	—
MBBC	50	3	0	141	0	10	0	0	B
MBFI	190	7	0	21	0	2	0	0	B
MMC	29,500	275	0	0	0	0	low	low	B
MOBE	19	15	0	97	0	4	0	0	B
MPH	240	15	950	37	5	2	26	2.5	S
OGLE	80	5	0	82	0	8	0	0	B
OPTN	300	16	450	0	1	0	high	high	—
OVER	2,000	57	865	0	10	0	high	high	S
PMSI	75	16	0	105	0	4	0	0	B
PPDI	1,675	52	25	150	1	1	0.2	1	—
PZZA	625	23	0	0	0	0	low	low	B

RYL	970	13	9	0	2	0	high	high	—
SRNA	875	40	400	0	1	0	high	high	—
STOR	600	97	1,325	0	8	0	high	high	S
STZ	1,600	37	0	0	0	0	low	low	B
SYMC	4,600	70	8	0	7	0	high	high	—
TDSC	185	13	0	141	0	1	0	0	B
THC	19,000	325	0	10	0	1	0	0	B
THER	1,000	39	0	91	5	4	0	0	B
TMPW	4,500	106	793	31	0	8	26	5	—
TRGL	30	6	0	208	0	3	0	0	B
TRKN	165	14	0	0	0	0	low	low	B
TW	1,660	85	2	203	1	1	0	1	—
VTA	275	35	0	146	0	6	0	0	B
WMB	13,100	515	13	46	1	2	0.3	0.5	—
WSBI	100	5	0	4	0	1	0	0	B
WYN	100	168	408	0	1	0	high	high	—

Table 7.4   Returns to Stocks Based on Trading Recommendations in Table 7.3

Ticker	Jan. 2002 Return (%)	Jan.–Mar. 2002 Return (%)	Jan.–Jun. 2002 Return (%)
Panel A: Sell Recommendations			
ADP	−8.3	−0.8	−25.7
AMHC	−15.1	−15.0	−44.3
BEN	6.2	19.1	21.1
BRCM	3.9	−12.2	−57.1
CAH	1.9	9.7	−5.0
CEFT	−11.1	1.5	−8.1
CLSR	0.3	−15.8	−40.1
COT	7.1	18.8	19.4
CSGS	−8.3	−29.7	−52.7
DELL	1.1	−3.9	−3.8
GNSS	−8.5	−60.7	−87.4
JAKK	6.9	20.0	−6.5
MPH	1.6	−12.3	−38.8
OVER	3.2	−21.2	−31.1
STOR	−16.8	−43.5	−68.3
Total (all 15 stocks)	−2.4	−9.7	−28.6
S&P 500 return	−1.6	−0.1	−13.8
S&P 500—adjusted return (all 15 stocks)	−0.8	−9.6	−14.8
Panel B: Buy Recommendations			
AHC	−1.8	27.5	33.0
APD	−1.4	10.5	8.5
AXR	32.6	13.5	28.7
BLS	5.4	−2.9	−16.6
CEC	3.6	6.5	−4.8
DBRN	7.1	18.4	23.7
FCBP	−3.2	30.4	15.8
GR	4.5	20.0	8.2
HMA	5.6	12.7	9.5
HU	4.7	11.8	1.2
ITT	5.1	25.1	40.5
MBFI	10.0	10.7	27.7
MBBC	2.8	9.7	16.1
MMC	−4.7	5.4	−9.2
MOBE	11.2	20.0	70.4
OGLE	−10.0	−34.8	−17.6
PMSI	23.6	56.6	140.1
PZZA	3.2	1.5	21.5
STZ	11.7	28.3	49.4
TDSC	−14.5	11.5	−14.4
THC	8.6	14.1	21.8
THER	−10.1	−23.8	−25.5
TRGL	−12.4	−13.0	−11.5
TRKN	4.0	24.9	−23.5
VTA	−11.0	−24.7	−46.0
WSBI	2.1	16.2	44.2
Total (all 26 stocks)	3.0	10.6	15.0
S&P 500 return	−1.6	−0.1	−13.8
S&P 500—adjusted return (all 26 stocks)	4.6	10.7	28.8

stocks lose an average of 28.6 percent, compared with a loss of 13.8 percent for the S&P 500. Thus, the net S&P 500 adjusted return is –14.8 percent for the six-month period, or an annualized return of –29.6 percent. The results for shorter periods are similar, suggesting that stocks that are aggressively sold by insiders underperform the market in subsequent months.

In contrast to the abnormal fall in prices for stocks with sell recommendations, stocks with buy recommendations outperform the market. Out of the twenty-six stocks with a buy, only nine stocks experience a fall in prices in the next six months. The overall return is 15.0 percent, compared with the S&P 500's return of –13.8 percent. Thus, stocks with a buy recommendation earn a whopping 28.8 percent abnormal return over a six-month period, or an annualized abnormal return of 57.6 percent! Similarly, the one-month abnormal return is 4.6 percent and the three-month abnormal return is 10.7 percent.

The large magnitude of returns following sells (–29.6 percent annualized) and buys (57.6 percent annualized) is surprising. Transaction costs will lower the returns by only about 1 percent over a six-month period. So, what can explain the large returns to insider

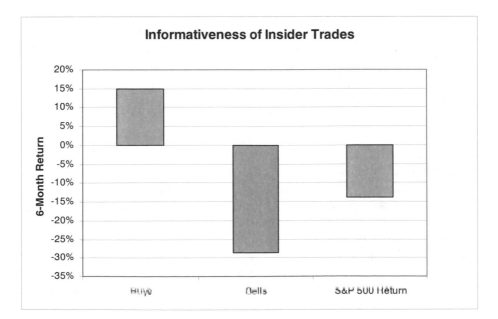

Figure 7.1   Returns to buy and sell recommendations based on insider trades are shown. The S&P 500 return is provided for comparison. The insider trades are taken from the "Insider Trading Spotlight" columns that appeared in the *Wall Street Journal* during December 2001. The trading strategies are implemented from January 2002 to June 2002.

trading in this analysis? Perhaps the sample size is too small, with only sixty firms and trading recommendations for only forty-one firms. It is also possible that insiders can predict their own company's performance in absolute terms rather than in relative terms. That is, they can predict what might happen to their stock price independent of market movements. Indeed, the average increase in the stock price following buys was only 15 percent. If the broader market had also risen during the same period, then the insider buys would not have generated the large abnormal profits witnessed. Nonetheless, it is sufficient to state that these abnormal returns are large and attractive.

Other Uses and Refinements of Insider Trading Information

OTHER USES

Besides a trading strategy for individual stocks discussed above, insider trading information can be used in at least two other ways. First, the information provided by insiders can be used to alter the timing of trades. As far as possible, outsiders should mimic the trades of insiders. If insiders are selling a stock aggressively, it does not seem reasonable to buy the same stock. Similarly, do not sell while insiders are postponing sales. An investor can follow steps 2 through 7 of the trading process for each stock he wants to trade. If the recommendation based on step 7 agrees with his desired action, then he should follow through. Otherwise, he should wait.

The second use of insider information is in trying to predict future direction of the broader market. If insiders can accurately predict how their company is likely to perform, then an aggregation of all insider recommendations should suggest whether the overall market or an industry is a buy, sell, or hold. The Vickers weekly insider report (go to vickers-stock.com) computes an "Insider Index" based on insider trading among all companies that is supposed to predict market direction. Similarly, Thomson provides its assessment of the market through its "Market Tearsheet" (go to insider.thomsonfn.com). The third source is WallStreetCity (go to www.wallstreetcity.com), which lists insider trading by industry. While these indices may be useful, the construction of the indices is critical. Detailed information on the construction of these indices is not available, and it is unclear whether these indices follow the criteria described above. However, for individuals and institutions with access to insider trading databases, it may be possible to construct an index that can accurately predict future market movements based on insider trades.

REFINEMENTS

The results reported above in "Strategy Implementation," based on broad analysis, are fairly good. However, analysts and newsletter pundits have attempted to further refine the analysis to improve the returns. Although the refinements discussed below have intuitive appeal, there is no empirical evidence to either support or refute the value added by these refinements.

The first refinement is based on the fact that different insiders may have different levels of predictability. An insider may repeatedly sell before the stock falls, or buy before the stock rises. A second insider's trades, on the other hand, may have no predictive power. So, past performances of insiders can be used to weight insider trades, with the first insider's trades getting a significantly higher weight than the second insider's trades.

The second refinement would use deviations from normal selling and buying patterns to make trading recommendations instead of using the absolute value of net insider sales. For example, suppose Bill Gates has established a normal pattern of liquidating $1,250 million worth of Microsoft stock every six months, but he sells only $100 million in the current six-month period. Is this a buying opportunity, or should you sell Microsoft stock? Looking at the absolute number of insider sales of $100 million, it may be prudent to sell. However, compared to the normal selling activity of $1,250 million, a $100 million sale might suggest a buy.

The final refinement is the use of information related to short sales concurrent with information from insider trading. Since short sellers are believed to possess superior information relative to the market, stocks with significant insider selling are likely to underperform the market if they also have an abnormally high level of short interest. Similarly, stocks with a buy recommendation based on insider trading are likely to outperform the market if they also have a low level of short interest. Thus, the level of short interest can be used to verify the information provided by insider trading.

Qualifications

The evidence presented in this chapter and the trading strategy recommendations are based on past data. Since future market conditions and market patterns may be completely different, insider trading may not continue to predict future price movements. Moreover, the refinements and other uses suggested in "Other Uses and Refinements of Insider Trading Information" are untested even with prior-period data. Finally, the trading strategies based on insider trading may be considerably riskier than holding funds in the broader market.

Key Points

- Contrary to popular belief, most trades by insiders are legal. Insiders may trade to raise funds, or they may believe that their company's stock is misvalued by the market. Whenever insiders trade for reasons other than liquidity, they convey information about their personal beliefs to the market. As insiders know and understand the company better than the market, it is reasonable to expect that mimicking insiders' trades is a profitable endeavor.

- The evidence suggests that top executives know more. Large trades (up to 500,000 shares) reveal more. Purchases have better predictive ability than sales. Consensus among insiders is important. It is easier to forecast returns for smaller firms than for larger firms. Copying carefully selected insider trades can generate large abnormal returns, typically between 10 and 15 percent per year.

- Recent changes in SEC reporting regulations and advances in sharing information via the Internet make the disclosure of insider trades much quicker than before. These changes should help in making insider trading more profitable to outsiders.

- Insider trading information can be used to construct trading strategies. However, it is difficult and expensive to get insider trading data. It may be necessary to rely on published information in secondary sources. Starting with stocks covered by the "Insider Trading Spotlight" of the *Wall Street Journal* and applying the criteria enunciated in "Evidence," it is possible to make definite buy and sell recommendations. The six-month returns to these buy and sell recommendations are quite large. Firms with a buy recommendation earn an abnormal return of 28.8 percent over a six-month period, whereas stocks with a sell recommendation lose 14.8 percent during the same period.

- Insider trading information can be used for other purposes as well. It can be used to predict the broad market direction. Also, investors can look up information on insider trades before executing their personal trades. If insiders have been selling, then it is advisable not to buy. But if insiders have been buying their own stock or not selling their stock, then buying that stock may be a smart decision.

Bottom Line

Copying insider trades is profitable. As insiders generally know a lot more about their companies than outsiders and the market, trades by insiders convey new information to vigilant outsiders. This information can be used in a variety of ways. First, trading strategies based on this information can generate annual abnormal returns of 10–15 percent. Second, the information can be used to review an investor's own trades. Third, the information can even suggest whether the overall market or a particular industry is likely to fall or rise.

Internet References

Information on Trades by Insiders for Individual Stocks

http://www.vickers-stock.com: This site has the most information compared to any other site. It offers subscriptions to a number of detailed reports where you can sort and search through insider trades to get the ones that you are particularly interested in. The site also reports its own "Insider Index" based on insider sells and buys for each stock. An exploration of the site reveals that the former chairman of the board of directors of Enron, Ken Lay, sold nearly half a million shares of Enron, worth more than $25 million, between January 2001 and July 2001.

http://www.wallstreetcity.com: Enter the ticker symbol, press Enter, and then click on "Insider Trading" to get details of trades by insiders. In addition to firm-by-firm insider trades, you can also get information on the best industries based on insider trading. To do that, click on "Industry Groups" below "Insider Trading." Thereafter, select "All Industries" and "Insider Trading" in the drop-down menus near the top of the site. Then click on "Insider Rank" to sort by the best industry down to the worst. The source of the data on this site is Vickers Stock Research.

http://www.realtimeinsider.com: This site provides alerts to SEC filings. Note that the actual trades would have taken several days earlier. However, SEC filing is when the information first becomes public. The service is expensive.

http://finance.yahoo.com: Type in the ticker symbol and go to "Insider Transactions" under "Ownership" in the left frame. Provides insider trading information by company. The sources of this data are EDGAR Online, Vickers Stock Research, and Computershare.

http://www.investor.reuters.com: Registration is required to access information on the website. Detailed insider trading information can be obtained by clicking on "Insider Trading." Summarized information is available under "Performance."

http://moneycentral.msn.com: Provides insider trading information by company. This list is updated weekly on Friday and is based on Form 4 SEC filings received from Disclosure Inc. The filings are delivered to MSN Money one week after they are received by Disclosure.

http://www.edgar-online.com: This site requires subscription. However, basic data from this site can be obtained through http://finance.yahoo.com without payment.

http://www.thomsoninvest.net: Thomson Financial's site for individual investors. The site has two recommendations under "Opinion." You can obtain insider trading information by typing in the company's ticker symbol. It also gives CDA/Investnet's rating based on trading by insiders. However, the site does not provide firm-level data on trading by insiders. Thomson Financial is the holding company for numerous financial companies such as First Call, Data Stream, Securities Data Company, Disclosure, Dialog, CDA/Investnet, Investment Dealers' Digest, and so on. It is also the publisher of the discontinued newsletters *Insider Chronicle* and *Insider Scores*.

http://www.quote.com: Information by company is freely accessible.

http://www.wsj.com: The *Wall Street Journal* lists the top ten insider sales and purchases in the "Insider Trading Spotlight" column every Monday online and on Wednesdays in print. The source of its data is "Ideas" on http://insider.thomsonfn.com. Thomson Financial.

http://www.sec.gov: For original filings by insiders.

Newsletters Based on Trading by Insiders

Discontinued newsletters: *Insider Chronicle, Insider Scores, Inside Track, Insider Report,* and *Insider Trading Monitor*.

http://www.argusgroup.com: Site of Vickers Stock Research. Offers a variety of reports for purchase: *Vickers Insider Trading Report* and *Vickers Weekly Insider. Vickers Insiders Portfolio* has been followed by *Hulbert Financial Digest* since December 1992. Outperforms the market on an absolute basis and a risk-adjusted basis. *Vickers Insiders Portfolio* earned an annualized return of 11.2 percent from 1993 to June 2002, compared with 10.5 percent for the Wilshire 5000.

http://www.jackadamo.com: Jack Adamo's weekly newsletter, called *Insiders Plus,* has been followed by *Hulbert Financial Digest* since January 2001. According to HFD, the newsletter has outperformed the market since January 2001, earning a return of −10.2 percent from February 2001 to June 2002, compared to −17.9 percent for the market. However, this is too short a period for evaluation. Jack Adamo's earlier newsletter, *Inside Track,* also did well but was discontinued by the publisher.

References for Further Reading

Benesh, Gary A., and Robert A. Pari. 1987. Performance of Stocks Recommended on the Basis of Insider Trading Activity. *Financial Review* 22(1), 145–58.

Bernhardt, Dan, Burton Hollifield, and Eric Hughson. 1995. Investment and Insider Trading. *Review of Financial Studies* 8(2), 501–43.

Bettis, Carr, Don Vickrey, and Donn W. Vickrey. 1997. Mimickers of Corporate Insiders Who Make Large-Volume Trades. *Financial Analyst Journal* 53(5), 57–66.

Bettis, J. Carr, Jeffrey L. Coles, and Michael L. Lemmon. 2000. Corporate Policies Restricting Trading by Insiders. *Journal of Financial Economics* 57(2), 191–220.

Chang, Saeyoung, and David Y. Suk. 1998. Stock Prices and the Secondary Dissemination of Information: The *Wall Street Journal*'s "Insider Trading Spotlight" Column. *Financial Review* 33(3), 115–28.

Damodaran, Aswath, and Crocker H. Liu. 1993. Insider Trading as a Signal of Private Information. *Review of Financial Studies* 6(1), 79–119.

Eckbo, B. Espen, and David C. Smith. 1998. The Conditional Performance of Insider Trades. *Journal of Finance* 53(2), 467–98.

Ferreira, Eurico J., and LeRoy D. Brooks. 2000. Re-Released Information in the *Wall Street Journal*'s "Insider Trading Spotlight" Column. *Quarterly Journal of Business and Economics* 39(1), 22–34.

Friederich, Sylvain, Alan Gregory, John Matatko, and Ian Tonks. 2002. Short-Run Returns Around the Trades of Corporate Insiders on the London Stock Exchange. *European Financial Management* 8(1), 7–30.

Kahle, Kathleen M. 2000. Insider Trading and the Long-Run Performance of New Security Issues. *Journal of Corporate Finance* 6, 25–53.

Lakonishok, Josef, and Inmoo Lee. 2001. Are Insider Trades Informative? *Review of Financial Studies* 14(1), 79–111.

Lee, Wayne Y., and Michael E. Solt. 1986. Insider Trading: A Poor Guide to Market Timing. *Journal of Portfolio Management* 12(4), 65–71.

Moreland, Jonathan. 2000. *Profit from Legal Insider Trading: Invest Today on Tomorrow's News* (Chicago: Dearborn Trade).

Pettit, R. Richardson, and P. C. Venkatesh. 1995. Insider Trading and Long-Run Return Performance. *Financial Management* 24(2), 88–103.

Roth, Greg, and Andy Saporoschenko. 1999. The Informational Effects of Large Insider Stock Purchases. *Managerial Finance* 25(1), 37–48.

Seyhun, H. Nejat. 1986. Insiders' Profits, Cost of Trading, and Market Efficiency. *Journal of Financial Economics* 16(2), 189–212.

———. 1992. Why Does Aggregate Insider Trading Predict Future Stock Returns. *Quarterly Journal of Economics* 107(4), 1303–32.

———. 1998. *Investment Intelligence from Insider Trading* (Cambridge, Mass.: MIT Press).

Trivoli, George William. 1980. How to Profit from Insider Trading Information. *Journal of Portfolio Management* 6(4), 51–56.

Notes

1. Besides the author's own analysis, this chapter is based on research in Lakonishok and Lee (2001), Chang and Suk (1998), Bettis, Vickrey, and Vickrey (1997), Ferreira and Brooks (2000), Roth and Saporoschenko (1999), and, especially, extensive work by Seyhun (1986, 1992, 1998). Seyhun's book on

trading by insiders (1998) is strongly recommended for anyone who wants to learn much more about insider trading.

2. See the section "Implementation Through Sector Fund Newsletters" for a discussion on evaluation of newsletters.

8

Changes to the S&P 500 Index

Firms in the S&P 500 are occasionally replaced by new firms because the existing firm is no longer representative of the economy or the firm ceases to exist (goes bankrupt or is acquired by another firm). In general, the changes are announced about a week before they become effective.

Evidence indicates that a firm added to the index typically rises in value, while a firm dropped from the index falls in value. Not all of this change takes place on the announcement date; rather, it continues to occur until the effective date. However, after the effective date, the price change reverses itself. The added firms give up some value, and the deleted firms regain nearly all of their lost value. There are several explanations for these price movements.

Investors and arbitrageurs can earn abnormal returns by buying (short-selling) the added firm (deleted firm) upon announcement and reversing the positions on the effective date. The new positions are held for about a month and then liquidated.

Description

The Standard and Poor's 500 (S&P 500) is a portfolio of five hundred stocks that represents leading industries in the U.S. economy.[1] The S&P 500 is considered to be a good proxy for the U.S. market and is commonly used in evaluating performance of money managers. The S&P 500 is considered an investable index, that is, individuals or institutions can easily invest in the stocks in the S&P 500. Currently, about $1 trillion out of a total market value of about $12 trillion is indexed directly or indirectly to the S&P 500. Changes to the index are widely followed.

Most but not all S&P 500 companies are large. At the end of 2002, 340 firms in the S&P 500 were in the top 500 firms by market capitalization. There are many large companies not in the S&P 500, such as USA Interactive ($11 billion market capitalization at the end of 2002) and Liberty Media ($23 billion). Similarly, there are many small firms in the S&P 500, such as McDermott International ($275 million) and Tupperware ($900 million). The median market value of S&P 500 firms is about $8 billion.

Not all S&P 500 companies are well-known firms. The typical investor is aware of companies usually through consumer products (Coke, Pepsi, Johnson and Johnson, Wal-Mart, etc.) or from coverage in the media (Enron [since dropped from the index], Honeywell, Tyco International). Companies with industrial products are hardly ever recognized. Some large companies that are not well known include Schlumberger ($32 billion), Applied Materials ($33 billion), Pitney Bowes ($10 billion), Fifth Third ($35 billion), Automatic Data Processing ($36 billion), Medtronic ($62 billion), and AIG ($207 billion).

The Process of Changing Index Components

Changes to the S&P 500 index are always initiated by deletions. About three-quarters of all deletions from the index are involuntary due to major restructurings, caused by a merger, spin-off, or bankruptcy. A deletion may occur when an S&P 500 firm merges with another company that is already a member of the S&P 500 (for example, Exxon's acquisition of Mobil) or is acquired by a foreign company (Nestlé's acquisition of Ralston Purina). The S&P 500 now contains no foreign companies; the remaining seven were deleted in July 2002. A spin-off can result in a deletion from the index if the firm becomes unrepresentative as a consequence of the spin-off. For example, FMC was deleted from the S&P 500 when it spun off FMC Technologies. In most cases, though the spun-off firm is added to the S&P 500. For example, when 3Com spun off Palm, 3Com was deleted from the S&P 500 and replaced by Palm. Firms filing for bankruptcy or those likely to file for bankruptcy, such as Kmart and Global Crossing, are also replaced.

In addition, firms may be deleted voluntarily by Standard and Poor's when they cease to represent the economy, either because the industry is no longer representative of the economy (railroads, for instance) or because the firm is no longer representative of the industry (such as Rite Aid for retail drug stores). Since the number of firms in the index is maintained at five hundred, additions to the index are almost always announced at the same time as deletions.[2]

Standard and Poor's uses four criteria to pick a firm, although the criteria are not always strictly enforced. The firm must have sufficient liquidity. Firm ownership must not be concentrated in a single or few entities. The firm must be profitable. The firm must be a leader in an important U.S. industry. Though no explicit market capitalization is specified as a criterion, the market capitalization of firms added in 2002 was at least $4 billion. However, because many firms meet the objective criteria, Standard and Poor's can ignore some of those criteria, making changes to the index subjective and unpredictable. Market observers, however, keep trying to predict changes to the index. For example, Lehman Brothers identified nineteen candidates for addition and ten candidates for deletion at the end of February 2002. Six months later, only four of the nineteen firms had been added, and two of ten firms had been deleted—not a very good record. On the other hand, the June 2002 issue of *Money* reported that Goldman Sachs would get added to the S&P 500 by year's end. Indeed, it was added to the index in July 2002. As much fun as it is to try to predict changes to the index, the focus here is on trading after the changes have been announced.

Changes to the index are announced after the market closes, and they take place at the close of the effective date. The amount of time between the announcement date and the effective date varies from one day to about one month, with an occasional lag of as much as three months. In most cases, the effective date is announced at the time of the initial announcement. In the remaining cases, especially when the merger consummation date is uncertain, the effective date is announced a few days after the initial announcement.

Evidence

A change to the S&P 500 index is a significant event for the firm that is added or deleted. An addition to the index means that there will be an additional demand for about 8 percent of the outstanding shares.[3] Second, publicity surrounding the addition will cause many investors to learn about the firm, and this may influence them to trade. Third, more analysts are likely to follow the newly added firm due to a greater interest in the firm. Finally, there will be more trading in the firm, which can make it more liquid.

The effect of additions on the stock price is presented in Table 8.1, and the effect of deletions is in Table 8.2. The first period is up to

Table 8.1 Price Impact of Additions to the S&P 500 Index

Period	Total Additions	Additions in the Sample	Abnormal Return on AD+1 (%)	Abnormal Return (AD+1 to ED) (%)	Abnormal Return to 20 Days After ED (%)	Abnormal Return tol 60 Days After ED (%)
July 1962–Aug. 1976	304	285	0.0		−0.5	0.9
Sept. 1976–Sept. 1989	297	274	3.0*		2.9*	3.5*
1990	13	11	3.1+	6.7*	3.1	−3.8
1991	13	9	5.8*	8.2*	4.5+	0.3
1992	7	6	4.6+	6.4+	6.6	2.3
1993	13	9	4.7*	7.3*	5.6+	6.3
1994	18	16	2.2*	4.7*	1.2	0.3
1995	32	21	4.3*	7.2*	3.0	2.5
1996	27	20	3.8*	7.5*	2.9	3.8
1997	28	24	8.1*	10.5*	7.5*	5.8
1998	48	37	5.5*	9.3*	3.5	0.5
1999	41	38	5.8*	8.5*	6.0	7.8
2000	33	29	7.1*	10.7*	13.5*	12.5+
1989–2000	278	224	5.3*	8.4*	5.6*	4.5*

All announcements are made after market close on the announcement date indicated in the table. AD+1 refers to the first trading day after announcement. ED refers to the effective date. All changes become effective at the close on the effective date. Volume is the sixty-day average prior to announcement date. Size is the market capitalization as of the day before announcement. Abnormal return is calculated as raw return minus the S&P 500 return. Statistical significance is at better than 1 percent for returns marked with * and at better than 5 percent for returns marked with +.

Table 8.2 Price Impact of Deletions from the S&P 500 Index

Period	Total Deletions	Deletions Considered Here	Abnormal Return on AD+1 (%)	Abnormal Return (AD+1 to ED) (%)	Abnormal Return to 20 Days After ED (%)	Abnormal Return to 60 Days After ED (%)
July 1962–Aug. 1976	304	170	−0.3		1.6*	3.5*
Sept. 1976–Sept. 1989	297	61	−1.6		−3.8⁺	−2.9
1990	13	5	−1.6	−4.6	−9.1	43.7⁺
1991	13	4	−19.3	−19.3	20.1	21.4
1992	7	5	−10.2	−32.4*	6.0	8.2
1993	13	6	−2.3	−7.2	−4.9	3.3
1994	18	10	−2.8⁺	−5.4⁺	1.4	2.3
1995	32	11	−5.8⁺	−15.7*	−10.7*	−16.7
1996	27	13	−4.0*	−7.4*	−0.1	3.0
1997	28	4	−5.2⁺	−7.4⁺	4.9	22.5
1998	48	8	−7.3*	−10.5⁺	−12.1	−2.8
1999	42	9	−3.2	−3.3	2.8	4.4
2000	32	12	−5.9*	−10.9*	−11.9⁺	−7.7
1989–2000	278	88	−5.4*	−10.3*	−3.3	2.6

Returns are reported in decimals. All announcements are made after market close on the announcement date indicated in the table. AD+1 refers to the first trading day after announcement. ED refers to the effective date. All changes become effective at the close on the effective date. Volume is the sixty-day average prior to announcement date. Size is the market capitalization as of the day before announcement. Abnormal return is calculated as raw return minus the S&P 500 return. Statistical significance is at better than 1 percent for returns marked with * and at better than 5 percent for returns marked with ⁺.

August 1976, when indexing was not considered important or popular. Until that time, no public announcements were made. The second period starts in September 1976, when Standard and Poor's began to formally announce the changes to interested investors, the media, and especially mutual fund managers. During this period, changes were announced after market close on Wednesdays, and the change in the index became effective the next morning upon opening. Since index fund managers are concerned with minimizing tracking error (the difference between the fund return and the S&P 500 return), index funds must buy the stock at the time of its addition to the index. However, with the growth in indexing, the buy orders from index funds at the market open increased order imbalances and volatility. To ease order imbalances, Standard and Poor's began preannouncing the changes on October 1, 1989. Thus, the third period covers changes to the S&P 500 from October 1989 to the present. Returns for both additions and deletions are reported after adjusting for the market return as measured by the total return to the S&P 500 index.

ADDITIONS

It is interesting to contrast the three periods. During the 1962–76 period (Table 8.1), when no public announcements were made, nothing abnormal happens to the stock price either on the first trading day after announcement or anytime after that. It is basically a non-event. During the 1976–89 period, when the stocks were added immediately after announcement, all the action is on the announcement date and nothing thereafter. The price goes up abnormally by 3 percent immediately after announcement but tracks the S&P 500 index's return for the next twenty trading days (about one calendar month) and for the next sixty trading days (about three calendar months). There is a lot of action in the 1989–2000 period. Overall, the return following the announcement date is an abnormal 5.3 percent, which climbs to 8.4 percent by the effective date and then falls back to the announcement date return twenty trading days later. It seems that there is a pop around the effective date that disappears later on.

DELETIONS

Since the number of firms is kept constant at five hundred, there must be one deletion for every addition. However, the sample of deletions considered in Table 8.2 is much smaller. Deletions that occurred due to a bankruptcy, merger, or other major corporate events are excluded from the table. Only deletions that are made voluntarily by Standard and Poor's and where the firm continues to exist are included.

Consider the three periods once again. For the 1962–76 period, when no public announcements were made, nothing abnormal happens around the announcement. During the 1976–89 period, again no significant abnormal change in price occurs around the announcement, and the magnitude of the change is also small. The abnormal return after announcement for the first and second periods are of opposite signs: the price rises abnormally in the first period but falls abnormally in the second period. Overall, for the first two periods, it is reasonable to conclude that the deletions have no impact on price.

As with additions, there is much action in the period after 1989. Deleted firms fall 5.4 percent on the day of announcement, fall another 4.9 percent by the effective date for a total loss of 10.3 percent, rebound back to a net loss of 3.3 percent twenty days later, and finally post a gain of 2.6 percent sixty days after the effective date. It can be seen that the net effect on stock price of deletions is zero. Although the year-by-year results from 1990 to 2000 vary widely, there is a common theme. The announcement date return is negative, and the return by the effective date becomes even more negative. Thereafter, in most years, the total return is less negative twenty days later and much less negative or even positive sixty days later.

Explanations

There are five explanations for the price impact of index changes: imperfect substitutes, price pressure (temporary), certification, liquidity, and investor recognition. However, none of the explanations seems capable of fully explaining the price effects.

The common starting point for these explanations is market efficiency. If markets are informationally efficient, then the price of a stock should not change unless there is new information. This means that excess demand or excess supply unaccompanied by new information should not affect security prices. How can that happen? The idea is that financial assets are perfect substitutes for one another, and the market is huge. Any single supply or demand shock is small compared to the overall size of the market. And since financial assets are perfect substitutes, excess demand for a stock will be met by arbitrageurs. They will short-sell that stock, increasing its supply, and will buy another stock with equivalent risk-return characteristics. In such an event, any price change will be imperceptible. However, as reported in the previous section, there is a permanent price impact. If there is no new information associated with index changes, then the only reason for the price impact is that financial assets do not have perfect substitutes.

The assumption of no new information, however, is questionable. For example, the observed change in stock prices could occur due to a change in expected future cash flows for at least two reasons. First, inclusion in the S&P 500 might convey positive information about the longevity and prospects of that firm, resulting in an upward revision of expected future cash flows. This is called *certification*.

The price impact could also be consistent with perfect substitutability if a decrease in required return accompanies an index addition. This could happen for several reasons. First, there may be an *improvement in liquidity* because of higher trading volume or lower asymmetry of information among traders. Second, the improvement in liquidity may occur because of greater production of information, resulting in the reduction of variability of earnings and other relevant estimates. Improvement in liquidity means that the cost of transacting will fall, causing the price to increase.

The third reason proceeds from *investor recognition*. An increase in investor awareness, for example, can affect the stock price in several ways. First, the firm's operating performance may improve because of increased monitoring by investors and by enhanced access to capital markets. Second, the firm's liquidity may improve due to less information asymmetry as a result of greater production of information by investors and analysts.

IMPERFECT SUBSTITUTES

The imperfect-substitutes argument relies on the concurrent growth in indexing and the price impact of changes to the S&P 500. There is a permanent price increase for firms added to the S&P 500 index (see Table 8.1). There are two arguments to suggest that there is no new information. First, before the advent of indexing (between 1962 and 1976), there was no price change. If an index addition is accompanied by information, then the price change should have occurred during that period. Second, in selecting firms Standard and Poor's relies only on publicly available information, which implies that no new information is implicit in an index change. Price changes could also occur if there is a permanent improvement in liquidity. However, in general, there is little evidence of an improvement in liquidity. Thus, the only remaining explanation is that the price increase must be due to the demand shock created by indexers. Since stocks have imperfect substitutes, the stock added to the index increases in price. If stocks did have perfect substitutes, the arbitrageurs would have ensured a negligible price effect.

There are two pieces of evidence that do not support the imperfect-substitutes explanation. First, in the post-1976 period, there is no relation between the level of indexing and the price impact. If the imperfect-substitutes argument is worthy of support, then the greater the demand shock, the greater should be the price impact. That does not happen. Second, the imperfect-substitutes explanation should work for both additions and deletions. Table 8.2 shows that firms deleted from the index do not have a permanent price impact. This is also inconsistent with the imperfect-substitutes explanation. Thus, it would seem that the imperfect-substitutes explanation is not the answer.

PRICE PRESSURE

The price pressure argument also relies on imperfect substitutes except that the focus is on short-term price changes. Under this explanation, adding a new stock to the index generates extra demand for the stock. This extra demand generates an upward price pressure to persuade investors to sell the stock prematurely. The price pressure abates once the momentary demand is satisfied.

Tables 8.1 and 8.2 show that until 1989 there is virtually no price pressure and the initial price impact is never reversed. The price pressure becomes more of an issue in the period after 1989, when the preannouncement procedure becomes effective. As discussed in the previous section, activities of the arbitrageurs seem to contribute to the price pressure. Thus, the price pressure does not occur due to demand shocks but is artificially created by market participants *in anticipation* of price pressure.

LIQUIDITY

There is conflicting evidence on improvement in liquidity, irrespective of its cause. If adding a stock to the Standard and Poor's index increases trading, then the increase in liquidity would cause lower bid-ask spreads. The lower cost of trading must be reflected in a price increase around the announcement. On the other hand, the number of shares available for trading will fall because index funds generally buy and then hold the shares. The reduction in the shares available for trading may negatively impact liquidity. There are a few studies that find a permanent increase in liquidity, as determined by permanent increases in trading volume, and permanent decreases in quoted and effective spreads. Other studies, however, find only a temporary improvement that disappears quickly after the effective date.

CERTIFICATION

The certification explanation maintains that the addition of a stock to the S&P 500 index conveys new positive information about the stock. Though Standard and Poor's relies on publicly available information, S&P's analysis of that information suggests longevity and/or leadership in the firm's industry. One test of certification is whether additions or deletions to supplementary indexes, where the level of indexing is small or nonexistent, affect prices. Indeed, they do. Additions to supplementary indexes also experience a significant abnormal return.

However, what is not easily explained is why there were no price reactions to additions to the index prior to 1976. Moreover, in the case of deletions, there is no permanent price impact even in the most recent years. These observations are inconsistent with a role of certification in index changes.

INVESTOR RECOGNITION

Investor awareness of a firm through addition to the S&P 500 index can help the firm with monitoring and improved access to capital markets. Monitoring by investors may induce the firm to become more efficient, thereby improving operating performance. Greater access to capital markets following membership in the S&P 500 index may enable it to accept projects that it could not otherwise pursue. Financial institutions may be more willing to lend to indexed firms, leading to higher debt capacity and/or lower cost of debt. The additional capital will allow the company to grow at a rate higher than that prior to inclusion in the index.

For deletions, however, investors cannot become "unaware" of the stock, though they may attempt to reduce their holdings. The investor recognition explanation suggests an asymmetric effect: positive price impact for additions and a muted price impact for deletions. The results in Tables 8.1 and 8.2 are consistent with this prediction.

How does this explanation square with other evidence? Since no public announcements of index changes were made before 1976, investors could not become aware of the stock, and hence there was no price impact. Besides index changes, a similar argument works for neglected stocks. Whenever neglected stocks are prominently featured in the media, they tend to become more widely held, resulting in a price increase. This implies that investor awareness is an important consideration for pricing of securities.

SUMMING UP

There are at least five explanations for the price impact of index changes. Of these, the investor recognition explanation is the one most consistent with the evidence. However, it is popularly believed that the imperfect-substitutes explanation is the more appropriate one. Reliance on an incorrect explanation can make market participants misjudge price patterns, especially with regard to deletions.

Persistence

Index effect can be divided into two parts: permanent and temporary. The permanent index effect is not a mispricing and cannot be arbitraged. In the case of additions, there are both permanent and temporary effects. The permanent index effect is the abnormal return on the day following the announcement. The abnormal return between the announcement date and the effective date is a temporary effect that eventually disappears. The evidence in Table 8.1 also shows the transitory nature of the price increase for additions. Standard and Poor's own evidence corroborates the conclusions enumerated here. It states that "a stock being added to the index would rise about 8.5 percent between announcement and implementation dates. . . . The stock would also give back half or more of that gain over the next year."

In the case of deletions, however, there is no permanent index effect. All of the abnormal return is temporary, as can be seen from Table 8.2. Again, Standard and Poor's essentially reaches the same conclusion: "The average market decline across all the deletions since 1998, a total of 53, was 11.7 percent. On average, this decline was nearly fully reversed by the sixth trading day."

Why does the temporary index effect occur, and why does it persist? The primary reason for persistence is the focus on tracking error by index fund managers. Index fund managers are evaluated strictly on the size and volatility of the tracking error (difference between the fund's return and the S&P 500 return) and not on the direction of the tracking error. A manager of a large index fund (more than $1 billion) is not expected to have a tracking error of more than 0.03 percent in a year. If it is more than 0.10 percent, the manager is likely to be fired. Therefore, it is easy to see that the managers are constrained, and must buy (sell) the firm added to (deleted from) the index on the effective date at the close.

Arbitrageurs know this. So they buy the stock added to the index before the effective date knowing that they will be able to unload the stock to the index fund managers at a higher price. The demand from the index fund managers is sufficient to absorb the entire supply of the arbitrageurs.

The situation is even more exciting in the case of deletions. Believing the imperfect-substitutes explanation, arbitrageurs force down the price of stocks deleted from the index on the first trading day after announcement by short selling. The price continues to fall until the effective date, when the arbitrageurs repurchase the deleted stocks from index fund managers. The price of the deleted stocks recovers soon thereafter.

There are two factors that cause the temporary index effect. If either of them changes, the temporary index effect will disappear. First, the preannouncements by Standard and Poor's allow the arbitrageurs to play this game. If the change in the index takes place immediately, the arbitrageurs will not be able to time their trades to the detriment of index fund managers. The second reason is the way owners of index funds evaluate the index fund managers. The performance of an index fund manager is measured by the tracking error, which forces the managers to trade exactly at the time that changes to the index are implemented. If the managers were free to trade the stocks deleted from or added to the index within a reasonable period around the effective date, they will not be forced to play into the hands of the arbitrageurs, and the investors will actually gain from this limited freedom given to the managers.

Trading Around the Effective Date

This section expands on the evidence presented above suggesting that a temporary price effect around the effective date is available for trading. Data for the year 2001 are selected for analysis for two reasons. First, they bring the evidence in prior sections more up to date. Second, observers have commented that 2001 was not a profitable year for arbitrageurs engaged in taking advantage of known price patterns around index changes. For example, Lehman Brothers' comment in the March 4, 2002, issue of *Outlook* is illustrative: "[W]e find that not only have stocks underperformed the index during their index inclusion period [announcement to effective date]

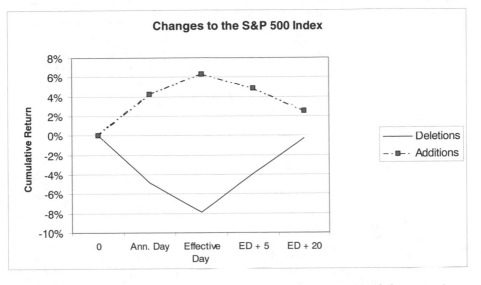

Figure 8.1   The cumulative return from the day of announcement of change to the effective date and until twenty days after the effective date is shown for additions and deletions from the S&P 500 index during 2001.

but they also underperformed the index post-inclusion date." There are two possible explanations for the weak index effect: either the negative market trend throughout the year attracted significantly more arbitrage funds or the shorter period between the announcement and effective date limited the ability of arbitrageurs to time index changes.

RETURN PATTERNS BEFORE AND AFTER EFFECTIVE DATE

Tables 8.3 and 8.4 contain the list of additions and deletions during 2001. Index changes along with the announcement date and the effective date are obtained from Standard and Poor's website. Standard and Poor's makes the announcement around 5:15 P.M. on the announcement date, and the change becomes effective at the close of trading on the effective date. A list of effective dates is available under "Index Changes," and announcements related to those changes are available under "News" on the S&P website (www.spglobal.com). The announcement states the reason for the change if the change is involuntary. Involuntary changes to the index are excluded from further consideration and the reasons for exclusion are recorded in Tables 8.3 and 8.4. In addition, if a major corporate event occurs in the week prior to the change announcement or if an earnings release is scheduled to occur anytime between the announcement date and the effective date, then that firm is also excluded from consideration.

Table 8.3   Additions to the S&P 500 Index During 2001

	Name	Ticker Symbol	Reason for Exclusion, if Any	Size Prior to Announcement (in $millions)	Daily Volume as a % of Shares Outstanding
1	Waters	WAT		5,000	0.46
2	Jones Apparel	JNY		4250	0.94
3	Genzyme	GENZ		12,200	1.02
4	Equity Residential	EQR		7,500	0.24
5	Nvidia	NVDA		7,425	3.24
6	Health Management	HMA		4,800	0.50
7	TECO Energy	TE		3,825	0.27
8	Equity Office	EOP		13,100	0.30
9	Immunex	IMNX		9,600	0.58
10	XL Capital	XL		9,750	0.40
11	International Game Tech	IGT		3,900	1.41
12	CIENA	CIEN		5,700	2.77
13	Amerisource	ABC	merged firm		
14	Zimmer Holdings	ZMH	spin-off		
15	Family Dollar Stores	FDO		4,950	0.47
16	PMC Sierra	PMCS		5,000	2.37
17	AT&T Wireless	AWE	spin-off		
18	Rockwell Collins	COL	spin-off		
19	John Hancock	JHF		12,000	0.26
20	Zions Bancorp	ZION		5,200	0.25
21	TMP Worldwide	TMPW		5,900	1.08
22	Pepsi Bottling	PBG		6,000	0.34
23	Mirant	MIR	spin-off		
24	Concord EFS	CEFT	earnings news		
25	Fiserv	FISV		5,880	0.40
26	Cintas	CTAS	earnings news		
27	Citizens Communications	CZN		3,550	0.15
28	Univision Communications	UVN		5,400	0.85
29	Jabil Circuit	JBL		4,375	2.60
30	Noble Drilling	NE		5,500	1.45
	Total (23)				

All announcements are made after market close on the announcement date indicated in the table. All changes become effective at the close on the effective date. Volume is the sixty-day average prior to announcement date. Size is the market capitalization as of the day before announcement. Abnormal return is calculated as raw return minus the S&P 500 return. Volume turnover is reported as volume divided by the number of shares outstanding. Since Nasdaq's reported volume is approximately two times the true volume, Nasdaq's volume is divided by two.

Announce-ment Date (AD)	Effective Date (ED)	Number of trading days between AD and ED	Abnormal Return on AD+1 (%)	Abnormal Return from AD+2 to ED (%)	Abnormal Return from ED+1 to ED+5 (%)	Abnormal Return from ED+1 to ED+20 (%)
12/27/2001	12/31/2001	2	1.7	−2.0	−3.4	−6.6
12/10/2001	12/14/2001	4	2.1	−0.3	−2.8	−2.9
12/12/2001	12/13/2001	1	2.0			
11/27/2001	11/30/2001	3	4.1	0.3	−0.8	−1.7
11/28/2001	11/29/2001	1	3.3			
11/1/2001	11/6/2001	3	2.3	−5.6	−1.6	−8.0
10/4/2001	10/9/2001	3	3.4	−2.9	−4.2	−6.5
10/3/2001	10/9/2001	4	0.6	−0.7	−5.5	−11.0
9/17/2001	9/20/2001	3	6.1	10.9	−2.6	12.4
8/27/2001	8/31/2001	4	3.7	6.5	2.4	9.6
8/29/2001	8/31/2001	2	3.9	−1.0	−0.6	−8.7
8/22/2001	8/29/2001	5	2.3	5.3	−18.4	−28.6
8/27/2001	8/29/2001					
7/31/2001	8/6/2001					
7/30/2001	8/3/2001	4	3.4	−5.9	5.4	12.8
8/1/2001	8/2/2001	1	10.2			
6/27/2001	7/6/2001					
6/25/2001	6/29/2001					
5/30/2001	6/27/2001	20	1.8	4.5	1.9	−0.7
6/19/2001	6/22/2001	3	3.1	−2.0	2.6	4.0
5/22/2001	6/1/2001	7	5.3	3.2	2.5	1.7
5/7/2001	5/11/2001	4	5.4	1.9	−2.2	−3.3
3/27/2001	4/2/2001					
3/26/2001	3/30/2001					
3/27/2001	3/30/2001	3	2.4	−9.1	9.9	15.9
2/27/2001	2/28/2001					
2/21/2001	2/26/2001	3	10.7	4.7	−1.0	−6.2
2/5/2001	2/6/2001	1	7.0			
12/27/2000	1/29/2001	21	12.4	37.4	−4.2	−33.9
12/19/2000	1/12/2001	16	2.7	−3.1	−1.1	16.2
			4.3	2.2	−1.2	−2.4

Table 8.4 Deletions from the S&P 500 Index During 2001

	Name	Ticker Symbol	Reason for Exclusion, if Any	Size Prior to Announcement (in $millions)	Daily Volume as a % of Shares Outstanding
1	FMC	FMC	spin-off		
2	Homestake Mining	HM	merger		
3	Ralston Purina	RAL	merger		
4	National Service	NSI	spin-off		
5	Enron	ENE	bankruptcy		
6	GPU	GPU	merger		
7	Global Crossing	GX	news		
8	Texaco	TX	merger		
9	Tosco	TOS	merger		
10	Wachovia	WB	merger		
11	Broadvision	BVSN	low price < $5		
12	American General	AGC	merger		
13	Oneok	OKE		1000	0.32
14	Timken	TKR		1000	0.18
15	Cabletron Systems	CS	spin-off		
16	Quaker Oats	OAT	merger		
17	Potlatch	PCH		1000	0.45
18	Long Drug Stores	LDG		900	0.46
19	Harcourt General	H	merger		
20	Alza	AZA	merger		
21	CIT Group	CIT	merger		
22	Adaptec	ADPT	spin-off		
23	Briggs& Stratton	BGG		900	7.4
24	Ceridian	CEN	spin-off		
25	Old Kent Financial	OK	merger		
26	Summit Bancorp	SUB	merger		
27	U.S. Bancorp	USB	merger		
28	Union Carbide	UK	merger		
29	Coastal	CGP	merger		
30	Time Warner	TWX	merger		
	Deletions (5)				

All announcements are made after market close on the announcement date indicated in the table. All changes become effective at the close on the effective date. Volume is the sixty-day average prior to announcement date. Size is the market capitalization as of the day before announcement. Abnormal return is calculated as raw return minus the S&P 500 return. Volume turnover is reported as volume divided by the number of shares outstanding. Since Nasdaq's reported volume is approximately two times the true volume, Nasdaq's volume is divided by two.

Announce-ment Date (AD)	Effective Date (ED)	Number of trading days between AD and ED	Abnormal Return on AD+1 (%)	Abnormal Return from AD+2 to ED (%)	Abnormal Return from ED+1 to ED+5 (%)	Abnormal Return from ED+1 to ED+20 (%)
12/27/2001	12/31/2001					
12/10/2001	12/14/2001					
12/12/2001	12/12/2001					
11/27/2001	11/30/2001					
11/28/2001	11/29/2001					
11/1/2001	11/6/2001					
10/4/2001	10/9/2001					
10/3/2001	10/9/2001					
9/17/2001	9/17/2001					
8/27/2001	8/31/2001					
8/29/2001	8/31/2001					
8/22/2001	8/29/2001					
8/27/2001	8/29/2001	2	−3.3	3.6	1.4	9.2
7/31/2001	8/6/2001	4	−7.5	−3.6	5.4	13.2
7/30/2001	8/3/2001					
8/1/2001	8/2/2001					
6/27/2001	7/6/2001	6	−5.1	−5.2	3.8	8.0
6/25/2001	6/29/2001	4	−5.4	−4.7	1.4	4.5
5/30/2001	6/27/2001					
6/19/2001	6/22/2001					
5/22/2001	6/1/2001					
5/7/2001	5/11/2001					
3/27/2001	4/2/2001	4	−2.7	−4.8	7.9	1.9
3/26/2001	3/30/2001					
3/27/2001	3/30/2001					
2/27/2001	2/28/2001					
2/21/2001	2/26/2001					
2/5/2001	2/6/2001					
12/27/2000	1/29/2001					
12/29/2000	1/12/2001					
			−4.8	−2.9	4.0	7.4

After screening based on the above criteria, twenty-three additions and five deletions remain out of the total sample of thirty additions and thirty deletions in 2001. Consider the additions in Table 8.3. Nearly all of the additions are firms with at least $4 billion in market capitalization. More importantly, in all but four cases, the waiting time is one week or less. Four cases had longer waiting times because of the uncertain completion of mergers. It seems that Standard and Poor's has deliberately reduced the waiting period for the change to become effective, possibly to curb arbitrage activity.

From Table 8.3, it can be seen that the average return on the first trading day after announcement of an addition is 4.3 percent. In addition, added firms earn an additional 2.2 percent thereafter through the effective date. After the effective date, the added firms lose 1.2 percent in the next five business days and lose a total of 2.4 percent in the twenty business days after the effective date.

It is instructive to compare and contrast the evidence for 2001 with the evidence given earlier. Prior evidence implies two trading strategies for additions. Both strategies are based on the price increase around the effective date. The first strategy calls for buying the added firm immediately upon announcement and selling it on the effective date. The second strategy requires short-selling the added firm on the effective date and repurchasing it several days later. Implementation of both strategies in 2001 is much weaker.

Five deletions remain, as shown in Table 8.4. The price pattern for deletions is much cleaner and stronger than for additions. The announcement return is –4.8 percent, which is followed by an additional –2.9 percent until the effective date. The loss in value is almost completely recouped in the twenty business days following the effective date. Thus, the strategies relating to deletions were as profitable in 2001 as in earlier years. Perhaps arbitrageurs don't fully understand price movements around deletions and are therefore unable to exploit them.

TEMPORARY PRICE EFFECT UNTIL THE EFFECTIVE DATE

Tables 8.1 and 8.2 reveal that the price of stocks added to the index increases until the effective date and the price of stocks deleted from the index decreases until the effective date. Why does this happen? The consensus is that arbitrageurs have started playing the "S&P game" with the preannouncements, as explained in the section titled "Persistence." With additions, arbitrageurs or market participants know that the index fund managers must buy the stock at the close of the effective date. Therefore, the arbitrageurs buy the stock before the effective date in the hope of unloading it to the index fund managers at a higher price on the effective date. For deletions, it is exactly the opposite.

A question that arises is why index fund managers don't buy immediately upon announcement instead of waiting till the effective date. The index fund managers must wait because their objective is *not* to beat the index but to minimize tracking error. To minimize tracking error, they must buy the added stock at the time and at the price that Standard and Poor's adds it to the index, neither before nor after. Since Standard and Poor's makes the change at the close on the effective date, index fund managers have no choice but to wait.

The most important determinant of the temporary price effect— that is, the change in price from announcement to the effective date— is the number of days in that period. If the change becomes effective the next trading day, then trading becomes almost impossible and arbitrageurs do not attempt to artificially affect the price. As the period lengthens, the potential for arbitrage activity increases. A span of at least three days between announcement and effective date is required for implementing any trading strategy.

The Trading Process

All trading strategies listed here are based on trading individual stocks. Exchange-traded funds, mutual funds, and futures cannot be employed because they contain a basket of stocks, whereas the strategy calls for a specific stock. Stock options are a possibility for trading on the temporary index effect and should be explored as an alternative. However, since the trading costs of options are usually high, they are not considered here.

ADDITIONS

The starting point for additions is the announcement of index changes by Standard and Poor's, usually between 5:00 P.M. and 6:00 P.M. Major news services will carry the press release. It is also possible to get the news from Standard and Poor's website. Once an addition is identified, follow these steps. There are two trading strategies that can be executed. One is from the announcement date to the effective date, and the other is from the effective date until about twenty trading days later.

Primary Strategy for Additions

Step 1: Almost all additions to the index are candidates for trading. Stocks added to the index are usually actively traded and have low bid-ask spreads, making the trading costs relatively low. The primary source of gains for additions is price patterns around the effective date (see "Trading Around the Effective Date"). If the effective date for the addition is one or two business days after the announcement, then those additions must be excluded because such additions are unlikely to garner a significantly large temporary price effect.

Step 2: Avoid stocks with scheduled announcements, such as earnings announcements, up to the effective date. These announcements will add unnecessary volatility. Moreover, the added firm should not be a new firm created from an existing firm, like a spin-off or a merger. The firm should be an existing firm not currently in the index.

Step 3: Place a market order to buy around the close of the first trading day following the announcement. The reason for waiting until the end of the day is to ensure that all the excess demand has been satisfied and the stock has settled to a stable price. The evidence presented for this strategy is based on the closing price. (To hedge against severe market movements and to reduce the risk of the trading strategy, consider short-selling the S&P 500 index [AMEX: SPY]. Also, see Appendix C.)

Step 4: Hold the stock till the effective date. Place a limit order at the market price to sell all shares held around 10:00 A.M. on the effective date. Remember the price tends to fall on the effective date. This concludes the first trading strategy. (If you hedged against market movements in the previous step, then undo the hedge by repurchasing the S&P 500 index.)

Secondary Strategy for Additions

Step 1: The second trading strategy requires short selling. Not all stocks may be candidates for this strategy. Two requirements must be satisfied. First, the stock must have a relatively narrow spread, not more than 0.5 percent in any case. Second, the temporary price effect must exceed 2–3 percent. Otherwise, it is not advisable to try to capture the post-effective date reversal.

Step 2: Assuming the reversal after the effective date is attractive, the ideal time to short-sell is in the morning on the day after the effective date. However, short selling at the close on the effective date will not be much worse, and the trading results are presented on this basis. After the short sell order is filled, place an open order to repurchase the stock at a price that reflects a drop in price equal to about one and a half times the expected reversal after the effective date. (Once again, to hedge against severe market movements and to reduce the risk of the trading strategy, consider purchasing the S&P 500 index.)

Step 3: If the open order does not get executed, then close the position twenty trading days later. (If you hedged against market movements in the previous step, then undo the hedge by selling the S&P 500 index.)

Deletions

The trading strategy for deletions from the index is similar to that of additions. However, there are some important differences, because the permanent price effect in the case of deletions is zero, unlike additions, where the permanent effect is positive. Moreover, for most investors who do not want to short-sell, the period between the announcement date and the effective date is attractive for additions, whereas the time after the effective date is most rewarding for deletions.

Deletions are identified from Standard and Poor's and the news media. Once a deletion is identified, follow these steps to ensure that the short-listed deletions consist of only those firms that have been voluntarily deleted from the index by Standard and Poor's and that do not have high trading costs. Two trading strategies exist for deletions. The primary source of gains for deletions is the reversal after the effective date. The main trading strategy is designed to capture that reversal. A secondary trading strategy requires short-selling the deleted stock on the announcement date to capture the downward price movement until the effective date.

The secondary strategy is described first because the period for this strategy (announcement date to effective date) occurs before the period for the primary strategy. If you are not interested in executing the secondary strategy, skip steps 5, 6, and 7 of that strategy. You still need to follow steps 1 through 4, which describe the selection of deletions for both strategies.

Secondary Strategy for Deletions

Step 1: Exclude any deletion that is related to a restructuring such as a merger, spin-off, or bankruptcy. Impending or likely bankruptcies should also be deleted. Look for and exclude deletions that have had any news related to a major structural change over the prior one month. This screen usually eliminates 75 percent of the deletions.

Step 2: Stocks with scheduled announcements within two weeks after the effective date should be avoided. Scheduled announcements by the firm, such as earnings announcements, add unnecessary volatility.

Step 3: The average daily trading volume should exceed one hundred thousand shares a day, so that it is easy to trade without affecting the price. The bid-ask spread should be less than 0.5 percent. Again, the intent is not to lose a significant portion of the profits to trading costs.

Step 4: Exclude any stocks that are below the $5 level. Some low-price stocks might perform as expected, but one must be particularly careful.

Step 5: The secondary strategy is based on short-selling the deleted firm after the announcement in anticipation of a further fall in price. Place an order to short-sell at close on the day following the announcement date. (To hedge against severe market movements and to reduce the risk of the trading strategy, consider purchasing the S&P 500 index.)

Step 6: If the order gets filled, then place an order to repurchase the stock around 10 percent below the price at which the order is filled.

Step 7: If the open buy order does not get executed, then buy to close the position as late as possible on the effective date. (If you hedged against market movements in step 5, then undo the hedge by selling the S&P 500 index.)

Primary Strategy for Deletions

Step 1: The primary trading strategy attempts to capture the rise in price of the deleted firm after the effective date. All deletions selected for the secondary strategy are not automatically candidates for this strategy. Since the average permanent price effect is zero for the deletions, the rise in the deleted firm's stock price, on average, will be equal to the fall in its price with the effective date. In order to cover transaction costs and still have a reasonable profit, the abnormal return until the effective date should be more negative than –2 percent.

Step 2: For the selected stocks, place an order to buy as close as possible to the close of trading on the effective date. The morning of the day following the effective date is preferred. Simultaneously, place a limit order to sell that reflects an appreciation equivalent to one and a half times the temporary price effect. Continue to adjust the limit price by changes in the S&P 500 index return. (Once again, to hedge against severe market movements and to reduce the risk of the trading strategy, consider short-selling the S&P 500 index.)

Step 3: If the open sell order does not get executed, then close the position twenty trading days later. (If you hedged against market movements in the previous step, then undo the hedge by repurchasing the S&P 500 index.)

Strategy Implementation

In this section, the index effect is implemented for the January-July 2002 period. The month of July 2002 is included because it provides nine new firms that were added by Standard and Poor's, including the replacement of all foreign firms from the index. The results are in Tables 8.5 and 8.6.

ADDITIONS: BUY ON ANNOUNCEMENT DATE AND HOLD UNTIL EFFECTIVE DATE

Based on the criteria established earlier, the following firms are bought at the close of trading on the day after the announcement: UPS, GS, PRU, EBAY, PFG, ERTS, SPG, MI, and RATL.

The remaining additions are excluded because the difference between the announcement and the effective date is not more than two trading days. All nine stocks bought upon announcement are sold at the 10 A.M. price on the effective date. For ease of computation, however, all sales are assumed to take place at the close on the effective date.

The mean number of days for which a position is held is 6.7 days, and the mean abnormal return during this period is 6.6 percent. Assuming a round-trip trading cost of 0.5 percent, the net return is 6.1 percent, which is equivalent to an annualized abnormal return of over 200 percent.

ADDITIONS: SHORT-SELL ON EFFECTIVE DATE AND HOLD FOR UP TO TWENTY DAYS

Of the firms selected in the previous subsection, ERTS, SPG, and RATL are dropped because the temporary price effect is less than +2 percent. The remaining stocks will be short-sold at the close on the effective date: UPS, GS, PRU, EBAY, PFG, and MI.

Assuming all of them are successfully short-sold, an open order to repurchase these shares is placed at a price equal to one and a half times the temporary price effect. Since the temporary price effect is

Table 8.5   Additions to the S&P 500 Index During January-July 2002

	Name	Ticker Symbol	Reason for Exclusion, if Any	Size Prior to Announce- ment	Announce- ment Date (AD)
1.	Anthem	ATH		8300	7/23/2002
2.	United Parcel Service	UPS*		68150	7/9/2002
3.	Goldman Sachs	GS*		35400	7/9/2002
4.	Prudential Financial	PRU*		18000	7/9/2002
5.	eBay	EBAY*		15850	7/9/2002
6.	Principal Financial	PFG*		10000	7/9/2002
7.	Electronic Arts	ERTS*		9200	7/9/2002
8.	SunGard Data	SDS	earnings announcement	6500	7/9/2002
9.	North Fork Bancorp	NFB		6250	7/12/2002
10.	Simon Property Group	SPG*		6,150	6/20/2002
11.	Apollo Group	APOL		6,350	5/13/2002
12.	BJ Services	BJS		6,000	5/13/2002
13.	American Standard	ASD		5,500	5/9/2002
14.	First Tennessee National	FTN		4,850	5/2/2002
15.	Marshall & Ilsley	MI*		6,200	2/5/2002
16.	Rational Software	RATL*		4,500	1/23/2002
17.	ACE	ACE	earnings announcement	9,150	1/23/2002
18.	MeadWestvaco	MWV	merged firm		1/23/2002
19.	Plum Creek Timber	PCL		5,300	1/15/2002
	Total (9)				

All announcements are made after market close on the announcement date indicated in the table. All changes become effective at the close on the effective date. Size is the market capitalization as of the day before announcement. Abnormal return is calculated as raw return minus the S&P 500 return.
*Selected additions.

Effective Date (ED)	Number of Days Between AD and ED	First-Day Abnormal Return (AD+1) (%)	Abnormal Return (AD+2 to ED) (%)	Abnormal Return (ED+1 to ED+5) (%)	Abnormal Return (ED+1 to ED+20) (%)
7/24/2002	1	3.4			
7/19/2002	8	7.5	13.8	−6.7	−11.1
7/19/2002	8	4.3	15.5	−10.2	−6.4
7/19/2002	8	4.3	14.0	−7.4	−11.1
7/19/2002	8	6.5	9.1	−8.3	−10.7
7/19/2002	8	8.4	6.5	−7.6	−6.3
7/19/2002	8	3.6	0.8	2.5	1.1
7/19/2002					
7/16/2002	2	0.3			
6/25/2002	3	3.3	1.9	3.3	0.0
5/14/2002	1	0.4			
5/14/2002	1	−1.4			
5/10/2002	1	2.2			
5/3/2002	1	2.2			
2/8/2002	3	2.3	0.5	0.9	−2.1
1/31/2002	6	4.8	−2.5	−11.2	−16.0
1/29/2002					
1/29/2002					
1/16/2002	1	5.9			
		3.6	6.6	−5.0	−7.0

Table 8.6   Deletions from the S&P 500 Index During January–July 2002

Name	Ticker Symbol	Reason for Exclusion, if Any	Size Prior to Announce-ment	Announce-ment Date (AD)
1. Conseco	CNC		509	7/23/2002
2. Royal Dutch Petroleum	RD	foreign firm	116,600	7/9/2002
3. Unilever NV	UN	foreign firm	37,628	7/9/2002
4. Alcan	AL	foreign firm	11,605	7/9/2002
5. Nortel Networks	NT	foreign firm	6,140	7/9/2002
6. Barrick Gold	ABX	foreign firm	9,900	7/9/2002
7. Placer Dome	PDG	foreign firm	3,600	7/9/2002
8. Inco Ltd.	N	foreign firm	4,065	7/9/2002
9. Immunex	IMNX	merger		7/12/2002
10. Conexant Systems	CNXT	spin-off		6/20/2002
11. WorldCom	WCOM	bankruptcy		5/13/2002
12. USAirways	U	bankruptcy		5/13/2002
13. Sapient	SAPE		225	5/9/2002
14. Compaq	CPQ	merger		5/2/2002
15. Williamette Industries	WLL	merger		2/5/2002
16. Niagara Mohawk	NMK	merger		1/23/2002
17. Westvaco	W	merger		1/23/2002
18. Mead	MEA	merger		1/23/2002
19. Kmart	KM	bankruptcy		1/15/2002
Total (0)				

All announcements are made after market close on the announcement date indicated in the table. All changes become effective at the close on the effective date. Size is the market capitalization as of the day before announcement. Abnormal return is calculated as raw return minus the S&P 500 return.

Effective Date (ED)	Number of Days Between AD and ED	First-Day Abnormal Return Return (%)	Abnormal Return (AD+2 to ED)	Abnormal Return (ED+1 to ED+5)	Abnormal Return (ED+1 to ED+20)
7/24/2002	1	−34.0			
7/19/2002					
7/19/2002					
7/19/2002					
7/19/2002					
7/19/2002					
7/19/2002					
7/19/2002					
7/16/2002					
6/25/2002					
5/14/2002					
5/14/2002					
5/10/2002	1	−11.5			
5/3/2002					
2/8/2002					
1/31/2002					
1/29/2002					
1/29/2002					
1/16/2002					
	1	−22.8			

an abnormal return, the limit price is adjusted at the end of each day to reflect the movement in the S&P 500. The results are given below:

Stock	Price Effect to be Captured (%)	Date Bought Back (days)	Abnormal Return (to a short position) (%)
UPS	20.7	Aug. 16, 2002 (20 days)	10.9
GS	22.5	Aug. 16, 2002 (20 days)	6.3
PRU	21.0	Aug. 16, 2002 (20 days)	11.0
EBAY	7.1	Jul. 31, 2002 (8 days)	7.1
PFG	9.8	Aug. 6, 2002 (12 days)	9.8
MI	3.9	Mar. 6, 2002 (17 days)	3.9

The total abnormal return from short-selling the added stocks is 8.2 percent over an average holding period of 16 days. Considering transaction costs of 0.75 percent, slightly higher for short selling, the net return is 7.5 percent. The annualized abnormal return is over 100 percent.

DELETIONS: SHORT-SELL ON ANNOUNCEMENT DATE
AND BUY BACK ON EFFECTIVE DATE

Unfortunately, there are no deletions that satisfy the criteria mentioned above. Only two firms are voluntarily deleted by Standard and Poor's: Conseco and Sapient.[4] Both of them are low-price stocks. Low-price stocks are especially risky because they could be delisted from the exchanges, which is devastating for a stock; they could reflect continuing problems with company's business or other factors. For example, after being booted out of the S&P 500 on July 24, 2002, Conseco defaulted on debt payments and filed for bankruptcy on August 8, 2002. On the other hand, Sapient gained 15.3 percent in the week following exclusion from the index.

DELETIONS: BUY ON EFFECTIVE DATE AND
HOLD FOR UP TO TWENTY DAYS

Again, the sample of deletions is zero. The data in Tables 8.2 and 8.4 suggest that this strategy would have been profitable had qualifying deletions been available.

Overall, the primary strategy for additions generated a return of 6.6 percent over 6.2 days; the secondary strategy for additions generated a return of 7.5 percent over 16 days. Both these strategies were very successful. Unfortunately, no deletions met the criteria for selection.

Qualifications

The evidence presented in this chapter and the trading strategy recommendations rely on past data. Since future market conditions and market patterns may change without notice, it is possible that trading on S&P 500 index changes will cease to be profitable. Furthermore, the analysis is based on abnormal returns, not raw returns, which means that if the market is falling, investors may lose money even though abnormal returns are positive.

In addition, the risk related to trading with index changes is not explicitly considered. The risk can be reduced by hedging with the S&P 500 index, and the results provided are actually based on the assumption of hedging. The hedging will require short-selling the S&P 500 index whenever a long position in the additions or deletions is taken, and buying the S&P 500 index whenever a short position in the additions or deletions is taken.

Key Points

- Firms are periodically deleted from the S&P 500 index because of major restructuring or because they no longer represent the U.S. economy. Each deletion is accompanied by an addition to keep the number of firms in the S&P 500 constant at 500. There are certain guidelines for changes made by Standard and Poor's. However, the process is largely subjective and unpredictable.

- Changes to the index are announced after the market closes and become effective either on the next day or several days later. Each change in the index is associated with a price effect called the index effect. The index effect is usually positive for additions and negative for deletions.

- The index effect has two components: temporary and permanent. The temporary component of the index effect is concentrated around the effective date. While additions have both a temporary and permanent effect, deletions have only a temporary effect. That is, firms deleted from the index usually regain their value.

- The index effect persists because index fund managers are intent on minimizing the tracking error (difference between the fund return and the S&P 500 index return). Therefore, they must buy added stocks and sell deleted stocks as close to the close on the effective date as possible, irrespective of whether they are paying more or receiving less. Other market participants know this and can trade to take advantage of the index funds.

- While the temporary effect occurs around the effective date and can be captured by arbitrageurs, the permanent effect occurs only for additions and cannot be captured through arbitrage.

- The four possible trading strategies (two each for deletions and additions) consist of two short sales and two purchases. For additions, an investor would buy the added stock after the announcement and sell on the effective date. Second, the investor would short-sell the added firm after it has been added and repurchase it up to twenty days later. For deletions, the first strategy is to short-sell immediately after the announcement and cover on the effective date. The second strategy is to buy after the stock has been deleted from the index and sell up to twenty days later.

- The trading strategies are tested with index changes that occurred between January 2002 and July 2002. Both trading strategies for additions are successful, generating 6.1 percent over 6.2 days and 7.5 percent over 16 days after costs. No deletions qualify for a trading strategy during this period.

Bottom Line

Changes to the S&P 500 index are not predictable. However, there is a pattern in prices after the changes to the index are announced. It is possible to capture the temporary index effect for both additions and deletions. The anticipated annualized abnormal return is between 15 percent and 25 percent.

Internet References

Information About Index Changes
http://www.spglobal.com: Standard and Poor's issues a press release and posts it on its website. In addition, all major news services carry the news.

SEC Filings for Accessing Annual Reports

http://www.secinfo.com: There are many sources for SEC filings. This is among the best. Go to Item 5 in the annual report to get the number of registered shareholders.

http://www.sec.gov/edgar/searchedgar/companysearch.html: This SEC site has all of the filings. But it is sometimes difficult to navigate.

http://www.freeedgar.com: This site collates information from the SEC's EDGAR database and makes it available in a more accessible format. The information is limited but free.

http://www.edgar-online.com: This site is good but is only accessible by paying users. To bypass the authorization, enter through http://finance.yahoo.com by clicking on SEC filings under the quotation for a stock.

Sources for Intraday Stock Data

Companies and brokerage firms that provide real time quotes also allow access to capture time and sales data for selected stocks. However, it is usually not possible to get historical tick by tick data. Historical data are available from the following sources.

http://www.tickdata.com: Tickdata has data for several hundred large companies for the past few years. In addition, they also sell futures price data. Their software is very useful for those uninitiated in handling large data sets and statistical packages. However, they are very expensive, and their customer service is not good.

http://www.nysedata.com: Look under Data Products, Stock Prices, and then Historical. The New York Stock Exchange's Trade and Quote database (TAQ) provides tick-by-tick data for all stocks (NYSE, AMEX, and Nasdaq) on CD from 1993. The cost is $1,000 per month for all stocks, but discounts for historical data can reduce the cost to $200 per month.

http://www.interquote.com: A data service provider. However, the investor is responsible for downloading, storing, and analyzing the data.

References for Further Reading

Arbel, Avner. 1985. Generic Stocks: The Key to Market Anomalies. *Journal of Portfolio Management* 11(4), 4–13.

Arbel, Avner, and Paul Strebel. 1982. The Neglected and Small Firm Effects. *Financial Review* 17(4), 201–18.

Beneish, Messod D., and Robert E. Whaley. 1996. An Anatomy of the "S&P 500 Game": The Effects of Changing the Rules. *Journal of Finance* 51(5), 1909–30.

———. 2002. S&P 500 Index Replacements: A New Game in Town. *The Journal of Portfolio Management*, fall, 51–60.

Blouin, Jennifer, Jana Raedy, and Douglas Shackelford. 2000. The Impact of Capital Gains Taxes on Stock Price Reactions to S&P 500 Inclusion. NBER working paper #8011.

Blume, Marshall, and Roger Edelen. 2003. On S&P 500 Index Replication Strategies. Working paper, Department of Finance, Wharton School, University of Pennsylvania.

Bos, Roger. 2000. Quantifying the Effect of Being Added to an S&P Index. Standard and Poor's report, September.

Chan, Louis K. C., Narasimhan Jegadeesh, and Josef Lakonishok. 1995. Evaluating the Performance of Value Versus Glamour Stocks: The Impact of Selection Bias. *Journal of Financial Economics* 38(3), 269–96.

Chen, Honghui, Greg Noronha, and Vijay Singal. 2004. The Price Response to S&P 500 Index Additions and Deletions: Evidence of Asymmetry and a New Explanation. Forthcoming in the *Journal of Finance*.

Chordia, Tarun. 2001. Liquidity and Returns: The Impact of Inclusion into the S&P 500 Index. Working paper, Department of Finance, Emory University.

Coval, Joshua D., and Tobias J. Moskowitz. 1999. Home Bias at Home: Local Equity Preference in Domestic Portfolios. *Journal of Finance* 54(6), 2045–73.

Dash, Srikant. 2002. Price Changes Associated with S&P 500 Deletions. Standard and Poor's report, July.

Denis, Diane, John McConnell, Alexei Ovtchinnikov, and Yun Yu. 2003. S&P 500 Index Additions and Earnings Expectations. *Journal of Finance*, forthcoming.

Dhillon, Upinder, and Herb Johnson. 1991. Changes in the Standard and Poor's 500 List. *Journal of Business* 64(1), 75–86.

Elliott, William B., and Richard S. Warr. 2003. Price Pressure on the NYSE and NASDAQ: Evidence from S&P 500 Index Changes. *Financial Management*, forthcoming.

Goetzmann, William N., and Mark Garry. 1986. Does Delisting from the S&P 500 Affect Stock Price? *Financial Analyst Journal* 42(2), 64–69.

Gosnell, Thomas, and Timothy Krehbiel. 2000. Market Liquidity and Changes in the Roster of the Standard and Poor's 500 Index. Working paper, Department of Finance, Oklahoma State University.

Harris, Lawrence, and Eitan Gurel. 1986. Price and Volume Effects Associated with Changes in the S&P 500: New Evidence for the Existence of Price Pressures. *Journal of Finance* 41(4), 815–30.

Hegde, Shantaram, and John McDermott. 2003. The Liquidity Effects of Revisions to the S&P 500 Index: An Empirical Analysis. *Journal of Financial Markets* 6(3): 413–59.

Jain, Prem C. 1987. The Effect on Stock Price of Inclusion in or Exclusion from the S&P 500. *Financial Analyst Journal* 43(1), 58–65.

Kaul, Aditya, Vikas Mehrotra, and Randall Morck. 2000. Demand Curves for Stocks Do Slope Down: New Evidence from an Index Weights Adjustment. *Journal of Finance* 55(2), 893–912.

Lynch, Anthony W., and Richard R. Mendenhall. 1997. New Evidence on Stock Price Effects Associated with Changes in the S&P 500 Index. *Journal of Business* 70(3), 351–83.

Merton, Robert C. 1987. Presidential Address: A Simple Model of Capital Market Equilibrium with Incomplete Information. *Journal of Finance* 42(3), 483–510.

Pruitt, Stephen W., and K. C. John Wei. 1989. Institutional Ownership and Changes in the S&P 500. *Journal of Finance* 44(2), 509–14.

Shleifer, Andrei. 1986. Do Demand Curves for Stocks Slope Down? *Journal of Finance* 41(3), 579–90.

Subrahmanyam, Avanidhar, and Sheridan Titman. 2001. Feedback from Stock Prices to Cash Flows. *Journal of Finance* 56(6), 2389–413.

Wurgler, Jeffrey, and Ekaterina Zhuravskaya. 2002. Does Arbitrage Flatten Demand Curves for Stocks. *Journal of Business* 75(4), 583–608.

Notes

1. This chapter is based on research by the author with Honghui Chen and Greg Noronha (2003) in "The Price Response to S&P 500 Index Additions and Deletions." Other work used in this chapter includes Arbel and Strebel (1982), Beneish and Whaley (1996, 2002), Blouin, Raedy, and Shackelford (2000), Blume and Edelen (2003), Chordia (2001), Coval and Moskowitz (1999), Denis et al. (2003), Dhillon and Johnson (1991), Elliott and Warr (2003), Goetzmann and Garry (1986), Gosnell and Krehbiel (2000), Harris and Gurel (1986), Hegde and McDermott (2003), Jain (1987), Kaul, Mehrotra, and Morck (2000), Lynch and Mendenhall (1997), Merton (1987), Pruitt and Wei (1989), Shleifer (1986), and Wurgler and Zhuravskaya (2002).
2. There are exceptions. Occasionally an involuntary deletion takes place before a suitable replacement is found.
3. The value of assets that track the S&P 500 index is about $1 trillion, and the total market value of all U.S. stocks is $12 trillion; dividing the second figure into the first gives a figure of about 8 percent.
4. Foreign firms are not considered because they operate in a different environment. Moreover, none of the evidence presented above includes deletion of any foreign companies.

9

Merger Arbitrage

When a merger is announced, the target's price should rise close to the bidder's offer for the target. However, in most cases it does not. Two reasons account for the difference. First, successful completion of the merger is not a certainty. Second, shareholders of the target firm must earn a positive return until consummation of the merger, which implies that the target's price must be less than the offered price. Based on past completion rates and completion periods, the difference in the bidder's offer and the actual target price after merger announcement is larger than what it should be.

Investors and arbitrageurs can earn annual abnormal returns of 4 to 10 percent by buying the target upon a cash merger announcement, and by buying the target and short-selling the bidder upon announcement of a stock merger. The profitability of merger arbitrage can be improved by carefully selecting mergers in which large arbitrageurs are unlikely to participate but which generate higher abnormal returns.

Description

Though merger arbitrage or risk arbitrage is used extensively by institutions and sophisticated investors, it is not frequently discussed in the media.[1] The first major public disclosure of merger arbitrage was made by Ivan Boesky in his 1985 book *Merger Mania—Arbitrage: Wall Street's Best Kept Money-Making Secret*, though a couple of stories had run in the popular press.[2] The purpose of merger arbitrage is to take advantage of a mispricing that might occur *after* the intended merger has been announced. This activity is perfectly legal. On the other hand, trading *before* merger announcement based on nonpublic information is illegal (see Chapter 7). Ivan Boesky, a well-known takeover speculator, became famous in the mid-1980s when he was charged by the Securities and Exchange Commission for insider trading related to mergers. Later, he was convicted and fined $100 million and sentenced to three years in jail.

THE MERGER PROCESS AND MERGER GAINS

A merger, also called a takeover or acquisition, occurs when one company buys another company. The steps in the merger process are initiation of merger discussions by one of the two parties, agreement to merge by the boards of the two companies, approval by any regulatory bodies pertinent to the merger, and approval by the stockholders of the two companies. Sometimes the boards of directors may not agree to a merger. In those cases, the acquiring company can commence a hostile tender offer (that is, directly approach the stockholders to tender their shares to the acquiring firm), bypassing the management of the company. Hostile bids were more common in the 1980s than in the 1970s or the 1990s. Hostile bids constituted about 8 percent of all bids during 1973–79, 14 percent during 1980–89, and 4 percent during 1990–98.

Firms merge because, in general, mergers create value by generating synergistic gains. Synergies may arise due to improvement in efficiency or enhancement of market power. The combined abnormal return to the target and acquirer around announcement is about 2 percent of the combined size. However, nearly all of the gain accrues to the target firm (about 16 percent of the target firm's size), whereas the acquiring firm gains nothing or loses due to the merger. Several explanations are offered for the poor performance of acquirers and why acquirers choose to merge in spite of negligible gains. These are discussed in the references listed for this chapter.

MODE OF PAYMENT IN MERGERS

The mode of payment (primarily cash or stock) for the target is important for merger arbitrage because it affects the division of gains between the target and the bidder and conveys information about the value of the bidder. During the 1990–98 period, 28 percent of the mergers were all-cash deals and 58 percent were all-stock deals. During the 1970s and 1980s, however, the fraction of cash deals was greater than that of stock deals. In terms of division of gains, bidders tend to lose about 2 percent when they pay for the merger in stock, whereas the announcement return to the bidder is near zero when bidders use cash to pay for the merger. Targets gain 13 percent with a stock deal and 20 percent with a cash deal. The difference in merger gains depending on the mode of payment has been explained by theoretical models based on differences in information available to investors and the management. One model suggests that the market assumes bidder equity is overpriced when bidders use stock to pay for an acquisition; a second model suggests risk sharing by target shareholders with a stock bid; a third one asserts that low-valued bidders pay for a merger using stock; yet another believes that a cash bid implies a higher valuation of the target than a stock bid.

Why do bidders pay stock or targets accept stock as a form of payment given the negative implications of a stock bid? Bidders like to pay with stock because as the value of the target firm to the bidder changes depending on market conditions, so does the price paid by the bidder in stock. If, on the other hand, the bidder makes a cash bid, then that amount doesn't change based on the bidder's ability to pay, or on whether the economy or the company's industry takes a downturn. Target shareholders are in a quandary. They prefer a stock payment because of tax implications but would like to receive cash because there is no uncertainty about the amount of money. As an example, consider the AOL–Time Warner merger, where AOL agreed to pay 1.5 shares of its stock for each share of Time Warner stock. AOL's price before announcement of the bid was $73 per share. With a 1.5 share ratio, Time Warner shareholders expect to receive $109.50 for each share. If AOL's stock price fell to $35, Time Warner shareholders would receive only $52.50, introducing uncertainty into the amount received by the target firm.

Collars are a recent innovation, a way of partially addressing both bidder and target concerns. When a collar is used, the bidding firm uses its stock to buy the target firm. However, the collar stipulates that if the bidder's stock drops (rises) to a certain level, then the number of shares that the bidding firm would give to the target firm is increased (reduced). There are many versions of a collar, but the most common is one where it is a fixed-price offer (payable in stock) if the stock price stays within predefined bounds. Outside that range, the offer becomes strictly a stock offer whose value changes with the bidder's stock price. For example, MCI WorldCom's aborted $115 billion bid for Sprint in October 1999 was structured as a stock bid with a collar as follows:

WorldCom's stock price	*Number of bidder shares per target share*
$0 to $62.15	1.2228 WorldCom shares per Sprint share
$62.15 to $80.85	Variable, such that the payment is $76 per Sprint share
Over $80.85	0.94 WorldCom shares per Sprint share

It is a fixed-price offer of $76 if WorldCom's price stays between $62.15 and $80.85. Otherwise, it becomes a typical stock offer.

Thus, collars make the amount payable to target shareholders more certain and make the bid look a little more like a cash transaction rather than a purely stock transaction. On the other hand, a big change in the stock price makes the bid appear more like a stock bid but with less risk for the bidding firm than a purely stock transaction. Researchers have found that the market does not penalize the bidding firm for using stock in conjunction with a collar; rather, the market interprets the use of a collar as a signal that the bidder's stock is currently not overvalued.

Characteristics of Merger Types

When a merger between two firms is announced, the stock price of the target firm may remain below the level promised by the bidding firm. The difference between the target's price and the bidder's offer price is referred to as the *speculation spread*. The idea is to capture the speculation spread in an efficient and selective manner. In the subsections below, the merger arbitrage process is considered for stock mergers, cash mergers, mergers with collars, and mergers where multiple bids are made for the same target.

STOCK MERGERS—SINGLE BID

When the target's stock price does not rise to the bidder's offer, traders can make arbitrage profits by strategic execution. An all-stock merger such as America Online's (NYSE: AOL) acquisition of Time Warner (NYSE: TWX) is a good example. The merger was announced after the close on January 7, 2000 (a Friday). AOL agreed to pay 1.5 shares for each share of Time Warner. On the next trading day (January 10, 2000), AOL closed at $71.88 and Time Warner closed at $90.06. Based on AOL's offer of 1.5 shares and it's closing price, Time Warner should have closed at $107.82. The speculation spread in this case is $17.76 ($107.82—$90.06), or 19.7 percent. An arbitrageur could buy one share of Time Warner at $90.06 (pays $90.06) and short-sell 1.5 shares of America Online at $71.88 (receives $107.82). The arbitrageur has no risk in this position, assuming successful completion of the merger on these terms. If AOL's price rises, the short position in AOL loses but the long position in TWX gains an equivalent amount. If AOL's price falls, the short position gains and the long position in

TWX loses. In addition, if there are zero transactions costs and the merger completion is immediate, then the arbitrageur makes a riskless profit of almost 20 percent with zero investment. Everyone would want to earn profits of this magnitude.

Obviously, the completion cannot be immediate. The AOL–Time Warner merger was completed on January 11, 2001—almost exactly one year later. The price of Time Warner had fallen to $71.19 but was 1.5 times AOL's price for that day, allowing the trader to close out both positions. Our arbitrageur would have earned a low-risk profit of 20 percent in one year—pretty good, considering that the S&P 500 lost about 10 percent during that period.

In addition to the time delay, there is uncertainty about the completion of the merger. If the merger is unsuccessful, then the loss to the arbitrageur can be substantial. The target firm's stock would lose the premium promised by the bidder and more, because the target firm has definitely lost time and energy in pursuing the merger. On the other hand, the bidder firm's stock might even rise due to relief on part of the bidder stockholders (recall that the bidding firms usually do not gain upon announcement of a merger). The aborted merger of General Electric (GE) and Honeywell is a good example. GE offered 1.055 of its shares for each share of Honeywell after the close of trading on October 20, 2000. GE's stock closed at $49.75 on the next trading day, while Honeywell's stock closed at $49.94. Since Honeywell's stock price is higher than GE's price by only 0.4 percent instead of 5.5 percent, the speculation spread is 5.1 percent. On June 14, 2001, it became clear that the GE-Honeywell merger would not go through, as the demands made by the European Union were too onerous for GE to accept. At the close of trading that day, Honeywell's price was $37.10 compared with GE's price of $48.86. Instead of making a profit of 5 percent, the arbitrageur would have lost 25 percent, not counting transaction costs.

The above examples illustrate the two primary reasons for the speculation spread: risk of failure and delay in completion of the merger. Several factors affect the probability of failure: the chance that the merger will not be approved by the local government, foreign government, target firm's stockholders, or bidder firm's stockholders; the delay in obtaining those approvals; and the operation of certain force majeure clauses (poor performance, fraud, severe industry or economic downturn, etc.) that preclude the completion of the merger. Besides the risk of failure and time delay, arbitrageurs must consider the difficulty and the significantly higher cost and risk of short selling.[3]

CASH MERGERS—SINGLE BID

The process for cash mergers is the same as for stock mergers except that the cash offered by the bidder is independent of the bidder's stock price. Thus, the arbitrageur's job is much simpler: buy the target, and there is no need to short-sell the bidder's stock. Take the example of Medtronic's $48 cash bid for MiniMed that was announced on May 30, 2001, before the market opened. MiniMed closed at $46.77 that day. An arbitrageur could have bought MiniMed at $46.77 and held it until completion of the merger. By the time of merger completion on August 28, 2001, MiniMed's price had risen to $47.99, giving a return of 2.6 percent over a three-month period, which is equivalent to an annualized return of approximately 11 percent.

As mentioned above, the fraction of cash deals is much smaller than the fraction of stock deals. Moreover, the targets are generally much smaller than the acquiring firms in cash deals. Due to the relative size and greater certainty for target stockholders, cash deals should have a higher probability of success. However, the evidence reported in the next section shows that cash deals do not necessarily have a greater probability of success.

MERGERS WITH COLLARS—SINGLE BID

As explained in the previous section, mergers with collars are like cash mergers or stock mergers, depending on the bidder's stock price. Broadly, the strategy is to buy shares of the target firm upon announcement without a corresponding short sale in the acquiring firm. However, if the bidder's stock price begins to fall and it seems as though the collar will be triggered, then the position in the target should be protected by short-selling the bidder's stock. Mergers with collars are usually somewhat complex and require close oversight.

MERGERS WITH MULTIPLE BIDS

A merger need not take place just with a single bid for the target. About 20 percent of mergers have multiple bids. When another bid from the same bidder or a new competing bidder is expected, the stock price of the target firm may rise above the initial bid. For example, Sabre Holdings made a cash offer of $23 for Travelocity on February 19, 2002, at a premium of 20 percent over Travelocity's previous day's closing price of $19.20. However, Travelocity jumped to $24.91 in anticipation of higher bids. On March 18, 2002, Sabre Holdings sweetened its offer to $28 and Travelocity's price held at

$27.97 on that date, with the market participants expecting that the deal would be completed at that price. The merger was completed on April 11, 2002.

Bidding contests can be much longer and more complex than Sabre's acquisition of Travelocity. Northrop Grumman's initial bid for TRW on the morning of February 22, 2002, was $47 in cash, a premium of 18 percent. However, TRW soared to $50.30 by the end of the day, indicating that another bid (or bidder) would be forthcoming. On April 15, 2002, Northrop raised the bid to $53, and then to $58 on June 25, 2002. In the meantime, several firms expressed interest in different business segments of TRW. Finally Northrop agreed to buy TRW for $60 on July 1, 2002, an offer that was accepted by TRW. As you can observe, multiple bids are rewarding for arbitrageurs who take positions after the first bid. This is borne out by the evidence in the next section.

Evidence

Table 9.1 summarizes the abnormal returns from merger arbitrage. The return is calculated assuming that the target firm's stock is purchased at the end of the first trading day after the announcement and sold upon merger completion or upon withdrawal of the offer by the bidder. In the case of stock mergers, shares of the acquiring firm are short-sold in the correct proportion and the position is liquidated upon merger completion or upon withdrawal of the offer. This is the raw return earned from merger arbitrage. The abnormal return is obtained after adjusting for return commensurate with this kind of risk. If the risk is assumed to be zero, then the abnormal return is simply the raw return minus the risk free rate. If risk is assumed to be market risk, then the abnormal return is the raw return minus the market return. The systematic risk in the case of merger arbitrage is usually less than the market risk because the risk of failure of the merger depends on many factors besides stock market movements.

In Table 9.1, annualized returns are reported for a better understanding of the magnitude of gains. To annualize the abnormal return, it is assumed that the same return can be earned for multiple mergers sequentially. For example, if an abnormal return of 5 percent is earned over a two-month period from merger announcement to merger completion, it is assumed that we will earn the same 5 percent abnormal return in a sequence of six merger arbitrage deals. Thus, the annualized return is calculated simply as the 5 percent

Table 9.1 Returns to Merger Arbitrage

Study	Sample Period	Sample Size	First Offers Only	Percent Cash (%)	Failure Rate[a] (%)	Days to Completion or Withdrawal	Annualized Raw Return (%)	Annualized Abnormal Return (%)	Special Notes	Source
1.	1997	37	Yes	100	14	57.3	52.3	33.9	Only Canadian mergers	Karolyi and Shannon (1999)
2.	1981–1995	362	Yes	100	3	72	46.5	24[b]		Jindra and Walkling (2001)
3.	1981–1996	1,901	No	70	16	NA	18.5	9.6	Pure cash or pure stock	Baker and Savasoglu (2002)
4.	1963–1998	4,750	No	73	15	59.3	10.6	4	Accounts for various kinds of costs and risk	Mitchell and Pulvino (2001)

[a]The failure rate is defined as the percent of targets that remain independent.
[b]Not reported in the study. Author's estimate.

abnormal return times six. This corresponds to the "Annualized Abnormal Return" column.

The failure rate represents the percentage of targets that remain independent. The percentage of unsuccessful bids will be higher than the figure listed here because some targets have multiple bids and only one of those bids can be successful.

It is interesting to note from Table 9.1 that all studies, without exception, report positive abnormal returns for merger arbitrage after controlling for risk. However, the annualized abnormal return varies from a low of 4 percent to a high of 33.9 percent. Four studies have investigated different aspects of merger arbitrage, and a discussion of the individual studies is instructive in highlighting and understanding various facets of merger arbitrage.

CASH MERGERS

The first study in Table 9.1 shows that the average merger arbitrage spread in thirty-seven Canadian cash deals that took place in 1997 and were valued at more than C $50 million each is 7.81 percent. Considering an average duration of 57.3 days, this translates into 52.3 percent annually. Only five deals out of thirty-seven (14 percent) generated zero or negative returns, while 30 percent generated more than 10 percent. Making a naive adjustment for risk based on the Toronto Stock Exchange 300 index generates an annual abnormal return of 33.9 percent. However, the actual risk levels are lower: the average preannouncement-period beta risk for the targets is 0.52, while the "in-play" beta is lower at 0.39. As the beta risk for the Toronto Stock Exchange is close to 1, it would seem that the risk adjustment is generous.

A similar but broader study of 362 cash mergers during 1981–95 that were valued at more than $10 million (see Table 9.2 below) gives the following main results based on the first bid for a target:

A 97 percent completion rate suggests that the risk of failure is relatively small in cash offers. In addition, offers are revised upward in 39 percent of the cases and revised down in only 4 percent of the cases. The revision in offers has a considerable impact and accounts for much of the returns. The revision return is 6.9 percent, whereas the arbitrage spread is only 1.9 percent. Indeed, a negative arbitrage spread suggests the likelihood of additional bidders or the first bidder upping its bid. Sabre's bid for Travelocity and Northrop's bid for TRW are examples of upward revisions.

The average lead time, from announcement to completion or withdrawal, is seventy-two days. A majority of the offers (62 percent) are

Table 9.2 Cash Mergers Valued at More than $10 Million, 1981–1995

Completions

Completed	350 (97%)
Withdrawn	12 (3%)
Total sample	362 (100%)

Revisions

Revised up	140 (39%)
Revised down	15 (4%)
Unrevised	207 (57%)
Total sample	362 (100%)

Returns	Mean	Minimum	Median	Maximum	% Negative
Arbitrage spread	1.9%	−30.1%	2.0%	41.5%	23.1%
Revision return	6.9%	−55.6%	0.0%	101.5%	4.1%
Total	8.8%	−51.9%	3.3%	91.0%	7.5%
Period (days)	72	14	48	565	

completed within two months, and only 6 percent last more than six months. A total of 7.5 percent of the deals result in negative returns. Based on the average duration of seventy-two days, the annualized raw return is 46.5 percent. Adjustment for risk results in a return of 2.0 percent per month, or approximately 24 percent annually.

Cash and Stock Mergers

The remaining two studies examine samples of both cash and stock mergers. The first study consists of 1,901 cash and stock merger offers during 1981–96. The definition of a cash deal is a fixed-price deal whether the consideration is paid in stock or cash. The 1,901 offers have only 1,556 targets. The remaining 345 offers are revised or new bids for the same target. Overall, 30 percent of the offers are stock deals. However, the fraction of stock deals increases substantially over time, from 19 percent in the pre-1990 period to 44 percent thereafter. In the sample, 16.3 percent of the targets remain independent, while 22.7 percent of the deals fail.

Targets of cash offers are bought upon announcement. No stake is taken in the bidder firm. In the case of stock offers, however, the bidder firm is short-sold in addition to buying the target firm. Besides adding stock mergers to the sample, this study computes abnormal returns based on sequential availability of merger deals. If no merger deals are available in a particular period, then the abnormal return for that period is zero. Based on these considerations, the raw return to an arbitrage portfolio is 1.5 percent per month for all offers. If only the first offer is considered, then the return is 1.6

percent per month. By comparison, the market earns 1.2 percent per month, and the risk-free rate is 0.6 percent per month. Adjusted for risk, the excess return is about 0.8 percent per month or 9.6 percent annually.

The other study of cash and stock mergers has the largest sample of bids (4,750 offers) over the longest period (1963–98). The sample includes both pure cash and pure stock bids, and bids that seek less than 100 percent of the target as long as the acquisition will result in the acquirer holding the entire 100 percent. For example, a company holding 75 percent of the target may seek to acquire the remaining 25 percent through a merger or a tender offer. For this sample of merger arbitrage deals, the risk-adjusted return is 0.7 percent per month if transaction costs and other slippages are not considered. The risk-adjusted return falls to 0.3 percent per month if all impediments and costs of transacting are considered. Further, the risk of the arbitrage portfolio is close to zero in stable or appreciating markets, but the systematic risk as measured by beta jumps to 0.50 in downtrending markets. Some other interesting information relating to the success of merger arbitrage is given in Table 9.3.[4]

Table 9.3   Success of Merger Arbitrage

	Cash Deals	**Stock Deals**	**Hostile Deals**
Total number of first bids	3,434	1,815	475
Arbitrageur loses money	778 (23%)	356 (20%)	143 (30%)
First bid fails	606 (18%)	295 (16%)	173 (36%)
Target not bought out	478 (14%)	272 (15%)	131 (28%)
Targets taken over	86%	85%	72%

It can be observed that the failure rate is high in the case of hostile deals. Also, stock deals are slightly more successful than cash deals. Further, the chance that the target will remain independent is only 14–15 percent.

Overall, the evidence presented in Tables 9.1 to 9.3 suggests that there is indisputable proof of positive abnormal returns from merger arbitrage. The excess returns to merger arbitrage vary between 4 percent and 33.9 percent.

Factors in Determination of Profits

To optimize the gains from merger arbitrage, it is necessary to predict which offers are likely to provide maximum gains. There are three main factors that affect the magnitude of arbitrage profits: probability of success, time from announcement to completion or withdrawal, and arbitrage activity. Arbitrage activity can directly influence the spread, and all three factors are interrelated.

PROBABILITY OF MERGER SUCCESS

First, consider the probability that an announced merger will be successful. The greater the chance of success, the greater the expected profit. And if the chance of success is 100 percent, then the profit is risk-free. This also implies that the greater the probability of success, the larger the number of investors and other arbitrageurs, and therefore a smaller merger arbitrage spread. Thus, a greater probability of success is accompanied by a smaller speculation spread. On the other hand, if investors assign a low probability of success to a merger, fewer investors will participate in the merger leading to a high speculation spread. It is, therefore, easy to judge the likelihood of success given the speculation spread. In general, mergers with high initial spreads are less likely to succeed. Studies have found that the average arbitrage spread is high (average > 15 percent) for failed deals but less than 10 percent for successful deals.

Besides what can be gleaned from the arbitrage spread, the probability of success depends on the characteristics of the deal. These are listed in Table 9.4. Managerial resistance seems to be the most important, and a decisive deterrent to success. However, there are large differences in the reported success of hostile bids. The probability of success is estimated to fall by anywhere from 4 percent to 45 percent for hostile bids compared to friendly bids. From Table 9.3 it can be seen that 72 percent of the targets that are subject to hostile bids are eventually taken over. Indeed, this is lower than the 85 percent of targets eventually acquired in the overall sample. However, the price of success is sweet. There is a very high likelihood that the hostile bid will be revised upward to induce the management to change its mind, giving much higher returns to the arbitrageurs.

The probability of success also depends on market conditions. If there is a downturn in market conditions, then the bidder is not as keen to acquire the target because of the uncertain nature of the economy. It may also have a difficult time securing funds to buy the target. In a stock deal, the bidder is somewhat protected because a fall in its stock price (due to the market downturn) also reduces the price it pays for the target, and the bidder does not need external funds to finance the acquisition. However, in a cash deal, the price

Table 9.4 Effect on Arbitrage Profits

Factor	Predicted Effect on Probability of Success, Duration and Arbitrage Activity	Support for the Prediction	Evidence Against the Prediction
Managerial resistance (hostile bid)	Reduces the probability of success; increases duration	Walkling (1985), Schwert (2000), Baker and Savasoglu (2002), Jindra and Walkling (2001), Mitchell and Pulvino (2001)	
Falling stock market	Reduces the probability of success	Mitchell and Pulvino (2001)	
Cash deal	Reduces the probability of success	Mitchell and Pulvino (2001)	No effect—Baker and Savasoglu (2002)
Large targets	Reduces the probability of success; reduces arbitrage activity	Baker and Savasoglu (2002), Jindra and Walkling (2001)	No effect—Mitchell and Pulvino (2001)
Large acquirers	Increases the probability of success	Baker and Savasoglu (2002)	No effect—Mitchell and Pulvino (2001)
Takeover premium	Increases the probability of success	Fishman (1988)—theory	No effect—Baker and Savasoglu (2002); Mitchell and Pulvino (2001)
Bidder and target in the same industry	Reduces the probability of success; increases duration		No effect—Baker and Savasoglu (2002)
Low stock price, low market capitalization, high merger activity, or low turnover volume	Reduces arbitrage activity	Cornelli and Li (2002)—theory; Jindra and Walkling (2001)	
High pre-bid runup or highly abnormal announcement volume	High arbitrage activity	Cornelli and Li (2002)—theory; Jindra and Walkling (2001)	

of the target remains unchanged and the bidder may need external financing. Therefore, there is a greater likelihood for the merger to fail. A 5 percent decrease in contemporaneous or lagged monthly market return increases the probability of failure by 2.25 percent. There is also some evidence to suggest that there is no difference in the probability of success between cash and stock offers. In addition, target size and bidder size do not seem to be important factors, though financing for the merger and possible antitrust challenges should be of concern. Higher takeover premium (price paid by the bidder above the premerger price of the target) should increase the probability of success, as the management and the stockholders of the target firm will be more sympathetic to a higher bid. However, none of the studies cited in Table 9.1 finds any effect of the takeover premium on the chance of success.

It would seem that if the bidder and target firms are in the same industry, then they are more likely to be subject to scrutiny for antitrust concerns, which would reduce the probability of success. However, there is no evidence to support that prediction either. Perhaps the merging firms evaluate the probability of an antitrust contest and desist from engaging in mergers that would raise serious objections from governmental authorities.

Time to Merger Completion

The second factor that affects arbitrage returns is the time for completion of the deal. If the expected time of completion is long, the arbitrage spread will be larger. Further, the longer the completion time, the lower the probability of success. The time of merger completion is likely to increase with managerial resistance and antitrust concerns. In addition, management holdings will have a significant impact. If the management holds a large stake in the firm, then it can be instrumental in accepting or rejecting the bid.

Arbitrage Activity

The role of arbitrageurs is important in merger arbitrage. They can become instrumental in the success or failure of a merger because they are more willing to trade their shares than individual shareholders or the management. If arbitrageurs are very interested in a merger (due to potential arbitrage gains), then they will step in and take large positions, which they will surrender at the appropriate time. Thus, the greater the arbitrageur interest, the greater the probability of success. Realizing the link between arbitrageur interest and the probability of success, arbitrageurs tend to have a herd mentality. However, this mentality is tempered by the size of profits: the greater the arbitrageur interest, the smaller the profit. Therefore, arbitrageurs would like to hide their trades to discourage other arbitraguers and consequently earn higher profits.

Holding all else constant, arbitrage activity has three implications for arbitrage profits. Since arbitrageurs are interested in hiding their trades, they will invest in targets where volume turnover (daily volume divided by the number of shares outstanding) is high. On the other hand, targets with low volume turnover will experience relatively low arbitrage activity and higher profits. Second, arbitrageurs are unlikely to invest in low-price stocks (less than $5) because those stocks are not marginable and, therefore, require a larger capital outlay. Moreover, as low-price stocks are generally low-market-capitalization stocks, they will have higher transaction costs and a larger price impact due to large trades. Third, assuming that capital available to arbitrageurs is limited, arbitrageurs must choose among various merger deals. The capital constraint means that arbitrageurs can't take large positions in large targets because of limited capital. In addition, in times of high merger activity, arbitrageurs' capital availability will act as a constraint. Thus, a period of high merger activity is particularly good for earning high arbitrage returns.

The evidence above suggests that to earn high arbitrage profits, investors should concentrate on small-size targets with low volume and low price, in times of enhanced merger activity, and where there is relatively little increase in price and volume around the announcement.

Persistence

The persistence of abnormal returns in a variety of studies indicates that the abnormal returns are real. There are three potential explanations. If the cost of transacting is high, then the documented returns may be unattainable. Further, annualizing short-period returns can result in large returns that cannot be realistically obtained. For example, if the AOL–Time Warner merger was consummated in ten days instead of one year, then the ten-day return would have been 20 percent and the annualized return more than 700 percent. It is difficult to repeat such high-yield events. Nonetheless, all of the studies in Table 9.1 explicitly account for transaction costs. Even with conservative assumptions, the minimum annual abnormal return is 4 percent. With less conservative and more realistic assumptions, the abnormal return is about 10 percent per year.

The second explanation relates to accounting for risk. Using historical risk measures are never appropriate for event-driven returns because the volatility (or risk) is unusually high around events. However, risk around mergers is different. Since the position of the arbitrageur is essentially hedged (except against a withdrawal), the risk of merger arbitrage is rather low. The systematic (market-related) risk is close to zero in most instances except in downtrending markets. Even in those cases, the beta of a merger arbitrage portfolio is only one-half of the market portfolio. The Merger Fund (see Table 9.5 below) estimates that its beta is less than 0.20. Nonetheless, accounting for risk is necessary. As noted in Table 9.1, all studies explicitly account for risk but still generate abnormal returns.

The third explanation refers to the limited capacity and risk-taking ability of the arbitrageurs. Arbitrageurs have limited access to capital and would like to take positions that generate the highest risk-adjusted returns. As more and more arbitrage capital enters the market, the abnormal returns are reduced. Why can't enough capital be available to arbitrageurs so that the abnormal returns become negligible? According to Mergerstat, the value of U.S. and U.S. cross-border merger deals was $108 billion in 1990, $356 billion in 1995, and $1,285 billion in 2000. Compared to this, the total market capitalization of all stocks on U.S. exchanges at the end of 2000 was $11,750 billion. That is, mergers in 2000 were in excess of 10 percent of the entire market. With such a high volume of merger activity, it is obvious that arbitrageurs are unable to command enough capital to participate fully in more than a few deals. Perhaps this is where the individual investors need to step in.

The Trading Process

Figures 9.1 and 9.2 depict a typical case. The speculation spread narrows and eventually disappears in a successful merger.

It is not possible to use index futures or exchange-traded funds for merger arbitrage because these financial instruments consist of several hundred stocks, whereas the focus of merger arbitrage is on single stocks. On the other hand, mutual funds, stocks, and options can be used for realizing returns related to merger arbitrage. These are discussed below. Among these, mutual funds are the easiest to use and generate reasonable returns.

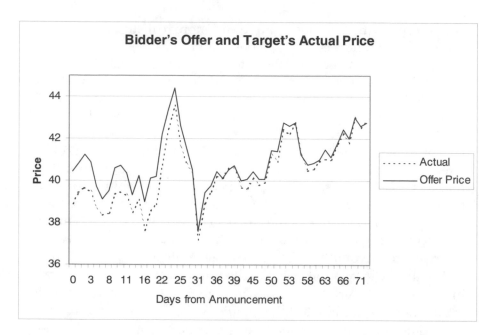

Figure 9.1   The figure shows the bidder's offer price and the target's actual price for a typical stock merger. Information is plotted for Cardinal Health's acquisition of Bindley Western Industries in December 2000.

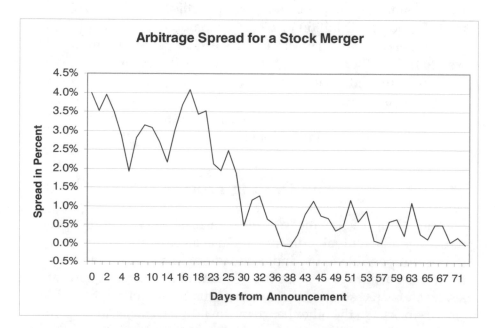

Figure 9.2   The figure shows the arbitrage spread or the difference between bidder's offer price and the target's actual price for a typical stock merger. Information is plotted for Cardinal Health's acquisition of Bindley Western Industries in December 2000.

USING OPTIONS

Options are not recommended for merger arbitrage because they are too expensive. The value of an option can be divided into its intrinsic value and its time value. The intrinsic value is the value an investor realizes if the option is exercised immediately. The time value of an option allows the investor to capture additional profits if the stock price moves in the desired direction. The distinction between these values is important, as the investor must pay for these values when buying an option. Since merger arbitrageurs do not attempt to time the market, the time value of the option is lost. Consequently, merger arbitrageurs tend not to use stock options. Perhaps for this reason the Merger Fund has only 5 percent of its deals hedged using options—the remaining positions are taken by trading in stocks.

There are, however, three conditions under which options might seem attractive. First, if there is significant risk of failure, then the option can limit the loss. Second, an option may be used to lock in gains already earned. For example, if the target in a cash offer has appreciated from $20 to $25, then buying an at-the-money put option would lock in a profit of $5 (less the put premium). Third, in the case of stock mergers, if it is not easy to short-sell, the investor can buy a put option on the acquiring firm's stock. Other than these special cases, trading the underlying stock is a superior strategy.

USING MUTUAL FUNDS

Mutual funds that specialize in merger arbitrage are the simplest vehicles for taking advantage of this mispricing. There are four mutual funds that use most of their assets for merger arbitrage: the Merger Fund, the Gabelli ABC Fund, the Arbitrage Fund, and the Enterprise Mergers and Acquisitions Fund. Details relating to these funds are in Table 9.5. The Merger Fund is the oldest and largest fund. Between 1993 and 2002, it earned an average return of 9.7 percent annually with relatively low risk, compared with 11.5 percent for the S&P 500 and 4.2 percent for one-month Treasury bills. Further, the Merger Fund has earned superior returns, and better than the risk-free interest rate in all years except 2001 and 2002. Adjusted for risk based on an estimated beta of 0.2, the Merger Fund earned an annual abnormal return of 4.0 percent.[5] Since the expense ratio goes toward compensating the managers and for marketing and administrative expenses, the true abnormal return of the Merger Fund is 5.3 percent (4.0 percent + 1.3 percent).[6]

Table 9.5 Availability and Performance of Merger Arbitrage Funds

Name of Fund	Merger Fund	Gabelli ABC Fund	Arbitrage Fund	Enterprise M&A Fund	Lipper Merger Fund	S&P 500	1-Month Risk-Free Rate (Annual)	Hedge Fund Research Merger Arb Index
Ticker Symbol	MERFX	GABCX	ARBFX	EMAAX, EMABC, EMACX	LMFRX	—	—	—
Date of Inception	January 1989	May 1993	September 2000	February 2001	August 2001	—	—	—
Assets as of December 2001 (in $ millions)	1,000	158	84	57	NA	—	—	—
Expense Ratio (%)	1.34	1.50	1.95	1.95	2.00	—	—	—
Beta of the fund	0.20					1.00	0.00	—
Total Return—2002 (%)	-5.67	0.86	9.27	-3.79	NA*	-22.1	1.75	-0.87
Total Return—2001 (%)	2.01	4.56	8.96	2.22	-0.70	-11.90	3.31	2.76
Total Return—2000 (%)	17.58	10.85				-8.49	5.67	18.02
Total Return—1999 (%)	17.39	9.00				21.68	4.52	14.34
Total Return—1998 (%)	5.35	11.14				29.53	4.60	7.23
Total Return—1997 (%)	11.65	12.75				33.73	4.96	16.44
Total Return—1996 (%)	9.95	7.90				23.28	4.98	16.61
Total Return—1995 (%)	14.15	11.07				37.82	5.32	17.86
Total Return—1994 (%)	7.13	4.53				1.35	3.91	8.88
Total Return—1993 (%)	17.69					9.90	2.85	20.24

Returns for EMAAX and LMRFX are for part of 2001.
*Ceased to exist in 2002.

Although the four funds invest primarily in merger arbitrage, they may (and do) follow many related strategies. Thus, the returns of these funds may be contaminated by other arbitrage activity. For example, the Merger Fund routinely picks stocks that may be potential targets or firms that were the subject of an unsuccessful takeover attempt. The Gabelli ABC fund can engage in any kind of arbitrage activity, though it concentrates on merger arbitrage. The Enterprise Mergers and Acquisitions Fund also looks for firms that are likely to be acquired.

To make sure the mutual funds are representative of pure merger arbitrage, they are compared with the Hedge Fund Research's Merger Arbitrage Index until 2002 (available at www.hfr.com). The returns are reported in the last column of Table 9.5. The average return for the ten-year period until 2002 based on the HFR Merger Arbitrage Index is 12.15 percent, which is comparable to the 11.06 percent (9.72 percent + 1.34 percent expense ratio) average return earned by the Merger Fund. This suggests that the return earned by the Merger Fund is representative of the actual returns earned by merger arbitrage.

Besides funds with direct interest in mergers, several other mutual funds practice merger arbitrage. For example, Fred Alger Management (manager of Alger mutual funds) changed its holdings to take advantage of the AOL–Time Warner merger that was announced in January 2000, as the numbers below illustrate. Fred Alger Management sold several million shares of AOL (acquirer) while at the same time increasing its stake in Time Warner (target).[7] Note that the reduction in AOL shares is larger than the increase in Time Warner, in part due to the exchange ratio of 1.5 AOL shares for each Time Warner share.

Holdings	December 1999	March 2000	Change
Time Warner	51,900	1,584,000	+1,532,100
AOL	6,915,790	4,297,950	−2,617,840

The above discussion shows that it is possible to get reasonable returns by using funds specializing in merger arbitrage. In addition to mutual funds, numerous hedge funds also engage in this activity.

Using Stocks

The remaining discussion focuses on the use of stocks in merger arbitrage. The advantage of relying on stocks over mutual funds is that the investor can hold potentially lucrative arbitrage positions that a large arbitrageur is not interested in holding or is unable to hold due to small target size, insufficient volume, or low price. Large arbitrageurs may have resources to pick deals with a high probability of success, but those deals generally have lower merger arbitrage spreads. To earn the returns documented in academic research, the investor does not require superior information to select any particular deals, since the research includes all available deals in computation of abnormal returns. Moreover, it may be possible to earn better returns for selections based on factors that affect the arbitrage spread.

The process for selecting deals and execution is as follows. Since most deals are announced before the open or after the close, there is enough time to obtain relevant information. If the time is insufficient, it is best to defer most trades toward the end of the day.

DEAL SELECTION

Factors for selecting deals are mentioned below.

1. Avoid deals with collars because they add uncertainty to an arbitrage position and require more frequent monitoring than pure cash or pure stock deals. Similarly, avoid deals that include warrants, units, preferred stock, and so on, because they complicate arbitrage positions.

2. Avoid deals that are likely to be subject to antitrust scrutiny. To identify such deals, look at the combined size of the target/ acquirer relative to the size of target's market. Any merger that will result in the merged firm accounting for more than 15–25 percent of the target's industry is cause for concern. This is especially true if no mergers have been attempted or if none has been successful. For example, it is prudent to avoid mergers in the airline industry, where several mergers have been attempted but none successfully. The only exception to antitrust scrutiny is a failing-firm merger, where the firm would go bankrupt unless it merges.

3. Choose deals where the target has a very large market capitalization (more than $50 billion) because arbitrageurs may not have the resources to fully participate in these deals.

4. Choose deals where the target has a low price (less than $10) because arbitrageurs are unlikely to participate in these deals due to high transactions costs.

5. Choose firms with low volume turnover (where volume of shares traded per day is less than 0.5 percent of the total number of shares outstanding). Arbitrageurs are unlikely to participate because they will not be able to hide their trades.

6. Choose deals with large arbitrage spreads carefully. Anything more than 15 percent is suspect, although such deals also have a high profit potential.

Actual Trading

Recall that arbitrage positions for stock mergers are different than those for cash mergers. Further, trading conditions on the NYSE are slightly different from those on Nasdaq. Accordingly, the strategies described below account for those differences.

Establishing Initial Position in Acquirers

1. *Cash mergers.* No action with respect to the acquirer is required in cash deals, or deals where the value of the acquirer's stock is fixed although payment is in stock instead of cash. For example, Johnson and Johnson's bid of $109 in common stock for each share of Cordis on October 19, 1995, is a cash deal even though the payment to target shareholders is in Johnson and Johnson stock. The reason it is treated as a cash deal is because the dollar amount received by the target does not change with a change in the acquirer's stock price.

2. *Stock mergers.* For stock deals where the exchange ratio is fixed (as in the AOL–Time Warner deal), the acquirer's stock must be sold short. The quantity to short-sell depends on the number of shares promised by the acquirer for each share of the target.

3. *NYSE acquirers for stock mergers.* Prices on the NYSE are less volatile than on Nasdaq and move more slowly because the specialist must maintain an orderly and continuous market. Since it is likely that the acquirer's price will fall soon after the market opens, place a market order before the market opens to short-sell the acquiring firm's stock. Note that execution of the order may take time, as the broker tries to find shares to short-sell. Cancel the order if it is not filled within the first fifteen to twenty minutes after opening of the stock for trading (often stocks with news open later than 9:30 A.M. on the NYSE). If the acquirer's stock cannot be short sold at the open, wait until later in the day and try again.

4. *Nasdaq acquirers for stock mergers.* Due to high premarket trading in Nasdaq stocks and high price volatility immediately after the market opens, it is always prudent to wait until about 10 A.M. to place orders. In addition, it is best to specify a limit price for short selling unless it is a very actively traded stock with a daily volume of more than 2 percent of the number of outstanding shares. In accordance with the strategy for stock mergers, place an order to short-sell.

Establishing Initial Positions in Targets

1. *Stock mergers.* For stock deals, always short-sell the acquirer before buying the target. Not only is it more difficult to short-sell, but sometimes it is not possible at all. If you buy the target before short selling, the profits could evaporate with a fall in the target's and acquirer's stock prices while you try to short-sell the acquiring firm's stock.

2. *Both stock and cash mergers.* For NYSE targets, place a market order at the open to buy the target. For Nasdaq targets, place a limit order to buy the target around 10 A.M. Market orders are appropriate only for actively traded Nasdaq stocks. The primary purpose of the limit is to remove any chances of a surprisingly high price at which a market order is filled. Unfavorable fills are common in illiquid stocks. The limit price can be set at the ask price, just above or just below the ask price, or just above the bid price.

3. *Cash mergers.* In the case of cash mergers, place a limit buy order before the market opens, where the limit price is set 4–5 percent below the bid price. In this way, the speculation spread will generate a sufficient return if the order is filled.

Closing Positions in Targets and Acquirers

The positions can be closed when the merger arbitrage spread has narrowed considerably and there is no chance of another competing offer or when the merger is close to completion. There is no need to wait until the merger is consummated.

Mergers During December 2000

Until now, all of the discussion has been based on prior research in merger arbitrage. This section and the next section concentrate on individual mergers, with a detailed discussion of one merger. Mergers that were announced during December 2000 are listed in Table 9.6. The month of December 2000 is selected to allow sufficient time for completion of mergers. The starting point for mergers is Thomson Financial's SDC Merger and Acquisitions database. To be included in Table 9.6, each merger must meet the following criteria:

- The merger is first announced during December 2000.

- The target and the bidder are both publicly traded companies in the United States. Foreign companies that trade on organized exchanges in the United States are also included. Bulletin board stocks and stocks trading under $1 are excluded.[8]

- The market capitalization of the target prior to the bid is at least $10 million.

- The mode of payment is either cash (90 percent or more) or stock (90 percent or more) or a simple combination of the two.

- The entire target firm is being sold, not merely a few assets of the target.

- The merger announcement is carried by news media such as Business Wire, PR Newswire, Associated Press, and so on.

Table 9.6 has twenty mergers. None of the mergers is hostile, and 100 percent of the target is sought by the acquirer. Terms of offer column gives details of the bid. "2.3 PEP" means that one share of the target firm, Quaker Oats (OAT), will be exchanged for 2.3 shares of the acquiring firm, PepsiCo. If a dollar amount is specified, then the bid is a fixed-price cash bid for the target. The last merger has a combination bid: $2 in cash plus 0.29 shares of the acquiring firm for each share of the target. "First Trade Date After Bid" refers to the first time an investor could have traded after the merger is announced. Thus, timing and date of the bid are very important. If the bid is made before close of the market (4 P.M.) on a business day, then that business day is the first trading day. If the bid is made after the market closes, the first trading day is the next business day. The speculation spread is the difference between the offer for the target and the target's closing price on the first trading day. In the case of the PepsiCo–Quaker Oats merger, the merger was announced in

Table 9.6 Arbitrage for Mergers Announced in December 2000

	Acquirer Name	Acquirer Ticker Symbol	Acquirer Size Prior to Offer ($million)	Target Name	Target Ticker Symbol
1	PepsiCo	PEP	61,150	Quaker Oats	OAT
2	Cardinal Health	CAH	27,770	Bindley Western Industries	BDY
3	BB&T	BBT	13,250	Century South Banks	CSBI
4	Best Buy	BBY	5,950	Musicland Stores	MLG
5	Nokia	NOKS	250,000	Ramp Networks	RAMP
6	United Community Financial	UCFC	250	Industrial Bancorp	INBI
7	American Skiing	SKI	43	MeriStar Hotels & Resorts	MMH
8	SouthTrust	SOTR	5,950	Bay Bancshares	BAYB
9	Swift Transportation	SWFT	1,275	MS Carriers	MSCA
10	Zions Bancorp	ZION	5,060	El Dorado Bancshares	ELBI
11	CKF Bancorp	CKFB	10	First Lancaster Bancshares	FLKY
12	FNB	FBAN	446	Citizens Community Bancorp	CCBI
13	LVMH (Moët-Hennessy, L. Vuitton)	LVMHY	31,770	Donna Karan International	DK
14	Regions Financial	RGBK	5,450	Morgan Keegan	MOR
15	Berkshire Hathaway	BRKA	104,000	Johns Manville	JM
16	Microsoft	MSFT	221,300	Great Plains Software	GPSI
17	Northrop Grumman	NOC	5,730	Litton Industries	LIT
18	Hughes Electronics	GMH	7,070	Telocity Delaware	TLCT
19	Fulton Financial	FULT	1,715	Drovers Bancshares	DROV
20	GenesisIntermedia .com	GENI	115	Fashionmall.com	FASH
	AVERAGE (ALL)				
	AVERAGE (EXCEPT #7, #20)[b]				

[a]Withdrawn bids.
[b]#7 and #20 are excluded because they have very high speculation spreads, suggesting that the mergers are likely to fail.

Target Size Prior to Offer ($million)	Terms of Offer	Trade Date After Bid	Speculation Spread (%)	Days to Completion/Withdrawal	Raw Return Earned (%)	Annualized Raw Return (%)
11,900	2.3 PEP	12/04/2000	10.7	241	10.7	16.6
1,350	0.4275 CAH	12/04/2000	4.0	72	4.0	22.0
330	0.93 BBT	12/05/2000	1.9	184	1.9	3.8
330	$12.55	12/07/2000	3.5	55	3.5	25.6
108	$5.80	12/07/2000	1.4	49	1.4	10.9
70	$20.38	12/11/2000	3.8	200	3.8	7.0
147	1.88 SKI	12/11/2000	39.9	102[a]	1.9	7.0
42	$26.42	12/12/2000	3.6	108	3.6	12.7
251	1.7 SWFT	12/12/2000	2.1	199	2.1	3.9
122	0.23 ZION	12/15/2000	2.8	105	2.8	10.1
10	$16.27	12/15/2000	4.1	167	4.1	9.2
24	0.543 FBAN	12/19/2000	4.2	132	4.2	12.0
108	$8.50	12/18/2000	0.0	344	26.2	28.0
550	$27	12/18/2000	2.6	101	2.6	9.7
1,600	$13	12/20/2000	1.0	69	1.0	5.4
715	1.1 MSFT	12/21/2000	2.6	104	2.6	9.4
2,800	$80	12/22/2000	2.6	159	2.6	6.1
117	$2.15	12/21/2000	5.9	103	5.9	22.5
108	1.24 FULT	12/28/2000	6.7	183	6.7	13.8
20	$2 + 0.29 GENI	12/29/2000	68.9	40[a]	−51	−98.5
			8.6	136	2	5.5
			3.5	143	5	13.2

the morning on December 4, 2000. PepsiCo's closing price that day was $43.813, while Quaker Oats' closing price was $91.06. However, PepsiCo's offer for Quaker Oats was $43.813 × 2.3 = $100.77. The difference between the offer and the actual price of the target is $9.71 or 10.7 percent. The merger was consummated 241 days later, and OAT ceased to trade at that time. The raw return of 10.7 percent is annualized to 16.6 percent based on the number of days to completion.

Table 9.6 shows several important points. About half the mergers are pure stock mergers, and the remaining are pure cash mergers. A collar is specified in only the PepsiCo–Quaker Oats merger. However, the collar did not get triggered because the price remained within the primary range. The speculation spread is an indicator of merger success. Typically, the spread is in single digits. However, the spread is especially wide for mergers 7 and 20. In those cases, the speculation spread is 39.9 percent and 68.9 percent. Such large spreads suggest that the mergers are unlikely to succeed—in fact, those are the only two bids that are eventually withdrawn. As discussed earlier and confirmed by the data in Table 9.6, it is prudent to avoid mergers with large speculation spreads.

In Donna Karan's merger, the speculation spread is zero. Very small or negative spreads suggest the likelihood of higher bids. Eventually DK was taken over at a price that was 26.2 percent above the initial offer. While the possibility of higher bids increases the returns to arbitrage, any such expectation must be tempered with the probability of failure.

Overall, excluding the two bids with high speculation spreads, the annualized return is 13.2 percent. This compares favorably with the results in Table 9.1. The actual annualized return may be lower for at least two reasons. First, transaction costs and bid-ask spreads are not considered. Second, it may not be possible to easily short-sell in all stock mergers.

The actual annualized return may be significantly higher in practice for other reasons. First, December 2000 was a particularly bad month for merger arbitrage. Due to deteriorating market conditions, the chance of merger failure was much greater than normal. Moreover, fewer mergers during that period meant that more arbitrage money was available for merger arbitrage driving down the speculation spreads. Second, it is possible and even desirable to close positions prior to merger completion so that they generate higher annualized returns due to the shorter holding period. Third, not all of the mergers listed would make good candidates for merger arbitrage.

Strategy Implementation

The following section evaluates several deals and provides a step-by-step execution of merger arbitrage for one deal.

Choosing Deals for Merger Arbitrage

It is useful to consider each deal individually to determine whether it would be desirable to take a position. The recommendations below are based on *the information available on the first trading day after announcement*. The process of arriving at the recommendation does not use any information not available at that time. Keep in mind that all mergers are friendly or neutral, and there is no attempt by the target management to reject the offer made by the acquiring firm.

Deal 1 (PEP-OAT) is a large merger in absolute terms. Since the merging firms are in related industries, it is likely to raise some antitrust concerns. Though it may not affect the probability of success or duration (see Table 9.5), the size of the target may still raise flags that might delay the completion of the merger. On the other hand, the speculation spread is large enough to make it attractive but not too large to suggest a high probability of failure. Therefore, the recommendation is to accept the deal for merger arbitrage.

Deal 2 (CAH-BDY) is not large either in absolute terms or relative to the acquirer's size. The merger is unlikely to encounter any significant problems. The speculation spread of 4 percent is attractive. The recommendation is to accept the deal for merger arbitrage.

Deal 3 (BBT-CSBI) is also not large either in absolute terms or relative to the acquirer's size. The merger is unlikely to encounter any significant problems. However, the speculation spread of 1.9 percent is small. Though BBT is actively traded, the daily volume of CSBI averages about ten thousand shares, which means that the bid-ask spread may be large. Indeed, the spread on CSBI prior to announcement averaged 1–2 percent. Therefore, the recommendation is to reject the deal for merger arbitrage.

Deal 4 (BBY-MLG) is not large either in absolute terms or relative to the acquirer's size. The merger is unlikely to encounter any significant problems. The speculation spread of 3.5 percent is attractive. Moreover, cash offers make it easier to trade by placing limit orders at the time of buying and at the time of selling. The recommendation is to accept the deal for merger arbitrage.

Deal 5 (NOK-RAMP) again is not large either in absolute terms or relative to the acquirer's size. The merger is unlikely to encounter any significant problems. However, the speculation spread of

1.4 percent is too small. Since it is a cash deal, it is possible to place an order at a preselected limit price that would allow sufficient speculation spread. For example, place an order to buy RAMP at $5.60 (giving a profit of 3.5 percent). You would initiate merger arbitrage only if your order gets filled at that price. In this particular case, the order would have remained unfilled because the target's price never fell below $5.66. The recommendation is to accept the deal for merger arbitrage only if the speculation spread is sufficient.

Deal 6 (UCFC-IBI) is not large in absolute terms but is large relative to the acquiring firm's size. The large relative size may increase the time for completion, but other than that no serious problems are anticipated. The speculation spread is attractive, and it is a cash bid. Therefore, the recommendation is to accept the deal for merger arbitrage.

Deal 7 (SKI-MMH) is not large in absolute terms but is large relative to the acquiring firm's size. The relative size and the extreme speculation spread of 39.9 percent raise serious questions about success of the deal. The deal should not be accepted for merger arbitrage.

Deal 8 (SOTR-BAYB) is similar to deal 4 and should be accepted.

Deal 9 (SWFT-MSCA) is large relative to the acquiring firm's size, and the time for completion is likely to be long. Coupled with a small speculation spread for a stock deal, the deal should not be accepted for merger arbitrage.

Deal 10 (ZION-ELBI) is similar to deal 2, though with a slightly smaller speculation spread. The recommendation is to accept the deal for merger arbitrage.

Deal 11 (CKFB-FLKY) is small in absolute terms but very large relative to the acquirer's size. The speculation spread is reasonable, and it is a cash bid. However, the average trading volume in FLKY is one hundred to two hundred shares a day with a wide bid-ask spread. If the merger fails, it will become very costly to sell the target's shares. Therefore, the recommendation is to reject the deal for merger arbitrage.

Deal 12 (FBAN-CCBI) is similar to deal 2 and quite attractive. The only downside is that the target firm is not actively traded. However, it seems very unlikely that the merger will fail. Thus, there is no clear recommendation for this deal.

Deal 13 (LVMHY–DK) is in many ways similar to deal 5, except that the speculation spread is zero. In fact, the speculation spread occasionally became negative on the first day of trading suggesting a strong possibility of higher bids for the target. Since revisions are typically very profitable, the recommendation is to accept the deal for merger arbitrage.

Deal 14 (RGBK-MOR) is similar to deal 4 and should be accepted.

Deal 15 (BRKA-JM) is similar to deal 5 with a similar recommendation.

Deal 16 (MSFT-GPSI) is similar to deal 10 with a slightly smaller speculation spread. The recommendation is to accept the deal for merger arbitrage.

Deal 17 (NOC-LIT) is large in absolute and relative terms. The time period for completion is likely to be long. Since it is a cash merger, the recommendation is to accept the deal only if a speculation spread of at least 4 percent can be obtained.

Deal 18 (GMH-TLCT) is similar to deal 8 with a larger speculation spread. The recommendation is to accept the deal for merger arbitrage.

Deal 19 (FULT-DROV) is similar to deal 2 and should be accepted.

Deal 20 (GENI-FASH) has an extremely high speculation spread at 68.9 percent, which means that the bid will fail. Therefore, the deal should not be accepted for merger arbitrage.

The average annualized return for the selected mergers is almost 16 percent. Coupled with low risk, this return far exceeds the normal market return.

EXECUTING A STOCK DEAL

A stock deal (deal 2: CAH-BDY) is selected for illustration because stock deals are more difficult to execute than cash deals.

Step 1: Information about the deal. Cardinal Health's (CAH) bid for Bindley Western Industries (BDY) was announced by all major media sources around 6:30 A.M. on December 4, 2000. Most deals are announced early in the morning, some in the evening, with very few deals announced when the market is open. The CAH-BDY deal seems to have a high probability of success. Four insiders holding 20 percent of the BDY stock have agreed to support the deal, and the merger is expected to be completed in the first half of 2001. The general consensus is that the deal will not be challenged by the Federal Trade Commission.

Step 2: Preopening stock prices. Obtain the preopening prices for the merging companies at www.island.com and www.archipelago.com. Preopening stock prices are easier to obtain for Nasdaq stocks than for NYSE/AMEX stocks.

Step 3: Short-sell the acquirer. First, it is necessary to calculate the number of shares to short-sell. If you buy five hundred shares of BDY, you would sell 213.75 shares of CAH. However, 213.75 shares is not a round lot. Therefore, you would short-sell 200 shares. It is desirable to err on the lower side than on the higher side when short-selling. Since CAH is an NYSE-traded stock, place a market order to short-sell 200 shares. Assume that the order is filled at $94.563, which is the closing price for December 4. Net receipt = $18,912.60 (price times quantity) minus $50 (one-half of bid-ask spread of $0.50) minus $10 (broker's fee) = $18,852.60.

Step 4: Buy the target. Immediately after the short sale order is filled, place an order to buy five hundred shares of BDY at the market, as BDY is a relatively actively traded NYSE stock. Assume that the order is filled at $38.875. Net payment = –$19,437.50 (price times quantity) minus $62.50 (one-half of bid-ask spread of $0.25) minus $10 (broker's fee) = –$19,510.

Step 5: Close the positions. The merger is actually consummated on February 15, 2001. However, it is not necessary to wait until the last day. On January 4, 2001, the closing price of $37.625 for BDY was almost exactly equal to 0.4275 times the closing price of $88 for CAH, giving a speculation spread near zero. Therefore, close positions on January 4, 2001. Net payment from repurchase of CAH = –$17,600 (price times quantity) minus $50 (one-half of bid-ask spread of $0.50) minus $10 (broker's fee) = –$17,660. Net receipt from sale of BDY = $18,812.50 (price times quantity) minus $62.50 (one-half of bid-ask spread of $0.25) minus $10 (broker's fee) = $18,740.

Step 6: Compute the return. Net profit = $18,852.60—$19,510—$17,660 + $18,740 = $422.60 on an initial investment of $19,510 is 2.2 percent. Period of holding = thirty-one days. Annualized return = about 26 percent.

Qualifications

The evidence presented in this chapter and the trading strategy recommendations rely on past data. Since future market conditions and market patterns may change without notice, there is no certainty that merger arbitrage will continue to be profitable. Furthermore, the analysis is based on abnormal returns, not raw returns, which means that if the market is falling, investors may lose money even though abnormal returns are positive.

In addition, merger arbitrage can become particularly risky if the deals are not carefully chosen. A broken deal can potentially wipe away a significant portion of the profits earned from other deals.

Key Points

- When a merger is announced, the stock price of the targeted firm may be above or below the price promised by the bidder. The difference between the actual price of the target and the bidder's offer is called *speculation spread*.

- A positive speculation spread (offer price > actual price) reflects the probability of failure and the duration between announcement and completion of the merger. A negative speculation spread (offer price < actual price) means that higher bids for the target, either from the same bidder or another bidder, are expected.

- The evidence indicates that the speculation spread is larger than what it should be based on the duration and probability of failure. The purpose of merger arbitrage is to capture the excess speculative spread.

- Studies have documented abnormal annual returns between 4 percent and 34 percent for different samples and periods. These returns are adjusted for risk, which is quite low for positions in merger arbitrage.

- The arbitrage profit is affected by probability of success, time from announcement to completion, and the degree of arbitrage activity. If the speculation spread is high, the probability of success is low. Although hostile bids are more likely to fail, successful hostile bids generate larger profits. The probability of success and the time to completion are negatively related. Arbitrage activity depends on the arbitrageurs' availability of investment capital and their ability to hide trades from other traders.

- Persistence of arbitrage profits can be attributed to transaction costs, risk of arbitrage, and limited capacity. The most important factor is limited capacity of arbitrageurs. Since capital must find the highest available risk-adjusted returns, arbitrageurs may only have restricted access to capital. Merger activity in 2000 was in excess of 10 percent of the entire market capitalization—clearly, such a large amount of capital cannot be earmarked for merger arbitrage.

- Investors can use mutual funds to capture returns from merger arbitrage or engage in merger arbitrage on their own using stocks. The Merger Fund has generated an average annual abnormal return of 4.0 percent over the last decade. Hedge Fund Research's Merger Arbitrage Index suggests an annual abnormal return of 6.4 percent without accounting for management expenses.

- An ad hoc sample of mergers from December 2000 generates an annualized raw return of 13.2 percent. Since the risk premium during 2001 was negative, the abnormal return could be higher.

- Not all announced deals are candidates for merger arbitrage. If only the recommended deals are accepted, the annualized raw return increases to more than 16 percent. Execution of one stock deal is illustrated.

Bottom Line

Merger arbitrage can generate continuous and sustainable abnormal returns of 4–10 percent annually. Evidence relating to the profitability of merger arbitrage is long-term and consistent.

Mutual funds specializing in merger arbitrage are a convenient way to earn a reasonable yet low-risk return. Stocks can be used to execute merger arbitrage transactions on an individual basis to possibly generate higher returns.

Internet References

Mutual Funds Specializing in Merger Arbitrage
http://www.gabelli.com/funds/products/408.html: The site for Gabelli's ABC Fund (GABCX).
http://www.thearbfund.com: The site for the Arb Fund (ARBFX).
http://www.enterprisefunds.com: The site for Enterprise M&A Fund (EMACX). Select "Sector/Specialty" from the left frame.

Information Regarding Merger Deals and Statistics
http://www.thedeal.com: Has current news regarding deals. A table shows speculation spreads of selected deals. A good source for active merger arbitrageurs. Subscription is required.
http://www.dealanalytics.com: A good source for real-time news relating to mergers, merging firms, arbitrage spreads, and so on.
http://www.mergerstat.com: Provides extensive statistics on mergers. Can also provide databases of historical merger activity.

http://www.thomsonfinancial.com: The data used in this chapter and many academic studies come from SDC Platinum, which is owned by Thomson. Go to "Solutions for Investment Banking", select "Bankers". Thomson Financial has many other M&A related products that tend to be quite expensive.

http://www.hfr.com: Hedge Fund Research's Merger Arbitrage Index gives performance of hedge funds primarily engaged in merger arbitrage.

http://www.nytimes.com: You can receive the daily DealBook by e-mail from the *New York Times* by registering on their website.

on-index_mergersacquisitions_d@e.moreover.com: Moreover.com will also send you daily e-mails with merger news if you register by sending an e-mail to the address given.

Stock Price Information

http://finance.yahoo.com: Contains historical and current stock price information. You must make sure that the prices account for cash dividends and stock splits.

http://www.archipelago.com and http://www.inet.com: These are electronic communication networks (ECNs) or electronic marketplaces that provide prices during trading hours and outside trading hours. However, unlike Yahoo!, which provides aggregate information for all exchanges, the ECNs provide prices only for trades executed through them.

References for Further Reading

Andrade, Gregor, Mark Mitchell, and Erik Stafford. 2001. New Evidence and Perspectives on Mergers. *Journal of Economic Perspectives* 15(2), 103–20.

Baker, Malcolm and Serkan Savasoglu. 2002. Limited Arbitrage in Mergers and Acquisitions. *Journal of Financial Economics* 64(1), 91–115.

Berkovitch, Elazar, and M. P. Narayanan. 1990. Competition and the Medium of Exchange in Takeovers. *Review of Financial Studies* 3(2), 153–74.

Boesky, F. Ivan. 1985. *Merger Mania—Arbitrage: Wall Street's Best Kept Money-making Secret* (New York: Holt, Rinehart and Winston).

Bradley, Michael, Anand Desai, and E. Han Kim. 1983. The Rationale Behind Interfirm Tender Offers. *Journal of Financial Economics* 11(1), 183–206.

———. 1988. Synergistic Gains from Corporate Acquisitions and Their Division Between the Stockholders of Target and Acquiring Firms. *Journal of Financial Economics* 21(1), 3–40.

Brown, Keith C., and Michael V. Raymond. 1986. Risk Arbitrage and the Prediction of Successful Corporate Takeovers. *Financial Management* 15(3), 54–63.

Cornelli, Francesca, and David D. Li. 2002. Risk Arbitrage in Takeovers. *Review of Financial Studies* 15(3), 837–68.

Dukes, William P., Cheryl J. Frohlich, and Christopher K. Ma. 1992. Risk Arbitrage in Tender Offers. *Journal of Portfolio Management* 18(4), 47–55.

Fishman, Michael J. 1989. Preemptive Bidding and the Role of the Medium of Exchange in Acquisitions. *Journal of Finance* 44(1), 41–58.

Hansen, Robert G. 1987. Theory for the Choice of Exchange Medium in Mergers and Acquisitions. *Journal of Business* 60(1), 75–96.

Hetherington, Norriss S. 1983. Taking the Risk out of Risk Arbitrage. *Journal of Portfolio Management* 9(4), 24–25.

Jarrell, Gregg A., James A. Brickley, and Jeffrey M. Netter. 1988. The Market for Corporate Control: The Empirical Evidence Since 1980. *Journal of Economic Perspectives* 2(1), 49–68.

Jensen, Michael C., and Richard S. Ruback. 1983. The Market for Corporate Control. *Journal of Financial Economics* 11(1), 5–50.

Jindra, Jan, and Ralph A. Walkling. 2001. Speculation Spreads and the Market Pricing of Proposed Acquisitions. Working paper, Department of Finance, Ohio State University.

Karolyi, Andrew, and John Shannon. 1999. Where's the Risk in Risk Arbitrage. *Canadian Investment Review* 12(1), 12–18.

Kim, E. Han, and Vijay Singal. 1993. Mergers and Market Power: Evidence from the Airline Industry. *American Economic Review* 83(3), 549–69.

Larcker, David F., and Thomas Lys. 1987. An Empirical Analysis of the Incentives to Engage in Costly Information Acquisition: The Case of Risk Arbitrage. *Journal of Financial Economics* 18(1), 111–26.

Marcial, Gene. Risk Arbitrage: Now Open to the Public. *Business Week*, April 29, 1983.

Mitchell, Mark, and Todd Pulvino. 2001. Characteristics of Risk and Return in Risk Arbitrage. *Journal of Finance* 56(6), 2135–75.

Schwert, G. William. 1996. Markup Pricing in Mergers and Acquisitions. *Journal of Financial Economics* 41(2), 153–92.

———. 2000. Hostility in Takeovers: In the Eyes of the Beholder? *Journal of Finance* 55(6), 2599–640.

Shleifer, Andrei, and Robert W. Vishny. 1997. The Limits of Arbitrage. *Journal of Finance* 52(1), 25–55.

Singal, Vijay. 1996. Airline Mergers and Competition: An Integration of Stock and Product Price Effects. *Journal of Business* 69(2), 233–68.

Walkling, Ralph A. 1985. Predicting Tender Offer Success: A Logistic Analysis. *Journal of Financial and Quantitative Analysis* 20(4), 461–78.

Welles, Chris. 1981. Inside the Arbitrage Game. *Institutional Investor,* August 1981, 41–58.

Notes

1. The academic and practitioner literature calls this "risk arbitrage." However, the term "merger arbitrage" is more descriptive because "risk arbitrage" can potentially refer to any arbitrage activity.

   This chapter draws from a large number of published and unpublished papers. Andrade, Mitchell, and Stafford (2001), Jensen and Ruback (1983), and Jarrell, Brickley, and Netter (1988) review the evidence related to mergers in different decades. Bradley, Desai, and Kim (1983, 1988), Kim and Singal (1993), and Singal (1996) have discussed causes of mergers. The effect on merger gains as determined by the mode of payment has been explored in Hansen (1987), Fishman (1989), and Berkovitch and Narayanan (1990). Finally, these works on merger arbitrage have been extensively used in this chapter: Baker and Savasoglu (2002), Brown and Raymond (1986), Cornelli and Li (2002), Dukes, Frohlich, and Ma (1992), Hetherington (1983), Karolyi and Shannon (1999), Larcker and Lys (1987), and especially Mitchell and Pulvino (2001). Mark Mitchell is on leave from Harvard Business School and runs a merger arbitrage fund along the lines discussed herein.

2. The only stories are Welles (1981) and Marcial (1983).
3. Appendix B has a primer on short selling. Short selling is significantly more costly than buying shares due to a variety of institutional and legal restrictions.
4. Personal communication, Todd Pulvino, March 2002.
5. The abnormal return is calculated as the actual return minus the expected return. Expected return is the risk-free rate plus market risk premium times the beta. Thus, abnormal return = 9.7% − (4.2% + 0.2) × (11.5% − 4.2%)).
6. Note that costs of trading are already accounted for in the returns. The expense ratio typically consists of management fees, distribution and service fees, and other administrative expenses. Thus, the expense ratio understates the true returns from a particular strategy. Lipper Merger Fund, another merger arbitrage fund, closed in 2002 due to lack of investor interest.
7. Institutional holdings in a stock are available at the end of each calendar quarter, that is, as of December 31, March 31, etc. Hence, it is not possible to report holdings exactly around the announcement of the merger.
8. Bulletin board stocks are not listed on NYSE, AMEX, or Nasdaq. Typically, a broker will take your order and post it on a bulletin board announcing to other traders that you are willing to buy a particular stock at a specific price. If someone else is interested, that person will contact the broker and offer to trade with you. Bulletin board stocks are difficult to trade and have wide bid-ask spreads.

10

International Investing
and the Home Bias

Financial economists have long maintained that all investors can improve the quality of their portfolios by investing a significant part of their portfolio in foreign securities. Including foreign assets reduces the risk of the portfolio due to low correlations between foreign stocks and domestic stocks without hurting return. However, individual investors routinely underweight foreign assets, perhaps due to their ignorance. While it is not possible to arbitrage home bias, investors should not suffer due to a home bias in their own portfolios.

Description

This chapter is about a long-term trading strategy.[1] Too many investors fail to realize the importance of investing internationally and consequently fail to obtain the best risk-return trade-off. This is known as the *home bias*. The tendency of investors to be insufficiently diversified is not limited U.S. investors, nor is it limited to foreign stocks. Investors are routinely underdiversified and take on much more risk than they are compensated for.

Background

RISK AVERSION

It is well known that investors are risk-averse. Such investors consider both the risk and return of an investment and demand a higher return for a riskier investment. It is no wonder that, in actual practice, higher-risk securities generate higher return. For example, the expected return on Treasury securities (about 6 percent) is the lowest because their risk is low. Corporate debt has the next higher return (about 9 percent) because corporate debt is riskier than T-bills. Stocks generate the highest return because stocks are the riskiest. Among stocks, small stocks are generally considered riskier and generate a higher return (18 percent) than large stocks (12 percent).

It is obvious that a risk-averse investor will choose the security with the lowest risk among securities with the same return, and the security with the maximum return among securities with the same level of risk. Therefore, when possible, it is highly desirable to reduce a portfolio's risk without affecting its return, or enhance the return of a portfolio without increasing its risk.

DIVERSIFICATION OF RISK

It is possible to reduce the risk of a portfolio by adding stocks that are not well correlated with the stocks in that portfolio. A simple example is illustrative. Assume that you hold the stock of a company that sells beachwear. The annual return from the company's stock is 20 percent in sunny years with many sunny days but falls to 0 percent in rainy years with few sunny days. Assume that the probabilities of a sunny year and a rainy year are equal at 50 percent. The average return is 10 percent, with a 50-percent chance of 20-percent return and a 50-percent chance of 0-percent return. Thus, the beachwear company's 10-percent return is risky.

How can you reduce the risk of your investment? Consider another firm that rents videos. The video rental company is similar to the beachwear company, except that its annual return is 20 percent in a rainy year and 0 percent in a sunny year, with an average return of 10 percent. The video rental company's 10 percent return is also risky, just like the beachwear company's return.

If you invest 50 percent each in video rental and beachwear, then the average return is still 10 percent—50 percent of 10 percent from video rental and 50 percent of 10 percent from beachwear. In a sunny year you would earn 10 percent (50 percent of 20 percent from beachwear + 50 percent of 0 percent from video rental). In a rainy year you would also earn 10 percent (50 percent of 0 percent from beachwear + 50 percent of 20 percent from video rental). Now, you have no risk because you earn 10 percent in both sunny and rainy years. Thus, by adding the video rental stock to the beachwear stock, you have reduced your risk without affecting your return. The result is tabulated in Table 10.1.

Table 10.1   Comparison of Returns with One and Two Stocks (in percent)

Type	Company	% Invested	Return in Sunny Year	Return in Rainy Year	Average Return
Single stock	Beachwear	100	20	0	10
Single stock	Video rental	100	0	20	10
Portfolio of two stocks	Beachwear	50	20	0	10
	Video rental	50	0	20	10
	Total	100	10	10	10

You can see from the above table that the return is the same in all cases—with a single stock or with both stocks. However, there is risk with a single stock. You get either 20 percent or 0 percent. Once you choose to invest in both stocks, the return becomes riskless because one of the two stocks does well and the other does poorly regardless of the kind of weather.

The key in diversification of risk is *correlation*. Notice that the returns from beachwear and video rental always go in the opposite direction. If one of them does well, the other does not. Therefore, adding stocks that do not behave like other stocks in your portfolio is good and can reduce risk. The correlation is measured by what is called a *correlation coefficient*. The correlation coefficient varies between –1 and +1. The two stocks in the above example have a correlation of –1. Unfortunately, most stocks have a positive correlation, and many of them have a correlation with the market portfolio that is close to +1. The challenge in diversifying risk is to find stocks that have a correlation of less than +1.

However, if you own only one stock, such as the stock of the company you work for, it is easy to find other stocks that are not well correlated with that stock. Adding more stocks to that one stock will certainly reduce risk. It is estimated that you must invest in thirty to forty randomly picked stocks to get a reasonably diversified portfolio. Did you know that a typical individual invests in less than ten stocks? How many different stocks does your portfolio have?

Correlation and risk are important for all financial decisions. For example, you protect your house and car against loss through insurance. Insurance has a negative correlation with your assets. Insurance pays off when your assets are destroyed but pays nothing if your assets are not destroyed. Moreover, the insurance actually generates a negative return for you. You are willing to accept that negative return because insurance reduces your risk. Thus, it is not unreasonable to accept negative returns if the addition of the investment generating the negative return reduces your overall risk significantly. This important point underscores the trade-off between risk and return: investors are happy to give up some return if the reduction in risk is sufficient. Therefore, it is not always necessary to ensure that the return is preserved.

A general rule to evaluate whether a new asset should be included in an existing portfolio is based on the risk-return trade-off relationship:

$$E(R_n) = R_f + \frac{\sigma_n \rho_{n,p}}{\sigma_p} \times \left[E(R_p) - R_f \right]$$

where $E(R)$ is the return from an asset, σ is the standard deviation, ρ is the correlation coefficient, and the subscripts n and p refer to the new stock and existing portfolio. R_f is the return on the risk-free asset. If the new asset's return is greater than the right-hand side in the above equation, then the asset should be included in the existing portfolio, otherwise not. That condition can be rewritten as below:

$$\frac{E(R_n) - R_f}{\sigma_n} > \frac{E(R_p) - R_f}{\sigma_p} \times \rho_{n,p}$$

Evidence

Before looking at the evidence, consider the potential benefits from international investing and the source of those benefits. Assume that the dollar return on U.S. stocks is 12 percent with a standard deviation of 18 percent, and the dollar return on non-U.S. stocks is also 12 percent with a standard deviation of 18 percent. Since the U.S. markets and foreign markets are not well correlated, let the correlation coefficient be 0.60. Putting the U.S. stocks and the non-U.S. stocks in a 50-50 combination would generate a new world portfolio with the following characteristics:

$$R_w = w_1 R_{US} + w_2 R_{non-US} = 0.50 \times 12\% + 0.50 \times 12\% = 12\%$$

$$\sigma_w = \sqrt{w_1^2 \sigma_1^2 + w_2^2 \sigma_2^2 + 2 w_1 w_2 \rho \sigma_1 \sigma_2}$$

$$= \sqrt{0.50^2 \times 0.18^2 + 0.50^2 \times 0.18^2 + 2 \times 0.50 \times 0.50 \times 0.60 \times 0.18 \times 0.18} = 0.16$$

The new world portfolio has a return of 12 percent and a risk of 16 percent. There is a reduction in risk from 18 percent to 16 percent without a concurrent reduction in return. Thus, even when the foreign markets do not generate a higher return, the overall risk can fall due to less than perfect positive correlation.

In this section, returns, risk, and correlations are presented along with an optimal portfolio.

RETURNS FROM INTERNATIONAL INVESTING

For the purpose of investing, the world has been divided into three main regions by the type of market: the United States, other developed markets, and emerging markets. All of the return data other than data for the U.S. market have been obtained from the Morgan Stanley Capital International indexes. The MSCI Europe, Australia, and Far East (EAFE) consists of developed markets other than the U.S. market. The emerging markets index (EMF) consists of emerging markets. There are two world indexes considered: the MSCI All Countries (AC) index consists of all three regions and the MSCI All Countries except the U.S. (AC-ex-U.S.) consists of MSCI EAFE and MSCI EMF countries. All indexes are constructed by weighting the constituents on the basis of the market capitalization of each country. You can see in Table 10.2 that the MSCI AC-ex-U.S. returns and the MSCI EAFE returns are similar because the emerging markets have a relatively small weight in the larger indexes.

Annual returns are reported for approximately fifteen years beginning with 1988. The return of the last year (2002) is annualized based on the first eight months of the year. The S&P 500's return varies from –27 percent to more than 37 percent, EAFE's return is between –20 percent and 35 percent, and the EMF return varies from –30 percent to more than 75 percent. Overall, the S&P 500 return is 13.2 percent compared with 13.7 percent for emerging markets and 5.3 percent for the developed markets. Out of the fifteen annual returns, emerging markets outperform other markets in eight years and the U.S. markets are the best in six years, while the other developed markets are better than other regions only in 1994. The emerging market returns exceed 50 percent in four out of fifteen years.

If a different set of markets is considered, the results do not change. Consider the developed markets alone: Japan, the United States, Europe except the United Kingdom, the United Kingdom, and all countries except the United States. Among these markets, the United States outperformed the remaining markets only two times between 1987 and 2001. Just like with the beachwear and video rental com-

Table 10.2   Annual Stock Returns by Region, 1988 to 2002 (in percent)

Year	S&P 500	Europe, Australia, and the Far East (EAFE)	Emerging Markets (EMF)	All Countries Except the U.S. (AC-ex-U.S.)	All Countries (AC)
1988	17.1	30.0	**41.8**	30.1	24.7
1989	32.5	12.3	**71.2**	13.0	18.7
1990	**−1.6**	−19.9	−6.8	−19.8	−14.5
1991	31.9	14.2	**62.6**	15.7	21.2
1992	7.9	−11.0	**12.1**	−10.1	−3.9
1993	10.3	34.8	**76.5**	36.9	25.6
1994	1.8	**8.9**	−5.5	7.9	5.7
1995	**37.7**	12.4	−4.1	10.4	19.9
1996	**23.6**	6.6	6.7	6.1	13.5
1997	**34.9**	3.3	−8.9	3.1	16.1
1998	**31.4**	22.4	−18.8	17.6	18.8
1999	22.0	28.3	**70.5**	31.4	33.8
2000	**−7.9**	−13.2	−29.7	−15.2	−13.1
2001	−10.2	−20.1	**2.0**	−18.2	−14.5
2002	−27.0	−15.4	**−5.1**	−14.5	−21.8
Average of Annual Returns	13.6	6.2	**17.6**	6.3	8.7

The highest returns in a year are in bold. The returns include dividends and other distributions. All returns and classifications are based on Morgan Stanley Capital International indexes, except that the S&P 500 returns are reported by Standard and Poor's. Data are from Global Financial Data and Barra. For 2002, only the return from January to August is used. The return for 2002 reported in the table is annualized based on the first eight months. Author's calculations.

panies, it is smart to use a combination of countries and regions than be restricted to the domestic market.

Though the results presented here are for the most recent fifteen-year period, using earlier periods only strengthen these conclusions. For example, if the 1971–88 period is considered, U.S. investors earned an annual return of 9.9 percent. Compared to this, an investor who held the EAFE portfolio would have earned 18.2 percent, nearly double the return in the U.S. market. No data are available for the emerging markets, as most of those markets were closed to foreign investors at that time. An investor holding the world portfolio would have earned 13.9 percent, 40 percent higher than the U.S. market.

What is obvious from Table 10.2 and other evidence cited is that no single market is consistently the best-performing market. A market may be good for one year, but a different market is likely to be the best performer in another year.

RISK OF INTERNATIONAL INVESTING

The average return and the associated risk for each of the three regions is in Table 10.3. The lowest risk, 14.3 percent, is for the U.S. stock market whereas the highest risk, 23.9 percent, is for emerging markets. The emerging markets also have the highest return of 17.6 percent compared to a return of 13.6 percent for the U.S. markets. As a stand-alone market, the U.S. market is better than the EAFE region but worse than emerging markets during the 1988–2002 period. However, it will soon be apparent that even though the U.S. market's return is very good, it is still advantageous to invest in foreign stocks.

The correlation matrix shows the correlations among different markets. The correlation between the S&P 500 and the emerging markets is only 0.42. With the developed markets, the S&P 500 has a correlation coefficient of 0.58. Both of these correlations are quite low. Similarly, the emerging markets and the developed markets are not well correlated. On the other hand, the correlation between the developed markets and the world without the United States is 1.00 because the contribution of emerging markets in the index for all countries except the United States is quite small.

Correlations in different periods and among individual countries provide a little more information about what can be expected in terms of correlations in the future. If the period 1971–98 is consid-

Table 10.3   Return, Risk, and Correlations by Region, 1988 to 2002

	S&P 500	Europe Australia, and the Far East (EAFE)	Emerging Markets (EMF)	All Countries Except the U.S. (AC-ex-U.S.)	All Countries (AC)
Annual Return	13.6%	6.2%	17.6%	6.3%	8.7%
Risk (standard deviation)	14.3%	17.0%	23.9%	16.9%	14.6%
Correlation Matrix					
S&P 500	1.00	0.58	0.42	0.60	0.70
Europe, Australia, and the Far East	0.58	1.00	0.48	1.00	0.88
Emerging Markets	0.42	0.48	1.00	0.52	0.64
All Countries except the US	0.60	1.00	0.52	1.00	0.88
All Countries	0.70	0.88	0.64	0.88	1.00

The data are as described in Table 10.2. The correlations are calculated based on monthly returns. The standard deviation reported is annualized. Author's calculations.

ered, the highest correlation between any two developed countries is 0.70 (Canada and the United States). The lowest correlation is 0.25, between Italy and Australia. The 1980–92 period exhibits similar correlations: the highest correlation, 0.70, is between Canada and the United States, and the lowest correlation, 0.24, is between Japan and the United States. For the 1970–2000 period, the correlations among developed countries vary from a low 0.25 to a high of 0.71. For the 1971–88 period, the correlations among developed nations vary between 0.14 and 0.70. The 1976–99 period shows correlations in the range of 0.24 and 0.71 among developed nations and between –0.05 and 0.48 among emerging markets and developed markets. If individual years are considered, the correlations between U.S. and developed markets vary between 0.3 and 0.8 over the last thirty years with an average of 0.5. The correlations suggest a continuing advantage from investing in foreign stocks.

Constructing an Optimal Portfolio

Since returns have been somewhat volatile over the years, the optimal portfolio can vary with different periods. However, return volatility underscores the need for controlling risk by diversifying aggressively. Optimal portfolios recommended by prior research are reported in Table 10.4. The recommendations have a common theme. If you invest at least 30 percent in other developed markets, the effect is a reduction in risk accompanied by an increase in returns. This is a win-win situation.

None of the optimal portfolios include exposure to emerging markets because emerging markets are small, they are considered to be very risky, and the correlations can increase significantly. However, the key is that the correlation between emerging markets and the U.S. market is still much less than the correlation between the U.S. market and other developed markets, and the return can be higher. Therefore, it is worthwhile to invest a nontrivial amount in emerging markets. The following allocation among global stock markets can be considered reasonable to obtain the benefits of diversification.

U.S. stocks	60%
Other developed markets	30%
Emerging markets	10%

An Estimate of the Home Bias

The evidence of optimal investment suggests significant investment in foreign stocks. How do investors compare with the recommended

Table 10.4 Optimal Portfolios for Different Periods

Period of Analysis	U.S. Portfolio (%) Return	U.S. Portfolio (%) Risk	Optimal Portfolio Allocation (%) U.S.	Optimal Portfolio Allocation (%) EAFE	Optimal Portfolio (%) Return	Optimal Portfolio (%) Risk	Comments
1970–2000	12.70	15.30			19.60	18.60	Much higher return and risk
1970–2000	12.90	15.40	70	30	13.00	14.00	Same return, lower risk
1971–1998	13.40	15.30			13.50	14.30	Same return, lower risk
1980–1992	17.20	15.80	41	59	20.00	14.50	Higher return, lower risk
1971–1988	9.90	16.20			13.90	14.50	Higher return, lower risk
1971–1988	9.90	16.20		100	18.20	17.50	Much higher return, higher risk

Table 10.5　Estimates of Home Bias (in percent)

Country	Market Capitalization as % of World	Investment in Domestic Stocks	Home Bias
Australia	1–2	88	>85
Canada	2–3	88	>85
France	5	83	>75
Germany	5	80	>70
Italy	2–3	93	>90
Japan	13	91	>75
Netherlands	2	75	>70
Spain	1–2	95	>90
Sweden	2	72	>65
UK	8–9	78	>65
US	47	90	>40

Adapted from Jeske (2001).

global allocations? The difference between the recommended allocation in foreign stocks and the actual allocation in foreign stocks is referred to as the home bias. Though the actual investment in foreign stocks has increased severalfold, from 1 percent in 1980 to 7 percent in 2000, U.S. investors remain woefully underdiversified. Compared with the recommended allocation in foreign stocks of 40 percent, the 7 percent allocation means that the home bias results in 33 percent excessive investment in domestic stocks.

There is another way of looking at the home bias. Some observers believe that investors should hold the world market portfolio passively, just as they do for domestic securities, where investment in a market index is considered appropriate. This means that if the capitalization of the U.S. markets is 47 percent of the worldwide total, then 47 percent should be invested in U.S. stocks and the remainder in foreign stocks. Using this measure of home bias, it is also possible to estimate the home bias for investors in other countries. Estimates of the home bias are reported in Table 10.5. American investors have the lowest home bias, perhaps because of the size of the market. Swedes and the Dutch invest the most in foreign equities among the developed countries. Thus, the incidence of home bias is not restricted to American investors alone but is a worldwide phenomenon.

Extensions

HOME BIAS ALSO EXISTS FOR DOMESTIC STOCKS

The term "home bias" is normally associated only with foreign stocks. However, "home" can be much closer to home. Home bias also exists for domestic stocks in addition to foreign stocks. Evidence shows that investors tend to invest in companies that they are aware of. For example, a disproportionately large number of investors in phone companies come from the states that the companies serve, though from an investment perspective the location of the company should be inconsequential. Even institutional investors, such as mutual funds, tend to invest in companies that are located close to their own corporate offices. Perhaps investors heed the advice of celebrities like Peter Lynch, who suggest that people should invest only in the companies they know well.

HOME BIAS IS WORSE THAN YOU THINK

Whenever an individual's portfolio is considered, *all* of the possible assets must be considered, financial and nonfinancial. However, the evidence presented above is based on equity markets only. In addition to marketable equity there is private equity in companies not publicly traded. There are fixed-income assets such as government bonds and corporate bonds. There is real estate. And, finally, even human capital is an asset.

Among all nonmarketable assets, human capital is probably the most important. Since human capital is highly correlated with an individual's job and eventually with the domestic economy, a large proportion of an individual's capital is invested in the domestic market. On the other hand, human capital is very weakly correlated with foreign markets. According to one estimate, once human capital is taken into account, a typical investor should not be invested in the domestic market at all. All marketable assets should be invested in foreign markets alone. Moreover, when you consider other assets such as bonds, real estate, and private equity, the home bias becomes much worse than that documented above.

BONDS CAN HELP WITH DIVERSIFICATION

If the correlation among different assets is important for minimizing risk, then bonds should play a critical role. Some correlation coefficients are illustrative. Based on the 1971–98 period, the correlation between U.S. stocks and Swiss bonds is –0.03, 0.21 between

U.S. bonds and Italian bonds, and 0.20 between Canadian bonds and French bonds. The correlation between U.S. stocks and U.S. bonds is also low: only 0.45 based on a fifteen-year period ending in 1985.

Therefore, an ideal portfolio should consist of U.S. stocks, foreign stocks, U.S. bonds, and foreign bonds. Due to ease of availability of data and analysis, the remainder of the chapter continues to focus on marketable equity assets only.

Concerns and Limitations

There are a variety of concerns with international investing and limitations of the analysis cited in previous sections. These limitations are discussed below and may weaken the case for international investing.

INCREASING AND VARYING CORRELATIONS

Concern

The key benefit from international investing arises because of low correlations between the domestic market and foreign markets. There are two criticisms of historical correlations. First, the correlations may be increasing due to greater global integration as evidenced by larger capital and trade flows. Moreover, as more and more emerging markets liberalize capital flows, the correlations will increase. If the correlations are increasing, the above analysis based on prior data overestimates the benefit from international investing. Reconsider the example in the preamble of "Evidence," above. With a correlation of 0.60, the new portfolio's risk fell from 18 percent to 16 percent. However, if the correlation is 0.70 instead of 0.60, then the new portfolio's risk falls less, from 18 percent to 16.6 percent. If the correlation is 0.8, then the risk is 17.1 percent.

You can see that the gains from international investing can quickly erode with an increase in correlations.

The second criticism stems from evidence that suggests that correlations increase in times of booms and crises. Since risk diversification is most useful and critical when markets are in a decline or in turbulent markets, increasing correlations at those moments make international investing less attractive. For example, all markets fell together during the 1974 oil price shock, the 1987 stock market crash, the 1991 Gulf crisis, and the 1997 East Asian currency crisis. Clearly, the higher correlation in times of crisis is not desirable.

Rejoinder

From Table 10.2, the average correlation is 0.58 for the developed markets and 0.42 for the emerging markets. The different periods considered in "Risk of International Investing" suggest that correlations vary between 0.20 and 0.70 for pairs of developed countries and that the range has not varied much over time. In any case, how high can the correlations go? The United States and Canada are probably as similar as two countries can be and trade a lot. However, the correlation has hovered around 0.70. The same thing is true of Switzerland and Germany. Thus, there seems to be an upper bound to how correlated U.S. markets and foreign markets can become.

Why is there an upper bound? The answer is in the two sources of diversification that cause the countries to be less than perfectly correlated. The first source is based on differences in the political and economic environment of different countries. The second source of low correlation is differences in the industrial makeup of countries. The argument goes as follows: the political outlook and economic structure of a country is important because a centrally planned economy will behave quite differently than a market-driven economy. Changes in the political climate do not affect more than one country or region. For instance, political turmoil in Indonesia may affect Singapore and Malaysia but is unlikely to affect the U.S. stock market. The political relationship between North Korea and South Korea is unlikely to have an effect on European markets. Similarly, national stock markets may continue to remain poorly correlated if those markets consist of different industries. For example, a country that specializes in textiles cannot be highly correlated with the U.S. stock market, which consists of high-tech and service-oriented industries.

Moreover, while globalization can increase correlations among countries due to integration, globalization can also lead to lower correlations. With greater trade and globalization, countries tend to specialize in industries depending on comparative advantage, their natural resources, labor skill, wages, and so on. As the developed countries move more toward services and concentrate on innovations, they will import more of other products. Therefore, globalization makes the countries more different due to specialization. This specialization in industries suggests that it is unlikely that the industrial base of countries will converge, and hence the stock markets are unlikely to become highly correlated.

The jury is still out on the relative importance of the two sources of diversification. Are differences in political and economic environment more important than differences in the industrial structure of countries? Whatever the cause, it is easy to see that countries will remain less than well correlated for a long time. From a historical perspective, global trade as a percentage of GDP was at a significantly higher level in the early 1900s than today, but the correlations among countries were not high. Individual country correlations have bounced around and increased a little, but the EAFE-U.S. correlations have remained between 0.50 and 0.60.

On the other hand, the correlations between emerging markets and the U.S. market are likely to increase as the emerging markets become more open to foreign capital flows. However, these correlations do not increase continually. Take the 1984–93 period. The correlation between the U.S. and a composite of emerging markets was 0.34 for 1984–88, but it fell to 0.20 between 1988 and 1990 and then to 0.19 for 1991–93. Though there is an increase in correlations, they will probably stagnate around 0.40 and 0.50. A low level of correlation with emerging markets is appropriate due to large differences in economic conditions and prosperity.

The second concern relates to higher correlations in times of crisis. There are two responses. First, other studies question the reliability of this finding and state that correlations only seem to be higher and in fact are actually the same. Second, the correlations mentioned above and used in calculations include both highly volatile and normal times. Since any equity investment, including international equity investment, ought to be long-term, very short-term correlations are not relevant.

COSTS AND TAXES

Concern

The cost of investing internationally is significantly higher than investing domestically because of many factors. First, gathering information about foreign stocks is more expensive. Foreign companies reveal much less information about their operations than their American counterparts because they do not have the same kind of disclosure requirements. Moreover, the information that is available in the public domain is more difficult to obtain and more expensive. Investors must subscribe to foreign database subscription services, fax services, and foreign newspapers and pay for expedited delivery to obtain the information in a timely manner. And differences in accounting practices mean that financial statements are not easily comparable. These difficulties make research required to value foreign company more expensive and more uncertain.

The second cost factor relates to the cost of trading. Trading costs consist of exchange commissions, brokerage commissions, transaction taxes, and market impact costs. Exchange costs must be incurred for converting dollars into another currency. Depending on the currency, these costs range between 0.05 percent and 0.1 percent for the more actively traded currencies and up to 0.25 percent for other currencies. In addition, foreign brokers charge higher commissions than U.S. brokers. Compared to a fee of 0.1 percent for large transactions in the United States, foreign brokerage commissions can run from 0.1 percent to more than 1.0 percent in other countries, including developed markets. Almost all governments impose taxes on stock trades. In the United States there is an SEC fee that is currently 0.00301 percent on all stock sales. Other governments may and do charge much higher fees, as much as 0.5 percent of the sale amount. Some countries charge fees on both buys and sells. Besides the fees and commissions, there is a market impact cost that must be borne by the investor. Whenever large trades are made, there is an impact on the price. If a large buy order is placed, the price increases to induce more market participants to part with their stock. Similarly, when a large sell order is placed, the price falls so that the stock becomes attractive to reluctant buyers. This impact on price occurs in all markets. However, the price impact of a trade is likely to be larger in foreign markets because they tend to be smaller and less liquid than U.S. markets. The high trading costs reduce the returns available from international investing.

Another form of tax is the withholding tax on dividends. This tax is usually about 15 percent and withheld by the foreign government. The investor must claim a set-off against other taxes. The withholding tax creates two problems. First, the extra hassle of paying taxes and then reclaiming those taxes with a time lag is a cost incurred by investors in foreign securities. Second, tax-exempt investors such as pension plans completely lose the withholding tax because they are not liable for payment of any income taxes.

All of the above costs due to information, trading, and taxes were ignored in prior analyses. The firm of Elkins and McSherry reports that costs directly related to trading vary considerably among the forty-five emerging and developed markets. It finds the highest trading costs among emerging countries for Venezuela (2 percent), highest among developed markets for Ireland (0.90 percent), and the lowest among developed markets for Japan at 0.22 percent. The trading costs in American and German markets are about 0.29 percent.

Rejoinder

Information costs, trading costs, and taxes can indeed reduce the net return earned from foreign investments. However, the costs are still smaller than the gains from international investing. In addition, for most individual investors, American depository receipts (ADRs, discussed below) provide an easy and inexpensive way to trade where the costs of trading foreign stocks are equivalent to those for trading domestic stocks.

CURRENCY RISK

Concern

Holding foreign securities denominated in foreign currencies entails currency risk, as dollars must first be converted into foreign currencies and the foreign currencies converted back into dollars at the future rate. As the future rate is unknown, investing in foreign markets suffers from an additional risk due to currency fluctuations.

Rejoinder

Yes, there is currency risk due to currency conversions and uncertainty with regard to future exchange rates. However, as all of the returns reported in the earlier tables are in dollar terms, those returns already incorporate associated currency risk. Thus currency risk is important in foreign investments but has already been accounted for. Currency risk can also be hedged if desired (see "Currency Hedging").

POLITICAL AND ECONOMIC RISK

Concern

Investors are also concerned about big changes in the economic conditions due to a change in the political orientation of the government. While this is of most concern in emerging markets, even the developed markets are not immune to a dramatic change in the environment. Obviously, large changes are risky for equity markets. In addition, foreign investors are also concerned about currency regulations that may hinder repatriation of capital/income. For example, Malaysia did not permit repatriation of capital for one year following the 1997 East Asian currency crisis. Other countries routinely make it difficult for investors to transfer funds out of the host country.

Rejoinder

This is a valid concern. However, there are numerous stock markets. It is easy to exclude countries that have an unstable political history or have restricted capital flows in the last decade. An investor can pick many developed markets and emerging markets where the political risk is relatively low. See "Internet References" for websites providing this information.

LIQUIDITY RISK AND MARKET INEFFICIENCY

Concern

The size of the markets can work against foreign investors in two ways. First, some securities and some countries may be illiquid. In such markets, any reasonably sized trades are sufficient to move the price. The price rises when one wants to buy and falls upon a sale. This is particularly painful because most foreign investors end up selling and buying around the same time.

The second concern with market size is inefficiency. Emerging markets are known to be inefficient, and prices can take several days to fully reflect new information. As a passive investor, you can lose money to more sophisticated investors who trade on the basis of the inefficiency.

Rejoinder

Liquidity risk exists in all markets, including the U.S. market, where small stocks are very illiquid. The challenge is for the investor to select markets and stocks that are likely to experience a smaller liquidity shock than other countries and stocks. So it would be smart for investors to trade only large, liquid stocks in large, liquid markets.

Market inefficiency can work both ways. It certainly worsens the returns for unsophisticated investors, but smart investors can take advantage of the inefficiencies, thereby forcing the market to become more efficient. In any case, passive investors can choose markets that are relatively less inefficient.

RISKINESS OF FOREIGN MARKETS

Concern

Foreign markets are very risky, much riskier than the U.S. markets. Risk-averse investors are unwilling to accept a higher level of risk.

Rejoinder

Foreign markets, especially emerging markets, are indeed riskier than U.S. markets. However, due to the low correlation between foreign markets and U.S. markets, a portfolio that includes stocks from both markets need not be as risky. The diversification of risk has been illustrated in Tables 10.3 and 10.4. As a matter of fact, holding U.S. stocks only is riskier than holding a world portfolio weighted by the market capitalization of each country.

Persistence

The home bias is nothing new and has persisted for decades. Though the investment in foreign equities has increased from 1 percent to 7 percent over the last two decades, it falls short of the level of optimal foreign investment.

Unlike the mispricings discussed in earlier chapters, it is not possible for arbitrageurs or anyone else to form short-term trading strategies. Over the long term, however, investors who hold foreign stocks will outperform portfolios that are restricted to domestic stocks only.

The only reason that can explain the persistence of the home bias is the ignorance of a typical investor. A comparison of investment in foreign stocks by individual and institutional investors is revealing. According to Fidelity and *Pensions and Investments*, only 3 percent of the assets held by individual investors are invested in foreign equity, compared with 13 percent for professionally managed pension funds. The two hundred largest corporate pension plans had an allocation of 16 percent to foreign stocks. On the other hand, mutual funds have only 3.5 percent invested in international stocks. The foreign allocation of mutual funds mirrors the individual investor allocation because individual investors can pick and choose mutual funds and exclude international mutual funds if they don't want to invest internationally. The pension funds can determine the allocation on the basis of portfolio theory, as discussed in this chapter.

Where and How to Invest Internationally

Buying foreign stocks is cumbersome for an individual investor because it requires currency conversion, opening an account with a foreign broker, taking custody of a foreign company's shares, and all the associated transactions. Many domestic brokers now offer trading in foreign stocks, but it is still a lot more difficult to buy and sell foreign stocks than it is to trade domestic stocks.

There are, however, alternatives available that do not require direct trading on foreign stock exchanges. These are American depository receipts (ADRs), mutual funds, exchange-traded funds, and multinational companies. Details are provided below.

American Depository Receipts (ADRs)

ADRs are negotiable registered certificates that stand in for the underlying stock of foreign companies. A U.S. bank (called a custodian bank) holds shares of foreign companies and issues receipts (ADRs) against those shares. There could be one ADR for several shares or several ADRs for one share of stock—the custodian bank picks a ratio that puts the ADR in a tradable range of $50–100. For example, each share of British Petroleum is subdivided into six ADRs and each share of British Airways is equal to ten ADRs, while two Honda shares make one ADR but one Sony share is equal to one ADR.

The Bank of New York holds the largest number of shares as a custodian, though J. P. Morgan created the first ADR in 1927 for investing in the British retailer Selfridge's. The certificates are quoted in U.S. dollars and dividends are paid in U.S. dollars. ADRs are traded on the major U.S. stock exchanges or over the counter. ADRs are issued in two basic versions: sponsored and unsponsored. The most popular version today is sponsored, and for these, the creation of the ADR is initiated and supported by the company. As of 2002 there were 1,450 ADRs, including 200 unsponsored ADRs. There are four kinds of sponsored ADRs.

- *Level I ADRs* trade on the pink sheets (OTC bulletin board), are exempt from the SEC reporting requirements, but cannot be used for raising capital, or be listed on organized stock exchanges in the United States. More than eight hundred ADRs, such as Roche, Nestlé, and Volkswagen belong to this category.

- *Level II ADRs* are listed and trade on U.S. exchanges—NYSE, AMEX, Nasdaq—but cannot be used for raising new equity capital. Financial statements must be partially reconciled with generally accepted accounting principles (GAAP).

- *Level III ADRs* can raise new capital from American investors and are listed on U.S. exchanges. These ADRs are just like domestic stocks and require full compliance with GAAP and SEC regulations.

- *Rule 144A ADRs:* Under Rule 144A, a company can raise new capital but only from qualified institutional buyers (QIB) and a limited number (thirty-five) of noninstitutional buyers. This provides another way of raising new capital but without compliance with GAAP/SEC regulations.

The biggest advantage of an ADR is the ease with which it can be traded. To buy Nokia, you would call your broker and tell him/her to buy Nokia just as you would tell him/her to buy IBM. You get all of the benefits of foreign ownership but are able to minimize the costs associated with foreign trading. With level II and III ADRs, you get more information and are better protected against fraud and misreporting.

Unfortunately, ADRs may not represent all industries and countries. Typically, ADRs are issued for companies that sell consumer goods because those companies will be known to American investors and will attract investment capital. ADRs have no voting rights because the investor does not actually hold the shares. Finally, liquidity may be an issue for some ADRs because the U.S. market shares typically represent less than 10 percent of all outstanding shares.

INTERNATIONAL MUTUAL FUNDS

Nearly all of the mutual fund families offer multiple funds that are geared toward international investing. The different kinds of funds can be categorized into index funds, international funds, regional funds, country funds, emerging market funds, and global funds. International mutual funds have higher expense ratios than domestic mutual funds to cover higher trading costs and higher management fees. The funds also tend to have redemption fees to control frequent trading. Examples of funds offered by major mutual fund companies are given below.

- *Index funds.* These include Fidelity Spartan International Index Fund, Vanguard Developed Markets Stock Index, Vanguard Emerging Markets Stock Index, and Price International Equity Index Fund.

- *International funds.* These funds do not invest in the domestic market. Funds include Fidelity International Growth, T. Rowe Price International, Fidelity Overseas, Vanguard International Growth, Fidelity Diversified International, and so on.

- *Global funds.* These funds invest in all countries, including the domestic market, and include Templeton World, GT Global

Worldwide, Dreyfus Global, Vanguard Global Equity, Price Global Stock, and so on.

- *Regional funds.* Examples include Fidelity Europe Capital Appreciation, Fidelity Nordic, Vanguard European Stock Index, and T. Rowe Price European Stock.

- *Country funds.* Examples include Fidelity Canada and Fidelity Japan Smaller Companies.

- *Emerging market funds.* Examples include Fidelity Emerging Markets Fund, Fidelity Latin America, and T. Rowe Price Emerging Markets Stock.

EXCHANGE-TRADED FUNDS AND CLOSED-END FUNDS

Both exchange-traded funds (ETFs) and closed-end funds trade on organized exchanges, just like stocks. Unlike mutual funds, which are priced at the end of the day, ETFs and closed-end funds can be traded at any time during trading hours with no restrictions or redemption fees.

Closed-end funds were started several decades ago, when many markets were closed to foreign investment. For example, Scudder Investments was permitted to invest $100 million in Korea in April 1984 with the condition that the money could not be taken out of Korea, nor more money brought in. As a result, the fund cannot redeem shares nor issue more shares. In other words, it is a closed-end fund. Any shareholders of the Korea Fund can sell shares only on an exchange, like the NYSE. Similarly, new investors must buy shares on the NYSE. One problem with the closed-end funds is that they usually trade at a discount (sometimes at a premium) to the underlying value of the securities held. The reasons for the discount/premium are not well understood, so many investors tend to avoid closed-end funds.

Exchange-traded funds track an index by holding the stocks in that index. There are iShares for twenty countries that track the MSCI (Morgan Stanley Capital International) country indexes, and three regional indexes. The regional ETFs are for the Pacific except Japan, EAFE, and the EMU. The EMU fund is for countries that participate in the euro. In addition to the ETFs that track MSCI indexes, there are four ETFs that track S&P international indexes: Latin America, Topix (Japan), Europe, and Canada. The ETFs track the underlying indexes quite well, with a correlation of about 0.97. At the same time, the correlation of ETFs with the S&P 500 is low. Thus, ETFs are effective in diversifying the risk of a domestic portfolio.

The expense ratio of the ETFs is less than 1 percent, which is less than the expense ratio for mutual funds. However, there are other costs of trading ETFs such as brokerage commissions and the bid-ask spread. Unlike the popular ETFs such as SPY (for the S&P 500) and QQQ (for the Nasdaq 100), international ETFs may not be actively traded. Investors may not want to trade ETFs if the daily average volume is less than a hundred thousand shares.

Multinational Companies

The last possible avenue for obtaining international exposure is multinational companies with large overseas operations. As these companies operate globally, their stocks should provide the diversification expected from foreign stocks. However, research suggests that multinational companies are not good substitutes for foreign investing.

The failure of multinational companies to diversify risk should not come as a surprise once you consider the correlation between the S&P 500 and companies with large overseas operations.

Company	Correlation with S&P 500
General Electric	0.97
Merck	0.96
Exxon Mobil	0.96
Pfizer	0.96
Microsoft	0.96
Chevron Texaco	0.94
Dell	0.93
AI Group	0.93
Citigroup	0.93
Intel	0.92

A correlation of more than 0.90 means that there is unlikely to be a significant improvement in risk by the addition of or overweighting of these companies in a domestic portfolio.

Effectiveness of These Instruments in Diversification

Though the ADRs and ETFs do not span the entire spectrum of foreign markets, they help in substantially diversifying risk. The addition of international mutual funds to ADRs and ETFs almost fully captures the benefits of international investing, eliminating the need for an individual investor to invest overseas directly.

Currency Hedging

One issue that has elicited different responses is the role of currency risk in overall risk and return. Currency risk has been accounted for in all of the evidence presented. So the existence of currency risk will not reduce the benefits of investing in foreign markets. Rather, the question is whether managing currency risk will improve the gains from international investing.

While the reduction of any kind of risk is good, there are two issues that must be considered with regard to currency risk. First, the correlation between currency risk and stock market risk is close to zero. That means that currency changes and stock returns are independent of one another. Though both currency risk and stock market risk contribute to the total risk of a portfolio of foreign stocks, the contribution of currency risk to the total risk is not very large because of the zero correlation. On average, currency risk contributes less than 20 percent of the total risk.

The second issue is the cost of hedging currency risk. To completely eliminate currency risk, a dynamic hedging strategy is required, which can be very expensive. Even incomplete hedging can be costly due to the time required and the expense of putting the hedge in place. Consider an investment in the EAFE index. For a given level of risk, the hedged portfolio has a return that is at most 0.5 percent higher than an unhedged portfolio. If the cost of hedging is less than that, hedging is worthwhile; otherwise it is not.

The case for hedging an investment in emerging markets is even weaker because the correlation between currency risk and stock market risk is very often negative. In such cases, hedging currency risk will increase the total risk instead of reducing total risk.

The performance of foreign portfolios including international mutual funds can depend a great deal on whether the funds hedge against currency risk or not. A comparison of the MSCI EAFE hedged and unhedged indexes is telling. The hedged MSCI EAFE index lost only 4.4 percent in 2000 compared with the unhedged index that lost 14.2 percent in the same period. On the other hand, the hedged index gained 11.0 percent in 1998 compared with 20.0 percent for an unhedged index. Note, however, that the hedged index does not include the cost of hedging.

Since it is difficult to predict which way the currency is going, is it worthwhile spending money on currency hedging? There isn't a good answer. But as an investor, you should be aware of whether or not the mutual fund you hold hedges currency risk.

Qualifications

The evidence presented in this chapter is based on past data. Since future market conditions and market patterns may be completely different, there is a small chance that home bias will not continue in the future.

Of greater concern are the relative returns, risks, and correlations of different markets. These may change in a way to make international investing less attractive. However, the discussion in "Concerns and Limitations" addresses these issues and continues to recommend investing in foreign markets.

Key Points

- Investors are risk-averse and would like to minimize risk or be compensated for assuming any risk. Portfolio risk can be reduced by adding stocks that are not well correlated with the portfolio. In particular, the risk can be reduced by adding foreign stocks to a domestic portfolio because foreign stocks are not highly correlated with domestic stocks. Though holding foreign stocks is optimal, investors tend not to hold portfolios that contain an optimal exposure to foreign stocks. The underweighting of foreign stocks in a portfolio is referred to as the home bias.

- The evidence shows that the correlation between emerging markets and the U.S. market is 0.42, and that between the developed markets and the U.S. market is 0.58. If emerging market stocks and other developed market stocks are included in a domestic portfolio, there is an improvement in the risk-return trade-off from a U.S. investor's portfolio. An optimal portfolio should contain about a 30 percent investment in other developed markets and another 10 percent in emerging markets. Compared to the optimal portfolio, U.S. investors invest only 7 percent in foreign stocks, emerging and developed markets combined. If other kinds of assets are considered, the home bias becomes even more severe.

- It is possible that the benefits of international investing are overstated, as the analysis does not account for varying correlations, trading costs and taxes, and different types of risk. These concerns are addressed along with the likely reasons for persistence.

- Avenues for investing internationally include American depository receipts, exchange-traded funds, and international mutual funds. With the availability of these instruments, an investor can realize the benefits of international investing without directly owning foreign stocks.

- Whether or not to hedge foreign portfolios against currency risk is a difficult question. While reducing risk is good, the cost of hedging currency risk may turn out to be too high. Some actively managed mutual funds do hedge currency risk, while others do not.

Bottom Line

Internationalizing a domestic portfolio is strongly recommended. Research based on the 1976–99 period estimates that an investment in developed countries and emerging markets would have increased a U.S. investor's annual return by 3.78 percent while reducing the investor's risk by 9.74 percent. Ideally, about 40 percent of the portfolio should be invested in foreign securities through ADRs, exchange-traded funds, and international mutual funds.

Internet References

Data Sources

http://www.msci.com: Morgan Stanley Capital International (MSCI) indexes are most widely used for measuring performance of international markets. The definition of the indexes and some performance data are available at this site.

http://www.globalfindata.com: Global Financial Data is a warehouse for a variety of financial data, including international stock returns and exchange rates.

http://www.barra.com: Barra provides a downloadable file that contains monthly S&P 500 total returns from 1975. These data are not available at the Standard and Poor's site (www.spglobal.com).

http://www.elkinsmcsherry.com: Estimates of trading costs mentioned in the chapter are obtained from Elkins/McSherry. However, their website does not provide this information.

http://www.ftmarketwatch.com and http://www.euronext.com: Information on European stocks.

http://www.beri.com and http://www.eiu.com: These sites provide information on political and business risk in different countries.

Benefits of International Investing

http://www.sec.gov/answers/adrs.htm, http://www.fidelity.com, http://www.troweprice.com: These sites of the SEC, Fidelity, and Vanguard have downloadable brochures on why international investing is good. Many other mutual fund companies and regulatory bodies provide similar information.

Avenues for International Investment

http://www.adr.com: J. P. Morgan's site. It explains how ADRs are created and the mechanics of trading. Contains a complete list of all ADRs.

http://www.adrbny.com: ADR site of Bank of New York. Contains a complete list of all ADRs.

http://www.citibank.com/adr/www: ADR site of Citigroup. Contains a complete list of all ADRs.

http://www.vanguard.com, http://www.fidelity.com, http://www.troweprice.com: Mutual fund sites of Vanguard, Fidelity and T. Rowe Price.

http://www.ishares.com: This site covers the exchange-traded funds managed by Barclays Global Investors.

http://www.amex.com: Select "ETFs," then "Product Information," then choose "International" from the drop-down list to get a list of exchange-traded funds.

References for Further Reading

General References

Solnik, Bruno. 2000. *International Investments*, 4th edition (Reading, Mass.: Addison-Wesley Longman Inc.).

Eun, Cheol, and Bruce Resnick. 2001. *International Financial Management*, 2nd edition (New York: McGraw-Hill).

Benefits of International Investing

Clarke, Roger G., and R. Matthew Tullis. 1999. How Much International Exposure Is Advantageous in a Domestic Portfolio? *Journal of Portfolio Management* 25(2), 33–44.

French, Kenneth R., and James M. Poterba. 1991. Investor Diversification and International Equity Markets. *American Economic Review* 81(2), 222–26.

Hunter, John E., and T. Daniel Coggin. 1990. An Analysis of the Diversification Benefit from International Equity Investment. *Journal of Portfolio Management* 17(1), 33–36.

Kim, E. Han, and Vijay Singal. 1997. Are Open Markets Good for Foreign Investors and Emerging Nations? *Journal of Applied Corporate Finance* 10(3), 18–33.

Michaud, Richard O., Gary L. Bergstrom, Ronald D. Frashure, and Bran K. Wolahan. 1996. Twenty Years of International Equity Investing. *Journal of Portfolio Management* 23(1), 9–22.

Sarkar, Asani, and Kai Li. 2002. Should U.S. Investors Hold Foreign Stocks? *Federal Reserve Bank of New York's Current Issues in Economics and Finance* 8(3), 1–6.

Wignall, Christian. 1994. Does International Investing Still Make Sense? Yes, and Here's Why. *Journal of Investing* 3(4), 12–17.

Explanations of the Home Bias

Coen, Alain. 2001. Home Bias and International Capital Asset Pricing Model with Human Capital. *Journal of Multinational Financial Management* 11(4–5), 497–513.

Coval, Joshua D., and Tobias J. Moskowitz. 1999. Home Bias at Home: Local Equity Preference in Domestic Portfolios. *Journal of Finance* 54(6), 2045–73.

Goetzmann, William N., and Alok Kumar. 2001. Equity Portfolio Diversification. NBER working paper no. 8686.

Hasan, Iftekhar, and Yusif Simaan. 2000. A Rational Explanation for Home Country Bias. *Journal of International Money and Finance* 19(3), 331–61.

Huberman, Gur. 2001. Familiarity Breeds Investment. *Review of Financial Studies* 14(3), 659–80.

Jeske, Karsten. 2001. Equity Home Bias: Can Information Cost Explain the Puzzle? *FRB Atlanta—Economic Review* 86(3), 31–42.

Lewis, Karen K. 1999. Trying to Explain Home Bias in Equities and Consumption. *Journal of Economic Literature* 37(2), 571–608.

Avenues for International Investment

Aiello, Scott, and Natalie Chieffe. 1999. International Index Funds and the Investment Portfolio. *Financial Services Review* 8(1), 27–35.

Dada, Joe, and T. Jon Williams. 1993. Is There a Shortcut to International Investing? *Journal of Investing* 2(4), 45–47.

Droms, William G., and David A. Walker. 1994. Investment Performance of International Mutual Funds. *Journal of Financial Research* 17(1), 1–14.

Errunza, Vihang, Ked Hogan, and Mao-Wei Hung. 1999. Can the Gains from International Diversification Be Achieved Without Trading Abroad? *Journal of Finance* 54(6), 2075–107.

Eun, Cheol S., Richard Kolodny, and Bruce G. Resnick. 1994. The Role of International Mutual Funds for U.S. Investors. *Advances in Investment Analysis and Portfolio Management* 2, 1–35.

Notes

1. Besides the author's own analysis, this chapter is based on Clarke and Tullis (1999), Coval and Moskowitz (1999), Huberman (2001), Errunza, Hogan, and Hung (1999), Sarkar and Li (2002), Eun and Resnick (2001), and Solnik (2000).

11

Bias in Currency Forward Rates

Currency forward rates are determined in accordance with interest rate parity, such that the total returns from investment in two risk-free assets are identical. Equivalence of returns implies that the forward rate foresees the currency with a higher interest rate falling in value. However, the evidence reveals that currencies with higher interest rates do not actually fall as much as implied by the forward rate, creating the forward rate bias. A trading strategy that short-sells currencies with low interest rates and buys currencies with high interest rates can generate abnormal profits.

Description

The topic of this chapter is different from other chapters: it is slightly more complex and related to currencies rather than stocks, but it is nonetheless extremely important.[1] From a trading perspective, the bias discussed in this chapter has been documented in several hundred research papers and many books. Institutional investors, hedge funds, banks, currency traders, and many other market professionals periodically try to take advantage of this bias. The *forward rate bias*, as it is generally known, is also related to international investing and currency hedging.

Before discussing the bias in forward rates, some knowledge of forward rates is desirable and is covered first. A spot exchange rate is the rate at which two currencies are exchanged in the spot market, which means that delivery will take place in two business days. If the delivery is scheduled to take place more than two business days later, then the forward rate applies. Thus, the forward rate is the rate at which two currencies are exchanged more than two business days later. The forward rate is set at the time the contract is entered into, not at the time of delivery. The obvious question arises: how is the forward rate determined? The forward rate is based on interest rate parity, which is described below.

Consider two investments that are completely risk-free. Let the first investment be one-year U.S. Treasury bills (investment A) and the second investment be another one-year claim fully guaranteed by the U.S. government (investment B). Assume further that there are no transaction costs and no restrictions on short selling, and both investments are equally difficult or easy to make. Under these circumstances, both investment A and investment B must provide the same return. If not, arbitrage profits can be earned. For example, assume that investment A generates a return of 2.0 percent, whereas investment B generates a return of 0.25 percent. As both investments are risk-free, an investor will short-sell B and use the proceeds to buy A. The investor will incur a cost of 0.25 percent in borrowing or short-selling B but earn a return of 2.0 percent from A. Thus, the net profit is 1.75 percent. This profit is risk-free and requires zero investment. Many investors will repeat this process. The higher demand for A means that its price will rise, reducing its return from 2 percent. At the same time, the excessive selling of B will lower B's price, raising its return from 0.25 percent. The process will continue until the returns from both investments become equal.

The basic idea is that two riskless securities or investments must earn the same return, or else arbitrage profits can be made. Consider introducing another currency by letting B be an investment in Japanese one-year Treasury bills. Investment A continues as an investment in U.S. T-bills. As the claim on Japanese T-bills is guaranteed by the Japanese government, investment B is still risk-free. Since both investments are risk-free, they must generate the same return. Consider an investor with $1 million who wants to invest for one year and get the money back in U.S. dollars. To invest in A, he just buys T-bills worth $1 million. After one year he will get $1.02 million. To invest in B, he must go through the following four steps:

1. Convert U.S. dollars into yen at the spot exchange rate. If the spot rate is S_0 per J¥, then the amount in J¥ = 1 million × $(1/S_0)$.

2. Invest the yen in Japanese T-bills at 0.25 percent.

3. Hold for one year and redeem the T-bills for yen after one year. The investor receives J¥ 1 million × $(1/S_0)$ × $(1 + 0.0025)$, in-

cluding interest. In a mathematical format, it is equal to $[(1/S_0) \times (1 + i^{FC})]$.

4. Convert the yen into dollars at the exchange rate. If the rate is $\$F_0$ per J¥, then the investor will receive \$1 million $\times (1/S_0) \times (1 + 0.0025) \times F_0$. In a mathematical format, it is equal to $[(1/S_0) \times (1 + i^{FC})] \times F_0]$.

The amount after the four steps, that is, the investment in B, must also equal \$1.02 million if it is risk-free. The first two steps are risk-free since they are executed right away and the third step is guaranteed by the Japanese government. Step 4 is potentially risky. Therefore, a forward contract signed at inception is required to make step 4 risk-free. With a forward contract, the investor is guaranteed exchange at the forward rate, which will take place a year later. Let the forward rate be F_0. With all four steps being risk-free, the amount that the investor receives at the end of one year with investment B should equal \$1.02 million, the amount that he will get with investment A. Thus, \$1 million $\times (1/S_0) \times (1 + 0.0025) \times F_0 = \$1.02$ million. In a mathematical format, it can be written as $[(1/S_0) \times (1 + i^{FC})] \times F_0] = 1 + i^\$$.

The only unknown variable is F_0. Upon calculation, it turns out that $F_0 = 1.0175 \times S_0$. More formally, the forward rate can be written in the form given below, called interest rate parity (IRP):

$$F_0 = \frac{\left(1 + i_0^\$\right)}{\left(1 + i_0^{FC}\right)} \times S_0$$

where the i's are the interest rates, F_0 and S_0 are the exchange rates expressed as dollars per unit of foreign currency, and the periods for the forward rate and interest rates are the same. That is, a six-month forward rate requires the interest rates also to be for six-month periods.

Reexamining the equation reveals that if $i^\$$ is greater than i^{FC}, as in the example here (2 percent for the U.S. and 0.25 percent for Japan), then $F_0 > S_0$. The calculations showed that $F_0 = 1.0175 \times S_0$. In such a case, one J¥ should buy more dollars a year later. This indicates that the forward rate reflects an appreciation of J¥ over the next one year and a depreciation of the dollar.

Look at it another way. As the return from both investments must be the same, the currency with the lower interest rate must reflect an appreciation relative to the other currency so that its total return can equal the interest earned by the higher-interest-rate currency. That can only happen if the forward rate reflects an appreciation of the currency with the lower interest rate. That way the forward rate ensures no difference in total returns and no opportunity for arbitrage.

The condition that the forward rate be set in accordance with interest rate parity is pretty unforgiving. In the example considered, the forward rate must reflect an appreciation of 1.75 percent for the yen. If it doesn't, then arbitrage profits can be earned and will continue to be earned until the forward rate does reflect an appreciation of 1.75 percent for the yen. In practice, violations of interest rate parity do not remain for more than a few seconds because arbitrageurs pounce to make a quick buck.

So far, so good. The problem is that the actual future spot rate, the exchange rate one year later, may not necessarily reflect an appreciation of the yen as predicted by the forward rate. The evidence indicates that currencies with high interest rates *do not fall sufficiently* to make the returns equal. That is, the returns on higher-interest-rate currencies tend to be higher than the returns on low-interest-rate currencies.

Evidence

In brief, the forward rate (F_0) is the rate at which currency exchanges take place later but the rate is decided at the time of signing the forward contract. The forward rate is determined based on interest rate parity, which ensures the same return for two risk-free assets. Any deviations from this condition are quickly arbitraged away. Second, under normal conditions, the future spot exchange rate (S_1) is expected to equal, on average, the forward rate. However, that does not seem to occur.

Table 11.1 will clarify some of these points. All rates are expressed in U.S. dollars per yen.

The forward rate on January 16 for delivery on March 15 is $0.009592/J¥, showing an appreciation of the yen relative to the spot exchange

Table 11.1   Spot Rates and Forward Rates

Time = 0	Spot (S_0)	Forward (F_0)	Actual Time = 1	Future Spot (S_1)
January 16	0.009445	0.009592	March 15	0.009446
March 15	0.009446	0.009567	June 17	0.009187
June 17	0.009187	0.009290	Sept. 16	0.009078
Sept. 16	0.009078	0.009191	Dec. 15	0.008754

rate of \$0.009445/J¥ on January 16 and reflecting the higher U.S. interest rate. However, the actual future spot rate on March 15 is \$0.009446/J¥, which did not reflect the anticipated appreciation of the yen. This trend continues for the remaining dates. On March 15, the forward rate for delivery on June 17 is \$0.009567/J¥ but it turns out that the yen actually depreciates to \$0.009187/J¥ instead of appreciating by June 17. The Japanese yen continues to depreciate in September and December, though the forward rate reflects an appreciation based on the lower interest on Japanese treasury securities.

The above table is only a snapshot and is not a scientifically selected period. The formal testing of forward rates vis-à-vis the actual future rates is set up below, beginning with interest rate parity. The interest rate parity equation can be rewritten so that the difference in exchange rates is equal to the difference in interest rates:

$$\ln F_0 - \ln S_0 = i_0^\$ - i_0^{FC}$$

Since the future spot rate (S_1) should equal the forward rate, the above equation can be rewritten as:

$$\ln S_1 - \ln S_0 = i_0^\$ - i_0^{FC}$$

This equation can be further generalized to the following form:

$$\ln S_1 - \ln S_0 = a + b\left(i_0^\$ - i_0^{FC}\right)$$

where a is expected to be 0 and b *is expected to be* +1 if the forward rate is unbiased, that is, on average equal to the actual future spot rate.

The empirical tests of the forward rate bias basically check whether b turns out be 1 or not. If b is not equal to 1, then the forward rate (F_0) is biased, as it is not equal, on average, to the future spot rate (S_1). The empirical evidence relating to the value of b varies with the time periods, currency pairs, observation periods, and the methods used. However, the value of b is generally negative, never equal to or greater than 1, and, on average, equal to –0.88 (negative, not positive or zero). This and similar evidence is the basis for the forward rate bias.

A few results are presented in Table 11.2 for three different periods. Note that much of the evidence here relies on the value of the dollar relative to other major currencies, such as the German mark

Table 11.2   Forward Rate Bias

Currency	*b* for 1980–87 (1-month period)	*b* for 1974–90 (1-month period)	*b* for 1980–98 (3-month period)
Canadian dollar	−1.94	−1.46	−0.52
German mark	−4.51	−3.54	−0.65
Japanese yen	−2.94	−1.81	−3.44
Swiss franc	−5.22		
British pound	−4.72	−2.31	−2.04

(until 1998), Japanese yen, British pound, Canadian dollar, and the Swiss franc. It can be seen that all values are negative, in fact, less than −1 in a majority of the cases, rather than being equal to +1.

The first two columns above report results based on a one-month forward rate, whereas the last one has the results based on a three-month forward rate. The values of *b* become smaller for the 3-month period, but they continue to be negative. So there is consistency in the results, though the magnitude of *b* varies.

There are two particular instances where the estimates of *b* change considerably. First, it seems that the value of *b* has increased in the 1990s, that is, become less negative, as shown in Table 11.3.

The second instance of a change is with the period for which the forward rate is estimated. The longer the period, the higher and more positive are the estimates of *b*, as in Table 11.4.

With a one-month forward rate, the estimates of *b* are negative in Table 11.4 (except for the German mark). However, when the period increases to one year, more of them become positive, and finally with the ten-year forward rate all of them become positive. The second column below incorporates a time series adjustment, making the results less comparable to the other results. What seems obvious, though, is that it takes a lot to make *b* close to 1. And remember that just as with other areas of empirical research, researchers have to try very hard to get a result that is different from what has been documented before. In this case, researchers have to use a

Table 11.3   Change in Forward Rate Bias During the 1990s

	b for 1980–88	*b* for 1989–98
British pound	−5.10	+1.06
Canadian dollar	−0.45	−0.69
German mark	−3.15	−0.54
Japanese yen	−4.52	−3.86

Table 11.4   Forward Rate Bias for Different Holding Periods

	b (1 month) for 1985–2000	b (1 year) 1985–2000	b (10 years) 1983–98
British pound	−1.94	1.00	0.57
Canadian dollar	−0.98	−0.46	1.10
German mark	1.21	1.67	0.83
Japanese yen	−1.38	−0.18	0.49
Swiss franc	−0.23	0.73	

variety of elaborate techniques to make the value of b close to 1, since numerous papers have already found that b is negative.

The reduction in bias for longer-term forward rates may result because the long periods probably smooth out all fluctuations. However, the long holding periods are uninteresting and unrealistic for currencies because most investors hold currencies, as an investment, for relatively short periods of time.

The evidence shows that the average value of b is −1 instead of +1. What does it mean? It implies that if U.S. interest rates are higher than foreign rates by 1 percent, then the U.S. dollar *appreciates* by 1 percent instead of *depreciating* by 1 percent, as implied by the forward rate. Thus, the forward rate seems to be severely biased. A trading strategy arising out of this evidence is to hold the currency with the higher interest rate. If that currency's interest rate is higher by 1 percent, you can expect to earn 2 percent more than if you held the currency with the lower interest rate.

While the return is higher, the risk associated with that return has not been explicitly considered. If an optimal currency portfolio, consisting of the German mark, Japanese yen, Swiss franc, and the British pound with the U.S. dollar as the risk-free asset, is formed, then it has been found that the portfolio would have generated an average excess return of 2.79 percent per year over the period November 1989 through June 1999. The Sharpe ratio for this portfolio is 0.69 compared with a Sharpe ratio of 0.53 for the U.S. Treasury index, 0.49 for an unhedged global Treasury index, 0.80 for a hedged global Treasury index, and 0.95 for the S&P 500. The Sharpe ratio for the S&P 500 is unusually high because of the high returns earned by stocks during this period.

Overall, the evidence suggests that holding currencies can be a superior form of investment than several other forms of investment, after accounting for risk, even during the 1990s. Strategies based on the forward rate bias are implemented and tested later with more current data.

Explanations

The previous section established that the forward rate is biased in the sense that, on average, the actual future spot rate is not equal to the forward rate. Moreover, the bias is predictable. The actual future spot rate reflects an appreciation of the high-interest-rate currency, whereas the forward rate suggests a depreciation of the currency with the higher interest rate.

The analysis above made certain implicit assumptions to claim that the forward rate should be an unbiased predictor of the future spot rate. It is time to make those assumptions explicit. Fuller details of these assumptions are in the explanations that follow.

- Investors are risk-neutral.

- Investors are rational.

- Markets are efficient, that is, prices reflect all available information.

INVESTORS ARE RISK-AVERSE

One assumption for the unbiasedness of forward rates is that investors are risk-neutral, that is, they do not care about risk but care only about total return. Such investors will always choose investments that have the highest expected return, irrespective of the associated risk. So they will be fully invested in biotech and information technology stocks but will never buy insurance.

In reality, investors are not risk-neutral, they are risk-averse. Being risk-averse means that investors care about risk, and their choices are based both on return and risk. Such investors may frequently turn down high-return investments if they contain high risk, and will always demand compensation for any risk that they assume. These investors will also buy insurance, which has a negative return, if that insurance will lower the risk of large losses.

The problem is that with risk-averse investors, the forward rate cannot be unbiased. Let us consider a risk-averse investor X who is holding dollars but needs yen after a year. X has two alternatives: either to hedge or to remain unhedged. To hedge, X would enter into a forward contract to buy yen for dollars at the forward rate, F_0. The hedged alternative removes all risk related to the exchange of currencies. With the unhedged alternative, he will just wait for a year to roll around and then exchange dollars for yen at the future spot rate, S_1. Since the unhedged position is riskier, X will choose to remain unhedged only if he has to pay fewer dollars per yen using the future spot rate than what he would have to pay if he had used the forward rate. Thus, to make X happy with an unhedged position, S_1 must be less than F_0, since the exchange rates are measured as dollars per yen ($S_1 < F_0$).

Reverse the previous example, and consider an investor who is holding yen and wants to convert to dollars after one year. The same two choices confront Y. Remaining unhedged means that he will get S_1 dollars for each yen. Or he could hedge by using a forward contract that ensures that he will receive F_0 dollars for each yen. Again, Y will choose to remain unhedged only if he gets more dollars per yen than with a forward contract. So he wants S_1 to be larger than F_0 ($S_1 > F_0$).

It is needless to say that both $S_1 < F_0$ and $S_1 > F_0$ can't be true. The result implies that if investors are risk-averse, then the *forward rate cannot be equal to the future spot rate*. In other words, the forward rate cannot be unbiased.

In addition, since risk-averse investors demand compensation for risk, riskier currencies must have higher returns. Which currency is riskier? Higher interest rates usually go with higher inflation, and higher inflation entails higher risk. Therefore, higher-interest-rate currencies must provide a higher return than lower-interest-rate currencies as a compensation for risk. This implication is consistent with the observed changes in currency values: higher-interest-rate currencies do not fall as much as suggested by the forward rate because the holder must be compensated for risk. The next question is whether the compensation for risk is too large or too small.

A b of -1 means that a 1 percent difference in interest rates must be compensated by a 2 percent difference in returns. That level of compensation for risk is too high. The theoretical risk premium even for the most risk-averse investors is less than one-fifth of the observed risk premium. Thus, the risk of the higher-interest-rate currency can only explain a small fraction of currency movements.

SMALL SAMPLE, OR THE PESO PROBLEM

The second explanation relates to a small-sample problem. The small sample is relevant in currency markets because exchange rates were generally fixed until 1971. Early studies in the 1980s that investigated the forward rate bias had only about ten years of data. The role of a small sample can be approached from two angles.

First, investors need time to learn. Initial errors in expectations might have occurred because investors and other market participants did not fully understand currency markets. Based on their prior beliefs, investors formed fully rational forecasts about the future spot rate. However, as they discovered errors in those beliefs, they revised and refined their expectations to be more realistic. Moreover, forward markets were not fully developed in the 1970s, so conclusions based on that sample are not necessarily representative of well-functioning currency markets.

The second part of the small-sample explanation assumes that investors do not err in setting expectations about the future. In their expectations, they incorporate the probability, albeit low, of certain events that may or may not actually take place. Given a sufficiently long time period, those expectations will be realized, the low-probability event will occur, and the value of b will come out close to 1. One example frequently cited is that of the Mexican peso. If you consider the sample period between 1955 and 1975, when the Mexican peso was fixed relative to the dollar at $0.25 per peso, you will find that there is a severe bias in forward rates. The peso, with its relatively high interest rate, did not fall relative to the dollar. Thus, anyone looking at the 1955–75 period would conclude that forward rates are biased. However, a large devaluation of the peso occurred in 1976. If the same analysis is redone with 1955–76 as the sample period instead of 1955–75, there is no forward rate bias. Thus, the investors and the markets were correctly valuing the peso all the time by incorporating the small probability of a devaluation—only the devaluation didn't occur until twenty years later. The small-sample problem is not unique to currencies alone. Similar small-sample limitations can explain returns on many other financial assets, such as junk bonds, emerging bond debt, and so on.

While this explanation is reasonable, when does the small sample problem cease to exist? How many years of data are sufficient? Given that there is strong evidence of a forward rate bias over a variety of different periods extending to thirty years and over many currency pairs and many forecast periods, it is probably reasonable to assume that the small-sample problem cannot adequately challenge the findings of a forward rate bias.

Biases in Expectations, or Market Inefficiency

Unlike prior explanations that were consistent with rational investors and efficient markets, this explanation assumes that investors make errors in forming expectations that are both biased and systematic. The persistent evidence of negative values of b suggests that the investors continue to make mistakes and repeat those mistakes. Why don't smart investors take advantage of irrational investors? These and related issues are discussed in the next section, on persistence of the forward rate bias.

Persistence

There are several reasons for the persistence of the forward rate bias. Arbitrageurs or other smart traders may not be able to trade on the forward rate bias due to transaction costs and risk of taking positions. Second, arbitrageurs may be wary of the forward rate bias due to the absence of a logical explanation. Third, limits on arbitrage exist, as currency markets are very large. Finally, the forward rate bias will continue to persist probably due to the structure of currency markets. Each reason for persistence is discussed in turn.

RISK OF TRADING ON THE FORWARD RATE BIAS

There is general consensus based on the evidence presented above that the forward rate is biased and a poor predictor of the future spot rate. There is also a consensus that trading on the forward rate bias can generate high returns. However, there is much disagreement over whether the excess return from trading the forward rate bias is adequate to compensate for the additional risk. Consider investor X, discussed in the section "Investors Are Risk-Averse," who holds dollars and wants to convert to yen after a year. Assume that the forward rate suggests an appreciation of the yen since the yen's interest rate is less than the dollar's. Should X contract at the forward rate, a strategy that is riskless but more expensive because he has to pay more dollars for the same yen, or should he wait for a year and assume currency risk but with the expectation of paying fewer dollars for the yen? Obviously the currency risk has to be matched with the expected return. Though the risk may justify the return based on past data, arbitrageurs and their principals may be unwilling to take the risk associated with exploiting the forward rate bias. If that is the case, the arbitrageurs may choose not to trade on the forward rate bias, and the bias will continue to persist.

LACK OF A RATIONAL EXPLANATION

The second reason for persistence of the bias is the absence of a logical explanation. As suggested in Chapter 1, if arbitrageurs are unsure about the cause of a mispricing, they are unlikely to trade on that anomaly due to much higher uncertainty relating to the success of a trading strategy. While many researchers have attempted to explain the bias, no satisfactory explanation exists. As a result, arbitrageurs may be reluctant to take a position.

SIZE OF CURRENCY MARKETS

Third, the size of the currency markets is too large relative to the arbitrageurs' risk capital. While arbitrageurs can tame any market that provides riskless profits, it is a different matter when a particular anomaly requires risky trading strategies. It is clear from the first reason discussed above that trading the forward rate bias entails risk. Since currency markets trade $2 trillion a day, they dwarf other financial markets. By comparison, all stock markets in the world trade less than $100 billion a day. Clearly, arbitrageurs do not have sufficient risk capital to make a huge impact on any mispricing. As a matter of fact, even the central banks (such as the Federal Reserve) are unable to *directly* influence currency rates in any significant way. Thus, the forward rate bias may continue to persist because arbitrage capital is not sufficiently large.

STRUCTURE OF CURRENCY MARKETS

Finally, the structure of the currency markets may work against elimination of the forward rate bias. Note that the forward rates depend *only* on the spot rate and the difference in interest rates. For arbitrage reasons, the forward rate cannot depend on anything else (see the discussion of interest rate parity in "Description," above). However, an exchange rate between two currencies reflects the relative state of the two economies. If the U.S. economy is expected to do better than the Japanese economy, then the spot exchange rate will reflect that. Any changes in growth expectations will promptly cause a change in the spot exchange rate and thereby in the forward exchange rate. For example, the dollar strengthened from 1995 to 2000 because of the relative strength of the U.S. economy. During 2002 and early part of 2003, when expectations about U.S. economic growth were constantly revised downward, the dollar kept losing ground to other currencies.

To understand how the structure of currency markets can affect the forward rate bias, it is necessary to comprehend the connection between interest rates, inflation, economic growth, and currency values. Central banks and financial markets are concerned about inflation because inflation adds to uncertainty or risk. If inflation is expected to rise, the Federal Reserve, in an attempt to control inflation, will raise short-term interest rates. Typically, inflation is expected to rise when the economy is growing too fast, and is expected to fall when the economy is not growing fast enough. The Japanese economy has been sputtering for the last decade and its interest rate is 0.1 percent per year, as there is no fear of inflation.

If this line of reasoning is stretched a bit, it means that interest rates and growth expectations are related. In general, countries that have interest rates less than their long-term steady-state interest rate are expected to grow less than countries that have interest rates more than their normal level. Look at the effect on the forward rate. If a country has a low interest rate, it is expected to underperform in terms of economic growth. Therefore, the currency should fall in value in the future. However, the forward rate suggests that low-interest-rate currencies must appreciate, not depreciate. Perhaps the negative b can be explained in this way. Currencies with lower interest rates tend to fall because of reduced growth expectations, in spite of what the forward rate predicts.

If markets are efficient and if market participants realize that growth expectations may be cut, then the currency value should depreciate immediately in the spot market, not sometime in the future, as implied above. Once the currency depreciates immediately in the spot market, the forward rate can still be unbiased. That brings up another issue relevant to currency markets: role of the government in trying to influence exchange rates. The exchange rate (dollar value or yen value) is one price that governments would like to control if they could. Why do they want to control a currency's value? Because the currency value affects the economy in many ways. A strong currency keeps inflation in check and makes foreign goods less expensive. At the same time, a strong currency hurts exporters. If the exchange rate is very volatile, it increases the risk of trading, meaning that firms will be less willing to trade with other countries. So a government would like to keep its currency value stable—not let it strengthen too much or weaken too much. For example, the Japanese government tries to keep the yen from strengthening against the dollar to protect its balance of trade. Though the currency markets are huge monsters, they cannot ignore a government's stance because the government can influence the spot exchange rate temporarily through direct intervention in the currency markets and permanently by changing interest rates.

A government may also use the exchange rate as a tool for jump-starting the economy. If the economy is doing poorly and inflation is not a threat, the government may want the currency to fall in value, so that exports increase along with domestic production. Japan fits this scenario perfectly—the Japanese government would like to see the yen fall in value. This is the same scenario as before:

low economic growth, low inflation, and low interest rates should be followed by a falling currency resulting in the forward rate bias. Thus, it seems that the role of government in currency markets may be an important factor in the forward rate bias. If the structure of currency markets contributes to the forward rate bias, it will persist until governments stop trying to influence exchange rates—something that is unlikely to happen.

The Trading Process

Whatever the explanation for the forward rate bias and whatever the reason for its persistence, we hope that the forward rate bias will continue to exist well into the future. Armed with this evidence, how can tradable profits be realized? The easiest way to trade the forward rate bias is to use currency futures. Futures contracts can be easily bought or short-sold, are easy to cancel, and have low trading costs. On the other hand, forward contracts are restrictive and difficult to cancel. The pricing of forward contracts and futures contracts is almost identical, so the trading profits will also be equivalent. The trading strategy consists of buying the currency with the highest interest rate and unwinding the position a month later. A one-month holding period is chosen because the forward rate bias is most prominent for shorter periods. The following steps are taken in choosing and executing the strategy.

Step 1: On the last trading day of each month, obtain the one-month interest rates for the major currencies: U.S. dollar, Japanese yen, British pound, Swiss franc, Canadian dollar, and euro. Select the currency that has the highest difference in interest rates relative to the U.S. dollar, whether below or above the U.S. dollar interest rate. (The last trading day is selected only for convenience. You can begin trading on any day.)

Step 2: If the currency selected in step 1 has a higher interest rate, then go long in that currency's futures contract. If the selected currency has a lower interest rate, then go short in its futures contract. More details about trading futures contracts are in Appendix A.

Step 3: At the end of the following month, close the position opened in step 2, and repeat steps 1 and 2.

Refinement of the Trading Strategy

Based on the discussion in "Structure of Currency Markets," a refinement to the strategy would probably improve its profitability.

Instead of using absolute differences in the nominal interest rates, as in step 1, use the difference between the country's current interest rate and its steady-state interest rate. For example as of May 2002, the average three-month interest rate over the past ten years was approximately 4.3 percent for the dollar. The three-month interest rate in June 2002 was 1.7 percent for the dollar, which is lower than the normal interest rate by 2.6 percent. In the case of Japan, the average overnight rate over the past ten years was approximately 1.0 percent. In June 2002 the overnight rate was 0.02 percent for the yen. Thus, the Japanese interest rate is lower by 0.98 percent. Based on these calculations, the U.S. interest rate is lower by 1.62 percent (2.6 percent—0.98 percent) than the Japanese rate compared to the steady-state levels in each country. Since the yen interest rate is higher relative to its steady-state interest rate when compared with the dollar interest rates, the investor should be long in Japanese yen in June 2002. Thus, for the trading strategy with refinement, steps 1 to 3 above are repeated except that the comparison of interest rates is based on the change from the steady-state interest rates.

Strategy Implementation

The trading strategy with and without the refinement is implemented using data from January 2000 to June 2002. This period is selected so that there are thirty monthly observations, the minimum required for most statistical tests. Historical interest rates are obtained from International Financial Statistics of the International Monetary Fund. Since the holding period is one month, the interest rate should represent the one-month period as closely as possible. However, the IMF does not report one-month interest rates: the data contain either overnight interest rates or three-month interest rates. Therefore, three-month interest rates are compared among different countries. Another problem arises because the IMF reports only twelve-month Treasury bills for Germany but has three-month interbank deposits, which are different from three-month T-bills. Japan has a two-month private bill rate that is likely to be very different from a three-month T-bill rate. In order to make rate comparisons as consistent as possible, the three-month T-bill rates are used except that the three-month interbank rate is used for Germany, and the overnight rate is taken for Japan. Fortunately, interest rates do not change dramatically with the holding period; therefore the approximations are appropriate.

Trading Strategy without Refinement

In accordance with the trading strategy, the first step is to identify the currency with the interest rate most different from the interest rate on the U.S. dollar. If the other currency has a lower interest rate at the end of the month, then the trading decision is to short-sell the foreign currency; otherwise, the foreign currency is bought.

The difference in nominal interest rates is reported in Table 11.5 at the end of every month preceded by the currency that exhibits the highest interest rate difference. The difference between the dollar interest rate and the yen interest rate is the maximum until October 2001, with the dollar having the higher interest rate. Thereafter, the British pound is the currency with the greatest interest rate differential, with the pound interest rate being greater than the dollar interest rate. Since the currency with the higher interest rate must be bought, the yen futures contract is short sold from the end of January 2000 to the end of November 2001. From the end of November 2001 to the end of July 2002, the investor would go long in pound futures.

The closing futures price at the end of each month is reported in the table. This is the price at which the position based on the trading strategy is opened. The closing futures price at the end of the next month is also reported, being the price at which the position is closed. For example, consider January 2000. At the end of January 2000 the three-month interest rate on the dollar was 5.34 percent, compared with 5.72 percent on the pound, 2.64 percent on the German mark (as a proxy for the euro), 5.07 percent on the Canadian dollar, 1.70 percent on the Swiss franc, and 0.02 percent on the yen. For the yen, it is the overnight rate as the three-month rate is unavailable. The largest difference between the interest rate on the dollar and another currency is 5.32 percent for the yen, as indicated in the first row of the table. On January 31, 2000, the March yen futures contract closed at $0.009368/¥. In accordance with step 2 of the trading strategy, the March yen futures contract is short sold on that day. The position is held until the end of February 2000, when the position is closed by buying back the March yen futures contract at the closing price of $0.009100/¥, thereby realizing a profit of $0.000268/¥ (0.009368—0.009100) or 2.86 percent. Since each yen futures contract has a size of ¥12.5 million, each one-point move at the sixth decimal place for the yen is worth $12.50, as ¥12.5 million × $0.000001/¥ = $12.50. A change of 286 points is equal to 286 × $12.5 = $3,575 per yen contract, a profit of $3,575 for the first month.

Table 11.5 Strategy to Trade on the Forward Rate Bias without Refinement

Month	Currency	Interest Rate Differential $I^\$-I^{FC}$ (%)	Position	Futures Price at the End of This Month (in $ per unit of foreign currency)	Futures Price at the End of This Month (in $ per unit of foreign currency)	Gain/ Loss (%)
Jan. 2000	J¥	5.3	Short J¥	0.009368	0.009100	2.86
Feb. 2000	J¥	5.5	Short J¥	0.009249	0.009908	−7.13
Mar. 2000	J¥	5.7	Short J¥	0.009908	0.009318	5.95
Apr. 2000	J¥	5.6	Short J¥	0.009318	0.009315	0.03
May 2000	J¥	5.9	Short J¥	0.009476	0.009577	−1.07
Jun. 2000	J¥	5.7	Short J¥	0.009577	0.009224	3.69
Jul. 2000	J¥	5.9	Short J¥	0.009224	0.009396	−1.86
Aug. 2000	J¥	6.0	Short J¥	0.009544	0.009373	1.79
Sep. 2000	J¥	5.7	Short J¥	0.009373	0.009247	1.34
Oct. 2000	J¥	5.8	Short J¥	0.009247	0.009085	1.75
Nov. 2000	J¥	5.9	Short J¥	0.009222	0.008827	4.28
Dec. 2000	J¥	5.6	Short J¥	0.008827	0.008647	2.04
Jan. 2001	J¥	5.0	Short J¥	0.008647	0.008536	1.28
Feb. 2001	J¥	4.7	Short J¥	0.008636	0.008008	7.27
Mar. 2001	J¥	4.4	Short J¥	0.008008	0.008132	−1.55
Apr. 2001	J¥	3.9	Short J¥	0.008132	0.008407	−3.38
May 2001	J¥	3.6	Short J¥	0.008488	0.008079	4.82
Jun. 2001	J¥	3.5	Short J¥	0.008079	0.008030	0.61
Jul. 2001	J¥	3.5	Short J¥	0.008030	0.008432	−5.01
Aug. 2001	J¥	3.4	Short J¥	0.008502	0.008415	1.02
Sep. 2001	J¥	2.9	Short J¥	0.008415	0.008198	2.58
Oct. 2001	J¥	2.2	Short J¥	0.008198	0.008103	1.16
Nov. 2001	GBP	−1.9	Long GBP	1.4156	1.4486	2.33
Dec. 2001	GBP	−2.1	Long GBP	1.4486	1.4066	−2.90
Jan. 2002	GBP	−2.2	Long GBP	1.4066	1.4158	0.65
Feb. 2002	GBP	−2.2	Long GBP	1.4088	1.4190	0.72
Mar. 2002	GBP	−2.2	Long GBP	1.4190	1.4534	2.42
Apr. 2002	GBP	−2.3	Long GBP	1.4534	1.4548	0.10
May 2002	GBP	−2.2	Long GBP	1.4464	1.5244	5.39
Jun. 2002	GBP	−2.3	Long GBP	1.5244	1.5582	2.22
					Annual Return	13.4
					Standard Deviation	10.9

Currency whose interest rate is most different from the dollar interest rate is selected. If the other currency has the lower interest rate, then short-sell that currency; otherwise, go long. The strategy is executed using futures contracts. Positions are initiated at the end of the current month and closed at the end of the following month.

The process is repeated for the next month again with yen. Note, however, that the closing futures price in the first row, $0.009100/¥, is not the opening price in the second row even though the yen contract continues to be short-sold. The reason for this difference is that the March futures contract will expire before the end of March, whereas for the second row, the contract must be held till the end of March. Therefore, the June yen futures contract is short-sold at the end of February 2000 at a price of $0.009249/¥ instead of the March yen futures contract.[2] To minimize trading costs, there is no need to close the contract at the end of March (second row) and reopen it immediately thereafter (third row). Instead, the position will be held unless the trading strategy requires a change in the position.

The annual return for the two-and-a-half-year period using this strategy is 13.4 percent. By comparison, a month-by-month investment in dollars would generate an annual return of 4.1 percent. Thus, the excess return is 9.3 percent with a standard deviation of 10.9 percent. The Sharpe ratio for the strategy is an impressive 0.85, which is greater than a typical Sharpe ratio of about 0.50 for government bills or bonds.

TRADING STRATEGY WITH REFINEMENT

The strategy is repeated with the changes discussed in "Refinement of the Trading Strategy." The main difference is that the strategy with refinement considers interest rates relative to the steady-state interest rate rather than the absolute interest rates. Consider January 2000. The dollar interest rate of 5.34 percent is 0.46 percent above the ten-year average interest rate of 4.88 percent. The yen interest rate of 0.02 percent is 2.70 percent below the ten-year average interest rate of 2.72 percent. The difference relative to the steady-state interest rates is 0.46 percent—(–2.70 percent) = 3.16 percent, or 3.2 percent, with the dollar interest being greater than the yen interest rate relative to steady-state interest rates.

The results are reported in Table 11.6. There is no difference in the trading strategy between Tables 11.5 and 11.6 until May 2001, as the yen is short-sold in both strategies. From June 2001 to November 2001, either the Swiss franc or the euro has the highest differential. From December 2001 until June 2002, both the yen and the euro are used because the difference between the dollar interest rate and the euro interest rate relative to the steady-state interest rates is very close (less than 0.1 percent) to the difference between the dollar interest rate and the yen interest rates relative to their steady-state interest rates.

Table 11.6 Strategy to Trade on the Forward Rate Bias with Refinement

Month	Currency	Interest Rate Differential (relative to steady-state rates) (%)	Position	Futures Price at the End of This Month (in $ per unit of foreign currency)	Futures Price at the End of This Month (in $ per unit of foreign currency)	Gain/ Loss (%)
Jan. 2000	J¥	3.2	Short J¥	0.009368	0.009100	2.86
Feb. 2000	J¥	3.3	Short J¥	0.009249	0.009908	−7.13
Mar. 2000	J¥	3.5	Short J¥	0.009908	0.009318	5.95
Apr. 2000	J¥	3.4	Short J¥	0.009318	0.009315	0.03
May 2000	J¥	3.6	Short J¥	0.009476	0.009577	−1.07
Jun. 2000	J¥	3.4	Short J¥	0.009577	0.009224	3.69
Jul. 2000	J¥	3.5	Short J¥	0.009224	0.009396	−1.86
Aug. 2000	J¥	3.5	Short J¥	0.009544	0.009373	1.79
Sep. 2000	J¥	3.3	Short J¥	0.009373	0.009247	1.34
Oct. 2000	J¥	3.3	Short J¥	0.009247	0.009085	1.75
Nov. 2000	J¥	3.3	Short J¥	0.009222	0.008827	4.28
Dec. 2000	J¥	2.9	Short J¥	0.008827	0.008647	2.04
Jan. 2001	J¥	2.3	Short J¥	0.008647	0.008536	1.28
Feb. 2001	J¥	1.9	Short J¥	0.008636	0.008008	7.27
Mar. 2001	J¥	1.9	Short J¥	0.008008	0.008132	−1.55
Apr. 2001	J¥	1.0	Short J¥	0.008132	0.008407	−3.38
May 2001	J¥	0.7	Short J¥	0.008488	0.008079	4.82
Jun. 2001	CHF	−0.8	Long CHF	0.5580	0.5795	3.85

(continues on next page)

Table 11.6 Strategy to Trade on the Forward Rate Bias with Refinement (continued)

Month	Currency	Interest Rate Differential (relative to steady-state rates) (%)	Position	Futures Price at the End of This Month (in $ per unit of foreign currency)	Futures Price at the End of This Month (in $ per unit of foreign currency)	Gain/Loss (%)
Jul. 2001	CHF	-0.8	Long CHF	0.5795	0.6001	3.55
Aug. 2001	CHF	-1.0	Long CHF	0.6006	0.6178	2.86
Sep. 2001	EUR	-0.9	Long EUR	0.9084	0.8983	-1.11
Oct. 2001	EUR	-1.3	Long EUR	0.8983	0.8954	-0.32
Nov. 2001	CHF	-1.4	Long CHF	0.6091	0.6020	-1.17
Dec. 2001	EUR/J¥	-1.5	Long EUR/J¥	0.8878/0.007629	0.8568/0.007436	-3.01
Jan. 2002	EUR/J¥	-1.6	Long EUR/J¥	0.8568/0.007436	0.8682/0.007489	1.02
Feb. 2002	EUR/J¥	-1.5	Long EUR/J¥	0.8650/0.007523	0.8659/0.007567	0.34
Mar. 2002	EUR/J¥	-1.5	Long EUR/J¥	0.8659/0.007567	0.8990/0.007802	3.47
Apr. 2002	EUR/J¥	-1.6	Long EUR/J¥	0.8990/0.007802	0.9317/0.008054	3.44
May 2002	EUR/J¥	-1.6	Long EUR/J¥	0.9280/0.008092	0.9885/0.008403	4.68
Jun. 2002	EUR/J¥	-1.6	Long EUR/J¥	0.9885/0.008403	0.9821/0.008341	-0.70
Annual Return						15.6
Standard Deviation						10.7

Currency whose deviation from the ten-year steady-state interest rate is most different from the dollar's ten-year steady-state interest rate is selected. The strategy is executed using futures contracts. Positions are initiated at the end of the current month and closed at the end of the following month.

The annual return over the period January 2000 to June 2002 is 15.6 percent, slightly better than the 13.4 percent return in Table 11.5. The excess return is 11.5 percent with a standard deviation of 10.7 percent and a Sharpe ratio of 1.07. The excess return is impressive, as is the risk-adjusted return as measured by the Sharpe ratio.

Overall, implementation of the trading strategy reveals annual excess returns of 9.3 percent and 11.5 percent. The strategy seems to be eminently successful with Sharpe ratios of 0.85 and 1.07.

Qualifications

The evidence presented in this chapter and the trading strategy recommendations based on the evidence rely on past data. Since future market conditions and market patterns may be completely different, and particularly as no valid and rational explanation for the forward rate bias is known, the forward rate bias may cease to exist without notice.

The trading strategy implemented *with the refinement* is based only on thirty months of data, as presented in this chapter. No other evidence exists. In addition, trading based on currencies is quite risky. Moreover, currency futures provide a high leverage ratio, which

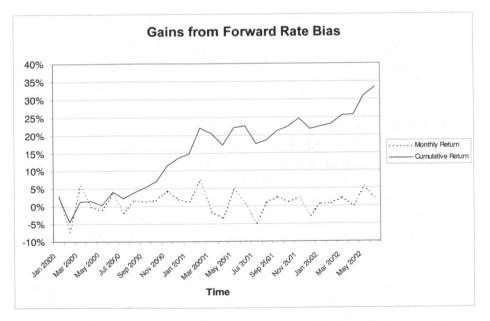

Figure 11.1   The figure shows the monthly return and the cumulative return from holding the currency with the higher interest rate from January 2000 to June 2002.

means the risk of loss may be much larger than the initial capital committed to the trading strategy.

Key Points

- When currencies are exchanged for delivery more than two business days later, the governing exchange rate is the forward rate. The forward rate is given by an inviolable interest rate parity that ensures that two riskless investments generate the same total return. Under normal circumstances, the forward rate should be an unbiased predictor of the future spot rate. However, the actual future spot rate is significantly different from the forward rate. This phenomenon is referred to as the *forward rate bias*. See figure 11.1 above.

- In order to satisfy the requirement of the same return generated by two riskless assets given by interest rate parity, the currency with the higher interest rate must depreciate relative to a currency with a lower interest rate as given by the forward rate. Evidence indicates that the currency with the higher interest rate actually appreciates instead of depreciating. This pattern is confirmed for a variety of currency pairs not including high-interest-rate currencies, for many different observation periods, and many different holding periods. It seems that the bias decreased a little during the 1990s and it disappears when the holding period becomes about ten years. However, the bias at short holding periods of about one month is of most interest to investors.

- Unfortunately, no reasonable explanation exists for the forward rate bias. Different explanations have been explored. Currencies with higher interest rates should be riskier and therefore must generate a higher return to risk-averse investors. However, the risk premium provided to risk-averse investors is unreasonably high. The second explanation relies on the small size of the sample. However, evidence over three decades and many currencies seems to suggest that the sample size may be large enough. Finally, it could be investor behavior. But the suggestion that investors in the world's largest financial market with daily trading in trillions of dollars have not learned over the last three decades is difficult to believe. Thus, the absence of a reasonable explanation continues to confound researchers.

- Why does the forward rate bias persist? It could be due to lack of availability of sufficient arbitrage capital because of the size of the market, or to the risk of trading, especially with the absence of a reasonable explanation. Another reason could be that governments tend to influence exchange rates, which makes the spot exchange rate less reflective of fundamentals. As the future spot rate is affected by government policies, it does not approach the forward rate as efficient markets would normally predict.

- A trading strategy based on the forward rate bias is constructed to identify the currency whose interest rate is most different from the dollar interest rate. The currency with the higher interest rate is bought using currency futures. The trading strategy is refined such that differences between deviations from steady-state interest rates are used instead of differences in absolute interest rates. The strategies are implemented during the January 2000–June 2002 period. The annual excess return is 9.3 percent with the simple trading strategy, and 11.5 percent with the refined trading strategy.

Bottom Line

There is overwhelming evidence that forward exchange rates are biased. Not only is the future spot rate different from the forward rate, the deviation is predictable. As per the forward rate, the higher-interest-rate currency should depreciate relative to the lower-interest-rate currency. However, the higher-interest-rate currency actually appreciates. Trading strategies designed to exploit the forward rate bias tend to be quite profitable. The forward rate bias can also help select foreign investments that should be hedged or not hedged against currency risk.

Internet References

Interest Rate Data

http://www.ny.frb.org/rmaghome/dirchrts/global.html: The New York Federal Reserve site has short-term and long-term interest rates for foreign countries, usually as of the previous week. Slightly stale interest rates are okay as interest rates do not change quickly.

http://www.imf.org. and http://www.imfstatistics.org: The International Monetary Fund is the premier source for international data. Historical interest rates by country can be obtained from the second site. The site allows for a sixty-day trial period, which is sufficient to get all of the data needed. International financial statistics are also available on CD-ROM with monthly updates.

http://www.ft.com: *Financial Times* contains yields on many foreign government bonds.

Foreign Exchange Rates and Futures Prices

http://online.wsj.com: The Wall Street Journal reports the prior day's spot exchange rate, one-month forward, three-month forward, and six-month forward rates for the Canadian dollar, British pound, Japanese yen, and the French franc.

http://www.cme.com: Currency futures contracts are most actively traded on the International Monetary Market of the Chicago Mercantile Exchange. Regular day trading for currency futures begins at 8:20 A.M. Eastern time and ends at 3:00 P.M. Though it is possible to trade currency futures after hours on CME's Globex market, the trading is usually thin and should be avoided. The initial margin for most currency contracts varies between $1,000 and $3,000 per contract. Mini currency contracts are also available that are one-half the full size. Full-size currency futures contracts are usually worth about $100,000.

http://www.futuresguide.com/historical-data.php: This is possibly the only site that provides historical data on futures contracts free of charge. The data are organized by date and contain the settlement prices on all contracts as put out by futures exchanges. Also see http://www.tickdata.com

http://www.federalreserve.gov/releases/H10/hist: Historical exchange rates with most of the world's currencies are available at the Federal Reserve site.

http://fx.sauder.ubc.ca/: The Pacific Exchange rate service at the University of British Columbia provides the exchange rates in addition several other useful bits of information.

References for Further Reading

Baz, Jamil, Francis Breedon, Vasant Naik, and Joel Peress. 2001. Optimal Portfolios of Foreign Currencies. *The Journal of Portfolio Management* 28(1), 102–11.

Engel, Charles. 1996. The Forward Discount Anomaly and the Risk Premium: A Survey of Recent Evidence. *Journal of Empirical Finance* 3(2), 123–92.

Froot, Kenneth A., and Richard H. Thaler. 1990. Anomalies: Foreign Exchange. *Journal of Economic Perspectives* 4(3), 179–92.

Meredith, Guy, and Menzie D. Chinn. 1998. Long Horizon Uncovered Interest Rate Parity. Working paper no. 6797, National Bureau of Economic Research.

Razzak, Weshah A. 2000. The Forward Rate Unbiasedness Hypothesis Revisited. Working paper, Reserve Bank of New Zealand.

Sercu, Piet, and Raman Uppal. 1995. *International Financial Markets and the Firm* (Cincinnati: South-Western College Publishing).

Szakmary, Andrew C., and Ike Mathur. 1997. Central Bank Intervention and Trading Rule Profits in Foreign Exchange Markets. *Journal of International Money and Finance* 16(4), 513–35.

Notes

1. Besides the author's own analysis, this chapter is based on research by Baz et al. (2001), Engel (1996), Meredith and Chinn (1998), Razzak (2000), Froot and Thaler (1990), Szakmary and Mathur (1997), and Sercu and Uppal (1995).
2. In actual practice, you would want to roll over a March futures contract to a June futures contract around the tenth of March instead of at the end of February because the trading in the June futures contract becomes large enough only after the first week of March.

12

Understanding and Learning from Behavioral Finance

While traditional finance is based on rational economic behavior of investors, behavioral finance claims that investors do not always behave rationally. This "irrational" behavior causes prices to move in anomalous patterns that cannot be explained by traditional finance theory but can be explained by behavioral finance. To be sure, traditional finance does allow some investors to behave irrationally, but those investors lose and are quickly driven out of the market by smart investors. Behavioral finance, on the other hand, believes that smart investors do not necessarily have the resources to dominate other investors. For example, limits of arbitrage (see Chapter 1) point to the limited nature of arbitrage activity, which may cause irrational investors to persist and may allow them to influence prices in a significant manner.

Whether or not the assumptions of behavioral finance are realistic, there are investors who suffer from behavioral biases. To earn optimal returns, investors should try to avoid those biases.

Why Behavioral Finance?

It is instructive to begin with two examples of human behavior.[1] Dick Thaler (2000) refers to the "guess the number" game that the *Financial Times* ran at his request, with a prize of two round-trip tickets between London and the United States. Contestants were told to guess an integer between 0 and 100, with the objective of making their guess as close as possible to two-thirds the average guess. If everyone thinks rationally, and it is fair to assume that almost all readers of the *Financial Times* are smart, then the winning number should be 0. Though some contestants guessed 0, the average guess was 18.19, and the winning number was 12. The example illustrates that all individuals do not process available information in a rational manner, that is, they behave irrationally. Or did the contestants try to guess what other people would guess?

Consider some anecdotal evidence related to salaries and wages. A worker who earns a pay raise of 4 percent in an environment of 10 percent inflation is likely to be happier than a worker who earns only a 2 percent raise in an environment of no inflation, even though the second worker is clearly better off. Have you also noticed that the salaries in San Francisco are not twice as much as those in Roanoke, Virginia, though the cost of living is twice as much? San Francisco may be a more desirable place to live in for many reasons. But a person earning $75,000 in Roanoke is clearly envious of another person in a similar position earning $100,000 in San Francisco.

The idea behind behavioral finance is that investors and other individuals behave in ways that are different from the unfeeling, rational individual assumed in standard finance. It does not mean that finance theory is wrong or should be abandoned, only that behavioral finance is needed to supplement the shortcomings of standard finance theory.

Assumptions Relating to Behavioral Finance

Traditional finance theory is based on actions of rational investors who can process information efficiently in a timely, unbiased manner and consistently make informed, value-maximizing decisions. However, as mentioned above traditional finance does not assume that all, or even most, investors are rational. But it does assume that irrational investors will be driven out of the market by smart, rational investors.

Behavioral finance theorists question the primary assumption of rational investor behavior. Based on concepts and models developed by cognitive psychologists, they claim that psychological forces prevent decision makers from acting in a rational manner. There are two basic themes of behavioral finance: heuristic-driven bias and frame dependence. Other characteristics of irrational behavior can usually be deduced from these themes.[2]

HEURISTIC-DRIVEN BIAS

The term *heuristic* refers to a rule of thumb that is developed by an individual based on trial and error. Note that the rule of thumb is developed not by scientific reasoning but simply on the basis of one's own experience or knowledge. Living in Blacksburg (home to Virginia Tech), a resident might believe that Virginia Tech is the best university in the nation. A New Yorker might believe that Fordham University is third only to NYU and Columbia. Or a Philadelphia resident might believe that Temple is just behind the University of Pennsylvania. Not only do people believe in what they think, they believe it so strongly that they suffer from *overconfidence*. Moreover, overconfidence becomes worse with self-attribution. Assume an investor "knows" that after a long bull run, Cisco is bound to fall. He has seen it happen before. So he sells Cisco once it rises by 10 percent. If Cisco falls thereafter, he pats himself on the back for having predicted the fall correctly. If Cisco rises, he doesn't blame himself for the error but just puts it down to bad luck. According to behavioral finance, investors take credit for occurrences that support their prior beliefs but dismiss any events that do not, making them more confident through self-attribution.

Reliance on rules of thumb also means that people are affected more by recent events even though those events may not represent the norm. Thus, their recent experiences will erroneously play a greater role in the formation of their expectations. Imagine a string of heads in a coin toss. According to behavioral finance, investors who are driven by heuristics will believe that either the probability of a head in a coin toss is greater than 0.5 or that the coin is biased.

The heuristic-driven bias has several implications for investor behavior. Investors will tend to change their beliefs slowly and only when presented with repetitive evidence. But then they swing to the other extreme that also causes swings in prices. Moreover, investors believe strongly in their ability where none exists, and they will continue to make wrong decisions due to their overconfidence. The overconfidence, like their other beliefs, is difficult to overcome.

FRAME DEPENDENCE

The second theme of behavioral finance is frame (or form) dependence. Rational economic theory argues that a dollar in your right pocket is the same as a dollar in your left pocket, or that a dollar earned in capital appreciation is the same as a dollar paid in dividends, assuming no taxes and no market imperfections. In a portfolio setting, rational investors consider only the risk and return of the entire portfolio, not the risk or return of individual securities. These assumptions of rational thinking are called frame (or form) independence, meaning that the form does not matter, only content does.

Behavioral finance enthusiasts contend that individual behavior is not consistent with frame independence. The example above regarding a salary raise of 4 percent versus a raise of 2 percent is a case of narrow framing. Even though the real change in salary is −6 percent for the first worker and 2 percent for the second worker, the pay raises are framed and compared separately from inflation rates. Consequently, the first worker is likely to be happier than the second. In the same vein, investors look at each stock individually, not as part of a portfolio as traditional economists assume. As a result, investors engage in mental accounting. They tend to value stocks that pay dividends more than stocks that pay capital gains. They tend to be loss-averse rather than risk averse. Some experiments find that investor behavior is consistent with frame dependence. For example, investors are known to hold losers for too long because they are averse to realizing a loss. On the other hand, investors sell winners too quickly because they don't want to see the winner become a loser.

Explaining Anomalous Price Patterns with Behavioral Finance

Since the behavior outlined with frame dependence and heuristics is not economically rational, what does it mean? Proponents of behavioral finance claim that behavioral characteristics can explain the anomalous price movements better than traditional finance. In particular, the behavioralists attempt to explain underreaction and overreaction observed in financial time series. Recall Chapter 4 on short-term price drift as a consequence of underreaction to news. Overreaction or reversal in returns occurs over longer periods and is briefly discussed in Chapter 13.

It is easy to see that the heuristic bias can cause underreaction at short intervals and overreaction at long intervals. The heuristic bias makes investors overconfident, so they trust their experiences more than they trust new information. Overconfidence means that investors do not change their existing beliefs quickly. For example, one negative earnings surprise after a string of good quarters is insufficient for investors to conclude that there is a change in the firm's prospects. That evidence must be supported by several instances of bad news before investors will alter their beliefs. If the same company continues to perform poorly in subsequent quarters, investors will slowly revise their beliefs to a stage where they now consider this company's performance abysmal. If the company announces bad earnings once again, they overweight that information because it is consistent with their new set of beliefs, forgetting that the company may announce surprisingly good earnings some time in the not-too-distant future. Effectively, investors give too much weight to recent patterns in the data and too little to the properties of the population that generate those numbers, leading to the observed overreaction. Thus, according to models of behavioral finance, investors will overreact to a string of good news and to a string of bad news but underreact to initial good news or bad news.

The underreaction/overreaction phenomenon can be explained in another behavioral finance context. If informed investors are smart and overconfident, then they may assign greater value to their own private information than to information revealed in public announcements. If the new public information is consistent with their private beliefs then these investors will overreact to this new information. On the other hand, if that information is inconsistent with their private beliefs, then these investors will underreact.

Another way of looking at the underreaction/overreaction story is through the eyes of two types of traders: traders who naively follow price trends (the momentum crowd) but ignore fundamental news, and traders who naively follow fundamental news (news watchers) but ignore price trends. In addition, assume that information diffuses gradually across the population. Since news watchers react to new information, the news watchers who receive the information first will trade first, followed by news watchers who receive the information next. It is easy to see that prices will underreact to information in the short run and will not reach the equilibrium level until all news watchers have received the information, which is assumed to diffuse slowly.

The addition of momentum traders is expected to accelerate the process of arriving at equilibrium quickly because those traders watch price trends and know that news watchers underreact to information. However, if momentum traders are allowed to condition their trades only on recent price changes, then they would not know whether or not prices have reached the equilibrium level, resulting in an overreaction. Thus, there is underreaction in the short run due to slow diffusion of information and the actions of news watchers. Momentum traders gain from the underreaction because they know that news watchers underreact. However, in the long run it leads to an overreaction because momentum traders continue to trade even after the equilibrium has been attained.

How Good Are These Explanations?

The primary limitation of all behavioral explanations is that these models *preclude learning*. The investors continue to make the same mistakes repeatedly. In reality, individuals and investors learn from their mistakes, especially when they are costly. The researchers acknowledge the limitation of the behavioral models but claim that the assumption is not unrealistic, as "people learn *slowly* and find it difficult to shake off pervasive biases."[3] Others dismiss learning by relying on episodes that are either materially different or so many years apart that limited memory impedes learning.

In addition, many assumptions seem contrived to arrive at the desired results. A relaxation of one assumption in these explanations can overturn the results. For example, the assumption of slow diffusion of information is critical to the success of the explanation based on momentum traders and news watchers. Similarly, the results will disappear if momentum traders are allowed to use the entire price history.

In any case, even if these limitations are ignored, do the behavioral finance models explain the anomalies more effectively? While these models accommodate initial underreaction and long-term overreaction to the same event, not all anomalies are of this kind. There are many anomalies (dividend initiations and omissions, stock splits, proxy contests, and spin-offs) where there is no long-term reversal predicted, unlike that predicted by behavioral models. On the other hand, models of behavioral finance imply underreaction to almost all events, as the investors underreact to any event that does not fit their priors. However, empirical evidence is consistent with this assertion for some events but inconsistent for others.

A Rational Explanation for Anomalies?

Is it possible to arrive at the results in behavioral models based on rational behavior? Note that the rational expectations asset pricing theory has two characteristic features: that investors have essentially complete knowledge of the fundamental structure of their economy, and that investors are completely rational processors of information.

The behavioral models relax the second assumption relating to rationality to accommodate mispricings that are inconsistent with traditional finance. The assumption made by behavioral models is that investors act irrationally despite having considerable knowledge about the fundamental structure of the economy.

However, there is a different way to explain the mistakes made by investors: allow the investors to be still completely rational, but relax the assumption that investors have complete information. Under this scenario, investors make rational decisions based on incomplete information available to them. These are termed rational structural uncertainty models.

There are a number of rational models based on incomplete information. One is an investor awareness model in which all investors know the basic structure of securities returns. However, not all investors know of the existence of all securities. Investors trade only in the securities they know about. In effect, in this model, capital markets are segmented, and the assumption that investors can use only the securities they know about in constructing their portfolios results in their being incompletely diversified. It follows that the equilibrium return demanded by less than fully diversified investors will be higher than that demanded in the full-information capital asset pricing model (CAPM).[4] As more investors become aware of the stock, the extent of incomplete diversification falls and the price rises. The investor awareness model can explain the empirical evidence with respect to neglected stocks, glamour stocks, stocks featured in the media, and S&P 500 index changes (see Chapter 8).

A structural uncertainty model with rational investors can also explain underreaction and overreaction. Assume that there is uncertainty about whether a structural shift in prices will occur, and a rational investor assigns a 50 percent probability to a positive shift in prices. If a structural shift in prices does not actually occur—that is, if prices remain unchanged—then the price pattern with rational learning looks much like a pattern with overreaction. On the other hand, if the structural shift in prices does occur, the price pattern is similar to that with underreaction. Since anomalous events are special occurrences, the price patterns could arise from a rational learning model rather than from a behavioral model.

Anomalies Explained

To convince skeptical investors, researchers and practitioners must explain any new anomalous price patterns. Otherwise, as explained in Chapter 1, investors are less likely to believe the anomaly. Typically, researchers try to explain the anomaly in a rational framework where market efficiency is not compromised because it is easier to sell a market-efficient explanation than a behavioral explanation.

In many cases the anomaly exists because of institutional reasons such as mispricing of mutual funds (discussed in Chapter 6). In some cases, no arbitrage opportunity exists due to trading costs and other restrictions, as with the January effect (Chapter 2). However, whenever a rational explanation *cannot* be found, though there may be one, it is easy to blame the anomaly on irrational investors.

Irrationality is an easy catchall explanation for any unexplained anomaly. Whenever a rational explanation is discovered, however, the realm of behavioral finance becomes less appealing. Take the example of the weekend effect from Chapter 3. According to the weekend effect, Friday returns are much larger than Monday returns. For more than two decades, no satisfactory rational explanation for this seasonality could be found. However, a variety of irrational explanations did seem to explain the anomaly. One explanation related to the distinction between institutional and individual investors goes like this: institutional investors do not trade actively on Mondays—they are sitting in meetings trying to figure out what to do. As institutional investors are the big buyers, their absence means lower prices. At the same time, individual investors do their homework over the weekend and for some irrational reason decide to sell on Mondays, causing prices to be lower on Mondays than on other days. Based on more recent research, the weekend effect is attributable more to the rational behavior of speculative short sellers than to the irrational behavior of individual or institutional investors.

In Defense of Behavioral Finance

Traditional finance or economics assumes all (or most) investors to be intelligent people who do extensive research before making any economic decisions and embraces what Herbert Simon called the "Olympian model." Not all investors have an IQ of 180. And people act based on their beliefs, whether to choose a home, a spouse, a college, or a stock. People suffer from relying on rules of thumb or heuristics. Heuristics are useful in facilitating decision making, but they can also be prone to error and resistant to change.

The traditional defense against such dumb investors was that irrational behavior would be priced out of the market by smart investors. However, limits of arbitrage, overconfident investors and the uncertain nature of mispricing can result in irrational traders actually surviving and driving out the smart traders. The main point is that the unpredictability of irrational traders' beliefs can add risk to stock returns. If risk aversion keeps rational investors from taking large arbitrage positions, then uninformed traders can affect prices. In this way, prices can move away from fundamental values for an extended period of time, which makes arbitrage positions riskier and less profitable.

Behavioral finance won worldwide recognition when the 2002 Nobel prize was awarded to Daniel Kahneman for having integrated insights from psychological research into economic science, especially concerning human judgment and decision making under uncertainty, and to Vernon Smith for having established laboratory experiments as a tool in empirical economic analysis, especially in the study of alternative market mechanisms. Amos Tversky (who died in 1996) deserves as much credit as Daniel Kahneman for explaining the role of human behavior in economic decision making.

Lessons from Behavioral Finance

Though behavioral finance is here to stay, it is not important whether one agrees with the assumption of pervasive irrational behavior. It is important, however, to learn from behavioral finance. This area of finance has convincingly highlighted the failings of normal human beings in making investment decisions. The challenge is to acknowledge those failings and implement changes to guard trading strategies from irrational behavior.

COMMON ERRORS INVESTORS MAKE

The common errors of investors are based on the biases discussed in "Assumptions Relating to Behavioral Finance," above. The errors are listed below with a brief explanation. The next subsection contains suggestions for foolproofing your investments.

Individual security decisions, underdiversification, and too much risk. As investors study and learn about a small subset of all stocks, they become overconfident in their evaluation of those stocks. Consequently, they invest in a few stocks, resulting in underdiversification and excessive risk. In addition, mental accounting causes investors to examine each security in isolation without looking at the overall portfolio, again creating inefficient portfolios. Research has found that a typical individual investor account holds only four stocks, with a median of three stocks, and nearly one-quarter of all individual accounts hold only one stock. While individuals may have multiple accounts, there seems to be uncontestable evidence of high concentration in a few stocks.

Investors hold losers for too long and sell winners too quickly. Most investors suffer from the tendency to hold on to losers for too long because they are loss-averse and do not wish to realize a loss. Investors are also overconfident and do not believe that they made a bad decision. They hope that the stock will turn around. By the time they accept an error in judgment, it is too late. Investors also make a sharp distinction between paper losses or gains and realized losses or gains, fooling themselves into believing that a paper loss/gain is not a real loss/gain. Similarly and based on loss aversion, there is a tendency to realize profits quickly before the investment becomes a loss.

Investors trade too much. Chasing winners and the ease of Internet trading causes excessive trading. As investors tend to place too much weight on more recent information, they think that a winning stock is likely to extend its winning streak, and so they buy the stock, only to sell it quickly thereafter when they find that another stock is doing better than the one they just bought. Average round-trip trading can cost about 0.50 percent, which is a deadweight loss for the portfolio.

Other common errors. One frequently made error involves confusing a good company with a good stock. Choosing good companies is the mantra of market observers, who base their decisions on corporate fundamentals. Warren Buffett of Berkshire Hathaway and Peter Lynch of Fidelity frequently tell investors to look for good companies, leaders in their industry, and so on. Unfortunately, that is only half the story. Not all good companies are good investments. In addition to being a good company, the company should also be attractively valued before it is considered for investment. Another common error is that investors tend to pay too much for dividend-paying stocks. This is a case of mental accounting. When returns are examined, it is necessary to look at the total return rather than at dividends and capital gains separately. Though dividends are more certain than capital gains, that certainty is already reflected in the risk of that stock and should not be counted twice.

How to Overcome Behavioral Biases

The behavioral biases arise from fear and greed associated with investing. And investors make mistakes in investing when they mix emotions with rational decision making. The primary objective for overcoming behavioral biases is to not allow emotions to play a significant role in investing. There are several things that can be done for achieving a separation of psychology and finance, assuming predefined and realistic goals with respect to the portfolio. If you are executing any of the strategies described in this book, the steps are clearly defined. However, some trading decisions still need to be made. Consider the following suggestions to move toward rational decision making by setting certain rules for execution.

New strategies, if any, should be developed based on several years of historic data. Further, there should be a dry run of at least six months when you implement the strategy without using real money. Stock challenges, available on many Internet sites, are a good testing ground because they keep track of all trades. The dry run ensures that the strategy you discovered was not the result of data mining or other biases.

Decisions to take a new position in a stock should include an exit strategy. If the decision is to buy, the decision should include the circumstances under which it will be sold: percent drop in price, percent rise in price, or time. Choosing the exit strategy is not easy and should depend on volatility of the stock, effect on the portfolio, expected return, and so on.

New decisions or changes to current decisions should not be executed until at least twenty-four hours have elapsed after the decision was made. In this way, the market condition or personal mood will be a smaller factor in making decisions. Execution of a strategy in place, however, is not considered a new decision.

Initiate or increase the use of stop orders and limit orders as an exit strategy. For example, if you buy a stock at $25 and decide to exit if the loss is 10 percent, then a stop order to sell at $22.50 will automatically put that decision into effect. Stop orders can also be moved if the stock price moves up. If the stock appreciates to $28, then a new stop order at $25.20 locks in the profit while keeping the loss at 10 percent from its last price. However, the stop price must not be lowered. For example, if the stock moves down to $24 instead of appreciating to $28, the stop order would remain at $22.50.

Try not to make decisions during market hours based on intraday prices. Instead, wait until the end of the day and make decisions based on closing prices. With the availability of trading on the Internet, it is very easy to make quick, impulsive decisions that investors regret later on. Setting aside time for a planning session once a day, once a week, or once a month, depending on the frequency of trading, saves time and helps you make more rational decisions.

From the previous discussion, it seems obvious that trading in individual stocks is more susceptible to behavioral biases. If you hold mutual funds instead of individual stocks, it can help reduce the impact of those biases as well as give you a more diversified portfolio. Not all mutual funds are well diversified. In fact, most mutual funds tend to be narrowly focused. Therefore, except for execution of certain trading strategies, investors should hold broad-based mutual funds or index funds for the long term.

Role of Behavioral Finance in Decision Making

There is probably a growing role for behavioral finance in modeling financial processes, but the current set of behavioral finance models do not provide better or more convincing explanations for the anomalous price patterns than the explanations provided by existing models based on traditional finance. It is, therefore, prudent to wait before trying to read the market through a behavioralist's eyes. Nonetheless, important weaknesses of individual investors have been uncovered by research, and all of us must recognize and limit the damage due to those weaknesses.

References for Further Reading

Arbel, Avner. 1985. Generic Stocks: The Key to Market Anomalies. *Journal of Portfolio Management* 11(4), 4–13.

Arbel, Avner, and Paul Strebel. 1982. The Neglected and Small Firm Effects. *Financial Review* 17(4), 201–18.

Barber, Brad M., and Terrance Odean. 2001. Boys Will Be Boys: Gender, Overconfidence, and Common Stock Investment. *Quarterly Journal of Economics* 116(1), 261–92.

Barberis, Nicholas, Andrei Shleifer, and Robert Vishny. 1998. A Model of Investor Sentiment. *Journal of Financial Economics* 49(3), 307–43.

Barsky, Robert B., and J. Bradford De Long. 1993. Why Does the Stock Market Fluctuate. *Quarterly Journal of Economics* 108(2), 291–311.

Brav, Alon, and J. B. Heaton. 2002. Competing Theories of Financial Anomalies. *Review of Financial Studies* 15, 575–606.

Chen, Honghui, Greg Noronha, and Vijay Singal. 2004. The Price Responses to S&P 500 Index Additions and Deletions. Forthcoming in the *Journal of Finance*.

Daniel, Kent, David Hirshleifer, and Avanidhar Subrahmanyam. 1998. Investor Psychology and Security Market Under- and Overreactions. *Journal of Finance* 53(6), 1839–85.

DeLong, J. Bradford, Andrei Shleifer, Lawrence H. Summers, and Robert J. Waldmann. 1990a. Noise Trader Risk in Financial Markets. *Journal of Political Economy* 98(4), 703–38.

———. 1990b. Positive Feedback Investment Strategies and Destabilizing Rational Speculation. *Journal of Finance* 45(2), 379–96.

———. 1991. The Survival of Noise Traders in Financial Markets. *Journal of Business* 64(1), 1–20.

Fama, Eugene F. 1998. Market Efficiency, Long-Term Returns, and Behavioral Finance. *Journal of Financial Economics* 49(3), 283–306.

Foerster, Stephen R., and G. Andrew Karolyi. 1999. The Effects of Market Segmentation and Investor Recognition on Asset Prices: Evidence from Foreign Stocks Listing in the United States. *Journal of Finance* 54(3), 981–1013.

Froot, Kenneth A., and Richard H. Thaler. 1990. Anomalies: Foreign Exchange. *Journal of Economic Perspectives* 4(3), 179–92.

Goetzmann, William, and Aloke Kumar. 2001. Equity Portfolio Diversification. Working paper, NBER.

Haan, Marco. 1997. Where Are the Motives? A Problem with Evidence in the Work of Richard Thaler: A Reply. *Journal of Economic Psychology* 18(6), 705–9.

Hong, Harrison, and Jeremy C. Stein. 1999. A Unified Theory of Underreaction, Momentum Trading, and Overreaction in Asset Markets. *Journal of Finance* 54(6), 2143–84.

Kadlec, Gregory B., and John J. McConnell. 1994. The Effect of Market Segmentation and Illiquidity on Asset Prices: Evidence from Exchange Listings. *Journal of Finance* 49(2), 611–36.

Kahneman, Daniel, Jack L. Knetsch, and Richard H. Thaler. 1991. Anomalies: The Endowment Effect, Loss Aversion, and Status Quo Bias. *Journal of Economic Perspectives* 5(1), 193–206.

Kahneman, Daniel, and Amos Tversky. 1979. Prospect Theory: An Analysis of Decision Under Risk. *Econometrica* 47(2), 263–92.

Mackenzie, Craig. 1997. Where Are the Motives? A Problem with Evidence in the Work of Richard Thaler. *Journal of Economic Psychology* 18(1), 123–35.

Merton, Robert C. 1987. Presidential Address: A Simple Model of Capital Market Equilibrium with Incomplete Information. *Journal of Finance* 42(3), 483–510.

Miller, Merton H. 1986. Behavioral Rationality in Finance: The Case of Dividends. *Journal of Business* 59(4), Part 2, S451–S468.

Nofsinger, John R. 2001. *Investment Madness: How Psychology Affects Your Investing . . . and What to Do About It* (Upper Saddle River, N.J.: Financial Times–Prentice Hall).

Odean, Terrance. 1998. Are Investors Reluctant to Realize Their Losses? *Journal of Finance* 53(5), 1775–98.

Shefrin, Hersh. 2000. *Beyond Greed and Fear: Understanding Behavioral Finance and the Psychology of Investing.* Boston: Harvard Business School Press.

Shefrin, Hersh, and Meir Statman. 1985. The Disposition to Sell Winners Too Early and Ride Losers Too Long: Theory and Evidence. *Journal of Finance* 40(3), 777–82.

Statman, Meir. 1999. Behavioral Finance: Past Battles and Future Engagements. *Financial Analyst Journal* 55(6), 18–27.

Thaler, Richard H. 1999. The End of Behavioral Finance. *Financial Analyst Journal* 55(6), 12–17.

———. 2000. From Homo Economicus to Homo Sapiens. *Journal of Economic Perspectives* 14(1), 133–41.

Notes

1. The discussion in this chapter draws extensively from Fama (1998), Shefrin (2000), Barberis, Shleifer, and Vishny (1998), Hong and Stein (1999), Daniel,

Hirshleifer, and Subrahmanyam (1998), Brav and Heaton (2002), and DeLong et al. (1990a, 1990b).

2. For example, Shefrin (2000) attributes the validity of the capital asset pricing model (CAPM) and "correct" prices to traditional finance. However, traditional finance has not claimed that security beta is the only risk factor; rather, traditional finance suggests only that prices depend on known (and unknown) risk factors. Nor does standard finance theory claim that prices are accurate; only that prices are unbiased based on available information.

3. See Barberis, Shleifer, and Vishny (1998), p. 320.

4. If all investors know about all securities, the model collapses to the CAPM. See Merton (1987).

13

A Description of
Other Possible Mispricings

Ten pricing anomalies are discussed in Chapters 2 through 11. However, there are many more perceived anomalies in financial markets—probably in the hundreds. Some of the so-called anomalies have little basis or research associated with them. For example, street folklore would have you believe that an NFC win in the Super Bowl is good for the stock market. Whether true or not, there is no scientific or economic basis for such an assertion. This chapter briefly discusses many other mispricings that have not been disproved by academic research. The list of references at the end of each mispricing allows the reader to learn more about that mispricing.

There are many mispricings that have been discovered by academic and practitioner research that have not been discussed in previous chapters. While it is not possible to list all possible anomalies and nonanomalies, a few popular or interesting anomalies are listed below, with a brief description relating to that anomaly. The following features characterize the mispricings selected for inclusion:

- The mispricing has been tested with different sample periods and different methods. Some popular mispricings that are *not* supported by the evidence are also included so that readers can see examples of failed anomalies.

- The mispricing appears interesting and profitable though more testing is warranted.

- Several long-term mispricings are included because there is much evidence to support the mispricing even though it is prudent to remain skeptical of long-term underperformance or overperformance for reasons explained in Chapter 1.

Note that the description of each anomaly is not intended to provide readers with a sense of the current state of research; rather, it is a starting point for further exploration. Readers interested in more information should refer to the list of references at the end of each mispricing. In the interest of conserving space, much of the earlier work on these anomalies has been omitted. However, recent work will generally cite earlier work in the area.

Technical Analysis or Charting

The basic idea behind technical analysis is to model price patterns that have been observed in the past. Technical analysis is different from the anomalies discussed in this book as it is not event driven. Short-term price drift in Chapter 4 comes closest to technical analysis, but that too requires a significant public announcement. Technical analysis or charting is probably one of the most, if not the most, popular ways of picking stocks on Wall Street. Thousands of analysts practice it and recommend the selections to their subscribers. Over the years it has become extremely sophisticated and technical. The evidence suggests that technical analysis by itself is not a good predictor of future returns.

References for Further Reading

Allen, Franklin, and Risto Karjalainen. 1999. Using Genetic Algorithms to Find Technical Trading Rules. *Journal of Financial Economics* 51(2), 245–71.

Bessembinder, Hendrik, and Kalok Chan. 1998. Market Efficiency and the Returns to Technical Analysis. *Financial Management* 27(2), 5–17.

Blume, Lawrence, David Easley, and Maureen O'Hara. 1994. Market Statistics and Technical Analysis: The Role of Volume. *Journal of Finance* 49(1), 153–81.

Brock, W. A., J. Lakonishok, and B. LeBaron. 1992. Simple Technical Trading Rules and the Stochastic Properties of Stock Returns. *Journal of Finance* 47, 1731–64.

Brown, David P., and Robert H. Jennings. 1989. On Technical Analysis. *Review of Financial Studies* 2(4), 527–52.

Gencay, Ramazan. 1998. The Predictability of Security Returns with Simple Technical Trading Rules. *Journal of Empirical Finance* 5(4), 347–59.

Lo, Andrew W., Harry Mamaysky, and Jiang Wang. 2000. Foundations of Technical Analysis: Computational Algorithms, Statistical Inference, and Empirical Implementation. *Journal of Finance* 55, 1705–65.

Neftci, Salih N., and Andrew J. Policano. 1984. Can Chartists Outperform the Market? Market Efficiency Tests for "Technical Analysis." *Journal of Futures Markets* 4(4), 465–78.

Pruitt, Stephen W., and Richard E. White. 1988. Who Says Technical Analysis Can't Beat the Market? *Journal of Portfolio Management* 14(3), 55–58.

Ready, Mark J. 2002. Profits from Technical Trading Rules. *Financial Management* 31(3), 43–61.

Sullivan, Ryan, Allan Timmermann, and Halbert White. 1999. Data Snooping, Technical Trading Rule Performance, and the Bootstrap. *Journal of Finance* 54(5), 1647–91.

Sweeney, Richard J. 1988. Some New Filter Rule Tests: Methods and Results. *Journal of Financial and Quantitative Analysis* 23(3), 285–300.

Treynor, Jack L., and Robert Ferguson. 1985. In Defense of Technical Analysis. *Journal of Finance* 40(3), 757–73.

The Value Line Enigma

The Value Line Investment Survey has been giving investment advice since 1965 based on its timeliness ranking of stocks, a system devised by Samuel Eisenstadt. The stocks are ranked from 1 (best) to 5 (worst) reflecting the attractiveness of a particular stock. According to *Hulbert Financial Digest,* an investor who bought stocks rated 1 and sold them when they fell in rank would have earned an annualized 16.3 percent over the period from July 1980 to June 2002, which is about 3.1 percent per year better than the Wilshire 5000 index return. Many other observers testify to the superior performance of the Value Line recommendations from 1965 to the present. Not only do the stocks ranked 1 and 2 outperform the market, stocks ranked at the bottom (rank 5) underperform the market.

The numbers below illustrate the difference in returns as computed from 1965 to 1996. The sum of $1,000 invested in broad-based funds at Value Line's inception would have grown to $27,246 by the end of 1996, whereas $1,000 invested in rank 1 stocks would have grown to a whopping $580,115 by the end of 1996, while $1,000 invested in rank 5 stocks would be worth a puny $4,912 by 1996.

Research has attempted to reconcile these returns with market efficiency. First, the excess returns earned by Value Line stocks seem to become much smaller once transaction costs are considered. Second, rank 1 stocks tend to be smaller, riskier firms and therefore should earn a higher return. Finally, it seems that the Value Line puzzle is simply a manifestation of the underreaction to earnings announcements and is not something new (see Chapter 4). That may explain the superior performance of rank 1 stocks, but it does not explain the underperformance of rank 5 stocks.

References for Further Reading

Affleck-Graves, John, and Richard R. Mendenhall. 1992. The Relation Between the Value Line Enigma and Post-Earnings-Announcement Drift. *Journal of Financial Economics* 31(1), 75–96.

Choi, James J. 2000. The Value Line Enigma: The Sum of Known Parts? *Journal of Financial and Quantitative Analysis* 35(3), 485–98.

Copeland, Thomas E., and David Mayers. 1982. The Value Line Enigma (1965–1978): A Case Study of Performance Evaluation Issues. *Journal of Financial Economics* 10(3), 289–322.

Felton, James. 1995. Teaching Market Efficiency with the Value Line Anomaly. *Journal of Financial Education* 21(1), 44–48.

Huberman, Gur, and Shmuel Kandel. 1990. Market Efficiency and Value Line's Record. *Journal of Business* 63(2), 187–216.

Waggle, Doug, Pankaj Agrawal, and Don Johnson. 2001. Interaction Between Value Line's Timeliness and Safety Ranks. *Journal of Investing* 19(1), 53–61.

Momentum and Reversal in Returns

Empirical evidence suggests that stocks experience momentum and reversals in returns depending on holding periods. Generally, there is momentum in short-term returns of about one month (see Chapter 4) and also in the medium term of about one year, but reversals in longer periods of three to five years. Since short-term momentum has been discussed in Chapter 4, this section is limited to medium- and long-term returns.

The most successful momentum strategy is to buy stocks that have performed the best over the past three to twelve months, and short-sell stocks that performed the worst over the same period. If these positions are held for the next three to twelve months, the positions generate an abnormal return of about 12 percent per year. Momentum strategies seem to be adopted extensively by mutual funds and other institutions.

Over longer periods, studies find that the returns reverse, that is, past winners become losers if held for three to five years and past losers become winners. According to long-term studies, 25–40 percent of the future return is predictable based on past returns.

References for Further Reading

Badrinath, S. G., and Sunil Wahal. 2002. Momentum Trading by Institutions. *Journal of Finance* 57(6), 2449–78.

Chan, Louis K. C., Narasimhan Jegadeesh, and Josef Lakonishok. 1996. Momentum Strategies. *Journal of Finance* 51(5), 1681–713.

————. 1999. The Profitability of Momentum Strategies. *Financial Analyst Journal* 55(6), 80–90.

Conrad, Jennifer, and Gautam Kaul. 1998. An Anatomy of Trading Strategies. *Review of Financial Studies* 11(3), 489–519.

DeBondt, Werner F. M., and Richard Thaler. 1985. Does the Stock Market Overreact? *Journal of Finance* 40(3), 793–805.

————. 1987. Further Evidence on Investor Overreaction and Stock Market Seasonality. *Journal of Finance* 42(3), 557–81.

————. 1989. Anomalies: A Mean-Reverting Walk down Wall Street. *Journal of Economic Perspectives* 3(1), 189–202.

Fama, Eugene F., and Kenneth R. French. 1988. Permanent and Temporary Components of Stock Prices. *Journal of Political Economy* 96(2), 246–73.

Grundy, B. D., and J. S. Martin. 2001. Understanding the Nature of the Risks and the Source of the Rewards to Momentum Investing. *Review of Financial Studies* 14(1), 29–78.

Jegadeesh, Narasimhan, and Sheridan Titman. 1993. Returns to Buying Winners and Selling Losers: Implications for Stock Market Efficiency. *Journal of Finance* 48(1), 65–92.

————. 1995. Overreaction, Delayed Reaction, and Contrarian Profits. *Review of Financial Studies* 8(4), 973–93.

————. 2002. Cross-Sectional and Time-Series Determinants of Momentum Returns. *Review of Financial Studies* 15, 143–57.

Lee, Charles M. C., and Bhaskaran Swaminathan. 2000. Price Momentum and Trading Volume. *Journal of Finance* 55(5), 2017–69.

Lewellen, Jonathan. 2002. Momentum and Autocorrelation in Stock Returns. *Review of Financial Studies* 15, 533–63.

Liew, Jimmy, and Maria Vassalou. 2000. Can Book-to-Market, Size and Momentum Be Risk Factors That Predict Economic Growth? *Journal of Financial Economics* 57(2), 221–45.

Short Selling and Returns

Heavily shorted stocks lose about 1 percent per month when compared with their peers, with stocks that are more heavily short-sold losing more than stocks that are less heavily short sold. Such stocks are also more likely to go bankrupt than other firms. It seems that short sellers are really smart at picking firms with poor performance that are overvalued by the market. The short sellers evaluate the firm in a great amount of detail, in particular with a critical examination of their financial statements. However, investors may short-sell for arbitrage reasons (see Chapter 9) in addition to speculative reasons. Therefore, before selling or short-selling a heavily shorted stock, it is best to make sure that the firm is not in the process of acquiring another company.

References for Further Reading

Asquith, Paul, and Lisa Meulbroek. 1996. An Empirical Investigation of Short Interest. Working paper, Department of Economics, Finance, and Accounting, MIT.

Aitken, Michael, Alex Frino, Michael McCorry, and Peter Swan. 1998. Short Sales ARE Almost Instantaneously Bad News: Evidence from the Australian Stock Exchange. *Journal of Finance* 53, 2205–23.

Chen, Honghui, and Vijay Singal. 2003. The Role of Speculative Short Sales in Price Formation: The Case of the Weekend Effect. *Journal of Finance* 58(2), 685–705.

Chen, Joseph, Harrison Hong, and Jeremy Stein. 2002. Breadth of Ownership and Stock Returns. *Journal of Financial Economics* 66, 171–205.

Choie, Kenneth, and S. James Hwang. 1994. Profitability of Short Selling and Exploitability of Short Information. *Journal of Portfolio Management* 20, 33–38.

DeChow, Patricia, Amy Hutton, Lisa Meulbroek, and Richard Sloan. 2001. Short Sellers, Fundamental Analysis, and Stock Returns. *Journal of Financial Economics* 61, 77–106.

Desai, Hemang, S. Ramu Thiagarajan, K. Ramesh, and Bala V. Balachandran. 2002. An Investigation of the Informational Role of Short Interest in the Nasdaq MARKET. *Journal of Finance* 57(5), 2263–87.

Senchack, A. J., and Laura T. Starks. 1993. Short-Sale Restrictions and Market Reaction to Short-Interest Announcements. *Journal of Financial and Quantitative Analysis* 28, 177–94.

Underpricing of Initial Public Offerings

There is evidence to suggest that IPOs are routinely underpriced, that is, they are issued for less than they are worth. On average over the 1980–2001 period, the closing price on the first day of trading after an initial issue is about 20 percent higher than the issue price. Excluding the late 1990s, the average gain on the issue day was about 9 percent, still a significant appreciation for a single day. There are many reasons why IPOs may be underpriced: uncertainty regarding valuation, asymmetric information with the issuer knowing more than the investors, reputation costs of the underwriters, inducement offered to investors to buy IPOs, preferential allocation practices, stabilization activities of the underwriters, compensation to institutional investors for information revelation, and so on. Moreover, evidence from actual pricing of IPOs shows that stocks with high offer prices tend to be underpriced more than stocks with low offer prices. Further, the level of underpricing depends on market conditions surrounding the IPO. Accurate estimates of underpricing based on market conditions and actual prices can be useful in predicting issue-day price movements.

The one-day return of 9 percent (or 20 percent) comes with several caveats. First, it is not easy to get an allocation of "hot" issues. Investors are usually allocated hot issues only if they have been accepting allocation of cold issues. Second, investors are prohibited by the brokers from selling their shares for about thirty days. Third, investors who do want to sell their shares immediately will be unable to do so because the shares are not actually distributed until several days after the issue date.

References for Further Reading

Aggarwal, Reena. 2003. Allocation of Initial Public Offerings and Flipping Activity. *Journal of Financial Economics* 68(1), 111–35.

Aggarwal, Rajesh, Laurie Krigman, and Kent Womack. 2002. Strategic IPO Underpricing, Information Momentum, and Lockup Expiration Selling. *Journal of Financial Economics* 66, 105–37.

Allen, Franklin and Gerald R. Faulhaber. 1989. Signaling by Underpricing in the IPO Market. *Journal of Financial Economics* 23(2), 303–24.

Asquith, Daniel, Jonathan D. Jones, and Robert Kieschnick. 1998. Evidence on Price Stabilization and Underpricing in Early IPO Returns. *Journal of Finance* 53(5), 1759–73.

Beatty, Randolph P., and Jay R. Ritter. 1986. Investment Banking, Reputation, and the Underpricing of Initial Public Offerings. *Journal of Financial Economics* 15(1–2), 213–32.

Booth, James R., and Lena Chua. 1996. Ownership Dispersion, Costly Information, and IPO Underpricing. *Journal of Financial Economics* 41(2), 291–310.

Busaba, Walid Y., Lawrence M. Benveniste, and Re-Jin Guo. 2001. The Option to Withdraw IPOs During the Premarket: Empirical Analysis. *Journal of Financial Economics* 60(1), 73–102.

Garfinkel, Jon A. 1993. IPO Underpricing, Insider Selling and Subsequent Equity Offerings: Is Underpricing a Signal of Quality? *Financial Management* 22(1), 74–83.

Hanley, Kathleen Weiss. 1993. The Underpricing of Initial Public Offerings and the Partial Adjustment Phenomenon. *Journal of Financial Economics* 34(2), 231–50.

Krigman, Laurie, Wayne H. Shaw, and Kent L. Womack. 1999. The Persistence of IPO Mispricing and the Predictive Power of Flipping. *Journal of Finance* 54(3), 1015–44.

Lee, Philip J., Stephen L. Taylor, and Terry S. Walter. 1999. IPO Underpricing Explanations: Implications from Investor Application and Allocation Schedules. *Journal of Financial and Quantitative Analysis* 34(4), 425–44.

Loughran, T., and J. Ritter. 2002. Why Don't Issuers Get Upset About Leaving Money on the Table in IPOs? *Review of Financial Studies* 15(2), 413–44.

Lowry, Michelle and Susan Shu. 2002. Litigation Risk and IPO Underpricing. *Journal of Financial Economics* 65(3), 309–35.

Ritter, Jay R., and Ivo Welch. 2002. A Review of IPO Activity, Pricing, and Allocations. *Journal of Finance* 57(4), 1795–828.

Rock, Kevin. 1986. Why New Issues Are Underpriced. *Journal of Financial Economics* 15(1–2), 187–212.

Schultz, Paul H., and Mir A. Zaman. 1994. Aftermarket Support and Underpricing of Initial Public Offerings. *Journal of Financial Economics* 35(2), 199–219.
Welch, Ivo. 1989. Seasoned Offerings, Imitation Costs, and the Underpricing of Initial Public Offerings. *Journal of Finance* v44(2), 421–50.

Underpricing of Seasoned Issues

Just like initial public offerings, seasoned equity issues are also underpriced.[1] The average underpricing for seasoned issues in the 1990s was about 3 percent. Why is there an underpricing of seasoned issues where there is much less uncertainty about valuation as shares of the firm are already traded in the market? Explanations include resolution of remaining price uncertainty, inducements offered to new investors especially for securities with relatively inelastic demand, and underwriting reputation and practices. The depressed price exists only for a few days immediately after pricing of the new issue. While it is not clear that there is a profitable strategy, investors can alter their trading patterns such that they sell before the issue is priced and buy on the day of pricing.

References for Further Reading

Altinkilic, Oya, and Robert S. Hansen. 2003. Discounting and Underpricing in Seasoned Equity Offers. *Journal of Financial Economics*, forthcoming.
Bayless, Mark, and Susan Chaplinsky. 1996. Is There a "Window of Opportunity" for Seasoned Equity Issuance? *Journal of Finance* 51(1), 253–78.
Corwin, Shane. 2003. The Determinants of Underpricing for Seasoned Equity Offers. *Journal of Finance*, forthcoming.
Gerard, Bruno, and Vikram Nanda. 1993. Trading and Manipulation Around Seasoned Equity Offerings. *Journal of Finance* 48(1), 213–46.
Guo, Lin, and Timothy S. Mech. 2000. Conditional Event Studies, Anticipation, and Asymmetric Information: The Case of Seasoned Equity Issues and Pre-Issue Information Releases. *Journal of Empirical Finance* 7(2), 113–41.
Loderer, Claudio F., Dennis R. Sheehan, and Gregory B. Kadlec. 1991. The Pricing of Seasoned Equity Offerings. *Journal of Financial Economics* 29(1), 35–58.
McLaughlin, Robyn, Assem Safieddine, and Gopala K. Vasudevan. 1998. The Information Content of Corporate Offerings of Seasoned Securities: An Empirical Analysis. *Financial Management* 27(2), 31–45.
Safieddine, Assem, and William J. Wilhelm Jr. 1996. An Empirical Investigation of Short-Selling Activity Prior to Seasoned Equity Offerings. *Journal of Finance* 51(2), 729–49.
Shin, Hyun-Han. 2001. The Book-Building Period of Seasoned Equity Offerings and Issue Costs. Working paper, Department of Finance, State University of New York at Buffalo.

Unlocking Value Around
Expiration of IPO Lockups

Most IPOs do not permit insiders and some other pre-IPO owners to sell their holdings for a specified period after the IPO. Typically, this lockup period is 180 days. On the unlock day, insiders are suddenly allowed to sell a significant part of their holdings, subject to certain constraints. Empirical research has found that there is abnormal return of –1.5 percent immediately surrounding the unlock day. The abnormal return is more negative, about –3.0 percent, for firms financed by venture capitalists and for firms not subject to SEC Rule 144. However, the relatively small returns and the need to short-sell probably preclude construction of trading strategies. Investors who intended to sell for other reasons can benefit if they choose to sell several days before lockup expiration.

References for Further Reading

Aggarwal, Rajesh, Laurie Krigman, and Kent Womack. 2002. Strategic IPO Underpricing, Information Momentum, and Lockup Expiration Selling. *Journal of Financial Economics* 66, 105–37.

Brau, James, and Grant McQueen. 2001. IPO Lockups: A Signaling Solution to an Adverse Selection Problem. Working paper, Department of Business Management, Brigham Young University.

Fields, L.C., and G. Hanka. 2001. The Expiration of IPO Share Lockups. *Journal of Finance* 56, 471–500.

Keasler, Terrill. 2001. Underwriter Lockup Releases, Initial Public Offerings and After-Market Performance. *The Financial Review* 37, 1–20.

Ofek, Eli, and Matthew Richardson. 2001. The IPO Lockup Period: Implications for Market Efficiency and Downward Sloping Demand Curves. Working paper, Department of Finance, New York University.

Aftermarket Returns from
Initial Public Offerings

Analysts and the management are prohibited from making any forward-looking statements for about twenty-five to thirty days after the IPO, referred to as the "quiet period." As a result, many analysts begin coverage of new issues at the same time. As most analysts tend to cover stocks where they are likely to have positive recommendations, their recommendations tend to have a positive impact on the stock price. A 4 percent abnormal return is expected for IPOs around that time. Moreover, it seems that stocks that are underpriced more are more likely to get covered. Thus, the extent of underpricing is a good predictor of the abnormal return a month later.

In addition to the abnormal returns after the quiet period, there is a tendency for IPO prices to drift after the initial publicity surrounding the IPO issuance has died down. The drift, either upward or downward, begins a few days after the issue date. It is believed that the drift occurs because informed traders break up their orders and spread them over several days to hide their superior information.

References for Further Reading

Affleck-Graves, John, Shantaram Hegde, and Robert E. Miller. 1996. Conditional Price Trends in the Aftermarket for Initial Public Offerings. *Financial Management* 25(4), 25–40.

Asquith, Daniel, Jonathan D. Jones, and Robert Kieschnick. 1998. Evidence on Price Stabilization and Underpricing in Early IPO Returns. *Journal of Finance* 53(5), 1759–73.

Bradley, D., B. Jordan, and J. Ritter, J. 2003. The Quiet Period Goes out with a Bang. *Journal of Finance* 58(1), 1–36.

Busaba, Walid Y., and Chun Chang. 2002. Bookbuilding vs. Fixed Price Revisited: The Effect of Aftermarket Trading. Working paper, Department of Finance, University of Minnesota.

D'Mello, Ranjan, and Stephen P. Ferris. 2000. The Information Effects of Analyst Activity at the Announcement of New Equity Issues. *Financial Management* 29(1), 78–95.

Ellis, Katrina, Roni Michaely, and Maureen O'Hara. 2000. When the Underwriter Is the Market Maker: An Examination of Trading in the IPO Aftermarket. *Journal of Finance* 55(3), 1039–74.

Krigman, Laurie, Wayne H. Shaw, and Kent L. Womack. 1999. The Persistence of IPO Mispricing and the Predictive Power of Flipping. *Journal of Finance* 54(3), 1015–44.

Schultz, Paul H., and Mir A. Zaman. 1994. Aftermarket Support and Underpricing of Initial Public Offerings. *Journal of Financial Economics* 35(2), 199–219.

Pricing of Closed-End Funds

Actively managed funds that trade on organized exchanges and are closed to new investors, also known as closed-end funds, usually trade at a premium or at a discount to the net asset value of the securities held by the fund.[2] The extant evidence suggests that closed-end funds are issued at a premium with respect to their net asset value, that discounts fluctuate widely over time and across funds, and that closed-end fund prices converge to their net asset values when they are either liquidated or open-ended. On average, they trade at a discount of about 10 percent to the net asset value. This is known as the closed-end discount puzzle. What are the explanations? Some studies have found that discounts vary with the sentiment of individual investors. Others relate it to management fees payable by the fund or to anticipated managerial performance. Still others find that funds that are more difficult to arbitrage have larger discounts. However, none of the theories, either individually or collectively, provides a sufficient explanation for the pricing (or mispricing) of closed-end funds.[3]

References for Further Reading

Barclay, Michael J., Clifford G. Holderness, and Jeffrey Pontiff. 1993. Private Benefits from Block Ownership and Discounts on Closed-End Funds. *Journal of Financial Economics* 33, 263–91.

Brauer, Greggory A. 1988. Closed-End Fund Shares' Abnormal Returns and the Information Content of Discounts and Premiums. *Journal of Finance* 43, 113–27.

Chay, Jong-Boon, and Charles A.Trzcinka. 1999. Managerial Performance and the Cross-Sectional Pricing of Closed-End Funds. *Journal of Financial Economics* 52, 379–408.

Chen, Nai-Fu, Raymond Kan, and Merton Miller. 1993. Are the Discounts on Closed End Funds a Sentiment Index? *Journal of Finance* 48(2), 795–800.

Chopra, Navin, Charles M. C. Lee, Andrei Shleifer, and Richard H. Thaler. 1993. Yes, Discounts on Closed-End Funds are a Sentiment Index. *Journal of Finance* 48(2), 801–8.

Coles, Jeffrey L., Jose Suay, and Denise Woodbury. 2000. Fund Advisor Compensation in Closed-End Funds. *Journal of Finance* 55, 1385–414.

Dimson, Elroy, and Carolina Minio-Kozeski. 1999. Closed-End Funds: A Survey. *Financial Markets, Institutions and Instruments* 8(2), 1–41.

Garay, Urbi, and Philip Russell. 1999. The Closed-End Fund Puzzle: A Review. *Journal of Alternative Investments* 2(3), 23–44.

Gemmill, Gordon, and Dylan C. Thomas. 2002. Noise Trading, Costly Arbitrage, and Asset Prices: Evidence from Closed End Funds. *Journal of Finance* 57(6), 2571–94.

Klibanoff, Peter, Owen Lamont, and Thierry Z. Wizman. 1998. Investor Reaction to Salient News in Closed-End Country Funds. *Journal of Finance* 53(2), 673–99.

Kumar, Raman, and Gregory N. Noronha. 1992. A Re-examination of the Relationship Between Closed-End Fund Discounts and Expenses. *Journal of Financial Research* 15, 139–47.

Lee, Charles M. C., Andrei Shleifer, and Richard H. Thaler. 1990. Anomalies: Closed-End Mutual Funds. *Journal of Economic Perspectives* 4(4), 153–64.

Malkiel, Burton G. 1995. The Structure of Closed-End Fund Discounts Revisited. *Journal of Portfolio Management* 21, 32–38.

Pontiff, Jeffrey. 1995. Closed-End Fund Premia and Returns: Implications for Financial Market Equilibrium. *Journal of Financial Economics* 37, 341–70.

———. 1996. Costly Arbitrage: Evidence from Closed-End Funds. *Quarterly Journal of Economics* 111, 1135–51.

Short-Term Price Drift Following Earnings and Analyst Recommendations

There is much research related to price drift following announcement of new information by the company, analysts, government, competitors, or other sources. The implications of this research have been subsumed in Chapter 4, where the release of news is combined with price changes and volume increases. No new references are listed here.

The Influence of Weather on Prices

There is a growing amount of literature that finds an effect of weather or other natural phenomena on stock returns. The weather in New York or other major centers for the relative international indexes seems to affect stock prices in a way consistent with psychological effects on human nature: stock prices rise on sunny days but are unaffected on other days. Similarly, stock returns around new-moon days are much higher than returns around full-moon days. Though there are documented differences in returns, it is probably a bit early to term it an anomaly. Moreover, the differences are small enough that trading strategies are unlikely to be profitable.

References for Further Reading

Goetzmann, William, and Ning Zhu. 2002. Rain or Shine: Where Is the Weather Effect. Working paper, School of Management, Yale University.

Hirshleifer, David, and Tyler Shumway. 2003. Good Day Sunshine: Stock Returns and Weather. *Journal of Finance* 58(3), 1009–32.

Kamstra, Mark J., Lisa A. Kramer, and Maurice D. Levi. 2000. Losing Sleep at the Market: The Daylight Saving Anomaly. *American Economic Review* 90(4), 1005–11.

Pardo, Angel and Enric Valor. 2003. Spanish Stock Returns: Where Is the Weather Effect? *European Financial Management* 9, 117–126.

Saunders, Edward M., Jr. 1993. Stock Prices and Wall Street Weather. *American Economic Review* 83(5), 1337–45.

Long-Term Price Drift After Open-Market Share Repurchases and Tender Offers

Instead of paying cash dividends, firms can pay stockholders by repurchasing stock. Repurchases (or buyback) of stock can be made in the open market or through tender offers by the company. Firms that announce repurchases outperform the market over the long term. The two-day announcement return is about 3 percent. However, this is followed by an abnormal return of 12 percent over the next four years. There are two main explanations for the initial reaction, but not necessarily for the continued drift. First, firms may repurchase stock when they believe the firm's stock is undervalued by the market. Second, firms may use repurchases as a way of returning excess cash to the stockholders. The undervaluation explanation is better supported by the evidence. As value firms are likely to be more undervalued than growth firms, their overperformance should be higher. Indeed, firms in the highest book-value-to-market-price quintile outperform their peers by about 45 percent over four years after the repurchase.[4]

As with other long-term studies, these studies suffer from the usual criticisms. Though there are excess returns, those returns come primarily from small firms and are not statistically significant.

References for Further Reading

Chhachhi, Indudeep S., and Wallace N. Davidson III. 1997. A Comparison of the Market Reaction to Specially Designated Dividends and Tender Offer Stock Repurchases. *Financial Management* 26(3), 89–96.

Dittmar, Amy K. 2000. Why Do Firms Repurchase Stock? *Journal of Business* 73(3), 331–55.

D'Mello, Ranjan, and Pervin K. Shroff. 2000. Equity Undervaluation and Decision Related to Repurchase Tender Offers: An Empirical Investigation. *Journal of Finance* 55(5), 2399–424.

Ikenberry, David, and Theo Vermaelen. 1996. The Option to Repurchase Stock. *Financial Management* 25(4), 9–24.

Ikenberry, David, Josef Lakonishok, and Theo Vermaelen. 1995. Market Underreaction to Open Market Share Repurchases. *Journal of Financial Economics* 39(2–3), 181–208.

———. 2000. Stock Repurchases in Canada: Performance and Strategic Trading. *Journal of Finance* 55(5), 2373–97.

Kahle, Kathleen M. 2002. When a Buyback Isn't a Buyback: Open Market Repurchases and Employee Options. *Journal of Financial Economics* 63(2), 235–61.

Lakonishok, Josef, and Theo Vermaelen. 1990. Anomalous Price Behavior Around Repurchase Tender Offers. *Journal of Finance* 45(2), 455–78.

McNally, William J. 1999. Openmarket Stock Repurchase Signaling. *Financial Management* 28(2), 55–67.

Mitchell, Mark, and Erik Stafford. 2000. Managerial Decisions and Long-Term Stock Price Performance. *Journal of Business* 73(3), 289–329.

Singh, Ajai K., Mir A. Zaman, and Chandrasekhar Krishnamurti. 1994. Liquidity Changes Associated with Open Market Repurchases. *Financial Management* 23(1), 47–55.

Stephens, Clifford P., and Michael S. Weisbach. 1998. Actual Share Reacquisitions in Open-Market Repurchase Programs. *Journal of Finance* 53(1), 313–33.

Long-Term Underperformance
Following Initial Public Offerings

Empirical evidence suggests that IPO firms underperform the market, as measured by a value-weighted index, by about 25 percent over a three-year period. As IPO firms are usually small growth firms, the market index that consists of large firms may not be an appropriate benchmark. Research has found that the IPO firms also underperform relative to their peers by about 5 percent over the same three-year period. There is much disagreement over the definition of peers, appropriate statistical methodologies, and the economic and statistical significance of the returns. Similarly, reasons for the underperformance are varied: constraints on short selling that cause the IPO prices to exhibit an upward bias in the first few days of trading, timing of IPOs during high valuation periods, poor financial performance after the IPO, and so on.

References for Further Reading

Brav, Alon. 2000. Inference in Long-Horizon Event Studies: A Bayesian Approach with Application to Initial Public Offerings. *Journal of Finance* 55(5), 1979–2016.

Brav, Alon, Christopher Geczy, and Paul A. Gompers. 2000. Is the Abnormal Return Following Equity Issuances Anomalous? *Journal of Financial Economics* 56(2), 209–50.

Brav, Alon, and Paul A. Gompers. 1997. Myth or Reality? The Long-Run Underperformance of Initial Public Offerings: Evidence from Venture and Nonventure Capital-Backed Companies. *Journal of Finance* 52(5), 1791–821.

Carter, Richard B., Frederick H. Dark, and Alan K. Singh. 1998. Underwriter Reputation, Initial Returns, and the Long-Run Performance of IPO Stocks. *Journal of Finance* 53(1), 285–311.

Gompers, Paul, and Joshua Lerner. 2003. The Really Long Run Performance of Initial Public Offerings: The Pre-Nasdaq Evidence. *Journal of Finance*, forthcoming.

Jain, Bharat A., and Omesh Kini. 1994. The Post-Issue Operating Performance of IPO Firms. *Journal of Finance* 49(5), 1699–726.

Loughran, Tim, and Jay R. Ritter. 1995. The New Issues Puzzle. *Journal of Finance* 50(1), 23–51.

Ritter, Jay R., 1991. The Long Run Performance of Initial Public Offerings. *Journal of Finance* 46(1), 3–28.

Ritter, Jay R., and Ivo Welch. 2002. A Review of IPO Activity, Pricing, and Allocations. *Journal of Finance* 57(4), 1795–828.

Teoh, Siew Hong, Ivo Welch, and T. J. Wong. 1998. Earnings Management and the Long-Run Market Performance of Initial Public Offerings. *Journal of Finance* 53(6), 1935–74.

Long-Term Underperformance Following Seasoned Issues

Empirical research finds that seasoned firms that issue equity underperform the market by 20 to 35 percent over the subsequent three-year period. Benchmarks become an issue, as with the underperformance for IPO firms. In some cases the abnormal returns disappear, while in other cases the underperformance is robust to a variety of specifications. Researchers have tried to avoid the benchmarking problem by studying the issuing firm's bonds and the mispricing as related to arbitrage costs. They tend to support the notion of underperformance of stocks following seasoned equity issues. Possible explanations for underperformance relate to poor operating performance, timing of equity issues in times of high valuation, and limits of arbitrage activity.

References for Further Reading

Alerson, Michael J., and Brian L. Betker. 2000. The Long-Run Performance of Companies That Withdraw Seasoned Equity Offerings. *Journal of Financial Research* 23(2), 157–78.

Brav, Alon, Christopher Geczy, and Paul A. Gompers. 2000. Is the Abnormal Return Following Equity Issuances Anomalous? *Journal of Financial Economics* 56(2), 209–50.

Brous, Peter A., Vinay Datar, and Omesh Kini. 2001. Is the Market Optimistic About the Future Earnings of Seasoned Equity Offering Firms? *Journal of Financial and Quantitative Analysis* 36(2), 141–68.

Clarke, Jonathan, Craig Dunbar, and Kathy Kahle. 2001. Long-Run Performance and Insider Trading in Completed and Canceled Seasoned Equity Offerings. *Journal of Financial and Quantitative Analysis* 36(4), 415–30.

———. 2003. Long-Run Performance of Secondary Equity Issues: A Test of the Windows of Opportunity Hypothesis. *Journal of Business,* forthcoming.

Eberhart, Allan C., and Akhtar Siddique. 2002. The Long Term Performance of Corporate Bonds (and Stocks) Following Seasoned Equity Offerings. *Review of Financial Studies* 15(5), 1385–406.

Eckbo, E. Espen, Ronald W. Masulis, and Oyvind Norli. 2000. Seasoned Public Offerings: Resolution of the "New Issues Puzzle." *Journal of Financial Economics* 56(2), 251–91.

Jegadeesh, Narashimhan. 2000. Long-Term Performance of Seasoned Equity Offerings: Benchmark Errors and Biases in Expectations. *Financial Management* 29(3), 5–30.

Jung, K., Y. Kim, and R. M. Stulz. 1996. Timing, Investment Opportunities, Managerial Discretion, and the Security Issue Decision. *Journal of Financial Economics* 42, 159–85.

Loughran, Tim, and Jay R. Ritter. 1995. The New Issues Puzzle. *Journal of Finance* 50(1), 23–51.

————. 1997. The Operating Performance of Firms Conducting Seasoned Equity Offerings. *Journal of Finance* 52(5), 1823–50.

————. 2000. Uniformly Least Powerful Tests of Market Efficiency. *Journal of Financial Economics* 55, 361–89.

Mitchell, Mark L., and Erik Stafford. 2000. Managerial Decisions and Long-Term Stock Price Performance. *Journal of Business* 73, 287–329.

Pontiff, Jeffrey, and Michael J. Schill. 2002. Long Run Seasoned Equity Offering Returns: Data Snooping, Model Misspecification, or Mispricing? A Costly Arbitrage Approach. Working paper, Department of Finance, University of Virginia.

Spiess, D. K., and J. Affleck-Graves. 1995. Underperformance in Long-Run Stock Returns Following Seasoned Equity Offerings. *Journal of Financial Economics* 38, 243–67.

Teoh, Siew Hong, Ivo Welch, and T. J. Wong. 1998. Earnings Management and the Underperformance of Seasoned Equity Offerings. *Journal of Financial Economics* 50(1), 63–99.

Long-Term Overperformance Following Spin-offs

A spin-off is a pro rata distribution of the shares of a subsidiary to the parent firm's stockholders. While a new independent entity is created, no new capital is raised since the existing shareholders get shares in the subsidiary. For example, Lucent Technologies was spun off by AT&T in 1996.

Companies spun off from parent companies earn returns that are about 33 percent larger than the returns earned by their peers over a three-year period. Parent companies earn abnormal returns of about 15 percent over the three-year period. Trading strategies designed to capture abnormal performance do not always perform satisfactorily.

The primary explanation for the overperformance of companies engaged in a spin-off seems to be related to corporate focus. When unrelated businesses are spun off, the focus of the management is sharper and the incidence of cross subsidies to keep poorly performing divisions alive is much reduced. There is an improvement in operating performance, and the empirical evidence suggests that focus-increasing spin-offs are the only ones that outperform their peers. The non-focus-increasing spin-offs do not outperform their peers. Another explanation for the abnormal performance is a reduction in asymmetry of information between the management and investors. When a company operates in a single segment, external earnings and performance estimates are more accurate than when a company operates in multiple segments. A reduction in information asymmetry means that there is less risk and, therefore, the stock price is higher.

References for Further Reading

Abarbanell, Jeffrey S., Brian J. Bushee, and Jana Smith Raedy. 2003. Institutional Investor Preferences and Price Pressure: The Case of Corporate Spin-offs. *Journal of Business,* forthcoming.

Allen, Jeffrey. 2001. Private Information and Spin-off Performance. *Journal of Business* 74(2), 281–306.

Cusatis, Patrick, James A. Miles, and J. Randall Woolridge. 1993. Value Creation Through Spin-offs: The Stock Market Evidence. *Journal of Financial Economics* 33, 293–311.

Daley, Lane, Vikas Mehrotra, and Ranjini Sivakumar. 1997. Corporate Focus and Value Creation: Evidence from Spin-offs. *Journal of Financial Economics* 45, 257–81.

Desai, Hemang, and Prem C. Jain. 1999. Firm Performance and Focus: Long-Run Stock Market Performance Following Spinoffs. *Journal of Financial Economics* 54(1), 75–101.

Dittmar, Amy. 2003. Capital Structure in Corporate Spinoffs. *Journal of Business,* forthcoming.

Johnson, Shane A., Daniel P. Klein, and Verne L. Thibodeaux. 1996. The Effects of Spin-Offs on Corporate Investment and Performance. *Journal of Financial Research* 19(2), 293–307.

Krishnaswami, Sudha, and Venkat Subramanian. 1999. Information Asymmetry, Valuation, and the Corporate Spin-off Decision. *Journal of Financial Economics* 53, 73–112.

Maxwell, William, and Ramesh P. Rao. 2003. Do Spin-offs Expropriate Wealth from Bondholders? *Journal of Finance,* forthcoming.

McConnell, John, M. Ozbilgin, and Sunil Wahal. 2001. Spin-offs, Ex Ante. *Journal of Business* 74(2), 245–80.

Miles, James, and James Rosenfeld. 1983. An Empirical Analysis of the Effects of Spinoff Announcements on Shareholder Wealth. *Journal of Finance* 38, 1597–606.

Long-Term Performance Following Mergers

Firms acquiring other firms tend to pay stock when they believe that their stock is overvalued and pay cash when they think that their stock is undervalued (see Chapter 9). So it is not surprising to find that firms do well following cash acquisitions but poorly after stock mergers. The question relates to whether the performance following mergers is significantly different from the norm. Some studies find no abnormal performance, while others find that merging firms underperform by up to −10 percent over a five-year period. The differences become sharper when the method of payment is factored in. Firms acquiring firms with cash seem to outperform their peers by 62 percent over the following five years, while stock mergers are associated with an underperformance of −25 percent.

Cash flows increase following cash mergers but decline following stock mergers. The usual disclaimer relating to long-term abnormal performance applies.

References for Further Reading

Agrawal, Anup, Jeffrey F. Jaffe, and Gershon N. Mandelker. 1992. The Post-Merger Performance of Acquiring Firms: A Re-Examination of an Anomaly. *Journal of Finance* 47(4), 1605–22.

Asquith, Paul. 1983. Merger Bids, Uncertainty and Stockholder Returns. *Journal of Financial Economics* 11, 51–83.

Franks, Julian R., Robert S. Harris, and Sheridan Titman. 1991. The Post-Merger Share Price Performance of Acquiring Firms. *Journal of Financial Economics* 29, 81–96.

Ghosh, Aloke. 2001. Does Operating Performance Really Improve Corporate Acquisitions? *Journal of Corporate Finance* 7(2), 151–78.

Healy, Paul M., Krishna G. Palepu, and Richard S. Ruback. 1992. Does Corporate Performance Improve After Mergers? *Journal of Financial Economics* 31, 135–75.

Linn, Scott C., and Jeannette A. Switzer. 2001. Are Cash Acquisitions Associated with Better Postcombination Operating Performance than Stock Acquisitions? *Journal of Banking and Finance* 25(6), 1113–38.

Loughran, Tim, and Anand Vijh. 1997. Do Long-Term Shareholders Benefit from Capital Acquisitions? *Journal of Finance* 52(5), 1765–90.

Rau, P. R., and T. Vermaelen. 1998. Glamour, Value and Post-Acquisition Performance of Acquiring Firms. *Journal of Financial Economics* 49, 223–53.

Walker, M. Mark. 2000. Corporate Takeovers, Strategic Objectives, and Acquiring-Firm Shareholder Wealth. *Financial Management* 29(1), 53–66.

Long-Term Price Drift
After Dividend Initiations and Omissions

When a firm initiates or omits dividends, it is conveying information about future earnings. As a result, the stock price falls immediately after a firm decides to omit or reduce dividend payment, but the price increases after a non-dividend-paying firm decides to start paying dividends. There is some evidence to suggest that the new information is not immediately reflected in price and the price continues to drift for several years. Firms initiating dividend payments outperform their peers by about 25 percent over the next three years, while firms omitting dividends underperform by about –15 percent. However, there is other evidence to suggest that the drift occurs only in certain periods and does not occur for large firms.

References for Further Reading

Boehme, Rodney D., and Sorin M. Sorescu. 2002. The Long-Run Performance Following Dividend Initiations and Resumptions: Underreaction or Product of Chance? *Journal of Finance* 57(2), 871–900.

Christie, William G. 1994. Are Dividend Omissions Truly the Cruelest Cut of All? *Journal of Financial and Quantitative Analysis* 29(3), 459–80.

Dyl, Edward A., and Robert A. Weigand. 1998. The Information Content of Dividend Initiations: Additional Evidence. *Financial Management* 27(3), 27–35.

Healy, Paul, and Krishna Palepu. 1988. Earnings Information Conveyed by Dividend Initiations and Omissions. *Journal of Financial Economics* 21, 149–75.

Howe, John S., and Yang-pin Shen. 1998. Information Associated with Dividend Initiations: Firm-Specific or Industry-Wide? *Financial Management* 27(3), 17–26.

Kohers, Ninon. 1999. The Industry-Wide Implications of Dividend Omission and Initiation Announcements and the Determinants of Information Transfer. *Financial Review* 34(1), 137–58.

Michaely, Roni, Richard H. Thaler, and Kent L. Womack. 1995. Price Reactions to Dividend Initiations and Omissions: Overreaction or Drift? *Journal of Finance* 50(2), 573–608.

Sant, Rajiv, and Arnold R. Cowan. 1994. Do Dividends Signal Earnings? The Case of Omitted Dividends. *Journal of Banking and Finance* 18(6), 1113–33.

Venkatesh, P. C. 1989. The Impact of Dividend Initiation on the Information Content of Earnings Announcements and Returns Volatility. *Journal of Business* 62(2), 175–98.

Long-Term Price Patterns After Stock Splits

Stock splits are almost always accompanied by an increase in the stock price around the announcement. However, the price drift continues for about a year, on average, with the firm announcing the stock split gaining about 9 percent more than its peers. Different sample periods and methods promise an abnormal return of at least 6 percent. Over longer periods extending to three years, however, the abnormal performance disappears. The limitations of measuring long-term abnormal performance remain.

References for Further Reading

Boehme, Rodney. 2002. Re-examining the Long-Run Stock Split Anomaly Puzzle. Working paper, Department of Finance, University of Houston.

Brennan, M., and P. Hughes. 1991. Stock Splits, Stock Prices, and Transaction Costs. *Journal of Finance* 46, 1665–91.

Brennan, M., and T. E. Copeland. 1988. Stock Splits, Stock Prices, and Transaction Costs. *Journal of Financial Economics* 22, 83–101.

Byun, Jinho, and Michael S. Rozeff. 2003. Long-Run Performance After Stock Splits: 1927 to 1996. *The Journal of Finance* 58(3), 1063–86.

Desai, H., and P. C. Jain. 1997. Long-Run Common Stock Returns Following Stock Splits and Reverse Splits. *Journal of Business* 70, 409–33.

Dharan, B. G., and D. S. Ikenberry. 1995. The Long-Run Negative Drift of Post-Listing Stock Returns. *Journal of Finance* 50, 1547–74.

Ikenberry, D. L., G. Rankine, and E. K. Stice. 1996. What Do Stock Splits Really Signal? *Journal of Financial and Quantitative Analysis* 31, 357–75.

Ikenberry, David L., and Sundaresh Ramnath. 2002. Underreaction to Self-Selected News Events: The Case of Stock Splits. *Review of Financial Studies* 15, 489–526.

Notes

1. If a publicly traded company issues more shares to raise capital, it is called a seasoned equity offering or a seasoned issue.
2. Unlike a typical mutual fund, shareholders in a closed-end fund cannot redeem their shares by returning them to the fund company. Instead, they must sell them to another investor through a stock exchange. Though closed-end funds are managed like open-end mutual funds, they trade like stocks.
3. Popular media claims a January effect for closed-end funds (see *Business Week* of December 2, 2002). However, there are no academic studies supporting or denying that claim. The low volume on most closed-end funds results in high trading costs. For more information, try www.herzfeld.com and www.cefa.com.
4. Theo Vermaelen, one of the authors of the repurchase studies, runs a buyback fund that invests in stocks announcing buybacks specifically due to undervaluation. As of January 2002, the fund had earned 37 percent since the fund's inception in July 1998, compared with 6 percent for the Nasdaq and 0 percent for the S&P 500.
5. Government taxes are not considered specifically because they are small. For individual stock sales, the SEC fee is 0.033 percent of the sale value. There is no tax on purchases.
6. Exceptions are Rydex Dynamic funds and Fidelity Select funds, which allow intraday trading.
7. Many brokerage firms do not allow account holders to short-sell a stock that is priced at less than $5 because low-priced stocks are riskier. This is not a condition imposed by the exchanges but internal to a brokerage house. You should be able to find another broker if you must short-sell a low-priced stock.
8. Options can also be used for hedging but are more complicated and unnecessary.

Appendix A: Financial Instruments

This appendix contains an overview of the financial instruments that can be employed: a description, availability, and a comparison of trading costs. Since arbitraging most of the anomalies discussed herein entails a substantial amount of trading, it is necessary to keep trading costs low. Besides translating into a higher profit margin, lower trading costs permit the arbitraging of anomalies that would otherwise be unprofitable.

Before talking about financial instruments, it is useful to get a feel for trading costs. There are three components of the total trading cost: the bid-ask spread, brokerage fees, and market impact cost. As any arbitrage activity consists of a round trip—one buy and one sell—the trader must buy at the ask and sell at the bid, resulting in the bid-ask spread as a trading cost for the arbitrageur. In addition, brokerage fees must be borne by the trader. Finally, any substantial trade will have an impact on the market price. If you want to buy a large block of shares, then many stockholders must be willing to part with their shares, and they may demand a price higher than the current ask price. This is referred to as the price impact of the trade. The price impact depends on the trade size relative to the normal trade size for that stock. The sum of the bid-ask spread, brokerage fees, and market impact cost constitutes the total trading cost.

There are five kinds of financial assets available for trading: individual stocks, stock options, index futures (and stock futures), open-end mutual funds, and exchange traded funds. Each of the five instruments is discussed in turn.

INDIVIDUAL STOCKS

The plain-vanilla financial instrument is the individual stock—the shares issued by a company. In the United States, there are about 7,700 stocks that trade on NYSE, AMEX, and Nasdaq. There are approximately 2,800 stocks on NYSE, 700 on AMEX, and 4,200 on Nasdaq.

The cost of trading individual stocks depends on the market value of the firm, trading volume, and size of trade. Small firms and low volume firms have a high cost of trading. Large trades entail a higher market impact cost. According to Elkins-McSherry (see www.elkins-mcsherry.com), the total weighted average trading costs are 0.28 percent on NYSE, 0.29 percent on AMEX, and 0.36 percent on Nasdaq. Academic studies estimate the average bid-ask spread to be approximately 0.50 percent. However, the bid-ask spread for low priced stocks and low volume stocks can be much higher, in the range of 2 to 10 percent.

In spite of relatively higher trading costs, investors may choose to trade individual stocks for several reasons. First, alternative instruments may not be available. Second, the trading can be focused in the single stock of interest rather than on a group of possibly unrelated stocks. Third, individual stocks can be short-sold to take a negative position that is sometimes more expensive with other instruments. Finally, the trading costs are reasonably small for large, actively traded stocks.

STOCK OPTIONS

Stock options are derivatives on individual stocks that give the investor a right to buy (call option) or sell (put option) the underlying stock at a specified price within a specified period. There is less risk with an option than with an individual stock. However, the option price reflects the lower risk. Options enable an investor to lever up exposure to stock movements without increasing the outlay.

On the downside, stock options are available for only about 2,000 stocks out of a universe of 7,700 stocks. Typically, options do not exist on small-cap stocks. Further, the minimum exercise price for options is $5, which means that few new options are written on low-priced stocks. Though options exist on many stocks, they are actively traded only on the large and high-volume stocks. For the top fifty stocks by option trading volume, the option volume is equivalent to 10–15 percent of the stock volume. For the next fifty stocks, the option trading volume falls to 5–10 percent of the stock volume. Thereafter, the option trading volume varies between zero and 5 percent of the stock volume. The low level of trading volume implies that trading costs can be high. Even for the top one hundred stocks by option volume, a bid-ask spread of 10–20 percent is the norm for near-term at-the-money options. For other options, the spreads are much higher.

Therefore, options should generally be avoided for investment strategies unless they are being used for a special reason.

INDEX FUTURES AND STOCK FUTURES

Stock index futures are available on many indexes, including the S&P 500, Nasdaq 100, Dow Jones Industrial Index, Fortune E-50, NYSE Composite, Russell 2000, S&P Midcap 400, S&P 500 Growth, and S&P 500 Value. Out of these, the S&P 500, Nasdaq 100, and Dow Jones are actively traded, while the Russell 2000 and S&P Midcap 400 have adequate trading. The remaining futures contracts do not have sufficient trading activity. Index futures are useful when a broad set of stocks must be followed and those stocks constitute a large fraction of one of the actively or adequately traded futures contracts. Index futures have relatively low transaction costs, including a much smaller price impact, than individual stocks. They should be the preferred mode of transacting when the index is representative of the stocks required for a trading strategy. Index futures are also useful for hedging market movements.

Individual stock futures first became available in October 2002. Stock futures work just like index futures. It is easy to short-sell the underlying stocks by using futures because futures contracts are not subject to the constraints of short selling. Stock futures are also less expensive to trade. However, they have not yet been able to generate significant interest and volume.

MUTUAL FUNDS

Mutual funds provide an alternative to stocks, options, and futures. Mutual funds usually trade at the end of the day at their net asset values. Though many mutual funds have front-end loads, back-end loads, or redemption fees, it is not difficult to find comparable funds with no loads or redemption fees. In general, mutual funds have very low transaction costs (almost zero) because you can buy and sell at the same price. As a result, mutual funds are probably the lowest-cost vehicle for arbitraging, provided a mutual fund appropriate for a particular strategy exists. However, mutual funds may have significantly higher costs than individual stocks for long-term investors. First, the fund charges fees for management, administration, and marketing, called the expense ratio. Second, the mutual fund's trading costs reduce the fund's overall return, though they are not explicitly reported. A fund is forced to trade whenever investors purchase or redeem shares in a fund. The cost of trading is borne by all investors, not just by the transitory investors that cause the trades.

Indexed mutual funds are available as an alternative to stock index futures. Indexed mutual funds are usually available for the major indexes only: the S&P500, Russell 2000, and Nasdaq 100. Unfortunately, no index funds track broader indexes such as the Wilshire 5000. There are other funds that are indexed to a subset of these primary indexes, such as the Russell 2000 Growth. True index funds hold all the stocks in the index in the correct proportion and will trade only when there are index changes or large investor flows. There are enhanced index funds that hold fewer stocks but still try to match or beat the performance of the index.

EXCHANGE-TRADED FUNDS

An exchange-traded fund (ETF) is a portfolio of individual stocks that trades just like a stock. The portfolio of stocks is static if it is based on a set of stocks selected by the manager of the ETF but may change if it is based on an index that is subject to change. The most common and actively traded ETFs are based on popular indexes: S&P Depository Receipts Trust Series 1 (SPDR) (AMEX: SPY) tracks the S&P 500, Nasdaq 100 Index Tracking Stock (Qubes) (AMEX: QQQ) tracks the Nasdaq 100, and Diamonds Trust (AMEX: DIA) tracks the Dow Jones Industrial Average. Similarly, other domestic indexes (such as Russell 2000, S&P MidCap 400, sector Spiders, and others) and international indexes (such as Morgan Stanley Capital International's Australia, Mexico, Japan, and others) are tracked by different ETFs. Vanguard Total Stock Market VIPER (AMEX: VTI) tracks Vanguard's Total Stock Market Index fund as a proxy for Wilshire 5000.

In addition, there are ETFs created by Merrill Lynch called Holding Company Depository Receipts (HOLDRs) that hold twenty stocks in one sector. No changes in the stocks take place except for corporate actions. For example, Biotech HOLDRs (AMEX: BBH) still has the twenty original stocks in the biotech ETF, while Internet HOLDRs (AMEX: HHH) is down to thirteen stocks in the Internet ETF because some companies went bankrupt or merged with other companies already in HHH.

Index-based exchange-traded funds are similar to index mutual funds. There are two basic differences: ability to trade and distributions. ETFs are easier to trade than mutual funds, can be traded at any time during the day, and can be short-sold because they trade like stocks. However, ETFs are more costly to trade due to brokerage commissions and the bid-ask spread. On the other hand, ETFs allow better tax planning because you can choose when to realize capital gains or losses. This is unlike mutual funds, where the fund is obligated to distribute its capital gains or dividends at the end of the year.

Internet References

Information on Stocks, Options, Mutual Funds, and Futures

http://www.nyse.com, http://www.amex.com, http://www.nasdaq.com: Sites of the national stock exchanges.

http://www.cboe.com, http://www.optionsclearing.com: Chicago Board Options Exchange (CBOE) is the primary options exchange. Options Clearing Corporation is the clearinghouse for all options listed on any U.S. options exchange.

http://www.cme.com: Site of the primary exchange for futures trading.

Information on Exchange-Traded Funds

http://www.amex.com: Go to "ETFs" or "HOLDRS." Most exchange traded funds trade on the American Stock Exchange.

http://www.ishares.com: Site of Barclays Global Investors, which manages the iShares that track S&P indexes, Russell indexes, Dow Jones indexes, and foreign country indexes. Almost all exchange-traded funds whose tickers begin with an I or E are managed by Barclays.

http://www.nasdaq.com: Information primarily on the Qubes (QQQ).

http://www.streettracks.com: Site of State Street Global Advisors, which manages select SPDRs.

http://www.holdrs.com. A group of stocks in selected and narrow industries managed by Merrill Lynch. All Holdrs begin with twenty stocks and a fixed number of shares, but the number of stocks can fall (with mergers or bankruptcies) or increase (with spin-offs), as the Holdrs are not actively managed.

Appendix B: Short Selling

This appendix describes the process and the restraints on short selling because some arbitrage strategies require short sales. Short-selling shares is a little more complicated than buying shares, as it involves selling shares that you do not own. How can you sell something that you do not have? You (or your broker) must borrow the shares that you want to short-sell. Brokerage houses and securities lenders lend shares for you to sell in return for a portion (or all) of the interest earned on the cash used to secure the shares borrowed. The transaction is profitable for the brokerage house or securities lender and carries little risk of default, since the loaned shares are secured by collateral. On the other hand, the short seller is able to implement various strategies that require short sales. The short seller hopes to be able to return the borrowed shares by buying them later in the market at a lower price.

However, it is important to realize the risks of short selling. In a long position (where you buy shares), your risk is limited to the amount of your investment. The shares you own can become worthless, but your loss is limited to the money invested. In a short position, however, your loss is theoretically unlimited because the stock you have sold short can increase in price to any level. For that reason, short sales must almost always be hedged. Some partial strategies in this book call for unhedged short sales. Those should be undertaken only after careful thought. Moreover, short sellers must be extremely well disciplined (see Chapter 12 on investor behavior) because emotional behavior can be devastating with short sales.

How to Make a Short Sale

To illustrate the differences between a purchase (going long) and a short sale (going short), consider two investors. Investor L wants to go long 100 shares of stock XYZ at the current price of $50, while investor S wants to short 100 shares of the same stock. L believes that XYZ will appreciate, while S thinks that the stock is overvalued. Assume that both investors have a cash, nonmarginable brokerage account. For simplicity, assume that the brokerage commission is zero, the bid-ask spread is zero, and the stock pays no cash or stock dividends.

If L has at least $5,000 available in the account, then L can call a broker and place a market order to buy 100 shares of XYZ. The broker executes that order, credits L's account with 100 shares of XYZ, and deducts an amount of $5,000 from the account to pay the seller. L can continue to hold XYZ indefinitely without any further concern with respect to the trade or any communication with the broker.

S's situation is quite different. S must first convert the cash brokerage account to a margin-enabled account and put up at least 50 percent of the short sale ($2,500), even though S is a seller. Once S tells the broker to short-sell, the brokerage firm looks at its other accounts to see whether it can borrow XYZ to short-sell. If the brokerage firm cannot find a long position in another account, it asks associate brokerage firms or securities lenders. If it can't find shares of XYZ to borrow from other firms, it will cancel S's order to short-sell XYZ, and S must try to short-sell again later in the day or on another day. Brokers do not hold orders to short-sell overnight. After several attempts, assume that S's brokerage firm is able to borrow shares of XYZ for a short sale. Now it sends the order, tagged as a short sale, to sell 100 shares of XYZ to the market maker. Seeing that the order is a short sale, the market maker must abide by the uptick rule. According to the uptick rule, short sales may be made only if the last executed price is above the previously executed price or if the last change in price was upward. Thus, S may not be able to sell XYZ if the stock is trending down.

Assume that XYZ moved up and the market maker is able to short-sell 100 shares of XYZ on S's behalf. The sale generates proceeds for S. However, S cannot use those proceeds for buying another security. The proceeds are given to the lender to secure the shares borrowed. Further, if S is an individual investor, then S can't earn any interest on the proceeds from the brokerage firm. If S is a large investor or large institution, it may be able to negotiate and obtain a fraction of the interest earned on the proceeds from selling XYZ.

The rate of interest depends on the Fed funds rate, the account size, and the difficulty in borrowing shares of XYZ. The greater the difficulty in borrowing shares, the lower the interest that large account holders receive from the broker. In any case, brokerage firms will pay interest that is always below the Fed funds rate.

That is not the end of the story. Loaned shares are "on call," meaning that the shares borrowed by S's broker must be returned anytime the lending firm or lending account needs them. When the shares are "called," S's broker can try to borrow shares from someone else, or may force S to buy shares from the market so that the shares can be returned. If many short sellers are forced to buy shares at the same time, then it results in a "short squeeze," with the price rising very quickly. This forces the short sellers to cover their positions, which causes the price to rise further, accentuating the loss in a short sale. Further, conditions relating to borrowed shares change on a daily basis: the shares may be put on "special," meaning that the short seller has to pay greater compensation to the lender, and the collateral is revised daily to ensure that the lender holds at least 102 percent of the value of shares lent.

Besides satisfying the lenders' conditions, short sellers are also subject to margin calls from the broker. Recall that S has short-sold 100 shares at $50 each. If the stock price rises to $105, then S's loss is $100 \times (\$105—\$50) = \$5,500$, which is more than the initial money in the short seller's account. Brokers cannot allow this situation to occur. Therefore, if the stock price rises, the brokers will call S to put up more margin money. Failing that, the broker will liquidate the position without further consultation. That will occur when the equity in S's account falls below a percentage determined by the brokerage firm, usually around 30 percent. In this case, if the price exceeds about $77, the brokerage firm will liquidate the position. Large brokerage houses will generally disallow short selling of low-priced stocks (less than $5) because they tend to be illiquid and highly volatile, increasing the risk for the broker.

While the process of short selling is complicated, it becomes easier to implement once a short seller has executed a couple of trades. Note that short selling is also riskier than going long. In the arbitrage strategies described, the short position will always be hedged to minimize that risk, but the hedge may break. For example, in stock mergers, a short position on the bidder is hedged with a long position on the target. However, if the merger is called off, the long position ceases to be a hedge.

RESTRAINTS ON SHORT SELLING

There are several reasons why short selling is complicated and discouraged. The main reason is that short selling, taken to the extreme, can result in a "bear raid," where the price is driven down significantly purely by short sales. To reduce the chance of bear raids, the SEC allows short sales only upon an uptick, that is, when the stock price is moving up.

Since short sales are risky, legal and institutional rules limit the use of short sales only to certain kinds of accounts and to traders who understand the risk of this strategy. Thus, short sales can be made only in marginable accounts. Government regulations forbid short sales by investment companies (such as mutual funds) and pension funds except under special circumstances. Similarly, custodial accounts and retirement accounts do not allow short sales.

WHY SHORT-SELL?

There are several reasons why traders may want to short-sell a stock. Most short sales are hedged to reduce the risk of a short position. However, traders do take naked or speculative short positions when they believe that the stock is overvalued. The reasons for short selling are discussed below.

Hedged Short Sales

Most of the transactions in this category occur from perceived mispricings, some of which are discussed in Chapters 2 through 11 of the book. Index arbitrage occurs when an index futures contract trades at a price different from that implied by the underlying cash index. For example, if the S&P 500 index futures contract is trading at a price below that implied by the stock market, then the arbitrageur will buy the futures contract in the futures market and hedge that by short-selling all five hundred stocks on the stock market. Differences between prices on different exchanges for the same security can be arbitraged by taking a long position on one exchange and a short position on the other. Intraindustry stock price differences are arbitraged by hedge funds by taking positions within an industry—for example, short-selling United Airlines and buying Delta Airlines on the belief that settlement of labor talks at Delta will have a negative impact on United. Merger arbitrage (see Chapter 9) takes place by short-selling the acquiring firm and buying the target firm.

Speculative Short Sales

Short sellers may believe that a security is overpriced and wish to take advantage from the expected drop in price by short-selling that security. Speculative short sales are not uncommon, and the market generally credits short sellers with possessing information superior to that of other traders due to the riskiness of short sellers' positions. There is evidence of a strong negative relation between the level of relative short interest and subsequent returns for stocks, both during the time the stocks are heavily shorted and over the following two years. Further, stocks with high short interest are more likely to file for bankruptcy.

References for Further Reading

Asquith, Paul, and Lisa Meulbroek. 1996. An Empirical Investigation of Short Interest. Working paper, Department of Economics, Finance, and Accounting, MIT.

Chen, Honghui, and Vijay Singal. 2003. Role of Speculative Short Sales in Price Formation: Case of the Weekend Effect. *Journal of Finance* 58(2), 685–705.

DeChow, Patricia, Amy Hutton, Lisa Meulbroek, and Richard Sloan. 2001. Short Sellers, Fundamental Analysis, and Stock Returns. *Journal of Financial Economics* 61, 77–106.

Desai, Hemang, S. Ramu Thiagarajan, K. Ramesh, and Bala V. Balachandran. 2002. An Investigation of the Informational Role of Short Interest in the Nasdaq Market. *Journal of Finance* 57(5): 2263–87.

Geczy, Christopher, David Musto, and Adam Reed. 2002. Stocks Are Special Too: An Analysis of the Equity Lending Market. *Journal of Financial Economics* 66(2): 241–69.

Senchack, Andrew J., and Laura T. Starks. 1993. Short-Sale Restrictions and Market Reaction to Short-Interest Announcements. *Journal of Financial and Quantitative Analysis* 28, 177–194.

Smith, Geoffrey. 1999. You Too Can Short Stocks. *Business Week,* March 22, 1999, 110.

Appendix C: Hedging Market Return

Performance of a trading strategy is evaluated by comparing its return with a benchmark. In most cases, the market return is used as a benchmark. A successful trading strategy is expected to generate positive abnormal returns. However, a positive abnormal return can still mean a negative return for the strategy, if the benchmark (market) return is negative. For example, Strategy 1 for trading of mispriced mutual funds in Table 6.5 generates a raw return of –5.8 percent. This compares favorably with the S&P 500 return of –13.2 percent and the mispriced fund's own buy-and-hold return of –17.1 percent. The strategy's abnormal return is +11.3 percent relative to the fund's buy-and-hold return and +7.4 percent relative to the S&P 500. Thus, neutralizing the market return would have generated a return of +7.4 percent for Strategy 1 instead of –5.8 percent.

Hedging the market means that the effect of market movements has been neutralized. Hedging market risk is good because it reduces the overall risk of the trading strategy and will significantly increase the probability of a positive return. At the same time, however, the expected return of a trading strategy will fall because the market return is usually positive. Continuing with the example in the previous paragraph, assume that in a different time period the S&P 500 return is 12 percent and Strategy 1's return is 18 percent. Since the abnormal return is 6 percent, hedging the market risk means that the net return to the strategy will be only 6 percent instead of 18 percent, albeit at a lower risk.

The choice between hedging and not hedging market risk depends on the preferences of an individual investor. Hedging is sometimes used in the book when institutional constraints force the investor to take on more risk than the strategy requires. Again, see Chapter 6, where fund supermarkets force the investor to hold the mispriced fund for two days, though the should be sold after one day for best returns.

The process of hedging is quite simple when futures or exchange traded funds are used. The first step in hedging is to identify the risk that is to be hedged. For example, buying the target in the case of a stock merger introduces the risk that the bidding firm's stock price will fall. Therefore, hedging requires short-selling the bidding firm's stock. In the case of S&P 500 index changes, buying the firm added to the index causes the investor to assume the risk of a drop in the S&P 500 index. Thus, one way of neutralizing the S&P 500 risk is to short-sell the S&P 500 index. Similarly, if you short-sell the firm deleted from the S&P 500 index immediately after announcement, the market risk can be hedged by buying the S&P 500 index.

When hedging the risk of an individual stock, you have no alternative but to use the stock itself. However, when the risk of the market (such as the S&P 500 index) is to be hedged, then several alternatives are available. First, the exchange-traded fund (AMEX: SPY) can be bought or short-sold. Second, the stock index futures can be bought or short-sold. Finally, index mutual funds can be bought, though not short-sold.

Though opportunities for hedging are usually indicated along with trading strategies, investors may be able to hedge other kinds of risk. It should be noted, however, that hedging is unlikely to eliminate all risk, and it may be expensive to undertake certain kinds of hedge. For example, currency hedging (see "Currency Hedging" in Chapter 10) is costly and probably undesirable.

Index

*Note: Page numbers in **bold** indicate chapters.
*Note: Page numbers in *italics* indicate charts and graphs.